S·A

Special A

HIKARI & YAHIRO
middle school

Volume 4

Story & Art by

Maki Minami

STORY

★At the tender age of 6, carpenter's daughter Hikari Hanazono suffered her first loss to the wealthy Kei Takishima in a wrestling match. Now the hardworking Hikari has followed Kei to the most elite school for the rich just to beat him! I call this story "Overthrow Takishima! Rise Above Perpetual Second Place!!" It's the story of Hikari's sweat, tears and passion, with a little bit of love thrown in!

★Last time, Tadashi asked Hikari on a "date" to prove to his mom he was not hopeless. But then a jealous Kei burst in and abducted Hikari in his helicopter!

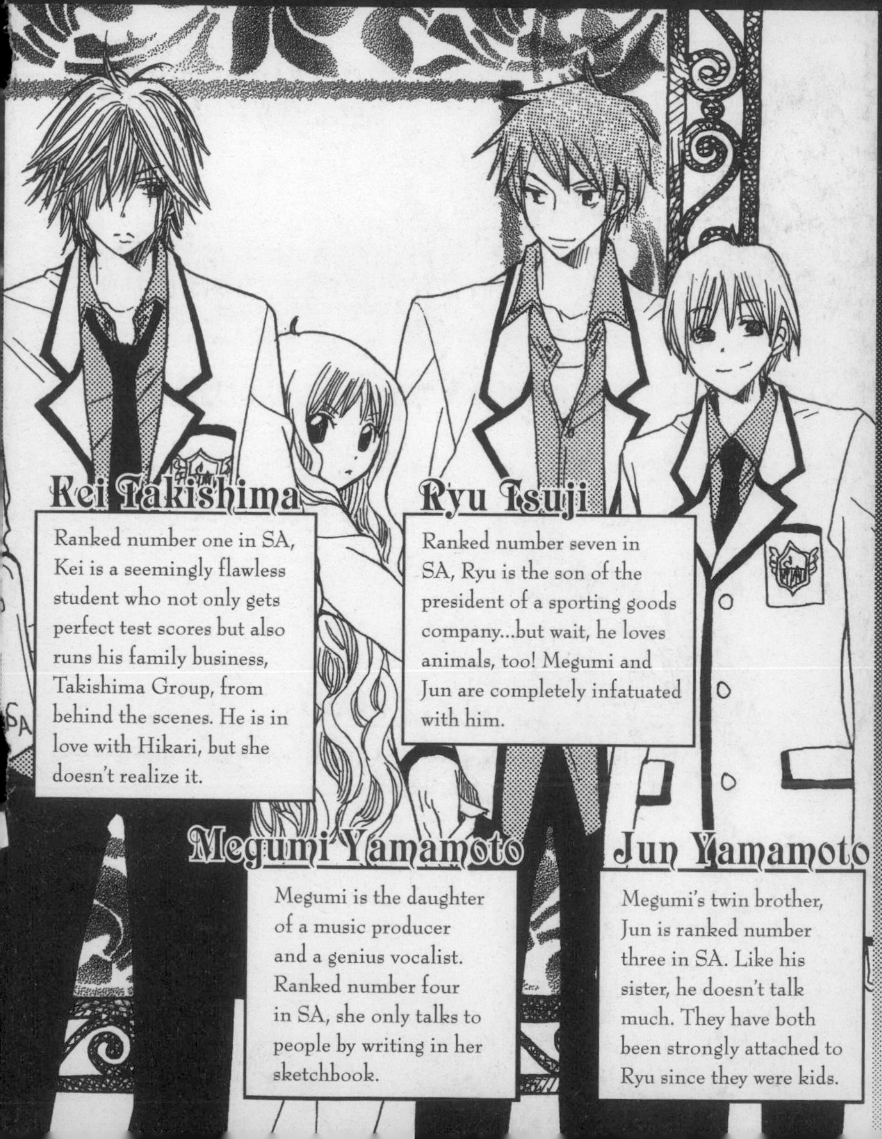
Kei Takishima
Ranked number one in SA, Kei is a seemingly flawless student who not only gets perfect test scores but also runs his family business, Takishima Group, from behind the scenes. He is in love with Hikari, but she doesn't realize it.
Ryu Tsuji
Ranked number seven in SA, Ryu is the son of the president of a sporting goods company...but wait, he loves animals, too! Megumi and Jun are completely infatuated with him.
Megumi Yamamoto
Megumi is the daughter of a music producer and a genius vocalist. Ranked number four in SA, she only talks to people by writing in her sketchbook.
Jun Yamamoto
Megumi's twin brother, Jun is ranked number three in SA. Like his sister, he doesn't talk much. They have both been strongly attached to Ryu since they were kids.

S·A CHARACTERS

Hikari goes to an elite school called Hakusenkan High School. This school divides each grade level into groups A through F, according to the students' test scores. Group A includes only the top seven students in each class. Then the top seven students from all grades' A groups are put into a group called Special A, which is considered much higher than all others. Known as SA, they are "the elite among the elite."

What is "Special A"?

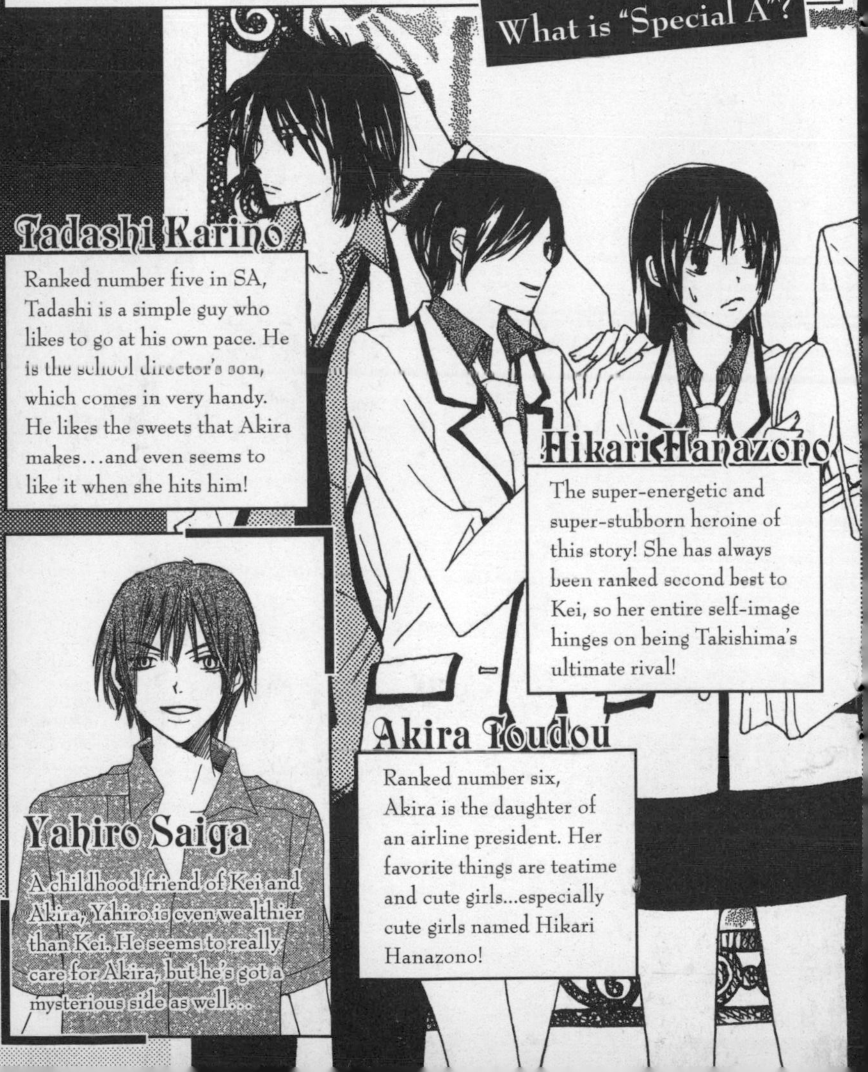

Tadashi Karino

Ranked number five in SA, Tadashi is a simple guy who likes to go at his own pace. He is the school director's son, which comes in very handy. He likes the sweets that Akira makes…and even seems to like it when she hits him!

Hikari Hanazono

The super-energetic and super-stubborn heroine of this story! She has always been ranked second best to Kei, so her entire self-image hinges on being Takishima's ultimate rival!

Yahiro Saiga

A childhood friend of Kei and Akira, Yahiro is even wealthier than Kei. He seems to really care for Akira, but he's got a mysterious side as well…

Akira Toudou

Ranked number six, Akira is the daughter of an airline president. Her favorite things are teatime and cute girls...especially cute girls named Hikari Hanazono!

Contents

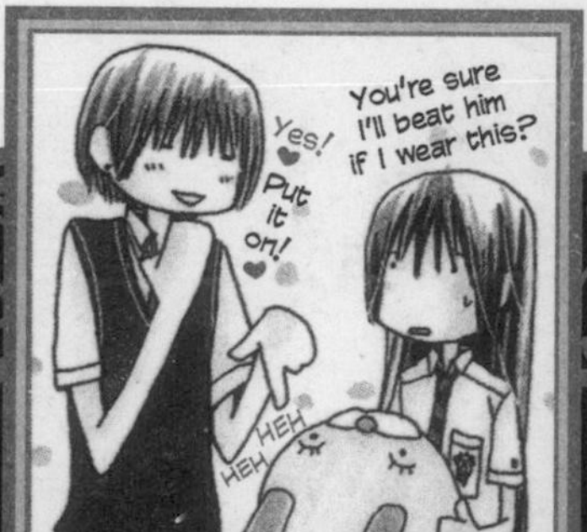

You're sure I'll beat him if I wear this?
Yes!
Put it on!
HEH HEH

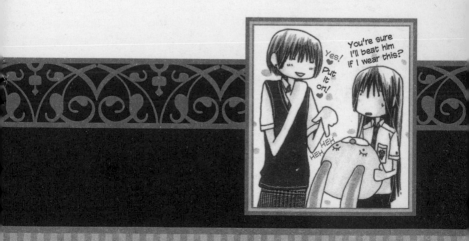

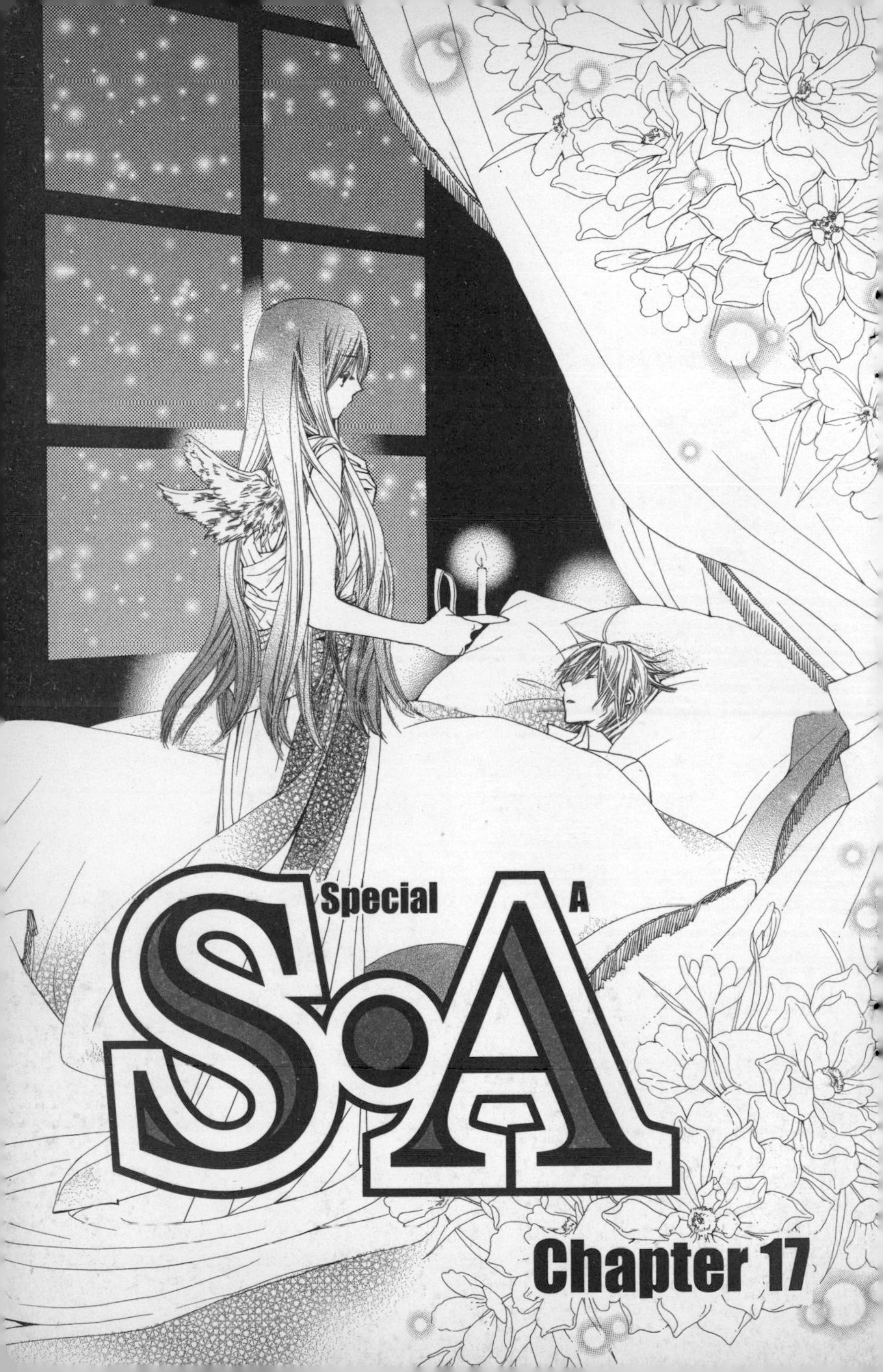
Special A
S·A
Chapter 17

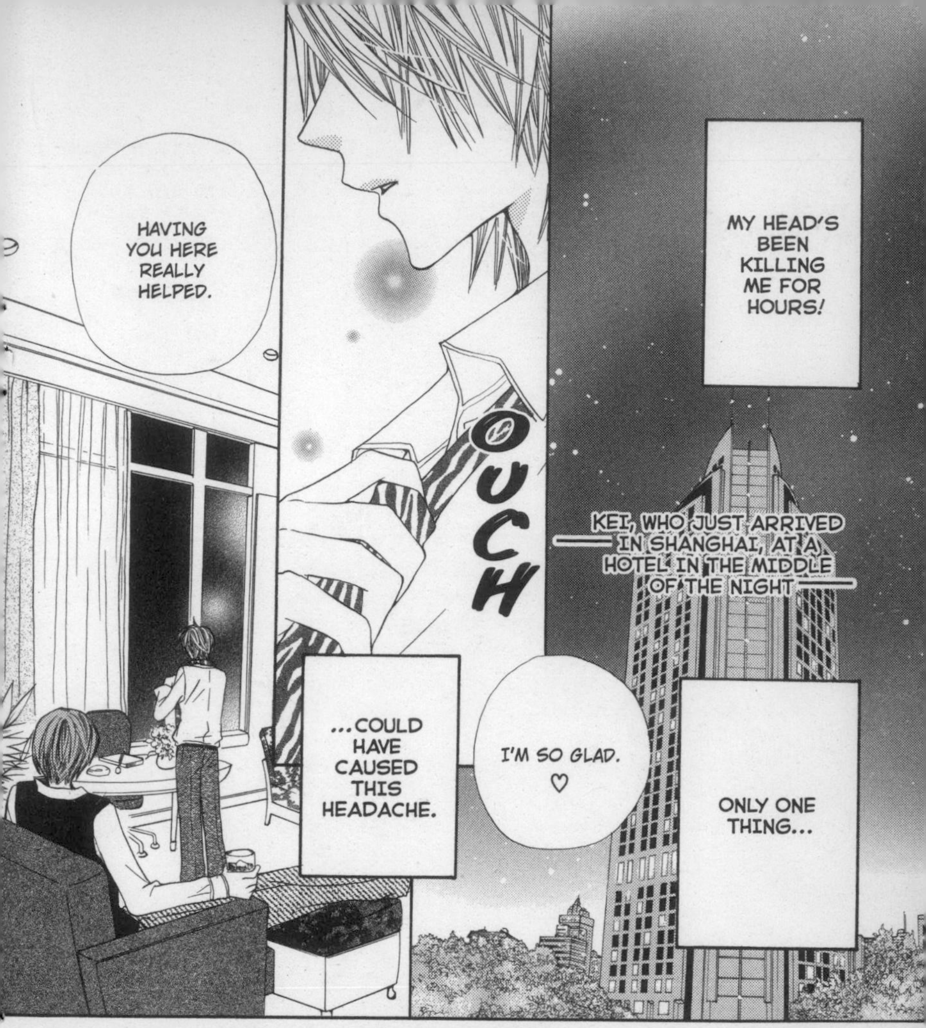
MY HEAD'S BEEN KILLING ME FOR HOURS!
—KEI, WHO JUST ARRIVED IN SHANGHAI, AT A HOTEL IN THE MIDDLE OF THE NIGHT—
ONLY ONE THING...
I'M SO GLAD. ♡
...COULD HAVE CAUSED THIS HEADACHE.
OUCH
HAVING YOU HERE REALLY HELPED.

•DUBBING•

AS A GIFT TO READERS, *HANA TO YUME* COMICS DECIDED TO MAKE CHAPTER 16 (THE END OF VOLUME THREE) AND CHAPTER 17 INTO A MANGA DVD! IT WAS AN ULTRA-SURPRISING EVENT THAT JUST THRILLED ME TO DEATH! AND IT'S ALL THANKS TO YOU!

AND I GOT TO GO TO A DUBBING STUDIO FOR THE FIRST TIME. WHAT CAN I SAY? THEY WERE ALL TRUE PROFESSIONALS AND I WAS TOTALLY IMPRESSED. TO ALL THE VOICEOVER ACTORS AND STAFF, THANK YOU SO VERY MUCH!

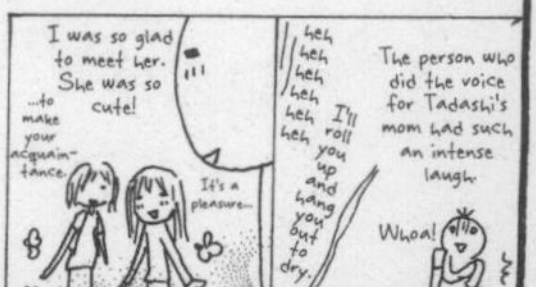
The person who did the voice for Tadashi's mom had such an intense laugh
heh heh heh heh heh heh
I'll roll you up and hang you out to dry.
Whoa!
I was so glad to meet her. She was so cute!
...to make your acquaintance.
It's a pleasure...

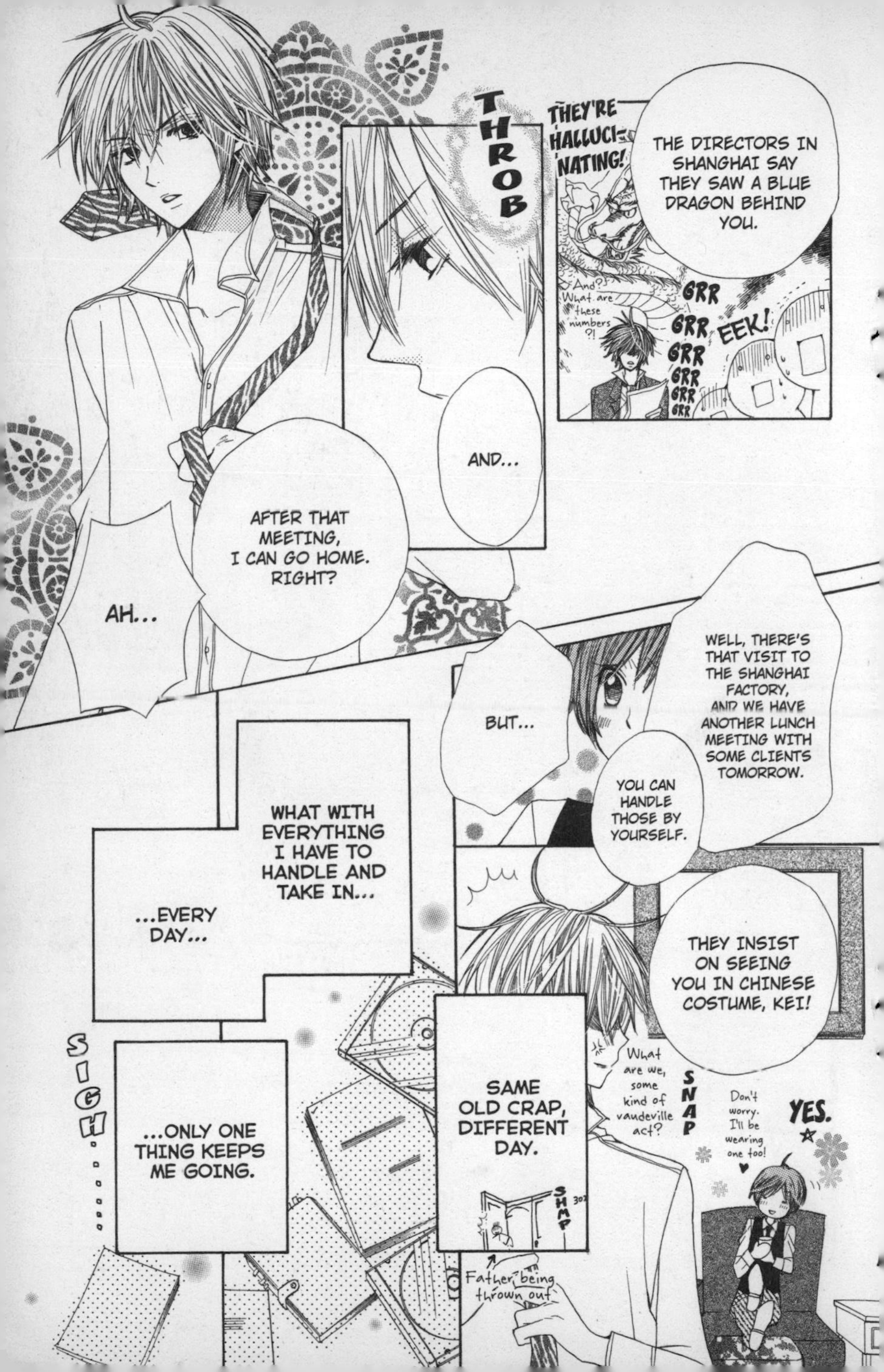
THE DIRECTORS IN SHANGHAI SAY THEY SAW A BLUE DRAGON BEHIND YOU.
THEY'RE HALLUCI-NATING!
And?! What are these numbers ?!
GRR GRR GRR GRR GRR GRR
EEK!
THROB
AND...
AFTER THAT MEETING, I CAN GO HOME. RIGHT?
AH...
WELL, THERE'S THAT VISIT TO THE SHANGHAI FACTORY, AND WE HAVE ANOTHER LUNCH MEETING WITH SOME CLIENTS TOMORROW.
BUT...
YOU CAN HANDLE THOSE BY YOURSELF.
THEY INSIST ON SEEING YOU IN CHINESE COSTUME, KEI!
What are we, some kind of vaudeville act?
SNAP
Don't worry. I'll be wearing one too!
YES.
SAME OLD CRAP, DIFFERENT DAY.
SHMP
Father being thrown out
WHAT WITH EVERYTHING I HAVE TO HANDLE AND TAKE IN...
...EVERY DAY...
...ONLY ONE THING KEEPS ME GOING.
SIGH......

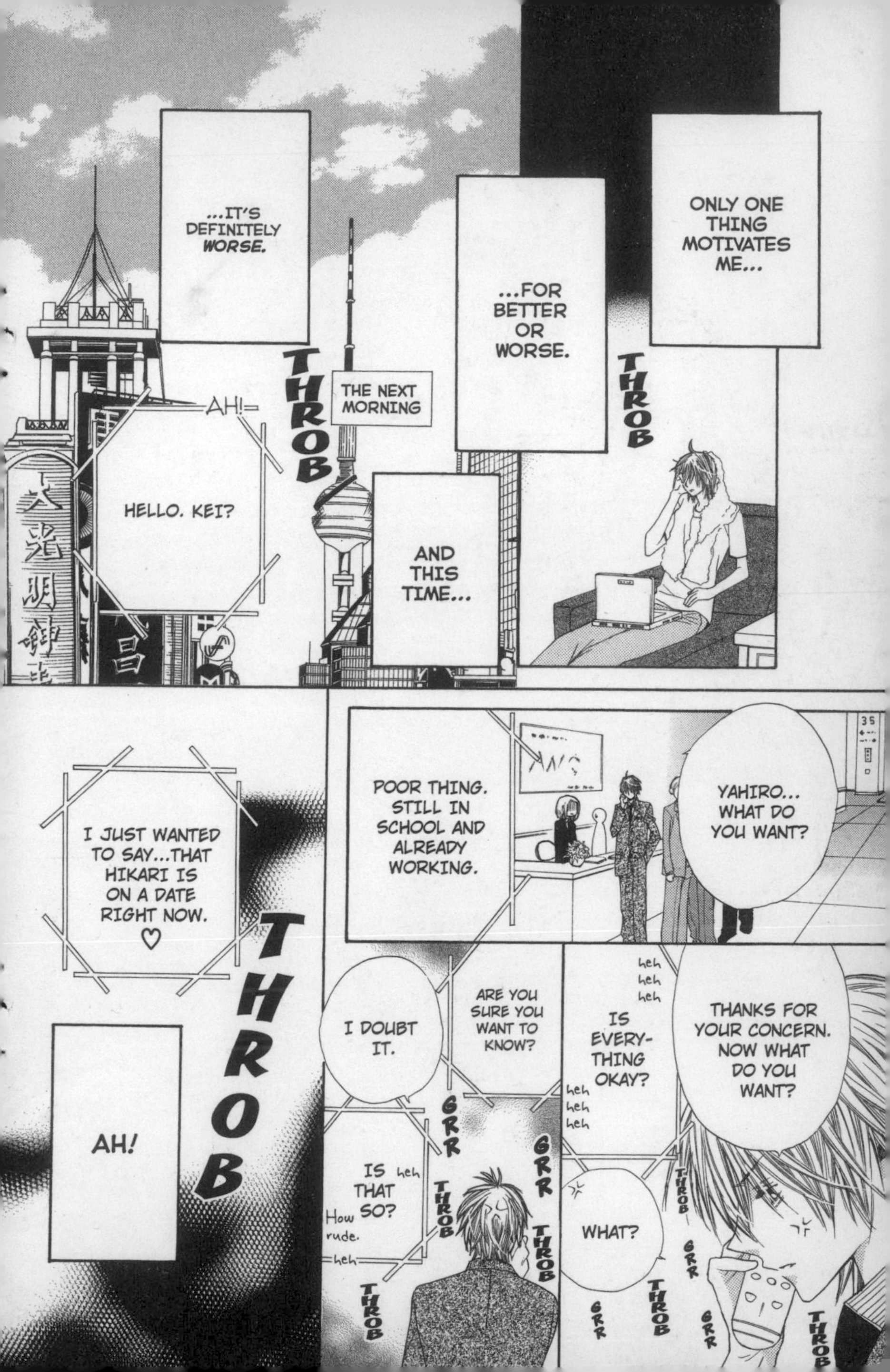
ONLY ONE THING MOTIVATES ME...
...FOR BETTER OR WORSE.
THROB
AND THIS TIME...
...IT'S DEFINITELY WORSE.
THROB
THE NEXT MORNING
AH!
HELLO. KEI?
YAHIRO... WHAT DO YOU WANT?
POOR THING. STILL IN SCHOOL AND ALREADY WORKING.
THANKS FOR YOUR CONCERN. NOW WHAT DO YOU WANT?
heh heh heh
IS EVERY-THING OKAY?
heh heh heh
THROB
GRR
WHAT?
GRR
THROB
GRR
THROB
ARE YOU SURE YOU WANT TO KNOW?
I DOUBT IT.
GRR
IS THAT SO?
heh
How rude.
heh
THROB
THROB
I JUST WANTED TO SAY...THAT HIKARI IS ON A DATE RIGHT NOW. ♡
THROB
AH!

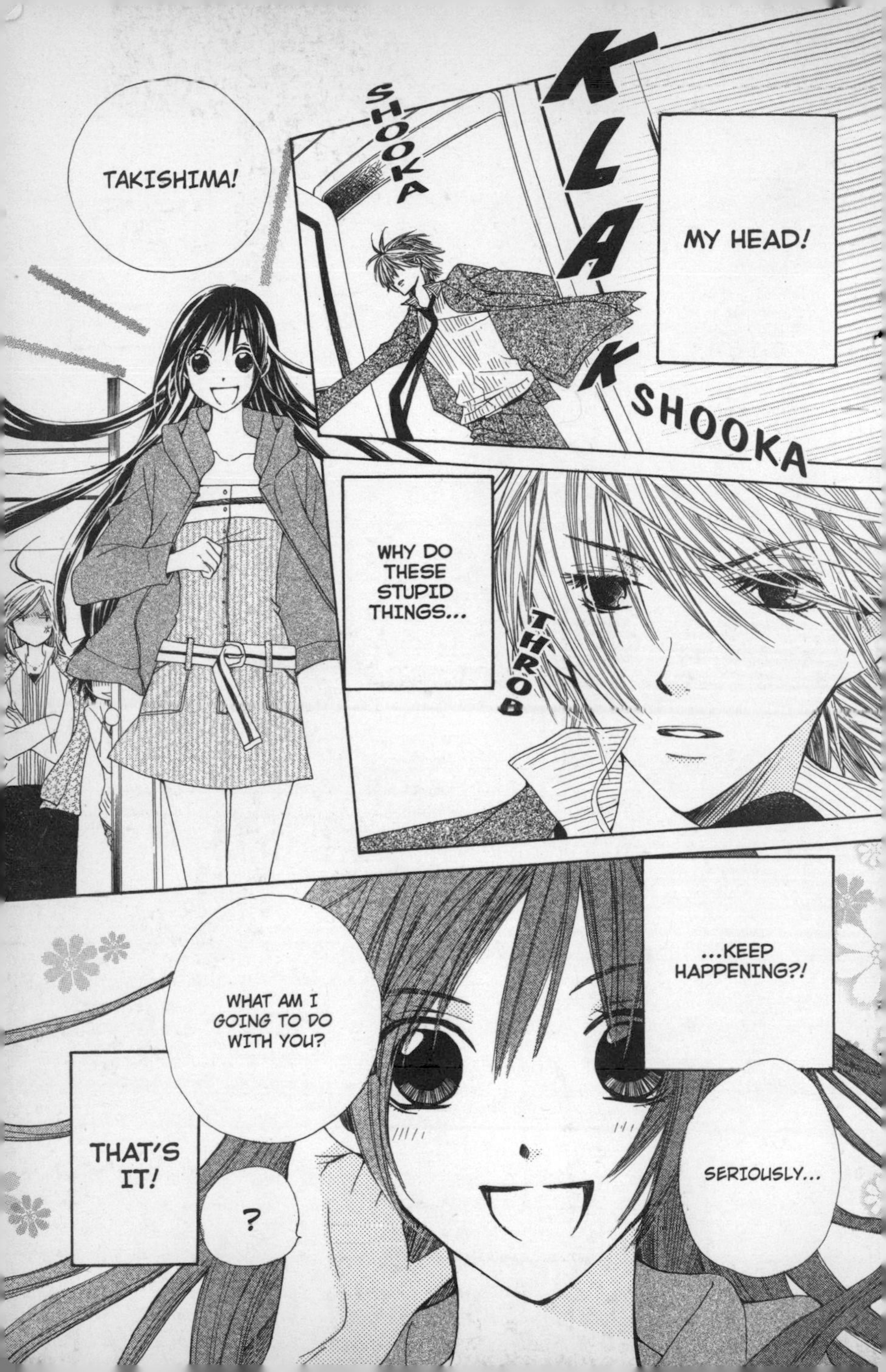
MY HEAD!
KLAK
SHOOKA
SHOOKA
WHY DO THESE STUPID THINGS...
THROB
TAKISHIMA!
...KEEP HAPPENING?!
SERIOUSLY...
WHAT AM I GOING TO DO WITH YOU?
THAT'S IT!
?

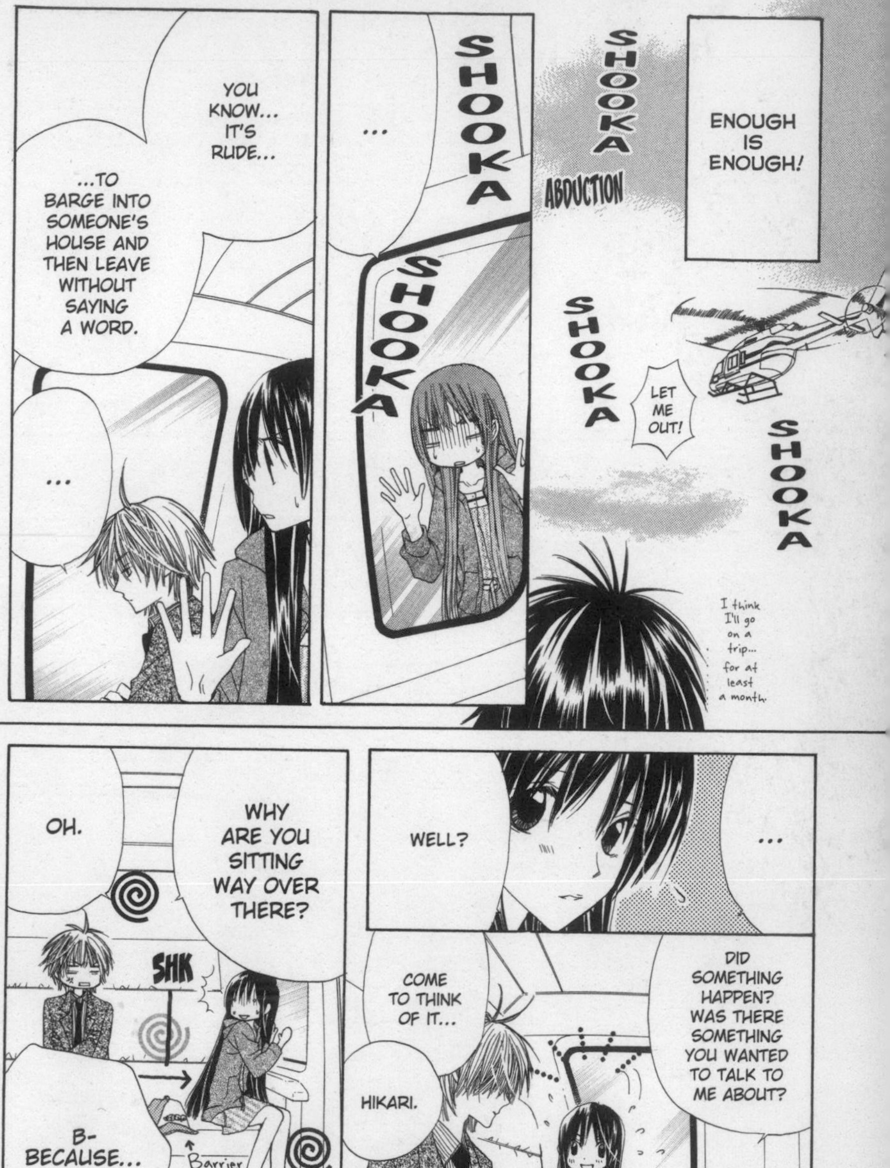

ENOUGH IS ENOUGH!
SHOOKA
ABDUCTION
SHOOKA
LET ME OUT!
SHOOKA
I think I'll go on a trip... for at least a month.
SHOOKA
SHOOKA
...
YOU KNOW... IT'S RUDE...
...TO BARGE INTO SOMEONE'S HOUSE AND THEN LEAVE WITHOUT SAYING A WORD.
...
...
WELL?
DID SOMETHING HAPPEN? WAS THERE SOMETHING YOU WANTED TO TALK TO ME ABOUT?
COME TO THINK OF IT...
HIKARI.
WHY ARE YOU SITTING WAY OVER THERE?
OH.
SHK
B-BECAUSE...
Barrier

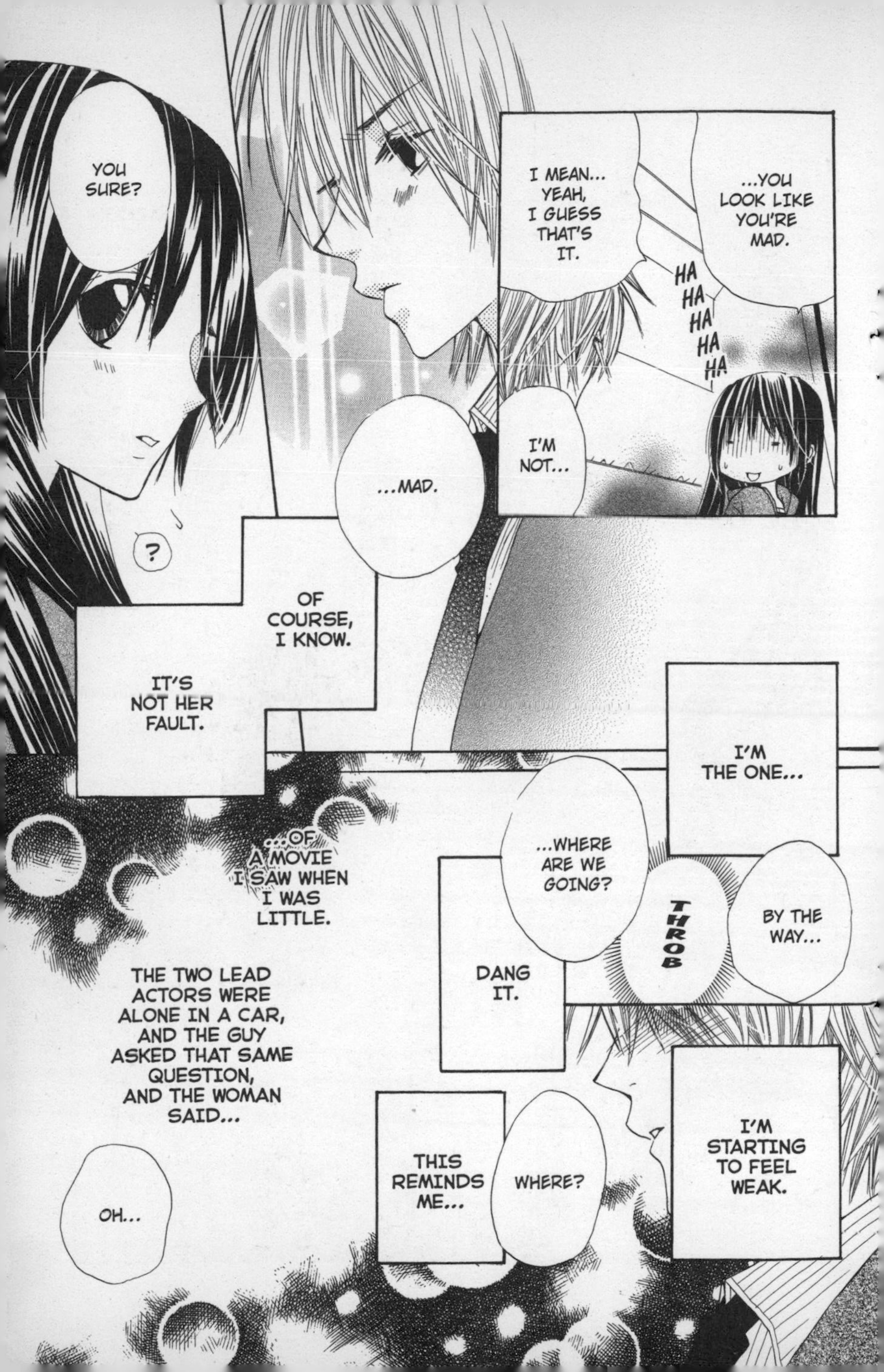
...YOU LOOK LIKE YOU'RE MAD.
HA HA HA HA HA
I MEAN... YEAH, I GUESS THAT'S IT.
I'M NOT...
...MAD.
YOU SURE?
?
OF COURSE, I KNOW.
IT'S NOT HER FAULT.
I'M THE ONE...
BY THE WAY...
THROB
...WHERE ARE WE GOING?
DANG IT.
I'M STARTING TO FEEL WEAK.
WHERE?
THIS REMINDS ME...
...OF A MOVIE I SAW WHEN I WAS LITTLE.
THE TWO LEAD ACTORS WERE ALONE IN A CAR, AND THE GUY ASKED THAT SAME QUESTION, AND THE WOMAN SAID...
OH...

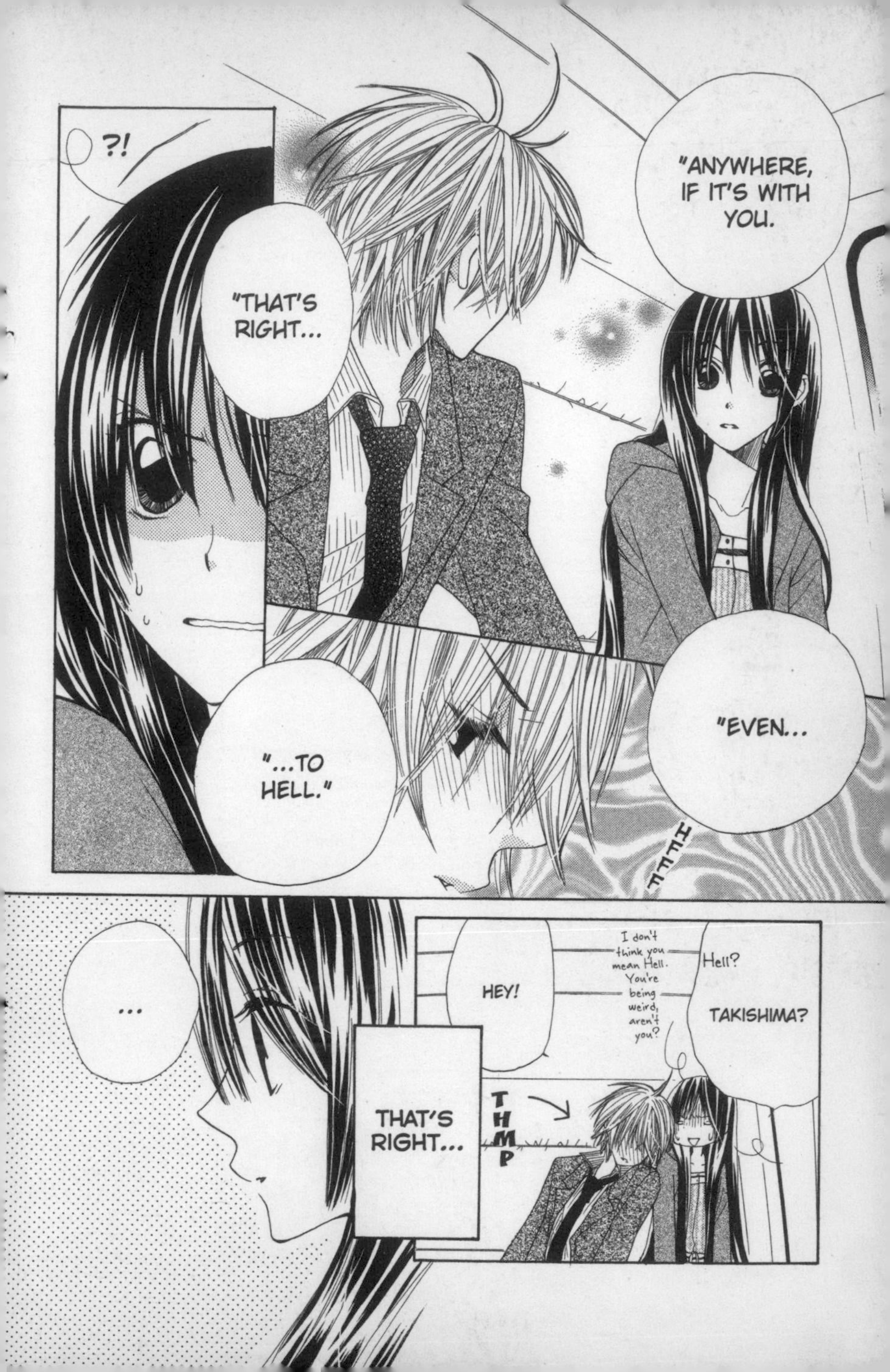
?!
"THAT'S RIGHT...
"ANYWHERE, IF IT'S WITH YOU.
"EVEN...
"...TO HELL."
HFFF
Hell? TAKISHIMA?
I don't think you mean Hell. You're being weird, aren't you?
HEY!
THMP
THAT'S RIGHT...
...

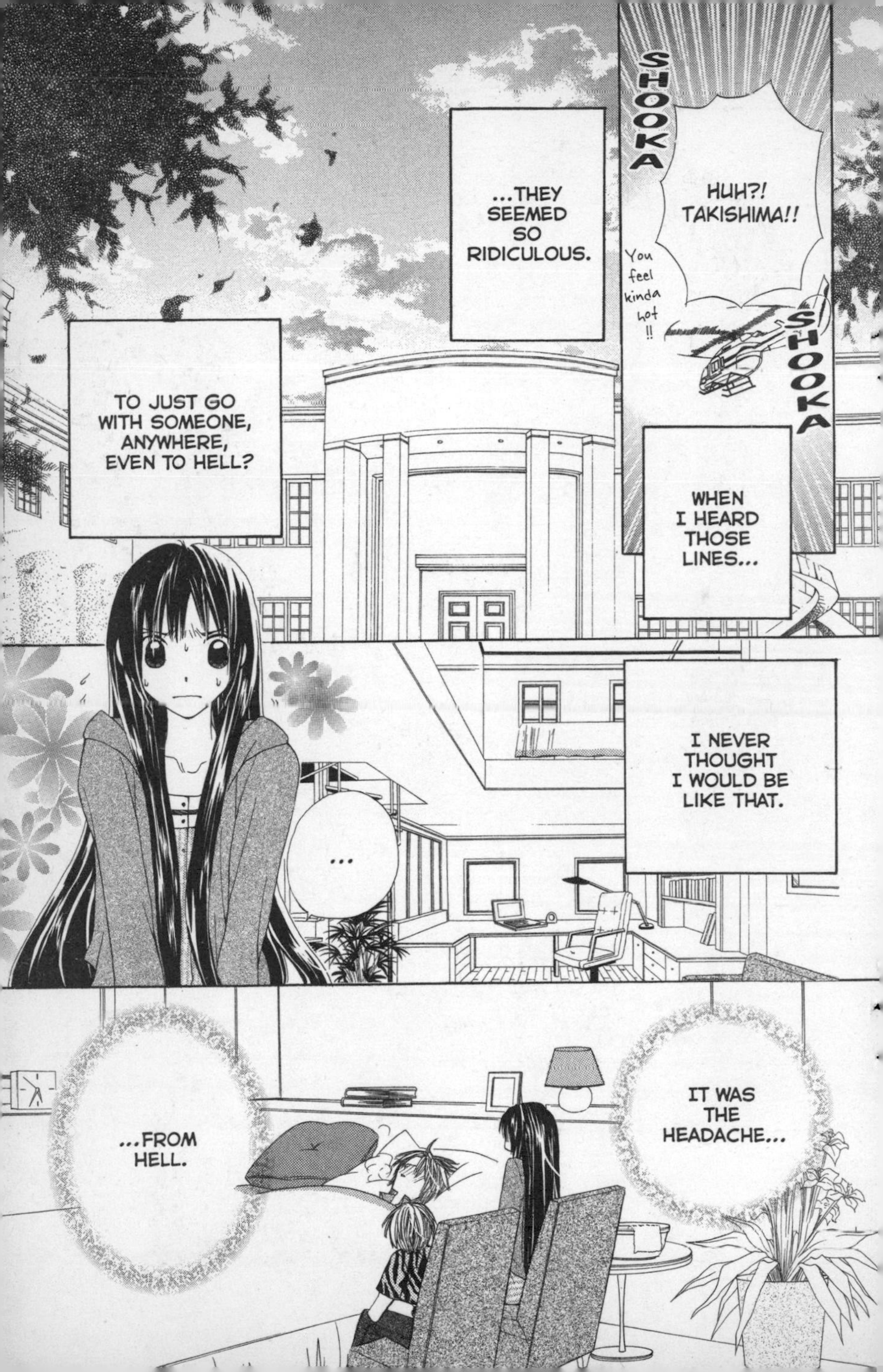
SHOOKA
HUH?! TAKISHIMA!!
You feel kinda hot!!
SHOOKA
TO JUST GO WITH SOMEONE, ANYWHERE, EVEN TO HELL?
WHEN I HEARD THOSE LINES...
...THEY SEEMED SO RIDICULOUS.
I NEVER THOUGHT I WOULD BE LIKE THAT.
...
IT WAS THE HEADACHE...
...FROM HELL.

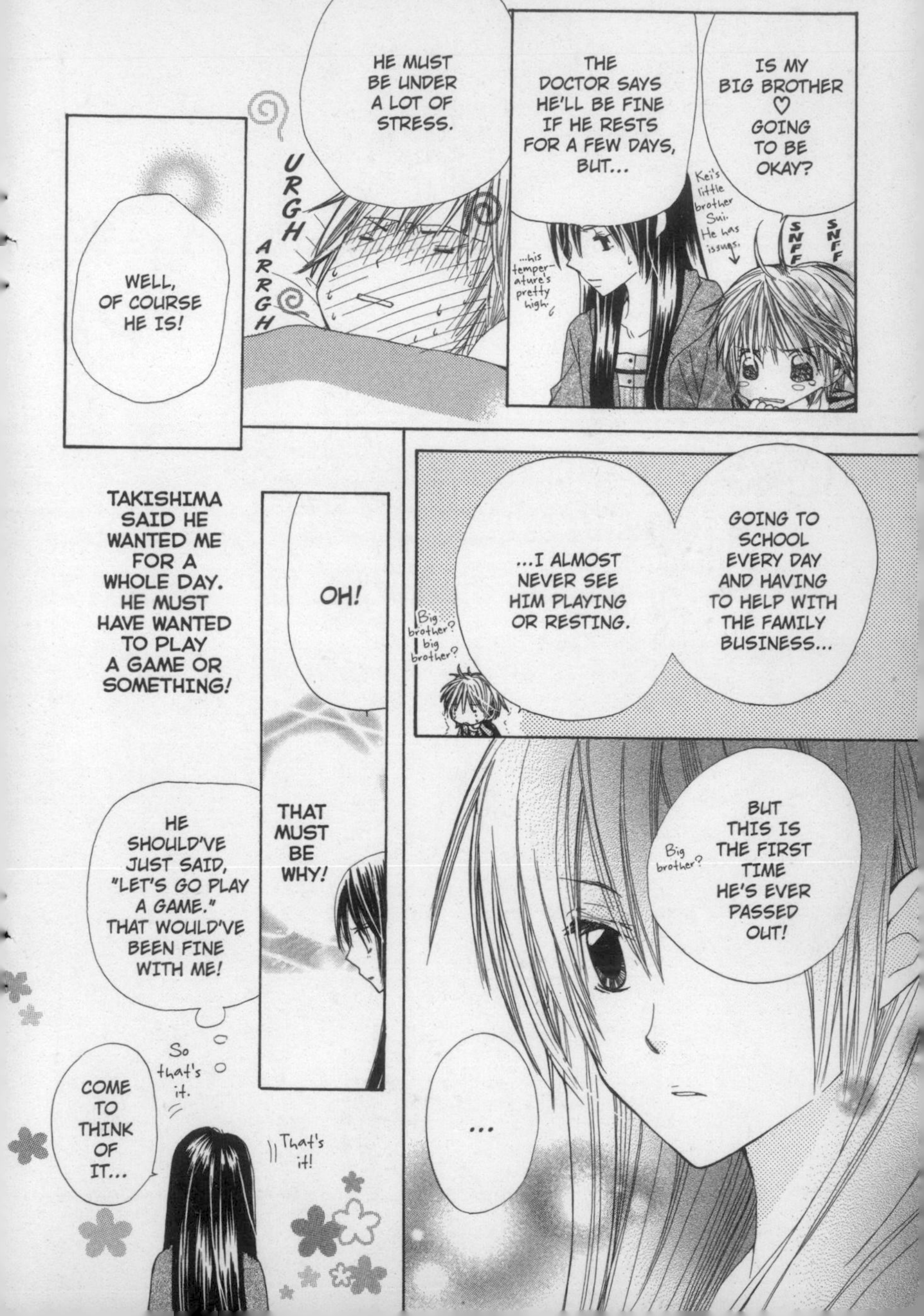

IS MY BIG BROTHER ♡ GOING TO BE OKAY?
Kei's little brother Sui. He has issues.
SNFF SNFF
THE DOCTOR SAYS HE'LL BE FINE IF HE RESTS FOR A FEW DAYS, BUT...
...his temperature's pretty high.
HE MUST BE UNDER A LOT OF STRESS.
URGH ARRGH
WELL, OF COURSE HE IS!
GOING TO SCHOOL EVERY DAY AND HAVING TO HELP WITH THE FAMILY BUSINESS...
...I ALMOST NEVER SEE HIM PLAYING OR RESTING.
Big brother? big brother?
BUT THIS IS THE FIRST TIME HE'S EVER PASSED OUT!
Big brother?
...
OH!
THAT MUST BE WHY!
TAKISHIMA SAID HE WANTED ME FOR A WHOLE DAY. HE MUST HAVE WANTED TO PLAY A GAME OR SOMETHING!
HE SHOULD'VE JUST SAID, "LET'S GO PLAY A GAME." THAT WOULD'VE BEEN FINE WITH ME!
So that's it.
COME TO THINK OF IT...
That's it!

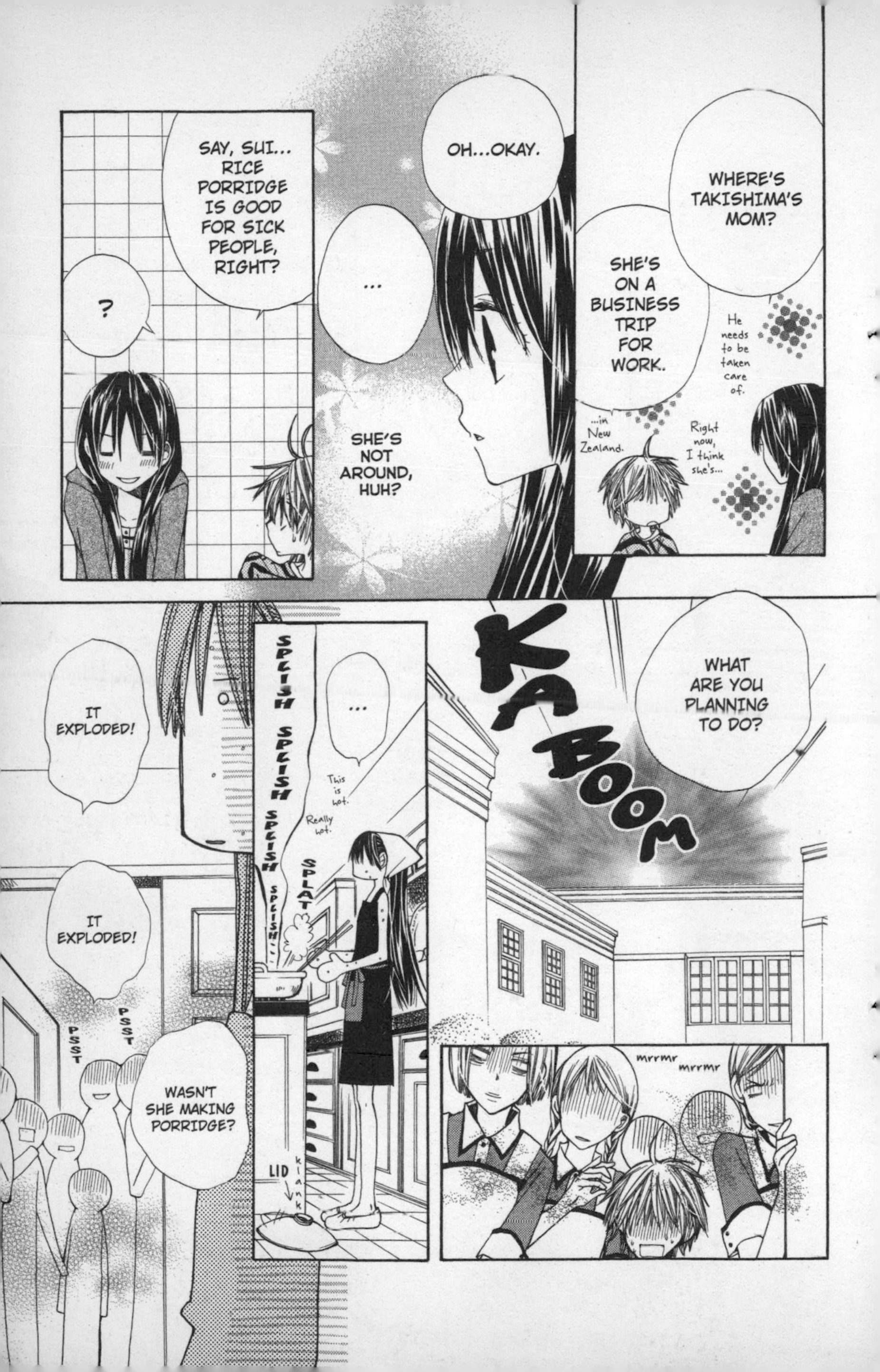
WHERE'S TAKISHIMA'S MOM?
SHE'S ON A BUSINESS TRIP FOR WORK.
Right now, I think she's...
...in New Zealand.
He needs to be taken care of.
OH...OKAY.
...
SHE'S NOT AROUND, HUH?
SAY, SUI... RICE PORRIDGE IS GOOD FOR SICK PEOPLE, RIGHT?
?
WHAT ARE YOU PLANNING TO DO?
KA BOOM
mrrmr mrrmr
SPLISH SPLISH
...
This is hot.
Really hot.
SPLISH SPLISH
SPLAT
LID
klank
IT EXPLODED!
IT EXPLODED!
PSST PSST
WASN'T SHE MAKING PORRIDGE?

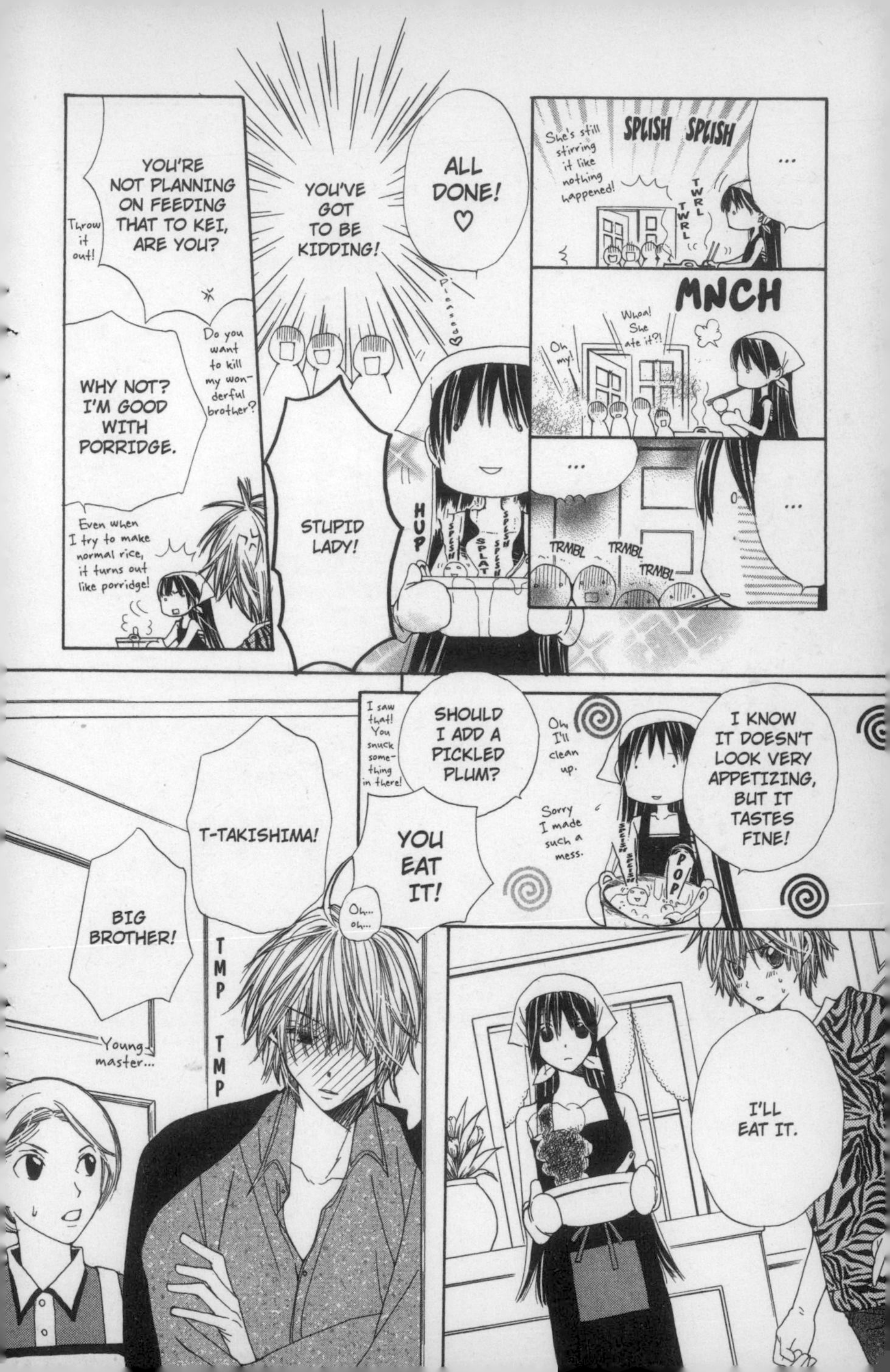

...
SPLISH SPLISH
She's still stirring it like nothing happened!
TWRL TWRL
MNCH
Whoa! She ate it?!
Oh my!
...
...
TRMBL TRMBL TRMBL
ALL DONE! ♡
YOU'VE GOT TO BE KIDDING!
HUP
SPLSH SPLAT SPLSH
STUPID LADY!
YOU'RE NOT PLANNING ON FEEDING THAT TO KEI, ARE YOU?
Throw it out!
Do you want to kill my wonderful brother?
WHY NOT? I'M GOOD WITH PORRIDGE.
Even when I try to make normal rice, it turns out like porridge!
I KNOW IT DOESN'T LOOK VERY APPETIZING, BUT IT TASTES FINE!
Oh, I'll clean up.
Sorry I made such a mess.
POP
SHOULD I ADD A PICKLED PLUM?
I saw that! You snuck something in there!
I'LL EAT IT.
YOU EAT IT!
Oh... oh...
T-TAKISHIMA!
BIG BROTHER!
TMP TMP
Young master...

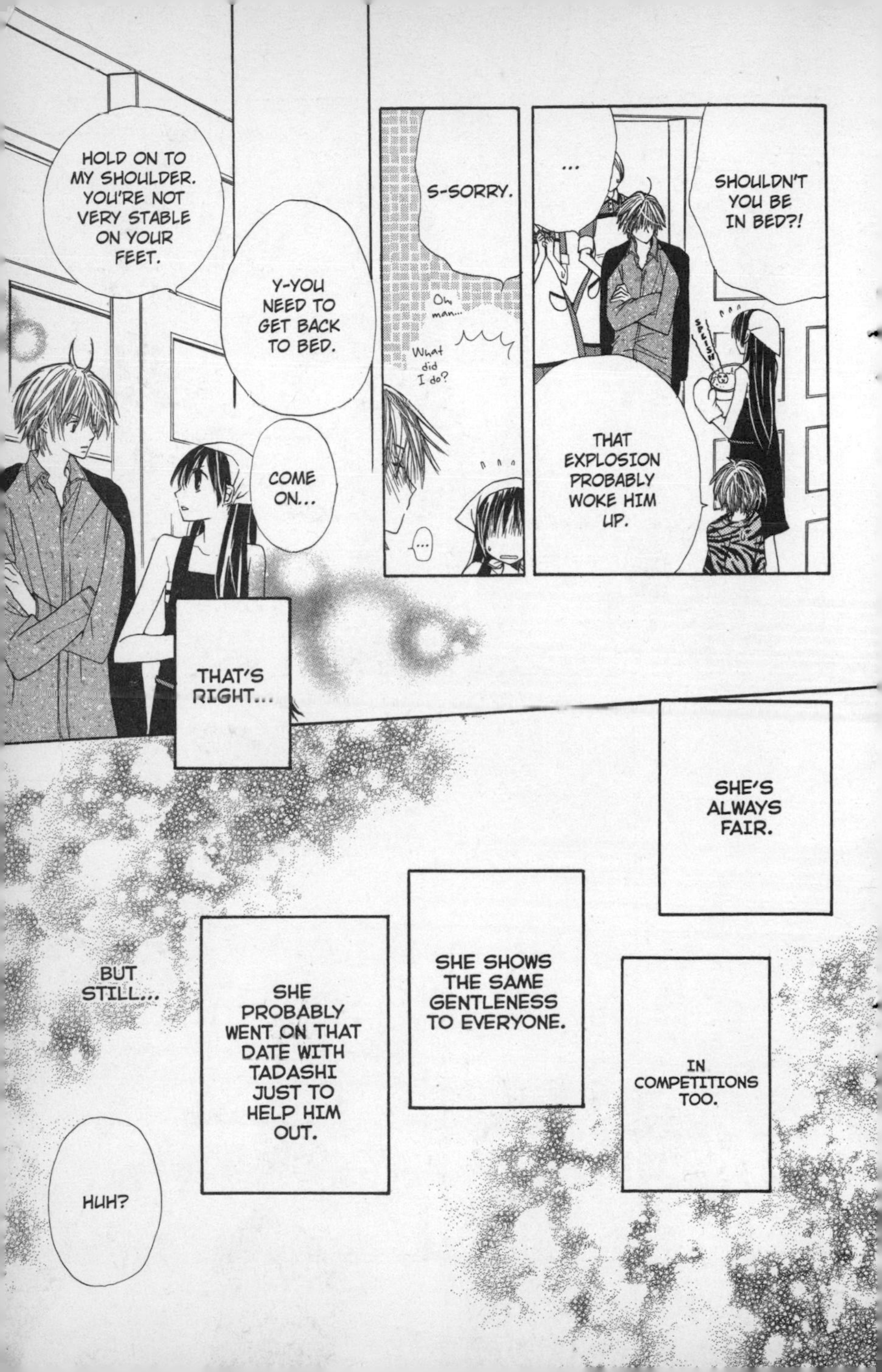
SHOULDN'T YOU BE IN BED?!
...
SPLISH
THAT EXPLOSION PROBABLY WOKE HIM UP.
S-SORRY.
Oh man...
What did I do?
...
Y-YOU NEED TO GET BACK TO BED.
HOLD ON TO MY SHOULDER. YOU'RE NOT VERY STABLE ON YOUR FEET.
COME ON...
THAT'S RIGHT...
SHE'S ALWAYS FAIR.
IN COMPETITIONS TOO.
SHE SHOWS THE SAME GENTLENESS TO EVERYONE.
SHE PROBABLY WENT ON THAT DATE WITH TADASHI JUST TO HELP HIM OUT.
BUT STILL...
HUH?

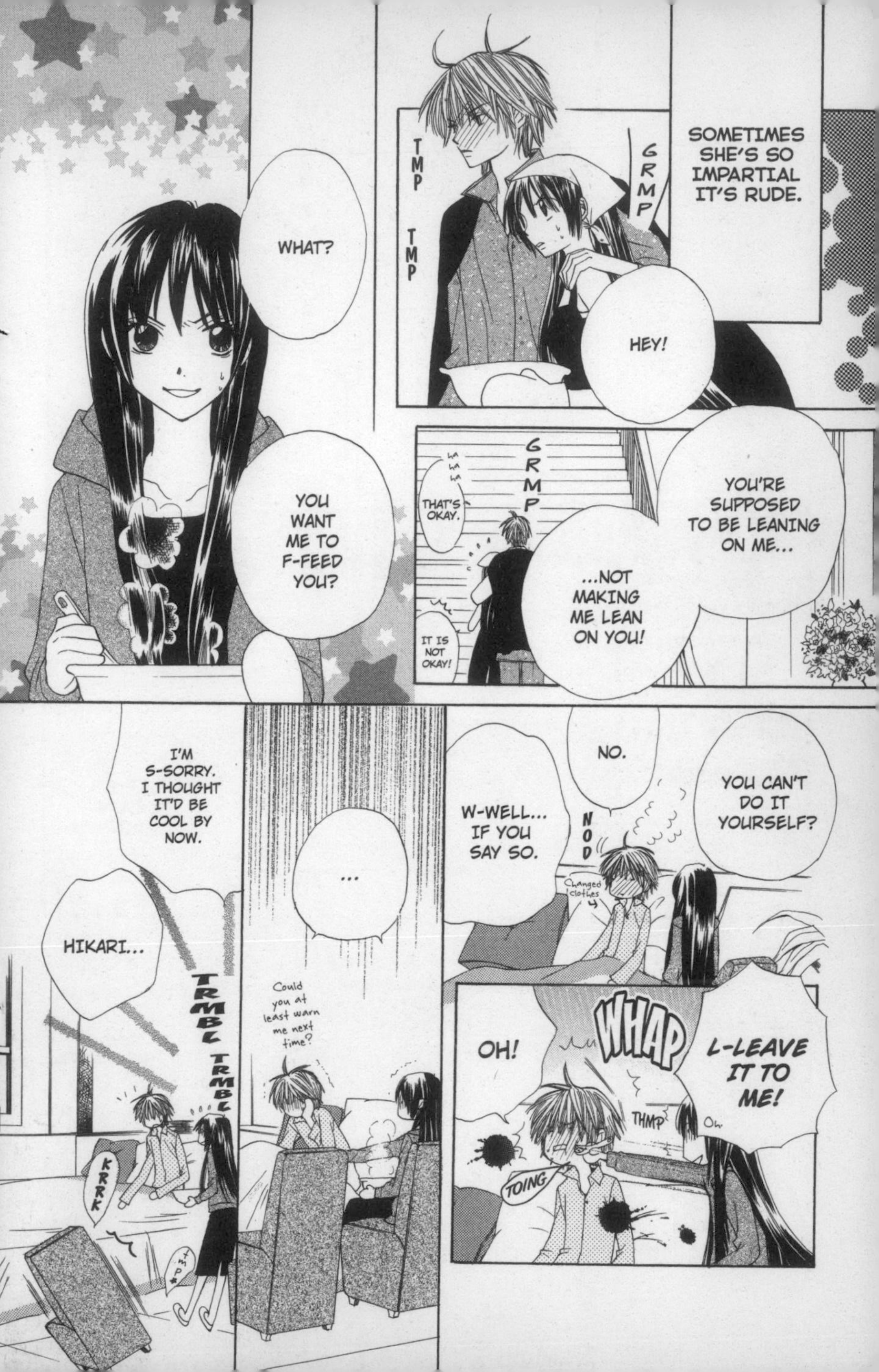
SOMETIMES SHE'S SO IMPARTIAL IT'S RUDE.
GRMP
HEY!
TMP TMP
YOU'RE SUPPOSED TO BE LEANING ON ME...
...NOT MAKING ME LEAN ON YOU!
GRMP
HA HA HA
THAT'S OKAY.
IT IS NOT OKAY!
WHAT?
YOU WANT ME TO F-FEED YOU?
YOU CAN'T DO IT YOURSELF?
NO.
NOD
W-WELL... IF YOU SAY SO.
Changed clothes
L-LEAVE IT TO ME!
WHAP
OH!
THMP
Ow
TOING
...
Could you at least warn me next time?
I'M S-SORRY. I THOUGHT IT'D BE COOL BY NOW.
HIKARI...
TRMBL TRMBL
KRRK
TMP

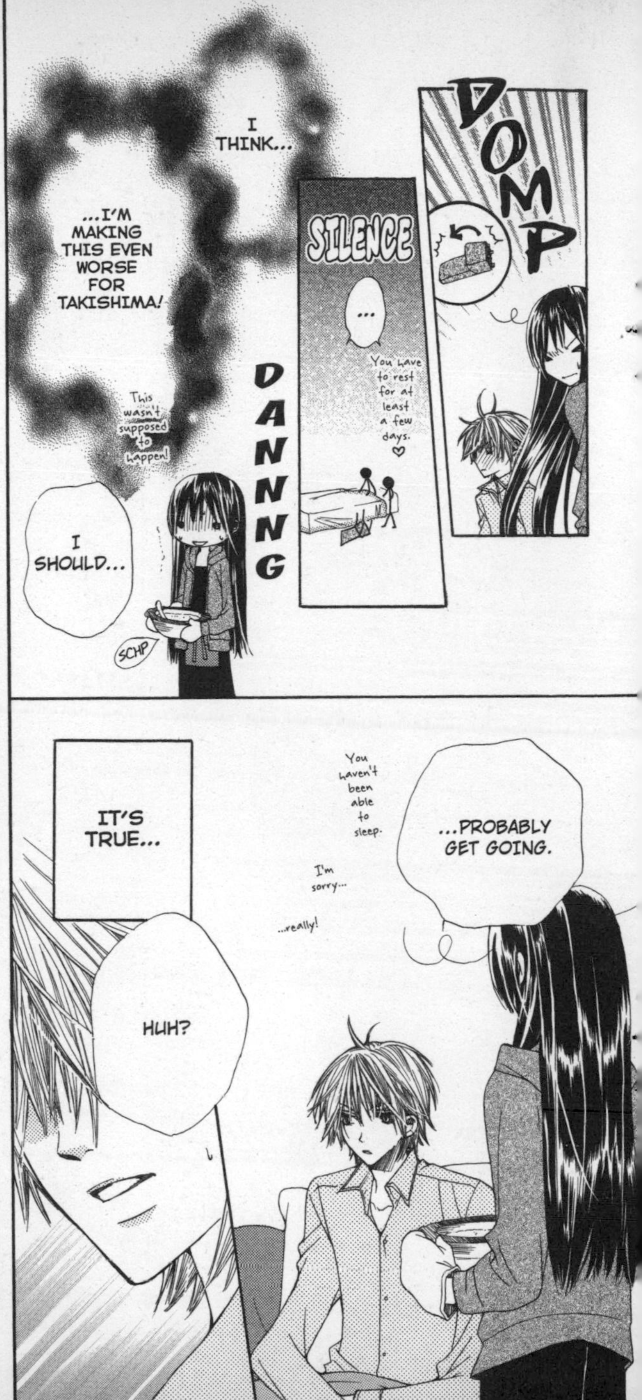
DOMP
SILENCE
...
You have to rest for at least a few days. ♡
DANNNG
I THINK...
...I'M MAKING THIS EVEN WORSE FOR TAKISHIMA!
This wasn't supposed to happen!
I SHOULD...
SCHP
...PROBABLY GET GOING.
You haven't been able to sleep.
I'm sorry...
...really!
IT'S TRUE...
HUH?

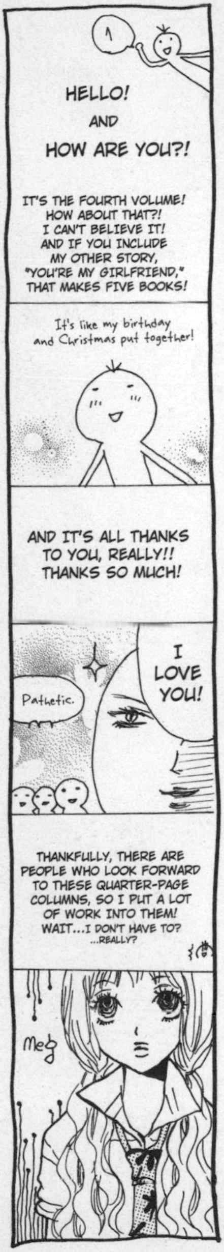
1
HELLO!
AND
HOW ARE YOU?!
IT'S THE FOURTH VOLUME! HOW ABOUT THAT?! I CAN'T BELIEVE IT! AND IF YOU INCLUDE MY OTHER STORY, "YOU'RE MY GIRLFRIEND," THAT MAKES FIVE BOOKS!
It's like my birthday and Christmas put together!
AND IT'S ALL THANKS TO YOU, REALLY!! THANKS SO MUCH!
I LOVE YOU!
Pathetic.
THANKFULLY, THERE ARE PEOPLE WHO LOOK FORWARD TO THESE QUARTER-PAGE COLUMNS, SO I PUT A LOT OF WORK INTO THEM! WAIT...I DON'T HAVE TO? ...REALLY?
Meg

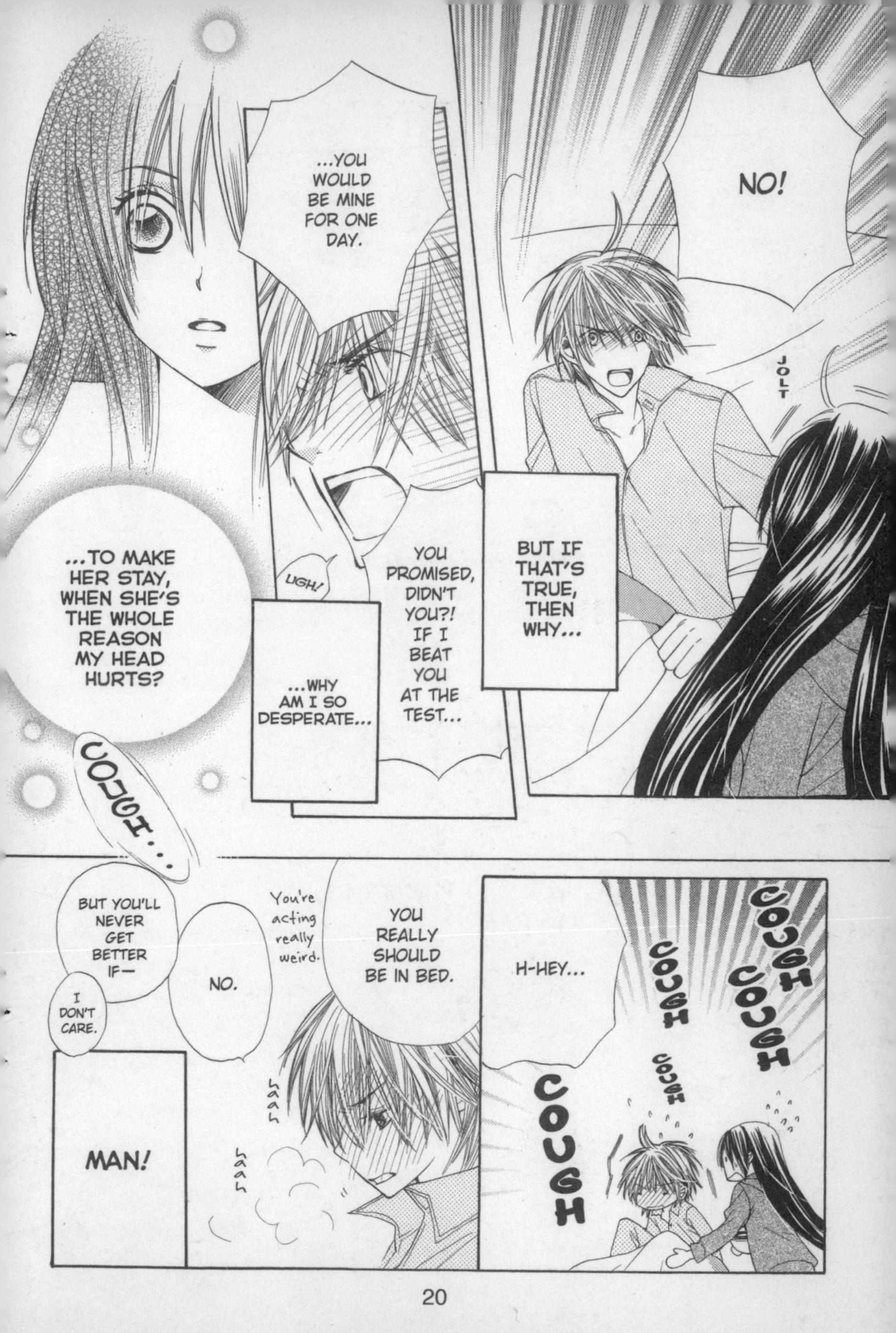
NO!
JOLT
BUT IF THAT'S TRUE, THEN WHY...
YOU PROMISED, DIDN'T YOU?! IF I BEAT YOU AT THE TEST...
...YOU WOULD BE MINE FOR ONE DAY.
UGH!
...WHY AM I SO DESPERATE...
...TO MAKE HER STAY, WHEN SHE'S THE WHOLE REASON MY HEAD HURTS?
COUGH...
COUGH COUGH
COUGH
COUGH
COUGH
COUGH
H-HEY...
YOU REALLY SHOULD BE IN BED.
You're acting really weird.
haah
haah
NO.
BUT YOU'LL NEVER GET BETTER IF—
I DON'T CARE.
MAN!

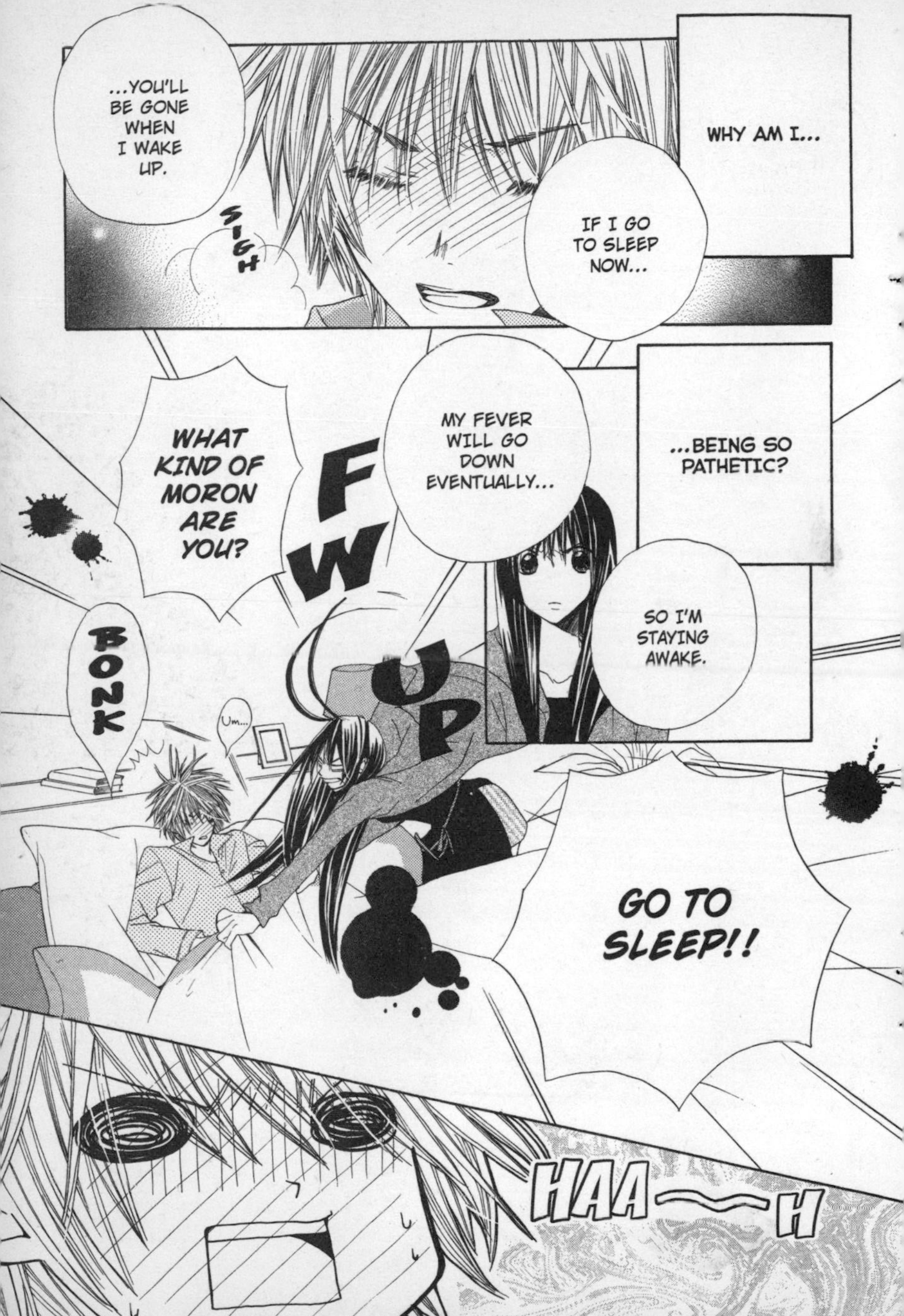
WHY AM I...
IF I GO TO SLEEP NOW...
...YOU'LL BE GONE WHEN I WAKE UP.
SIGH
...BEING SO PATHETIC?
SO I'M STAYING AWAKE.
MY FEVER WILL GO DOWN EVENTUALLY...
WHAT KIND OF MORON ARE YOU?
FWUP
BONK
Um...
GO TO SLEEP!!
HAA——H

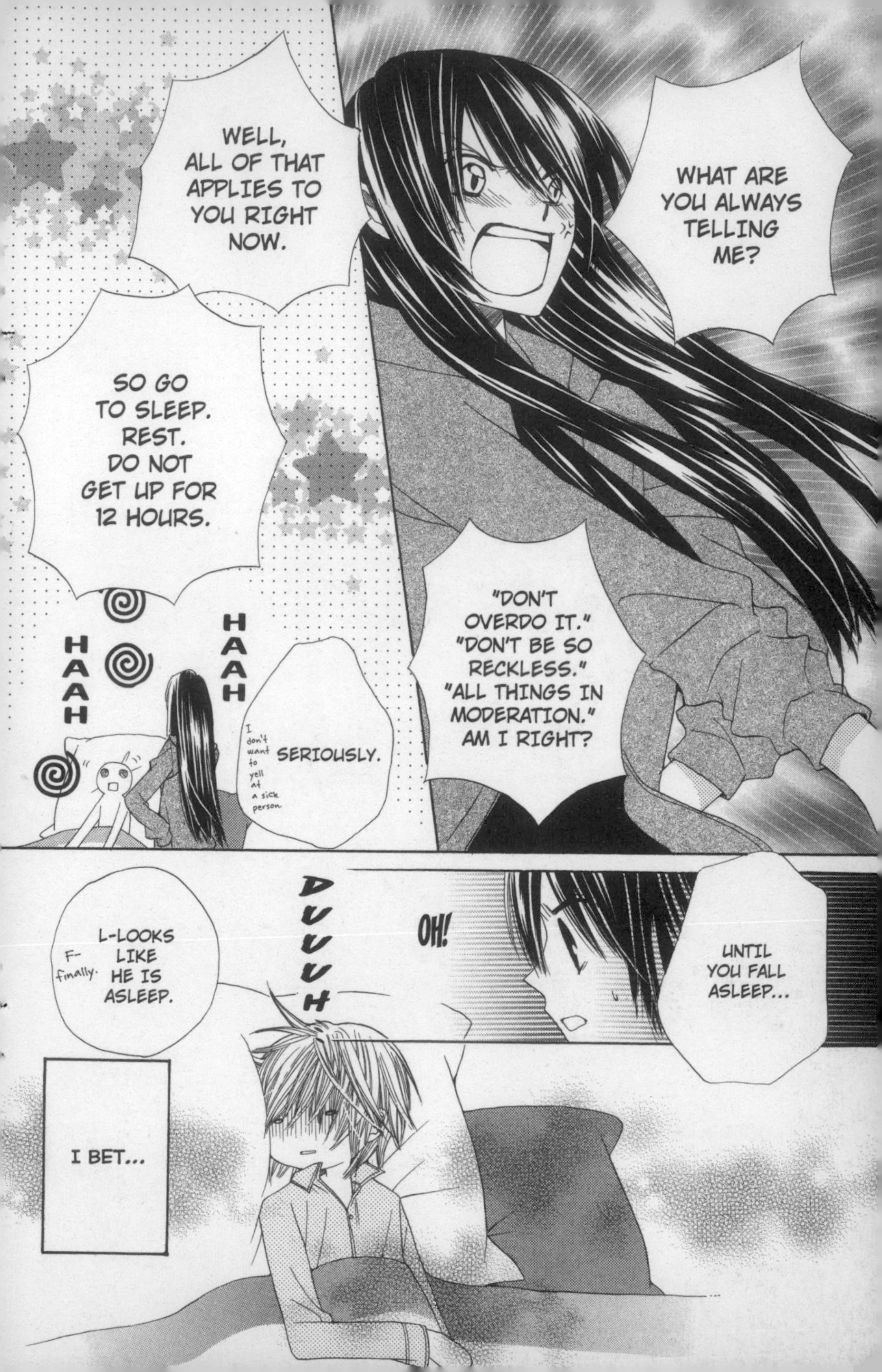
WHAT ARE YOU ALWAYS TELLING ME?
"DON'T OVERDO IT." "DON'T BE SO RECKLESS." "ALL THINGS IN MODERATION." AM I RIGHT?
WELL, ALL OF THAT APPLIES TO YOU RIGHT NOW.
SO GO TO SLEEP. REST. DO NOT GET UP FOR 12 HOURS.
HAAH
HAAH
SERIOUSLY.
I don't want to yell at a sick person.
UNTIL YOU FALL ASLEEP...
OH!
DUUUUH
L-LOOKS LIKE HE IS ASLEEP.
F-finally.
I BET...

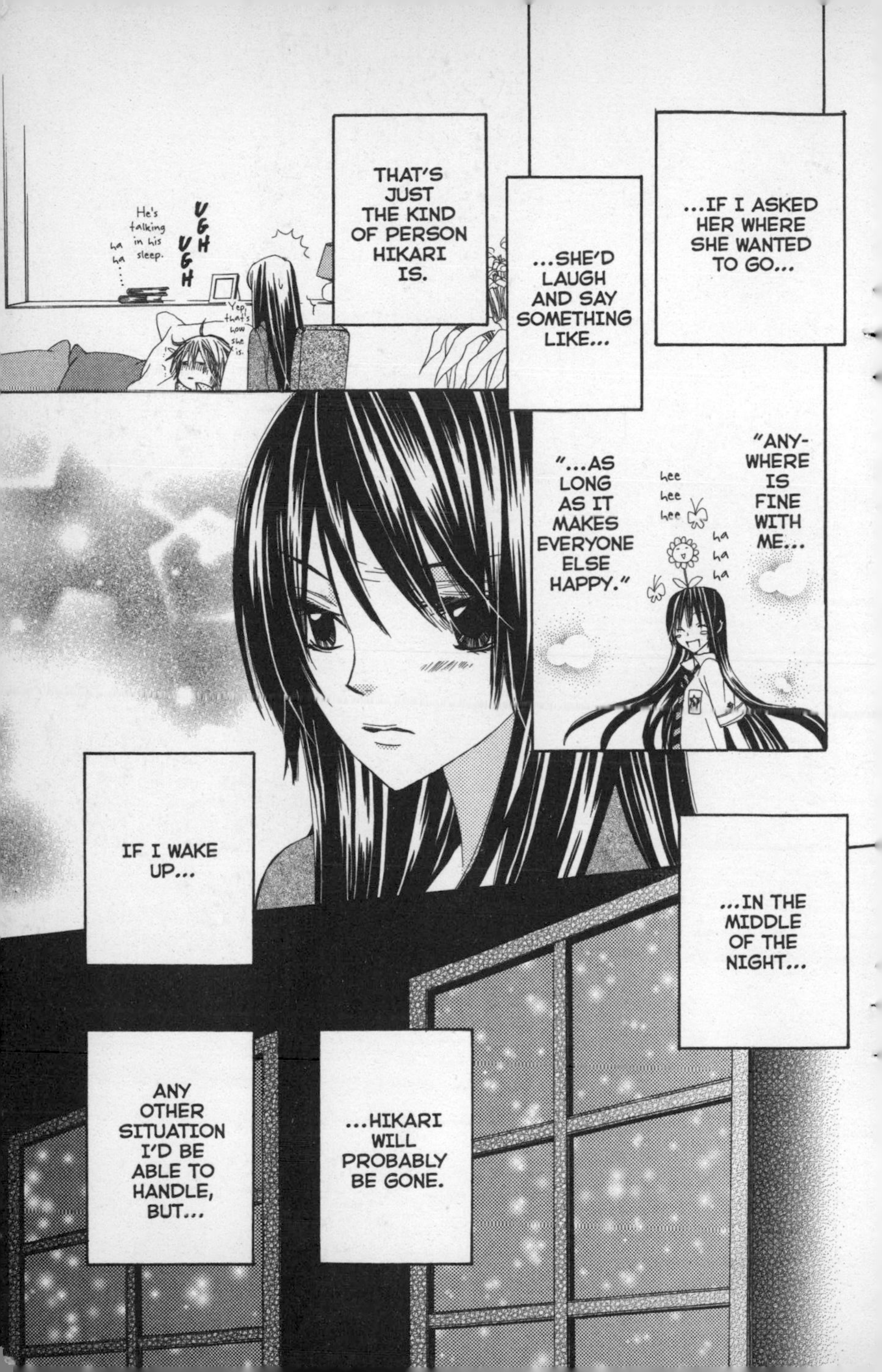
...IF I ASKED HER WHERE SHE WANTED TO GO...
...SHE'D LAUGH AND SAY SOMETHING LIKE...
"ANY-WHERE IS FINE WITH ME...
hee hee hee
ha ha ha
"...AS LONG AS IT MAKES EVERYONE ELSE HAPPY."
THAT'S JUST THE KIND OF PERSON HIKARI IS.
UGH UGH
He's talking in his sleep.
ha ha...
Yep, that's how she is.
...IN THE MIDDLE OF THE NIGHT...
IF I WAKE UP...
...HIKARI WILL PROBABLY BE GONE.
ANY OTHER SITUATION I'D BE ABLE TO HANDLE, BUT...

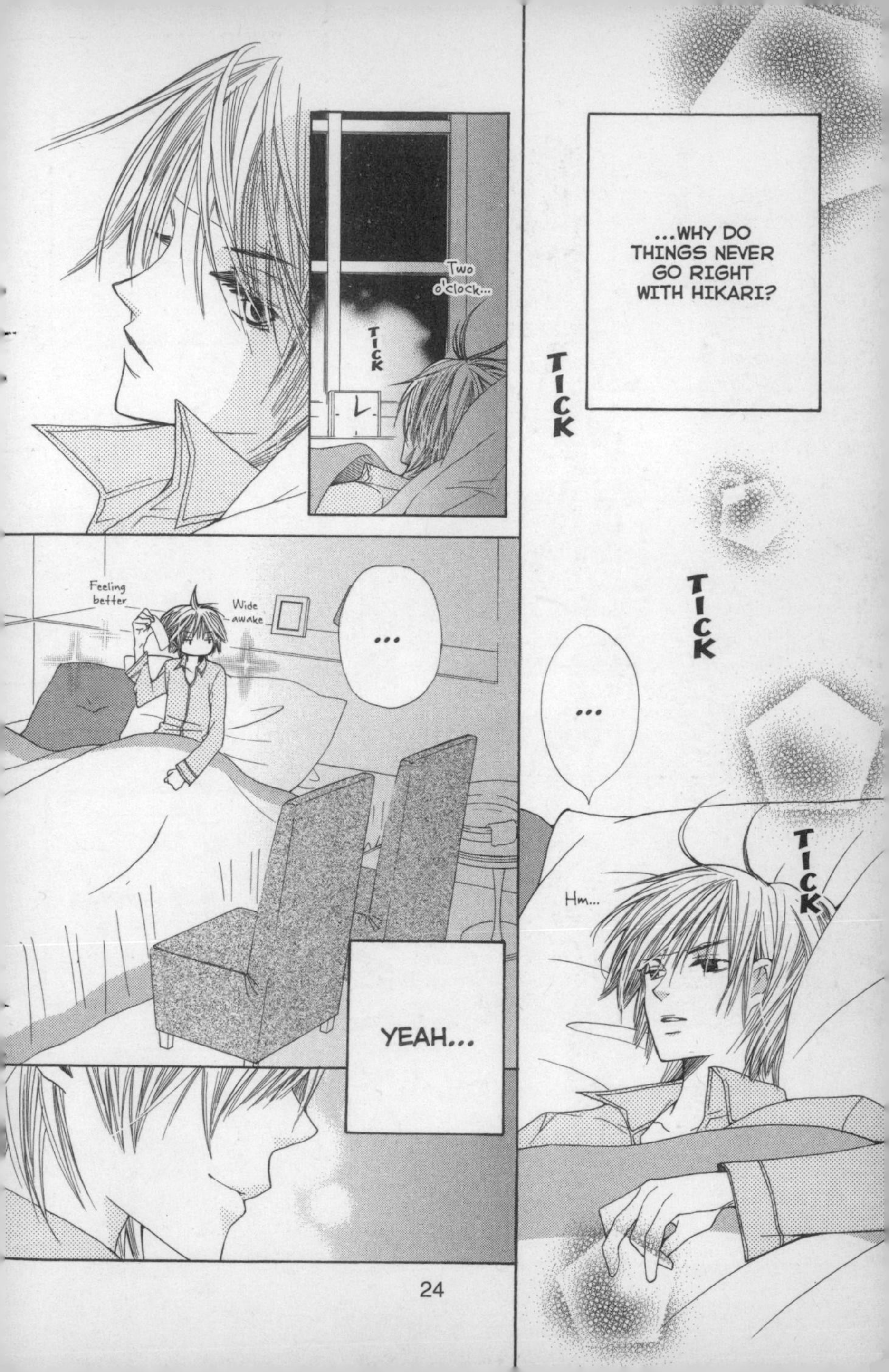
...WHY DO THINGS NEVER GO RIGHT WITH HIKARI?
TICK
TICK
...
TICK
Hm...
Two o'clock...
TICK
...
Feeling better
Wide awake
YEAH...

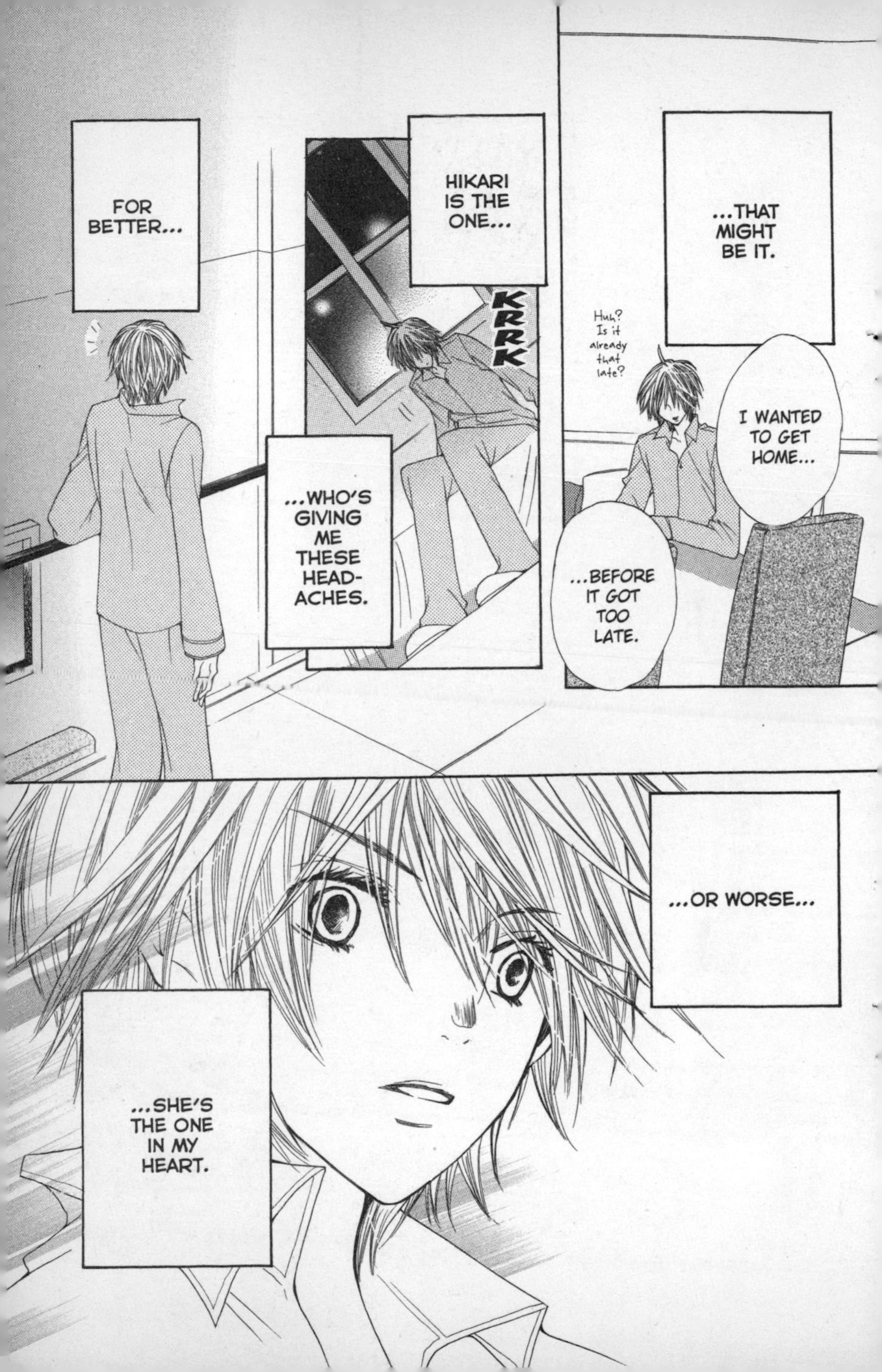
...THAT MIGHT BE IT.
Huh? Is it already that late?
I WANTED TO GET HOME...
...BEFORE IT GOT TOO LATE.
HIKARI IS THE ONE...
KRRK
...WHO'S GIVING ME THESE HEAD-ACHES.
FOR BETTER...
...OR WORSE...
...SHE'S THE ONE IN MY HEART.

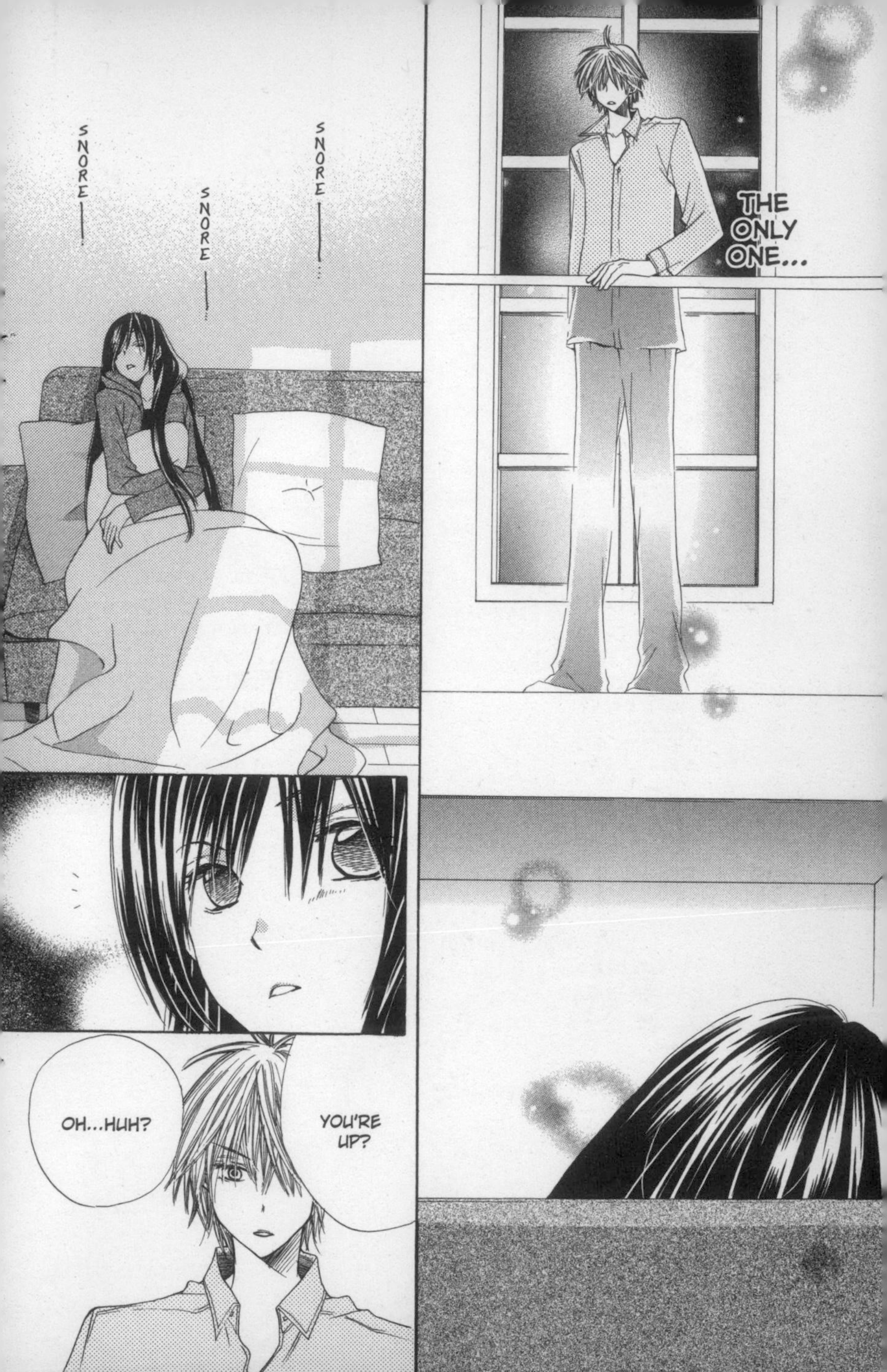
THE ONLY ONE...
SNORE
SNORE
SNORE
YOU'RE UP?
OH...HUH?

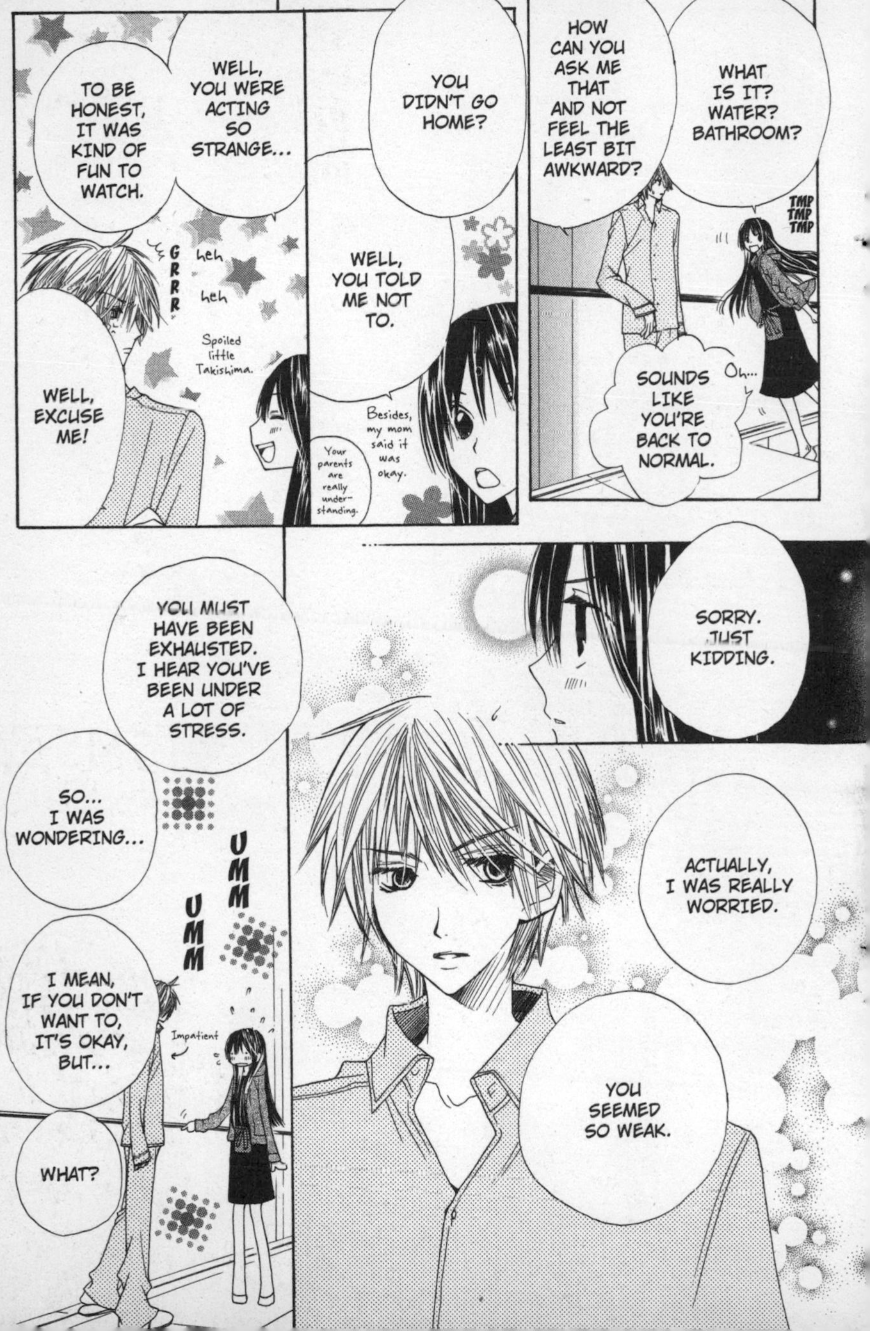
WHAT IS IT? WATER? BATHROOM?
TMP TMP TMP
HOW CAN YOU ASK ME THAT AND NOT FEEL THE LEAST BIT AWKWARD?
Oh...
SOUNDS LIKE YOU'RE BACK TO NORMAL.
YOU DIDN'T GO HOME?
WELL, YOU TOLD ME NOT TO.
Besides, my mom said it was okay.
Your parents are really understanding.
WELL, YOU WERE ACTING SO STRANGE...
TO BE HONEST, IT WAS KIND OF FUN TO WATCH.
heh heh
GRRR
Spoiled little Takishima.
WELL, EXCUSE ME!
...
SORRY. JUST KIDDING.
ACTUALLY, I WAS REALLY WORRIED.
YOU SEEMED SO WEAK.
YOU MUST HAVE BEEN EXHAUSTED. I HEAR YOU'VE BEEN UNDER A LOT OF STRESS.
SO... I WAS WONDERING...
UMM UMM
I MEAN, IF YOU DON'T WANT TO, IT'S OKAY, BUT...
Impatient
WHAT?

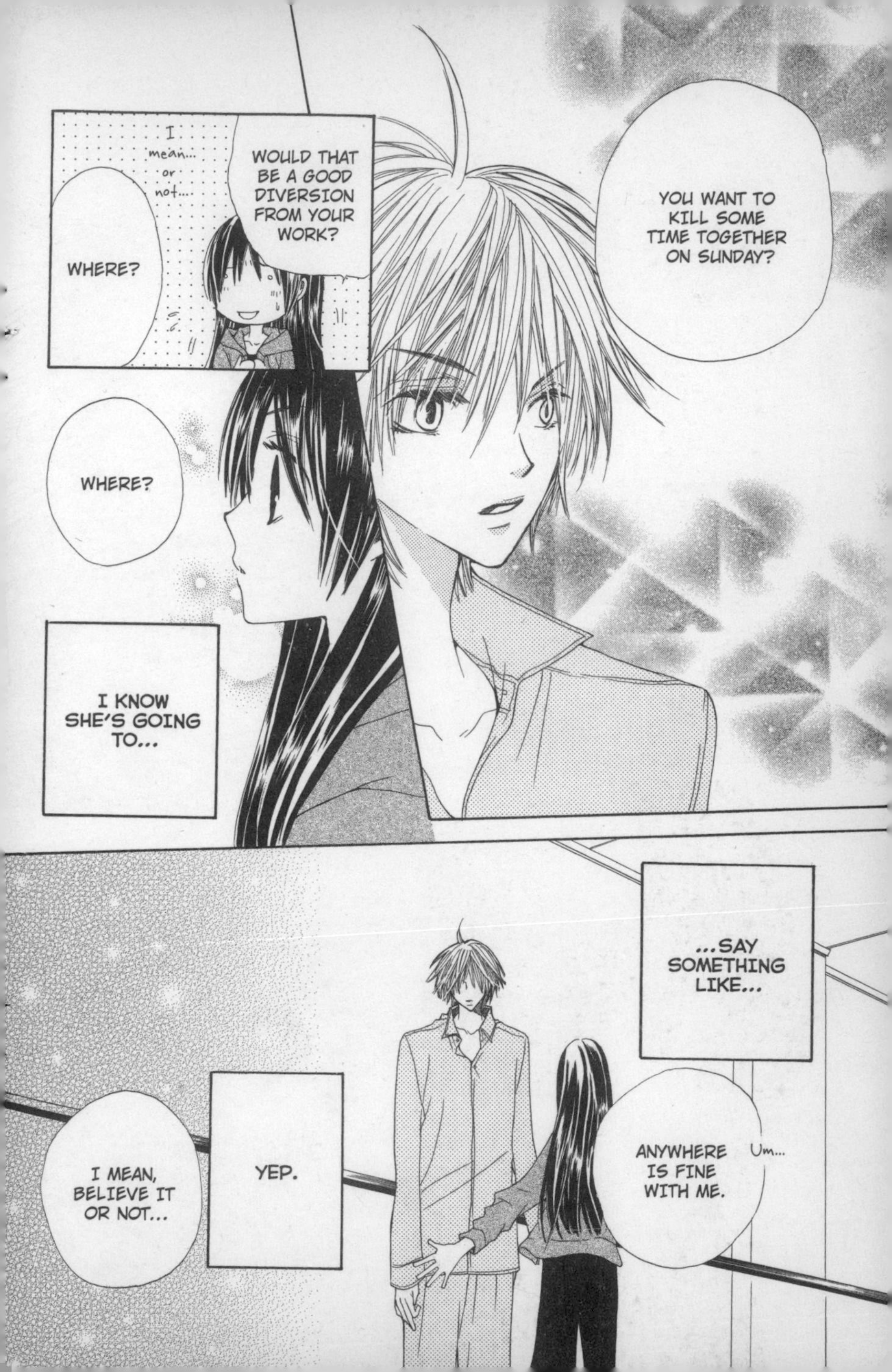

YOU WANT TO KILL SOME TIME TOGETHER ON SUNDAY?
WOULD THAT BE A GOOD DIVERSION FROM YOUR WORK?
I mean... or not...
WHERE?
WHERE?
I KNOW SHE'S GOING TO...
...SAY SOMETHING LIKE...
ANYWHERE IS FINE WITH ME.
Um...
YEP.
I MEAN, BELIEVE IT OR NOT...

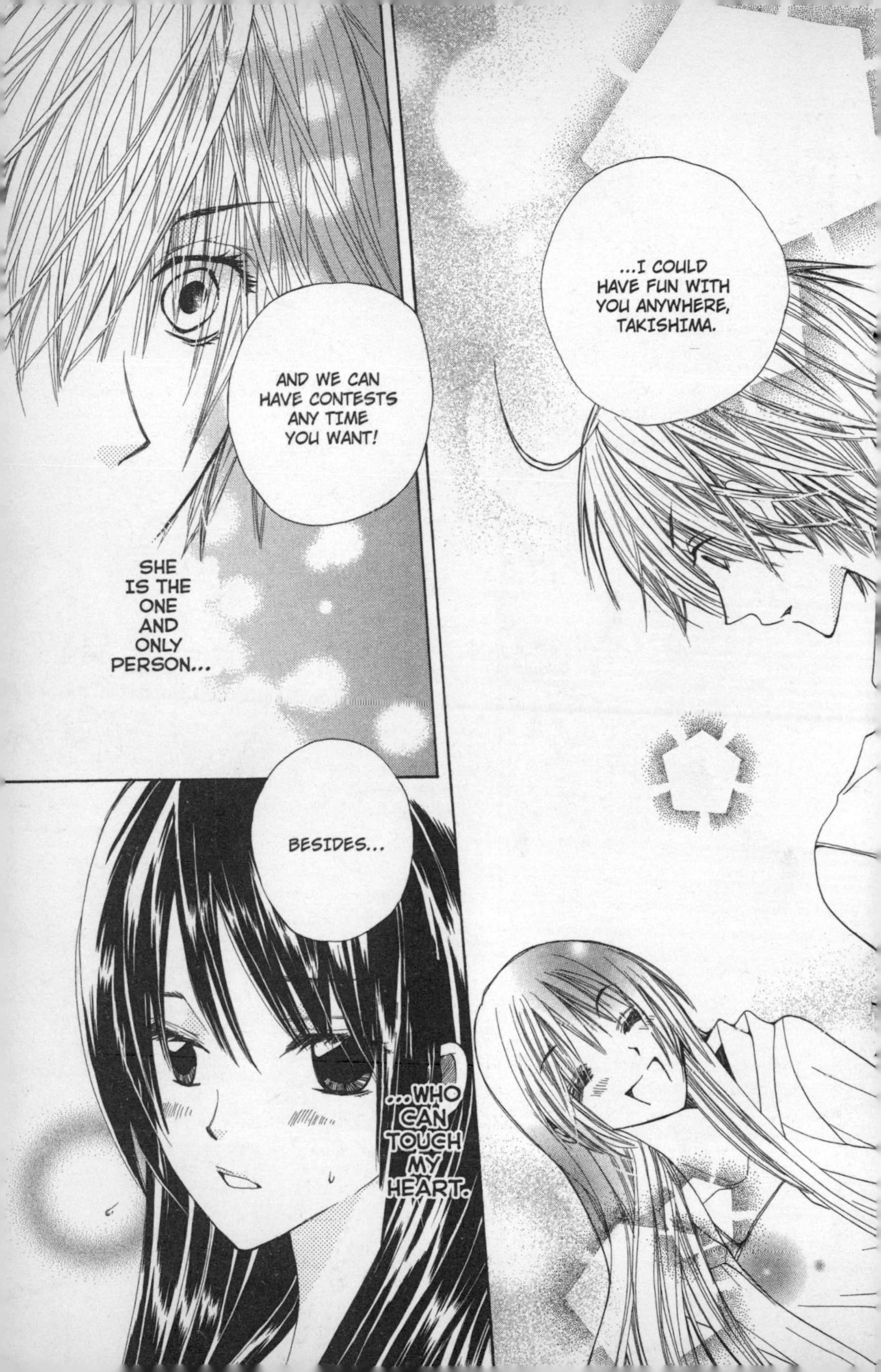
...I COULD HAVE FUN WITH YOU ANYWHERE, TAKISHIMA.
AND WE CAN HAVE CONTESTS ANY TIME YOU WANT!
SHE IS THE ONE AND ONLY PERSON...
BESIDES...
...WHO CAN TOUCH MY HEART.

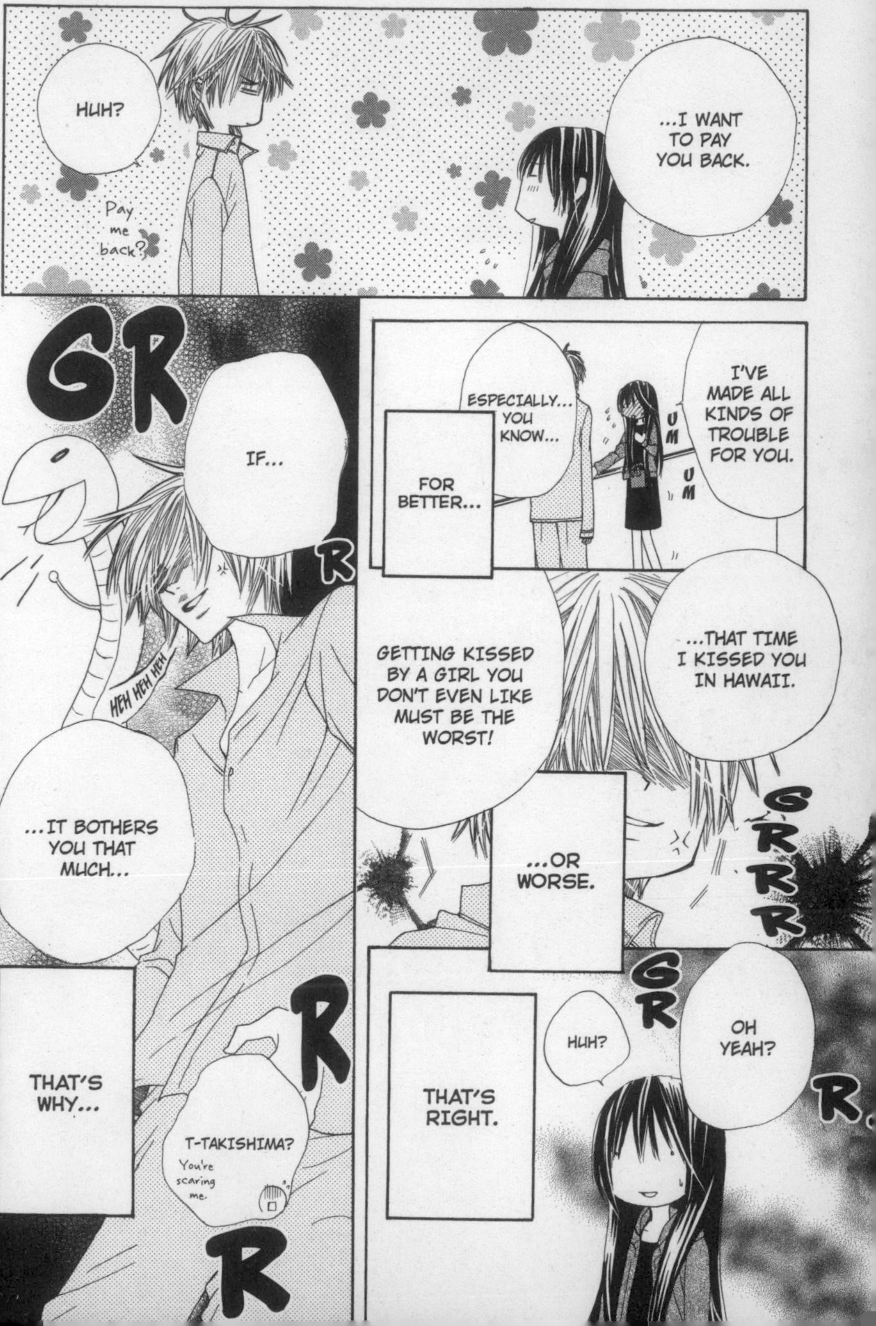
...I WANT TO PAY YOU BACK.
HUH?
Pay me back?
I'VE MADE ALL KINDS OF TROUBLE FOR YOU.
UM UM
ESPECIALLY... YOU KNOW...
FOR BETTER...
...THAT TIME I KISSED YOU IN HAWAII.
GETTING KISSED BY A GIRL YOU DON'T EVEN LIKE MUST BE THE WORST!
GRRRR
...OR WORSE.
OH YEAH?
GR
R.
HUH?
THAT'S RIGHT.
GR
IF...
R
HEH HEH HEH
...IT BOTHERS YOU THAT MUCH...
R
THAT'S WHY...
T-TAKISHIMA?
You're scaring me.
R

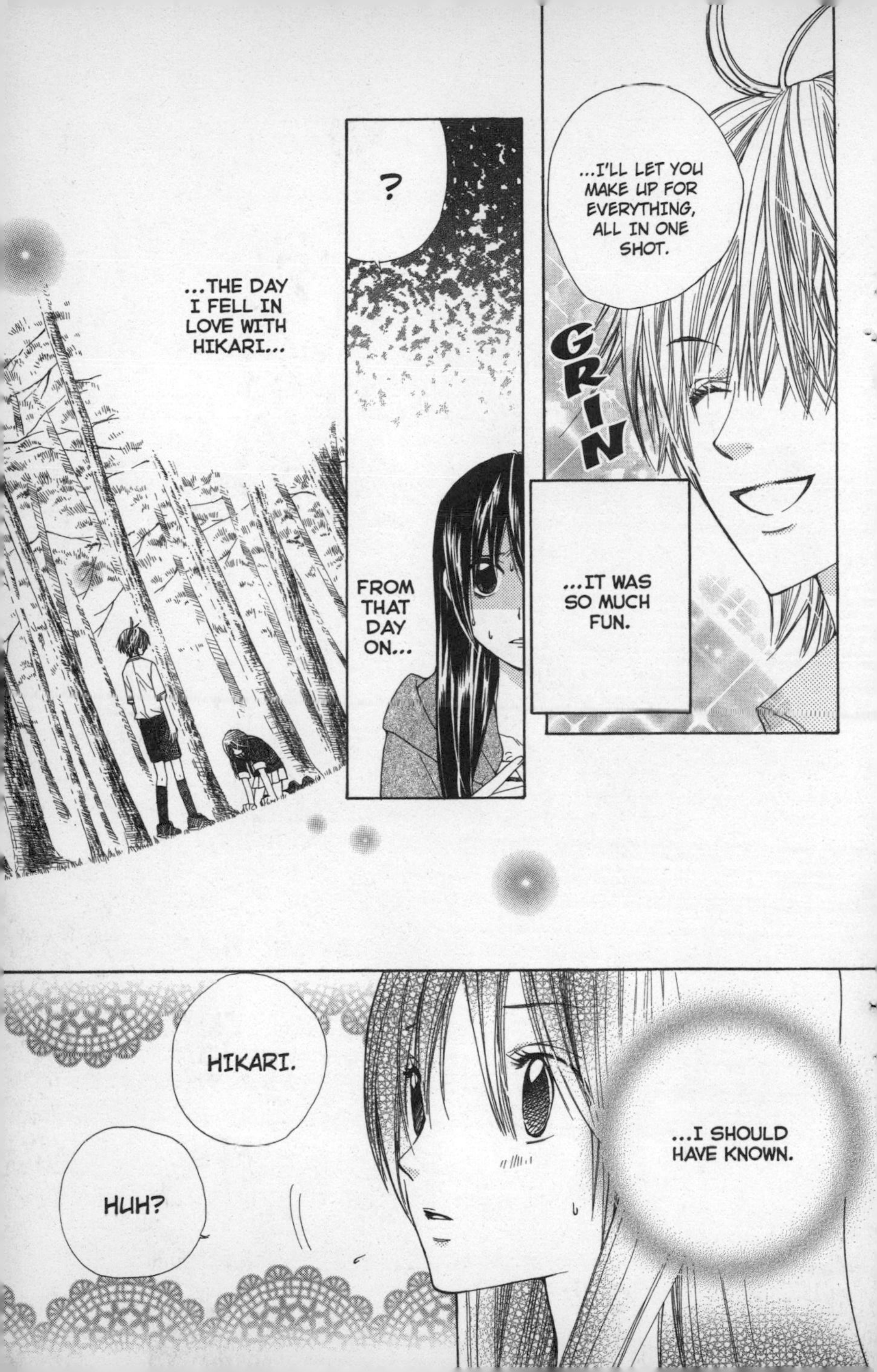
...I'LL LET YOU MAKE UP FOR EVERYTHING, ALL IN ONE SHOT.
GRIN
...IT WAS SO MUCH FUN.
?
FROM THAT DAY ON...
...THE DAY I FELL IN LOVE WITH HIKARI...
...I SHOULD HAVE KNOWN.
HIKARI.
HUH?

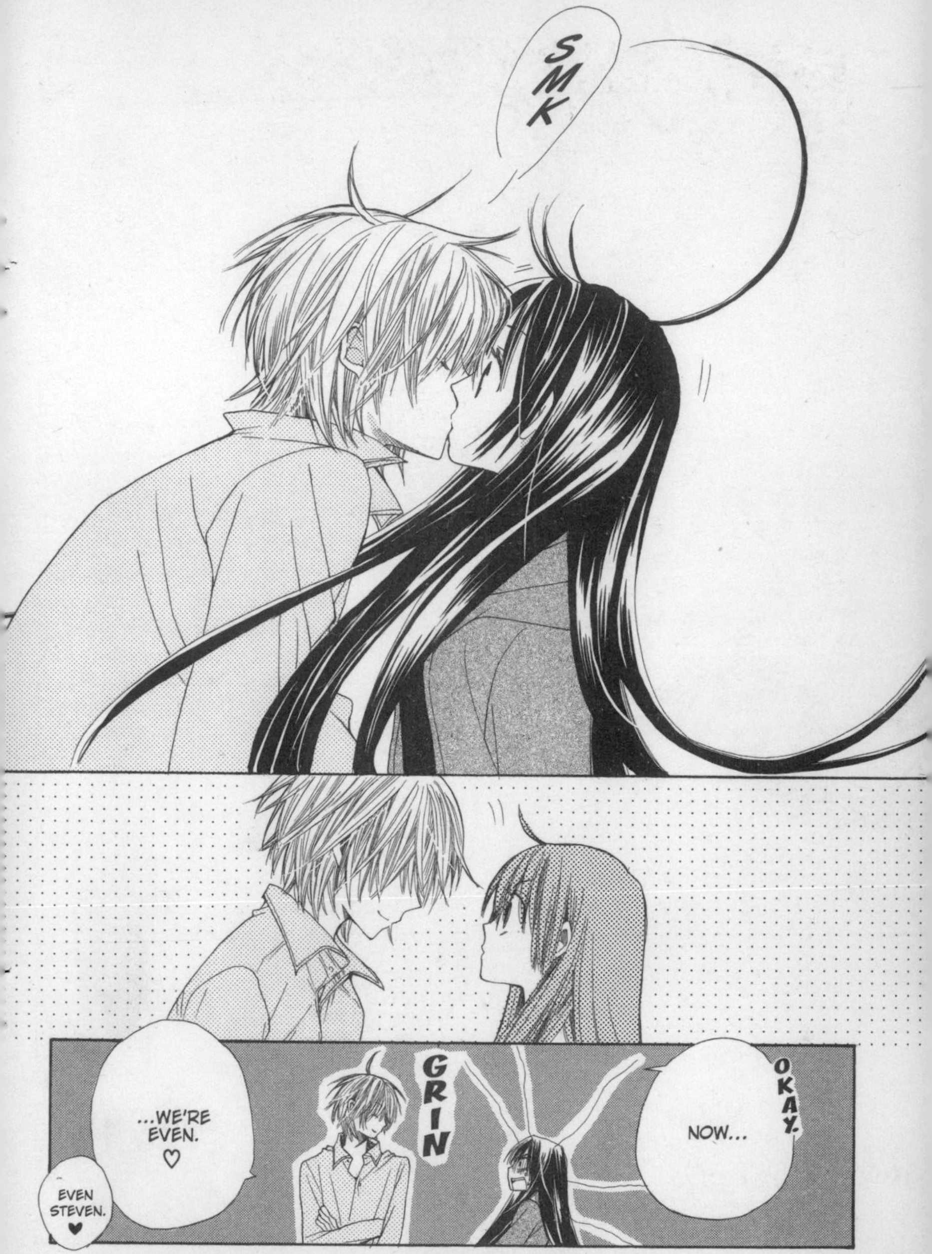
SMK
OKAY.
NOW...
GRIN
...WE'RE EVEN. ♡
EVEN STEVEN. ♥

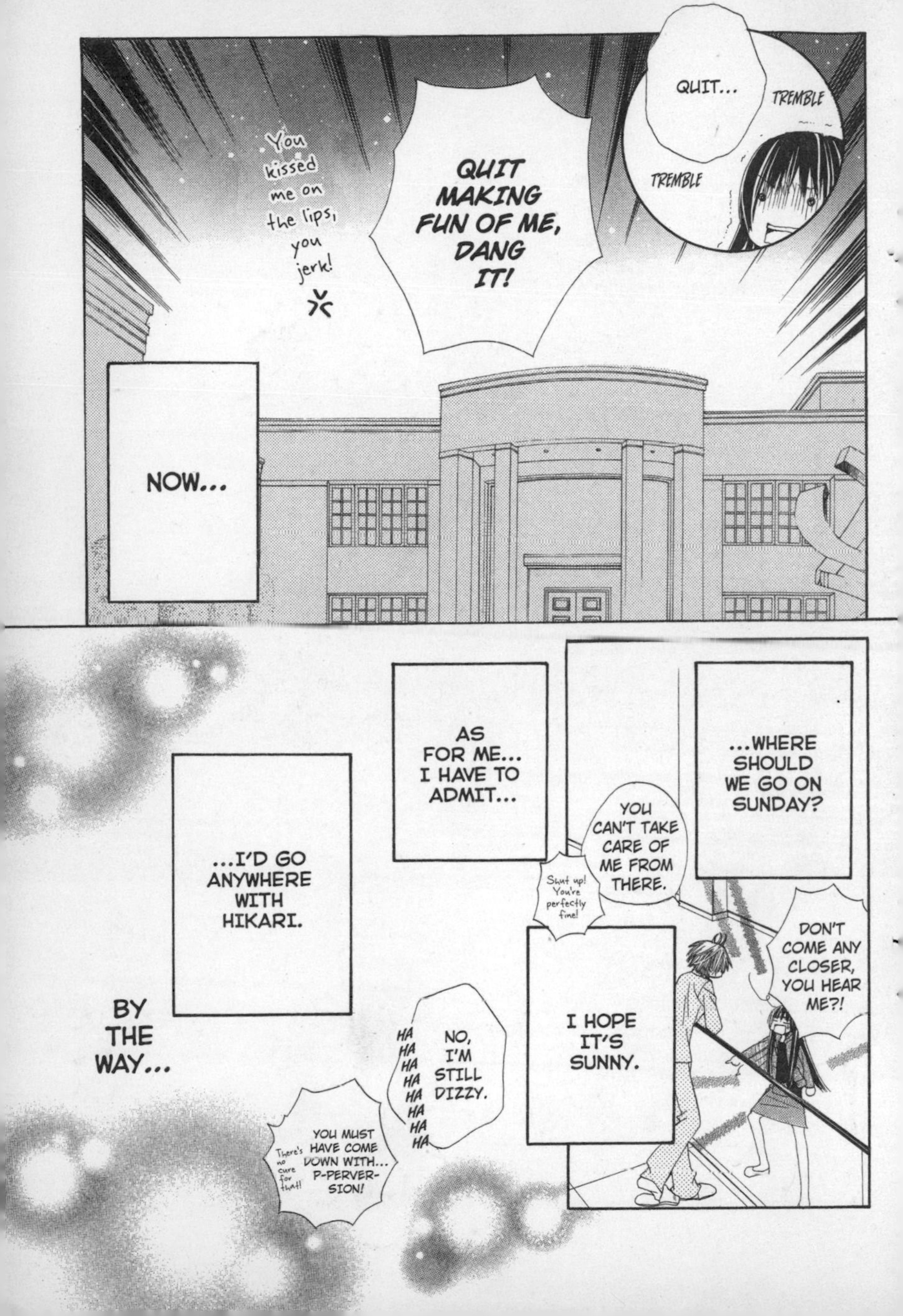
QUIT...
TREMBLE
TREMBLE
QUIT MAKING FUN OF ME, DANG IT!
You kissed me on the lips, you jerk!
NOW...
...WHERE SHOULD WE GO ON SUNDAY?
DON'T COME ANY CLOSER, YOU HEAR ME?!
YOU CAN'T TAKE CARE OF ME FROM THERE.
Shut up! You're perfectly fine!
I HOPE IT'S SUNNY.
AS FOR ME... I HAVE TO ADMIT...
...I'D GO ANYWHERE WITH HIKARI.
NO, I'M STILL DIZZY.
HA HA HA HA HA HA HA HA
YOU MUST HAVE COME DOWN WITH... P-PERVER-SION!
There's no cure for that!
BY THE WAY...

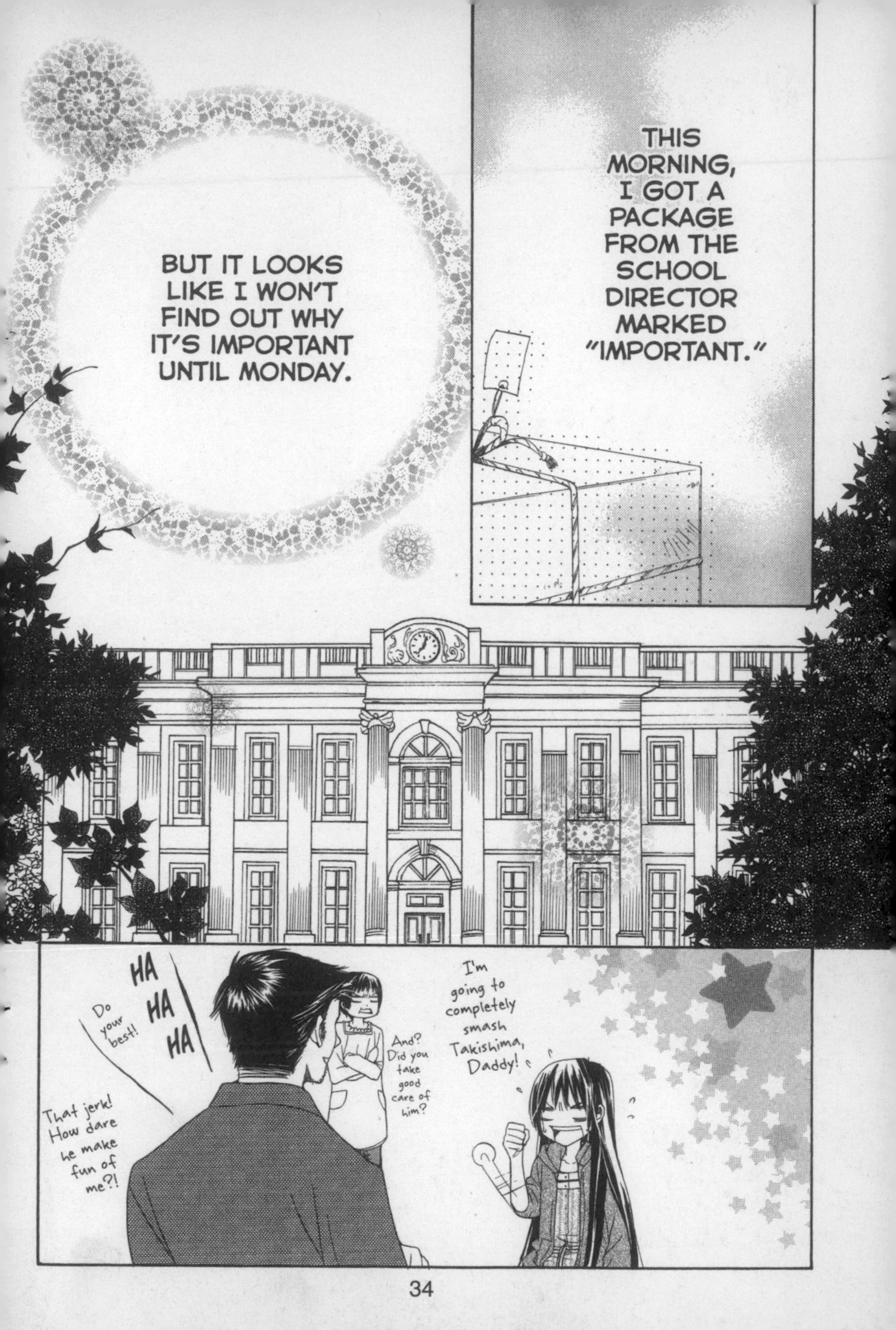
THIS MORNING, I GOT A PACKAGE FROM THE SCHOOL DIRECTOR MARKED "IMPORTANT."
BUT IT LOOKS LIKE I WON'T FIND OUT WHY IT'S IMPORTANT UNTIL MONDAY.
I'm going to completely smash Takishima, Daddy!
And? Did you take good care of him?
HA HA HA
Do your best!
That jerk! How dare he make fun of me?!

Chapter 18

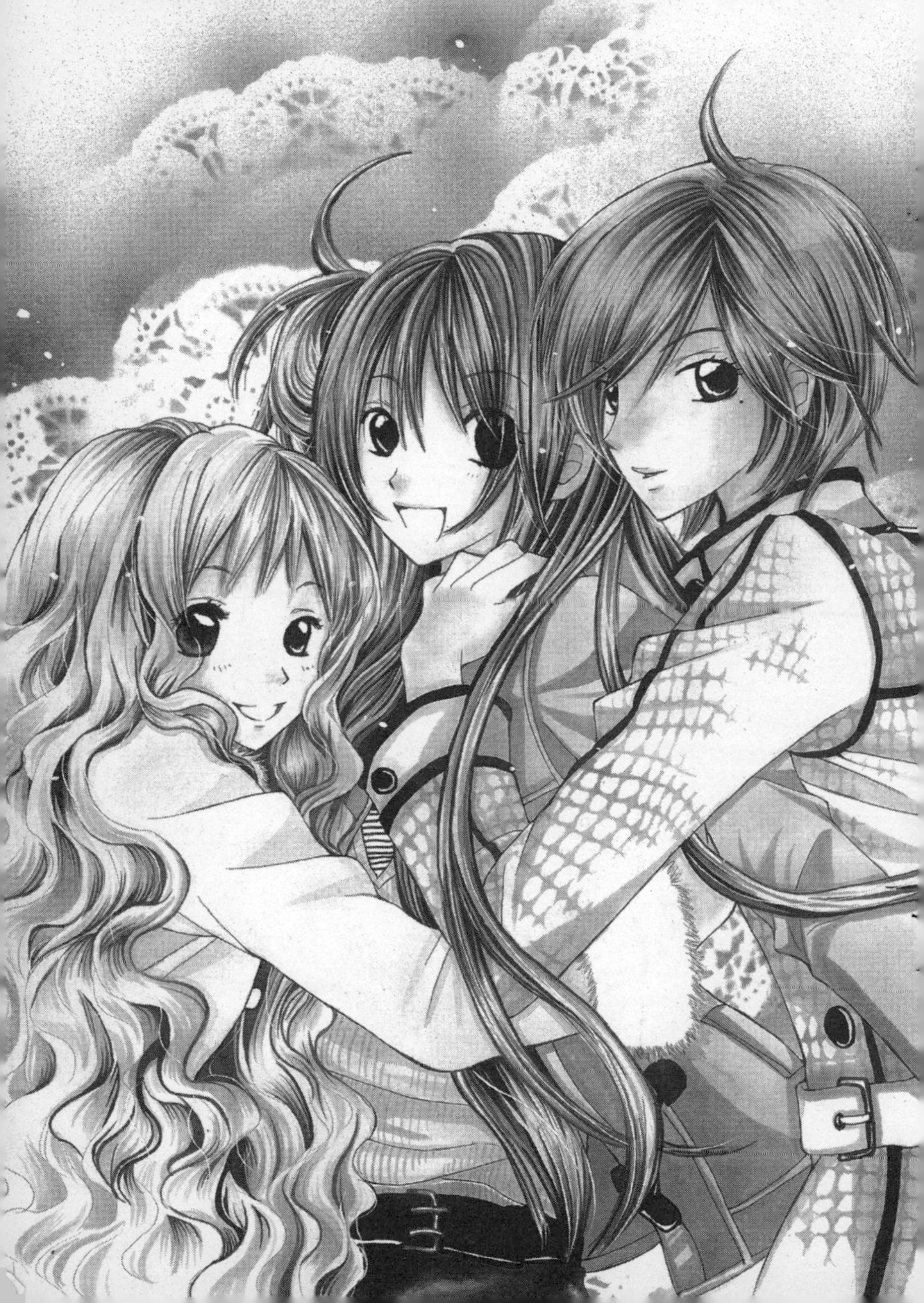

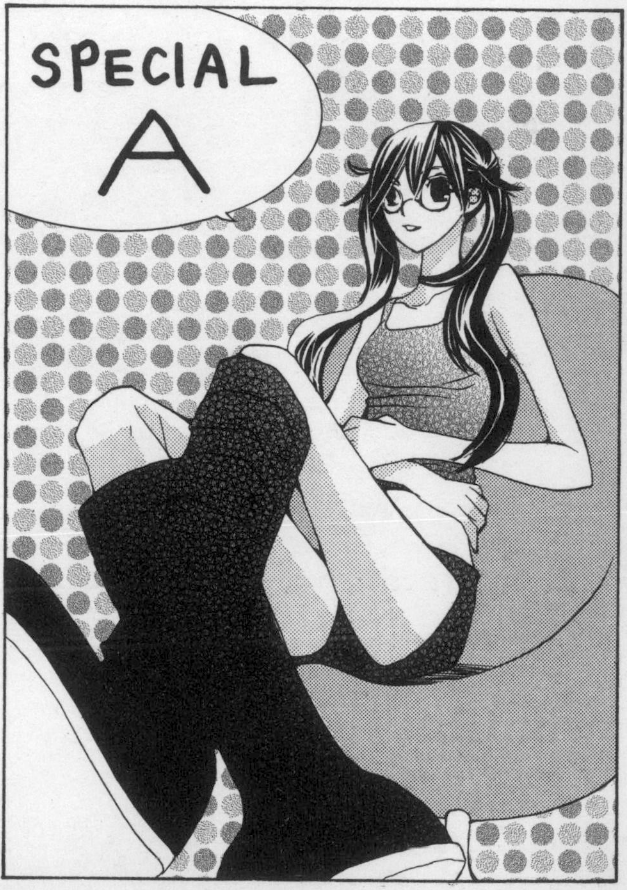
SPECIAL
A

··● Fuji?

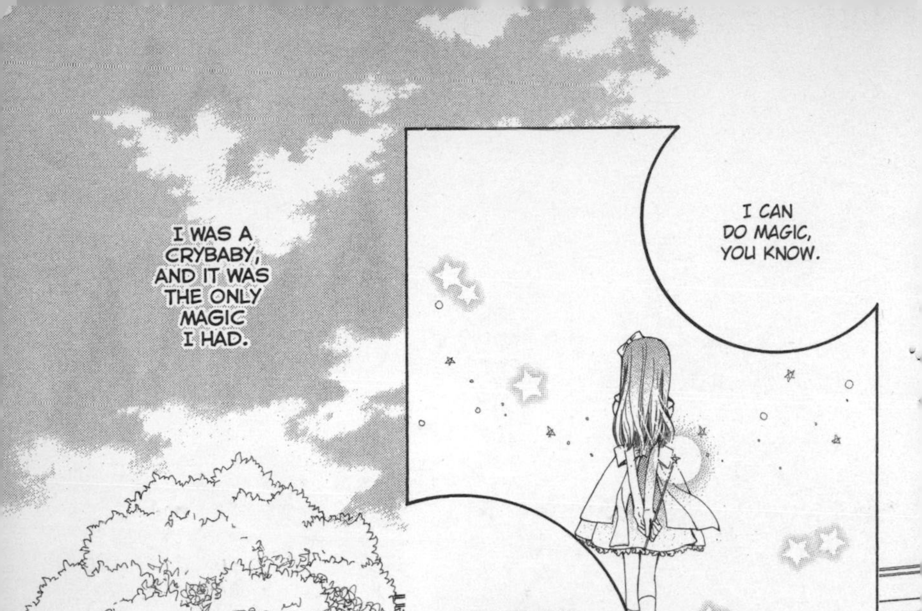
I CAN DO MAGIC, YOU KNOW.
IT'S THE KIND OF MAGIC THAT CAN PUT ANYONE IN A BETTER MOOD.
I WAS A CRYBABY, AND IT WAS THE ONLY MAGIC I HAD.
THE TOUDOU MANSION, SUNDAY
WHAT?!

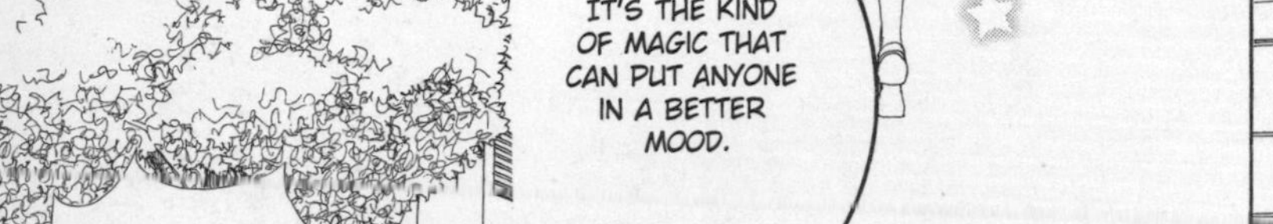
•SONGS•
B
I COULDN'T THINK OF A TOPIC THIS TIME, SO I'M GOING TO SING.
strumm
One... two... three...
TAP
TAP
1
A TOPIC? NO, I HAVE NOTHING TO SAY. WHAT I DID? NO, I FORGOT MY WHOLE DAY. NOT MUCH TO SING, BUT I DO KNOW ONE THING...
CHORD
CHANGE!
2
I ALWAYS...
strum
3
...REMEMBER WHAT I ATE! OH YEAH... I ALWAYS REMEMBER WHAT I ATE... OHHH... CHICKEN KEBABS MONDAY, POT-STICKERS TUESDAY, WEDNESDAY PLUM AND CAKES OF RICE! I ALWAYS REMEMBER WHAT I ATE, BECAUSE WHAT I EAT IS SO VERY NICE! CHICKEN KEBABS MONDAY, POT-STICKERS TUESDAY, WEDNESDAY PLUM PUDDING AND CAKES OF RICE! AND BEFORE THAT AN OMELET, YEAH...! WHOA...! AND EVEN BEFORE THAT, COLD NOODLES, OHHH...!
strumm
Somebody make it stop!
4

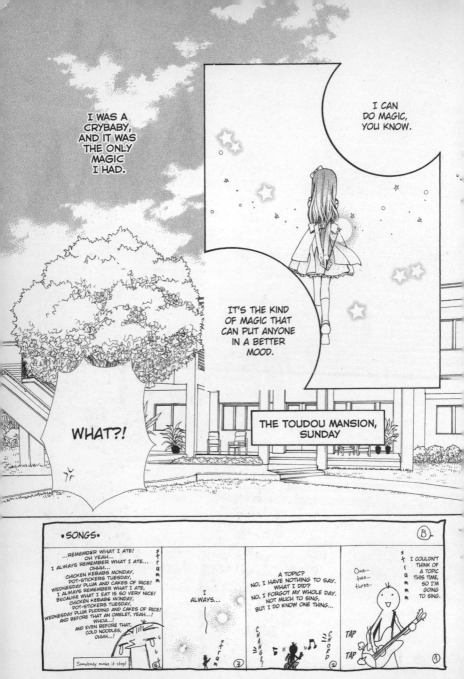

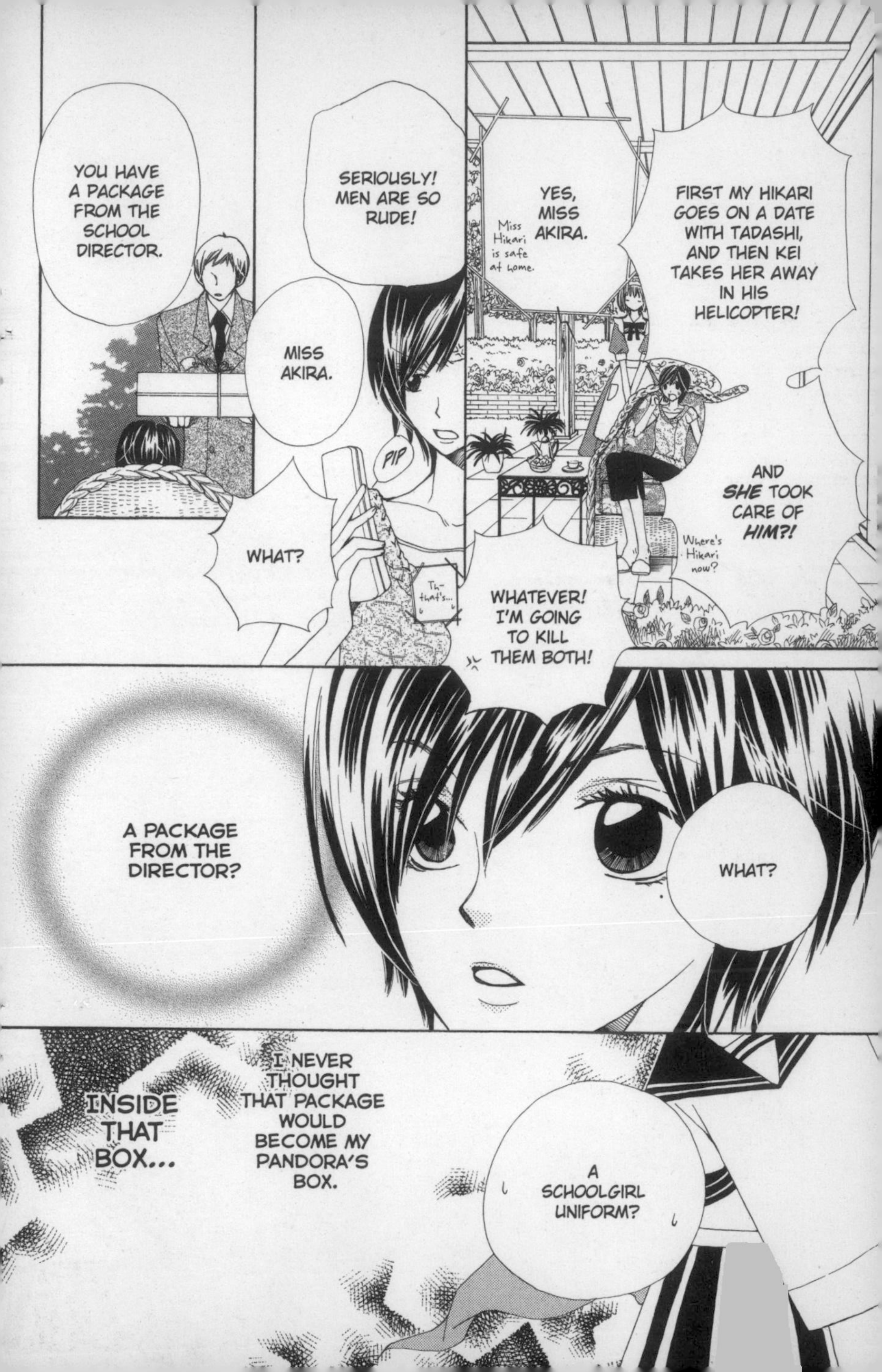
FIRST MY HIKARI GOES ON A DATE WITH TADASHI, AND THEN KEI TAKES HER AWAY IN HIS HELICOPTER!
YES, MISS AKIRA.
Miss Hikari is safe at home.
AND SHE TOOK CARE OF HIM?!
Where's Hikari now?
WHATEVER! I'M GOING TO KILL THEM BOTH!
SERIOUSLY! MEN ARE SO RUDE!
PIP
MISS AKIRA.
YOU HAVE A PACKAGE FROM THE SCHOOL DIRECTOR.
Th-that's...
WHAT?
WHAT?
A PACKAGE FROM THE DIRECTOR?
A SCHOOLGIRL UNIFORM?
I NEVER THOUGHT THAT PACKAGE WOULD BECOME MY PANDORA'S BOX.
INSIDE THAT BOX...

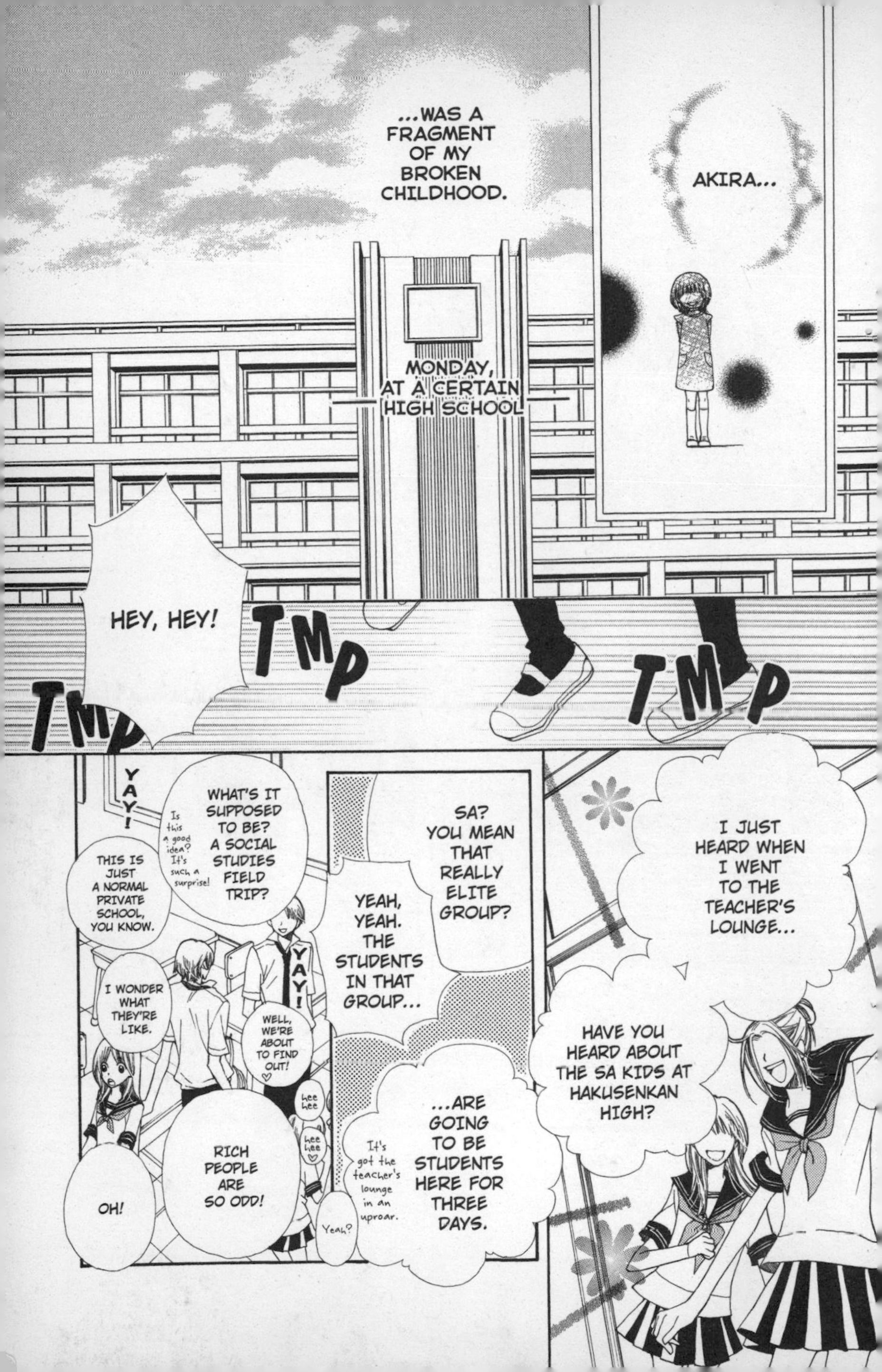
AKIRA...
...WAS A FRAGMENT OF MY BROKEN CHILDHOOD.
MONDAY, AT A CERTAIN HIGH SCHOOL
TMP
TMP
HEY, HEY!
TMP
I JUST HEARD WHEN I WENT TO THE TEACHER'S LOUNGE...
HAVE YOU HEARD ABOUT THE SA KIDS AT HAKUSENKAN HIGH?
SA? YOU MEAN THAT REALLY ELITE GROUP?
YEAH, YEAH. THE STUDENTS IN THAT GROUP...
...ARE GOING TO BE STUDENTS HERE FOR THREE DAYS.
It's got the teacher's lounge in an uproar.
Yeah?
YAY!
WHAT'S IT SUPPOSED TO BE? A SOCIAL STUDIES FIELD TRIP?
Is this a good idea? It's such a surprise!
THIS IS JUST A NORMAL PRIVATE SCHOOL, YOU KNOW.
YAY!
I WONDER WHAT THEY'RE LIKE.
WELL, WE'RE ABOUT TO FIND OUT! ♥
hee hee
hee hee ♥
RICH PEOPLE ARE SO ODD!
OH!

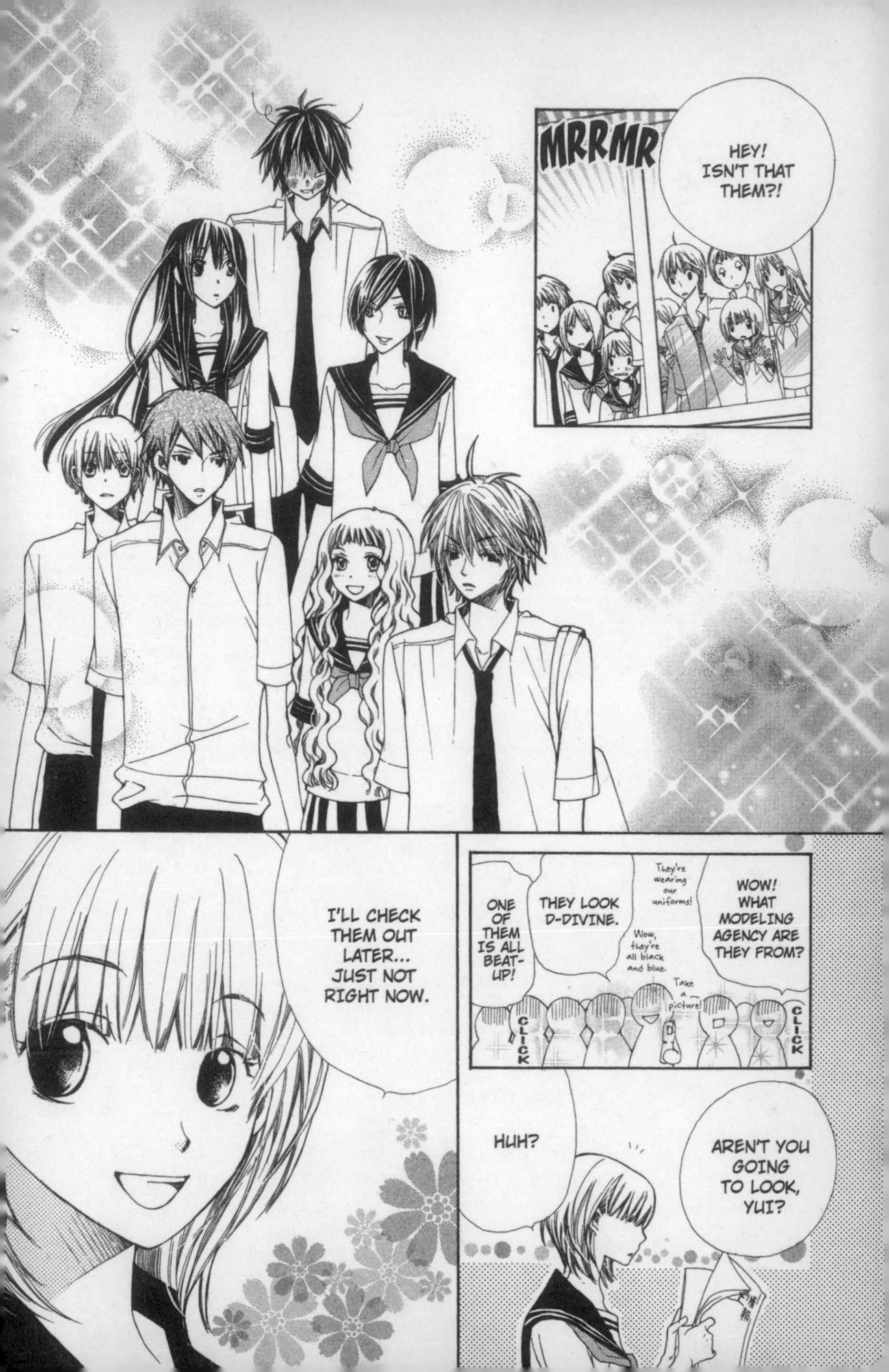
MRRMR
HEY! ISN'T THAT THEM?!
WOW! WHAT MODELING AGENCY ARE THEY FROM?
They're wearing our uniforms!
Wow, they're all black and blue.
THEY LOOK D-DIVINE.
ONE OF THEM IS ALL BEAT-UP!
Take a picture!
CLICK
CLICK
AREN'T YOU GOING TO LOOK, YUI?
HUH?
I'LL CHECK THEM OUT LATER... JUST NOT RIGHT NOW.

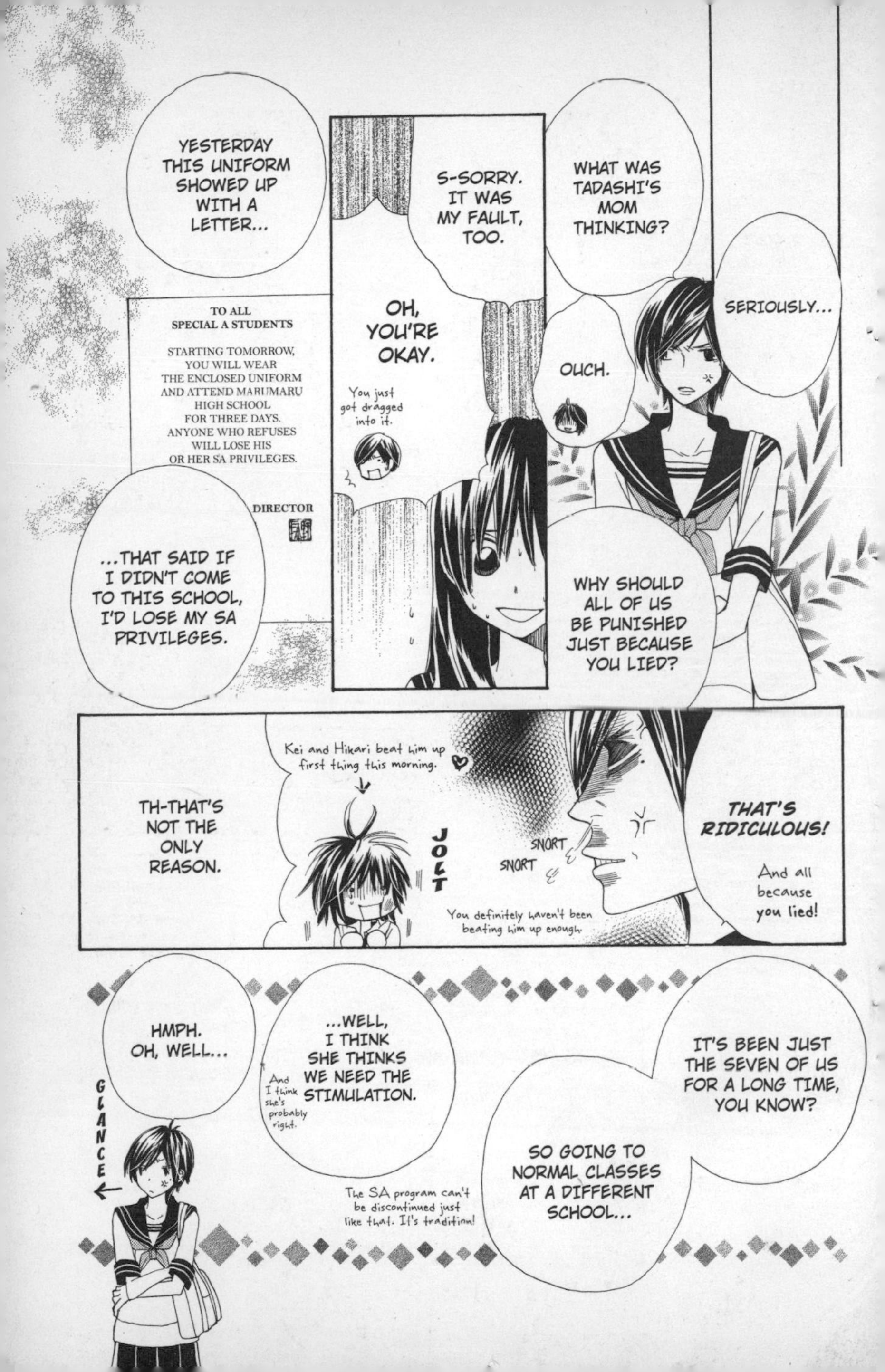
WHAT WAS TADASHI'S MOM THINKING?
SERIOUSLY...
OUCH.
WHY SHOULD ALL OF US BE PUNISHED JUST BECAUSE YOU LIED?
S-SORRY. IT WAS MY FAULT, TOO.
OH, YOU'RE OKAY.
You just got dragged into it.
YESTERDAY THIS UNIFORM SHOWED UP WITH A LETTER...
TO ALL SPECIAL A STUDENTS
STARTING TOMORROW, YOU WILL WEAR THE ENCLOSED UNIFORM AND ATTEND MARUMARU HIGH SCHOOL FOR THREE DAYS. ANYONE WHO REFUSES WILL LOSE HIS OR HER SA PRIVILEGES.
DIRECTOR
...THAT SAID IF I DIDN'T COME TO THIS SCHOOL, I'D LOSE MY SA PRIVILEGES.
THAT'S RIDICULOUS!
And all because you lied!
SNORT
SNORT
You definitely haven't been beating him up enough.
Kei and Hikari beat him up first thing this morning.
JOLT
TH-THAT'S NOT THE ONLY REASON.
IT'S BEEN JUST THE SEVEN OF US FOR A LONG TIME, YOU KNOW?
SO GOING TO NORMAL CLASSES AT A DIFFERENT SCHOOL...
...WELL, I THINK SHE THINKS WE NEED THE STIMULATION.
And I think she's probably right.
The SA program can't be discontinued just like that. It's tradition!
HMPH. OH, WELL...
GLANCE

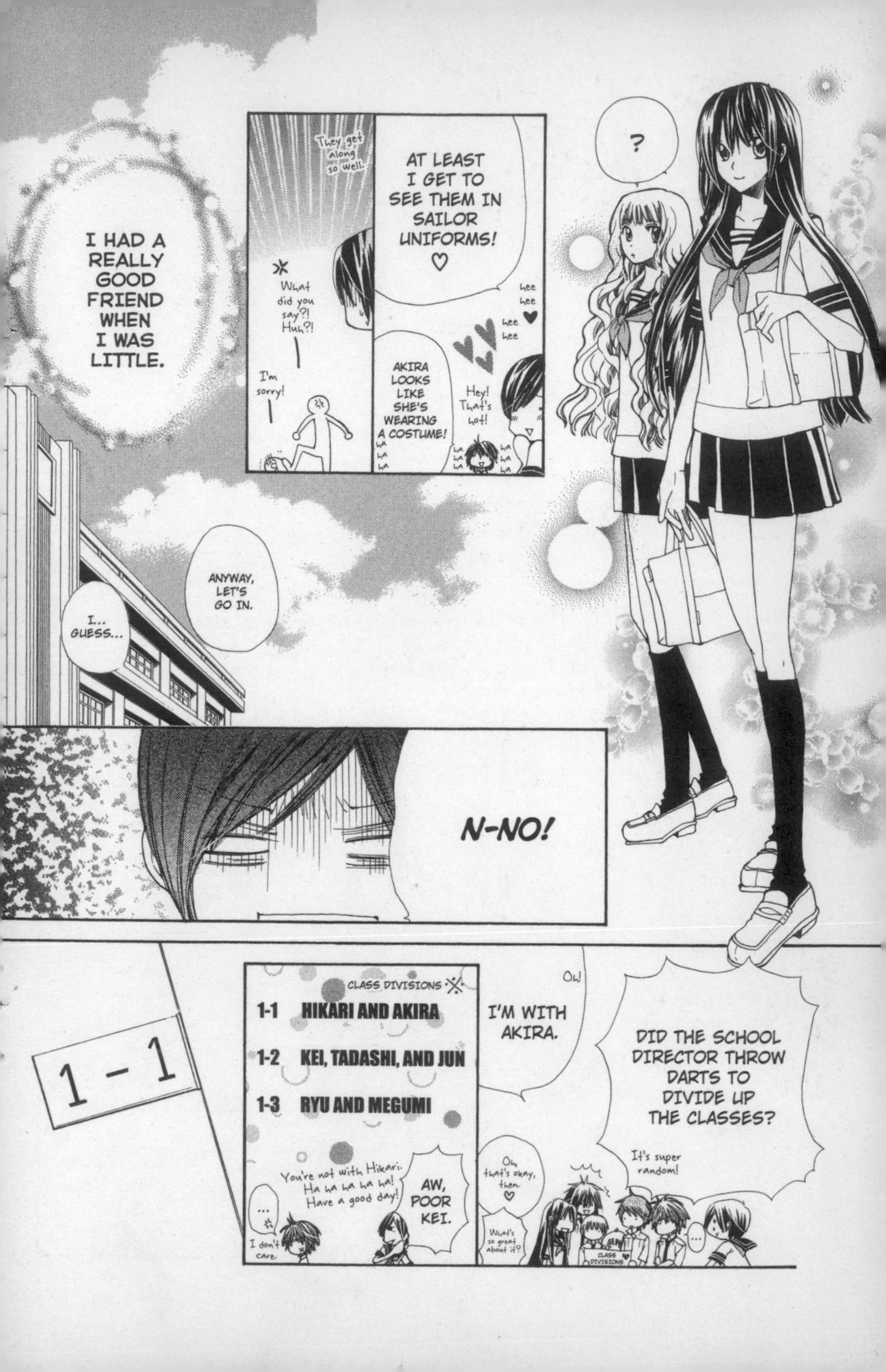
?
AT LEAST I GET TO SEE THEM IN SAILOR UNIFORMS! ♡
hee hee hee hee
Hey! That's hot!
AKIRA LOOKS LIKE SHE'S WEARING A COSTUME!
ha ha ha
ha ha ha
ha ha ha
ha ha ha
They get along so well.
What did you say?! Huh?!
I'm sorry!
I HAD A REALLY GOOD FRIEND WHEN I WAS LITTLE.
ANYWAY, LET'S GO IN.
I... GUESS...
N-NO!
DID THE SCHOOL DIRECTOR THROW DARTS TO DIVIDE UP THE CLASSES?
It's super random!
...
Oh that's okay, then. ♡
What's so great about it?
CLASS DIVISIONS
Oh!
I'M WITH AKIRA.
CLASS DIVISIONS
1-1 HIKARI AND AKIRA
1-2 KEI, TADASHI, AND JUN
1-3 RYU AND MEGUMI
AW, POOR KEI.
You're not with Hikari. Ha ha ha ha ha! Have a good day!
...
I don't care.
1-1

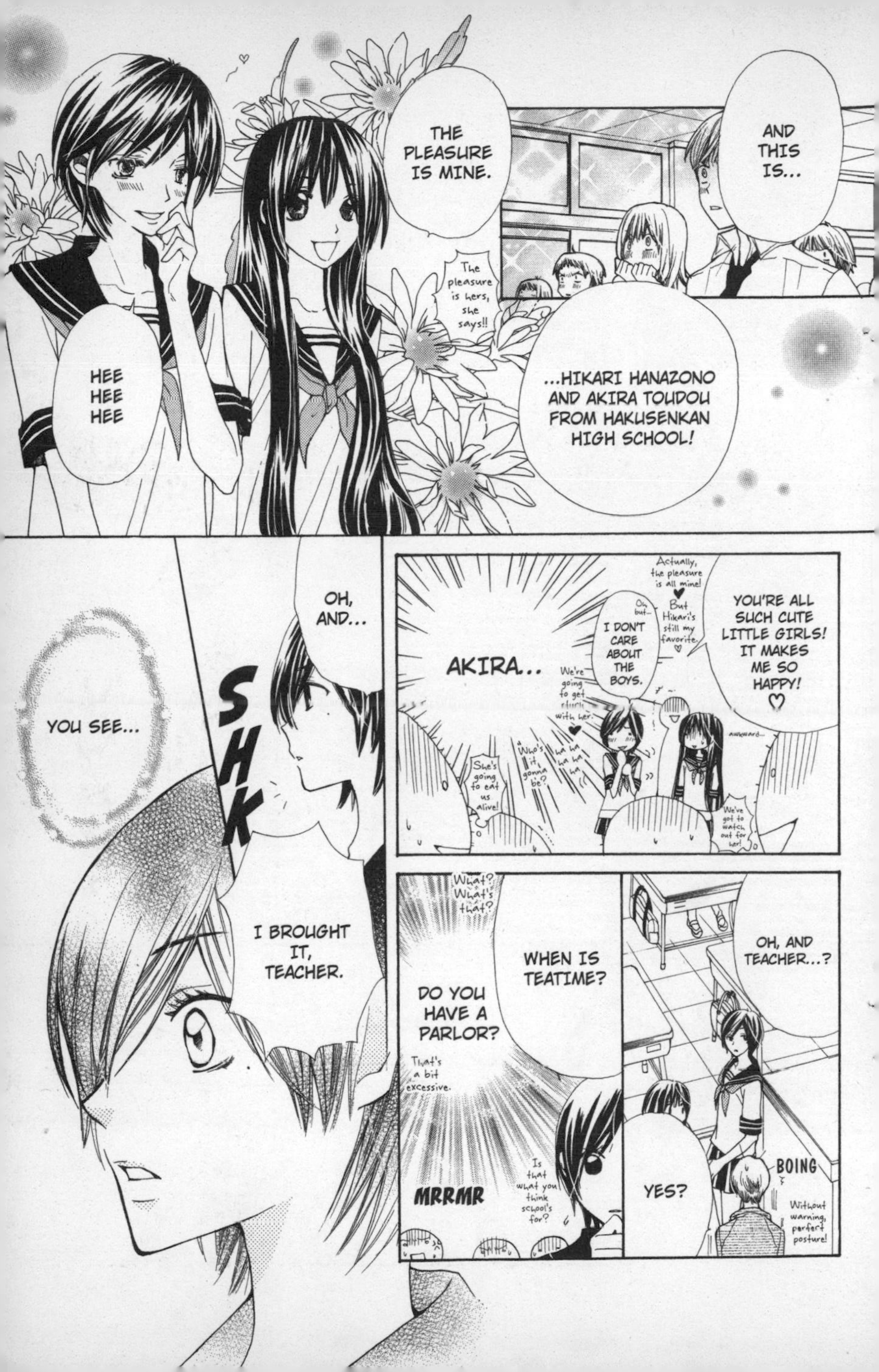
AND THIS IS...
...HIKARI HANAZONO AND AKIRA TOUDOU FROM HAKUSENKAN HIGH SCHOOL!
THE PLEASURE IS MINE.
The pleasure is hers, she says!!
HEE HEE HEE
YOU'RE ALL SUCH CUTE LITTLE GIRLS! IT MAKES ME SO HAPPY! ♡
Actually, the pleasure is all mine! ♥
But Hikari's still my favorite. ♡
Oh, but...
I DON'T CARE ABOUT THE BOYS.
AKIRA...
We're going to get stuck with her. ♥
awkward...
Who's it gonna be?
ha ha ha ha ha
She's going to eat us alive!
We've got to watch out for her!
OH, AND TEACHER...?
BOING
Without warning, perfect posture!
YES?
WHEN IS TEATIME?
What? What's that?
DO YOU HAVE A PARLOR?
That's a bit excessive.
Is that what you think school's for?
MRRMR
OH, AND...
SHK
YOU SEE...
I BROUGHT IT, TEACHER.

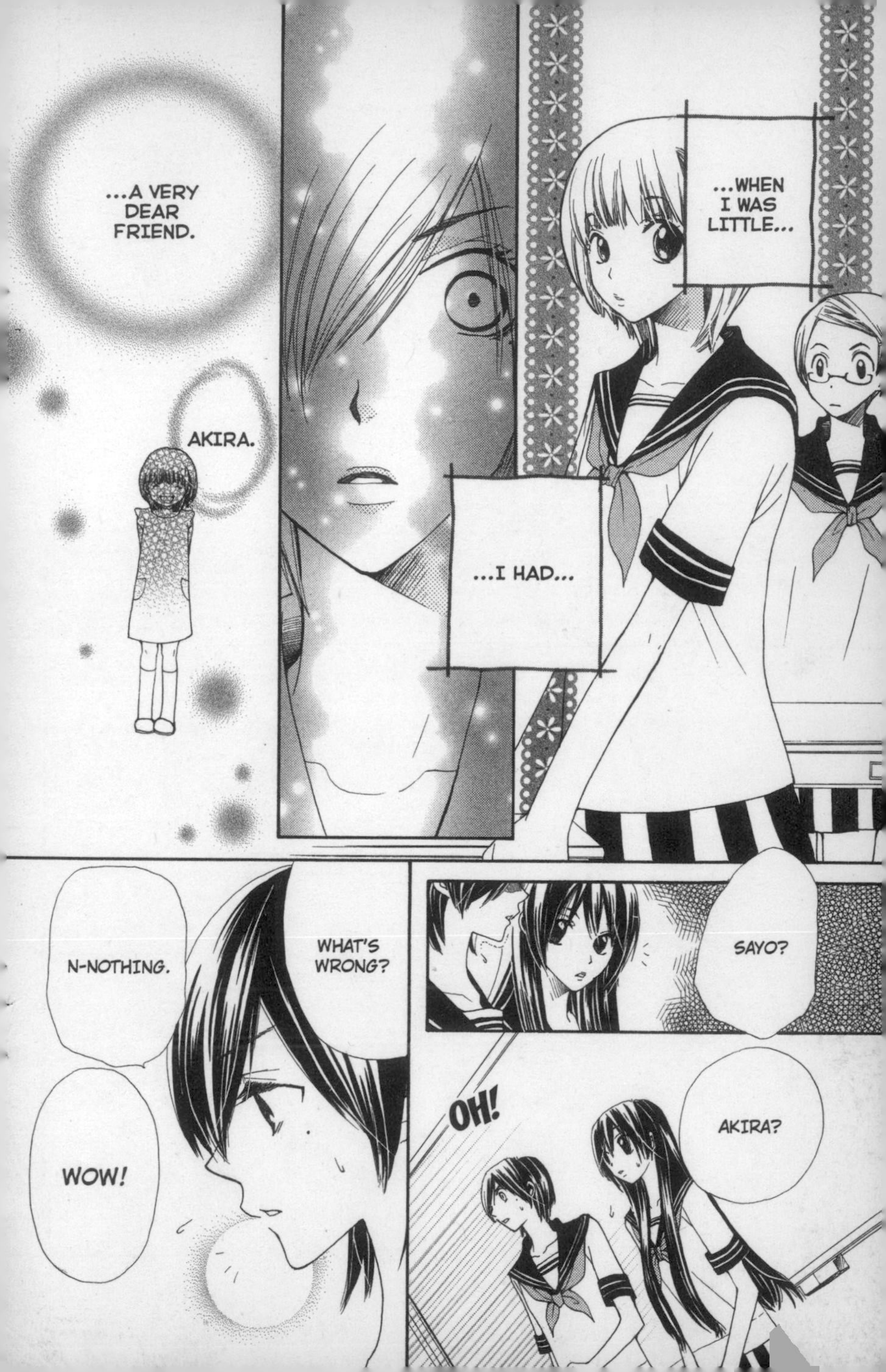
...WHEN I WAS LITTLE...
...I HAD...
...A VERY DEAR FRIEND.
AKIRA.
SAYO?
AKIRA?
OH!
WHAT'S WRONG?
N-NOTHING.
WOW!

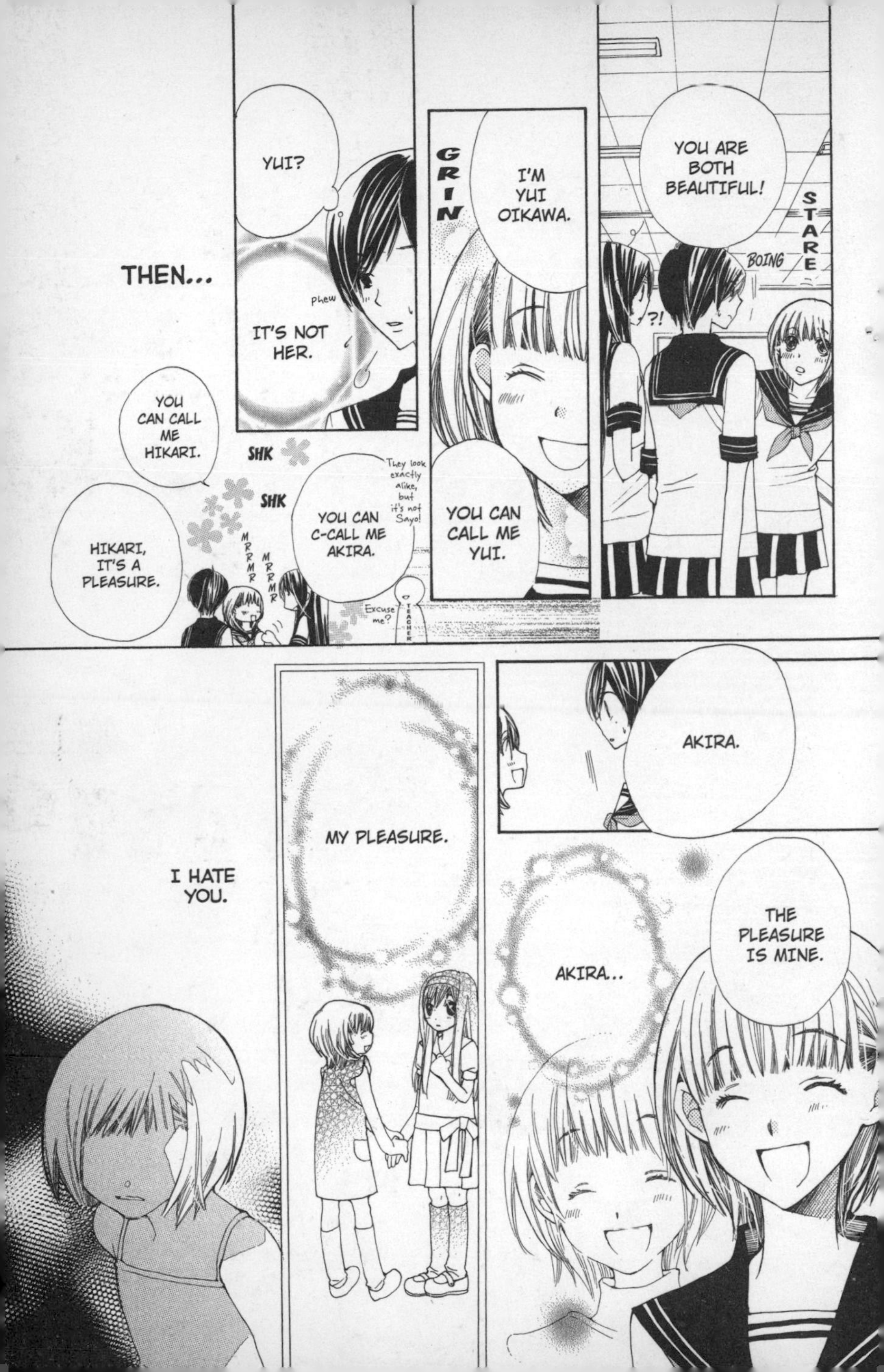
YOU ARE BOTH BEAUTIFUL!
STARE
BOING
?!
GRIN
I'M YUI OIKAWA.
YOU CAN CALL ME YUI.
YUI?
Phew
IT'S NOT HER.
THEN...
YOU CAN C-CALL ME AKIRA.
They look exactly alike, but it's not Sayo!
Excuse me?
TEACHER
SHK
YOU CAN CALL ME HIKARI.
SHK
MRRMR
MRRMR
HIKARI, IT'S A PLEASURE.
AKIRA.
THE PLEASURE IS MINE.
AKIRA...
MY PLEASURE.
I HATE YOU.

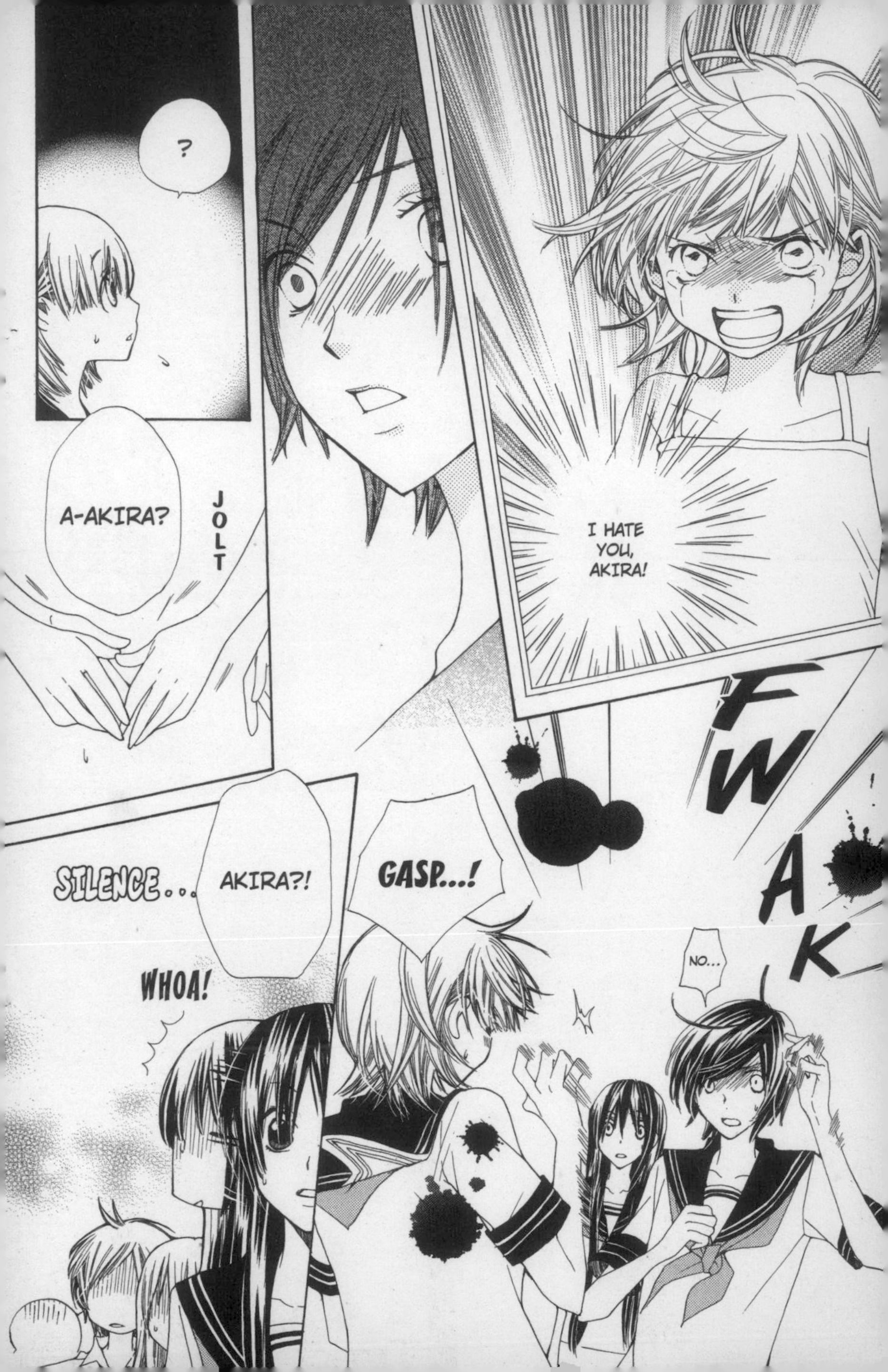
I HATE YOU, AKIRA!
?
A-AKIRA?
JOLT
FWAK
NO...
GASP...!
AKIRA?!
SILENCE...
WHOA!

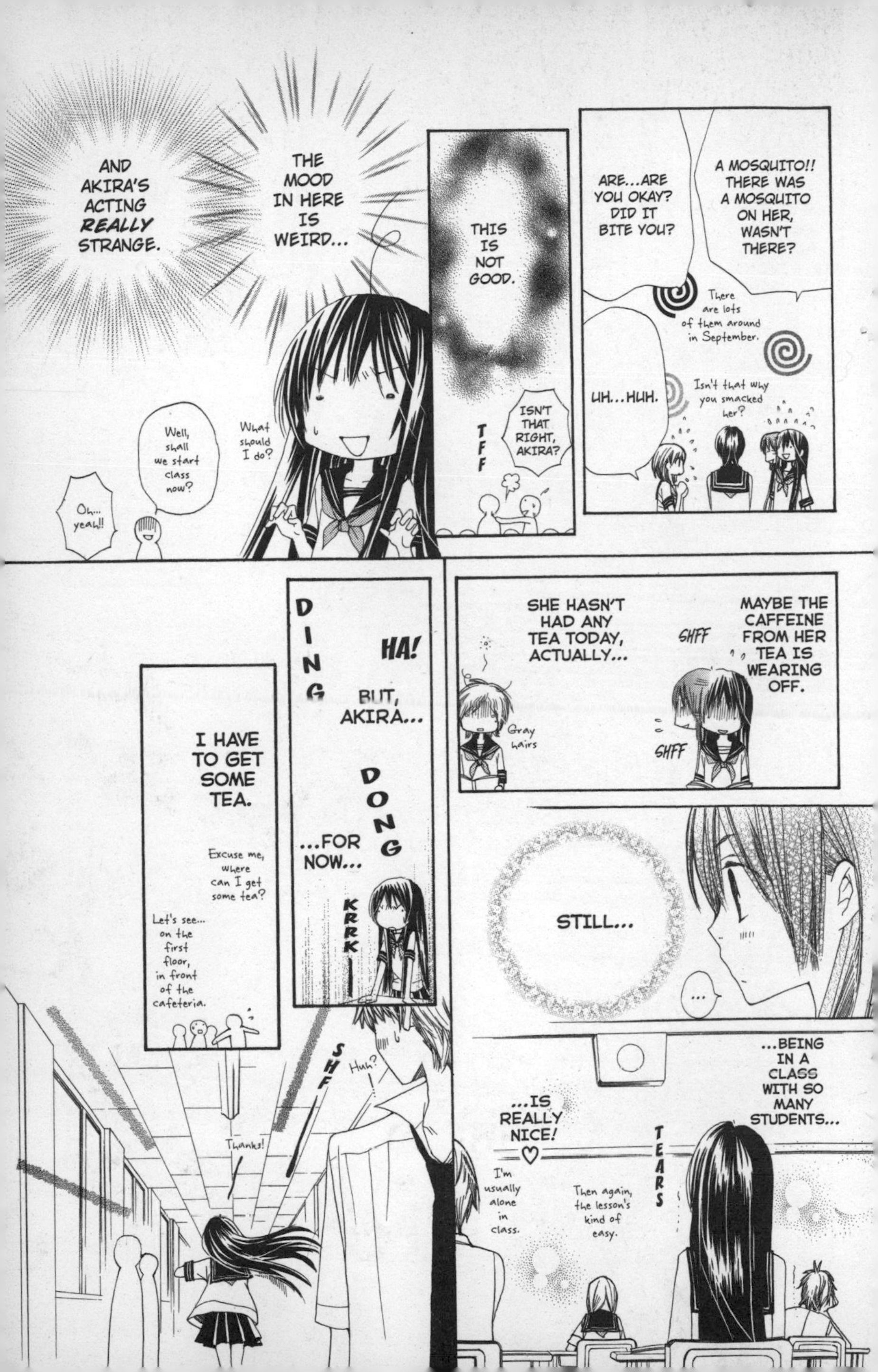
A MOSQUITO!! THERE WAS A MOSQUITO ON HER, WASN'T THERE?
ARE...ARE YOU OKAY? DID IT BITE YOU?
There are lots of them around in September.
UH...HUH.
Isn't that why you smacked her?
THIS IS NOT GOOD.
ISN'T THAT RIGHT, AKIRA?
TFF
THE MOOD IN HERE IS WEIRD...
AND AKIRA'S ACTING *REALLY* STRANGE.
What should I do?
Well, shall we start class now?
Oh... yeah!!
MAYBE THE CAFFEINE FROM HER TEA IS WEARING OFF.
SHFF
SHFF
SHE HASN'T HAD ANY TEA TODAY, ACTUALLY...
Gray hairs
DING
HA!
BUT, AKIRA...
DONG
...FOR NOW...
KRRK
I HAVE TO GET SOME TEA.
Excuse me, where can I get some tea?
Let's see... on the first floor, in front of the cafeteria.
STILL...
...
...BEING IN A CLASS WITH SO MANY STUDENTS...
TEARS
...IS REALLY NICE! ♡
Then again, the lesson's kind of easy.
I'm usually alone in class.
SHF
Huh?
Thanks!

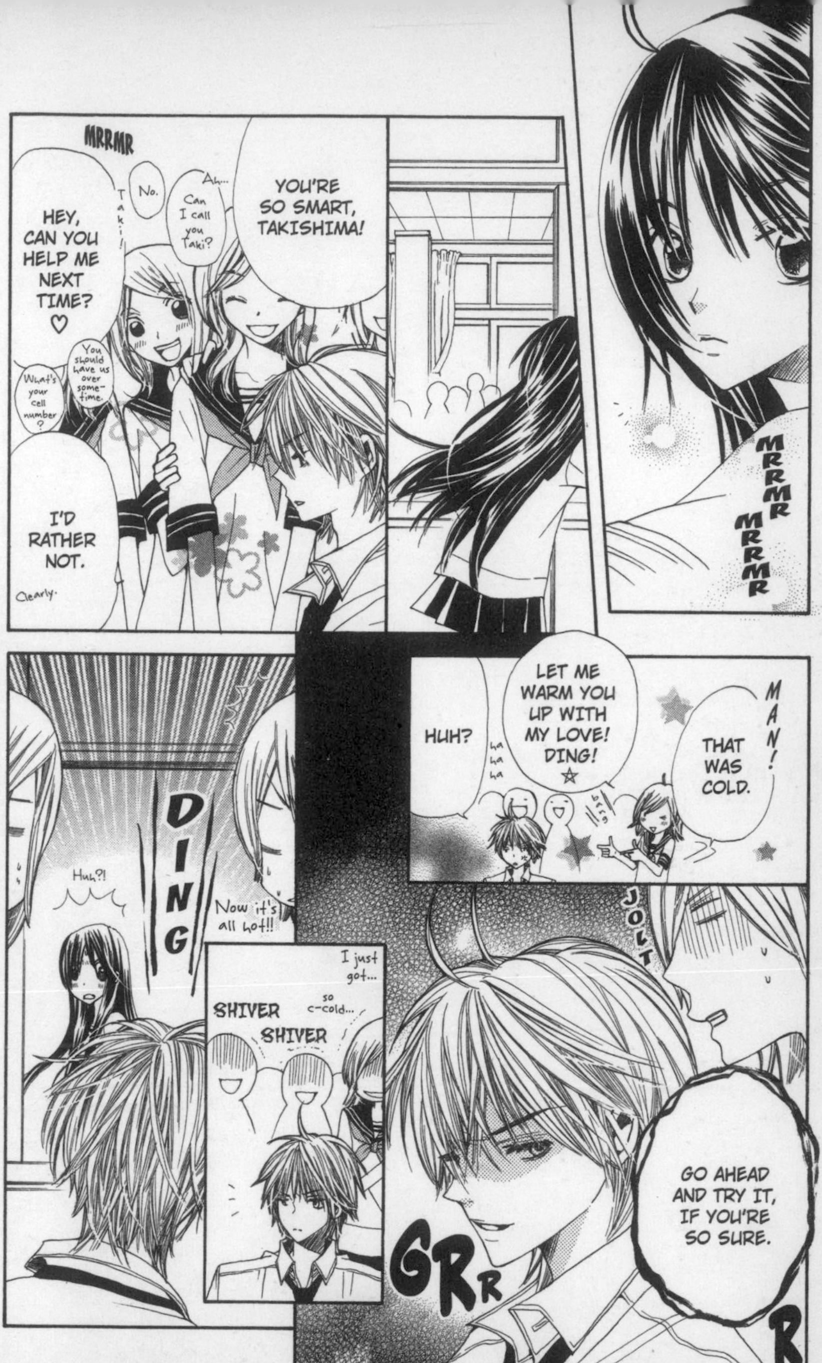
MRRMR
MRRMR
YOU'RE SO SMART, TAKISHIMA!
Ah... Can I call you Taki?
No.
Taki!
MRRMR
HEY, CAN YOU HELP ME NEXT TIME? ♡
You should have us over sometime.
What's your cell number?
I'D RATHER NOT.
Clearly.
MAN! THAT WAS COLD.
LET ME WARM YOU UP WITH MY LOVE! DING! ☆
ha ha ha
HUH?
JOLT
GO AHEAD AND TRY IT, IF YOU'RE SO SURE.
GRRR
DING DING
Now it's all hot!!
Huh?!
I just got... so c-cold...
SHIVER SHIVER

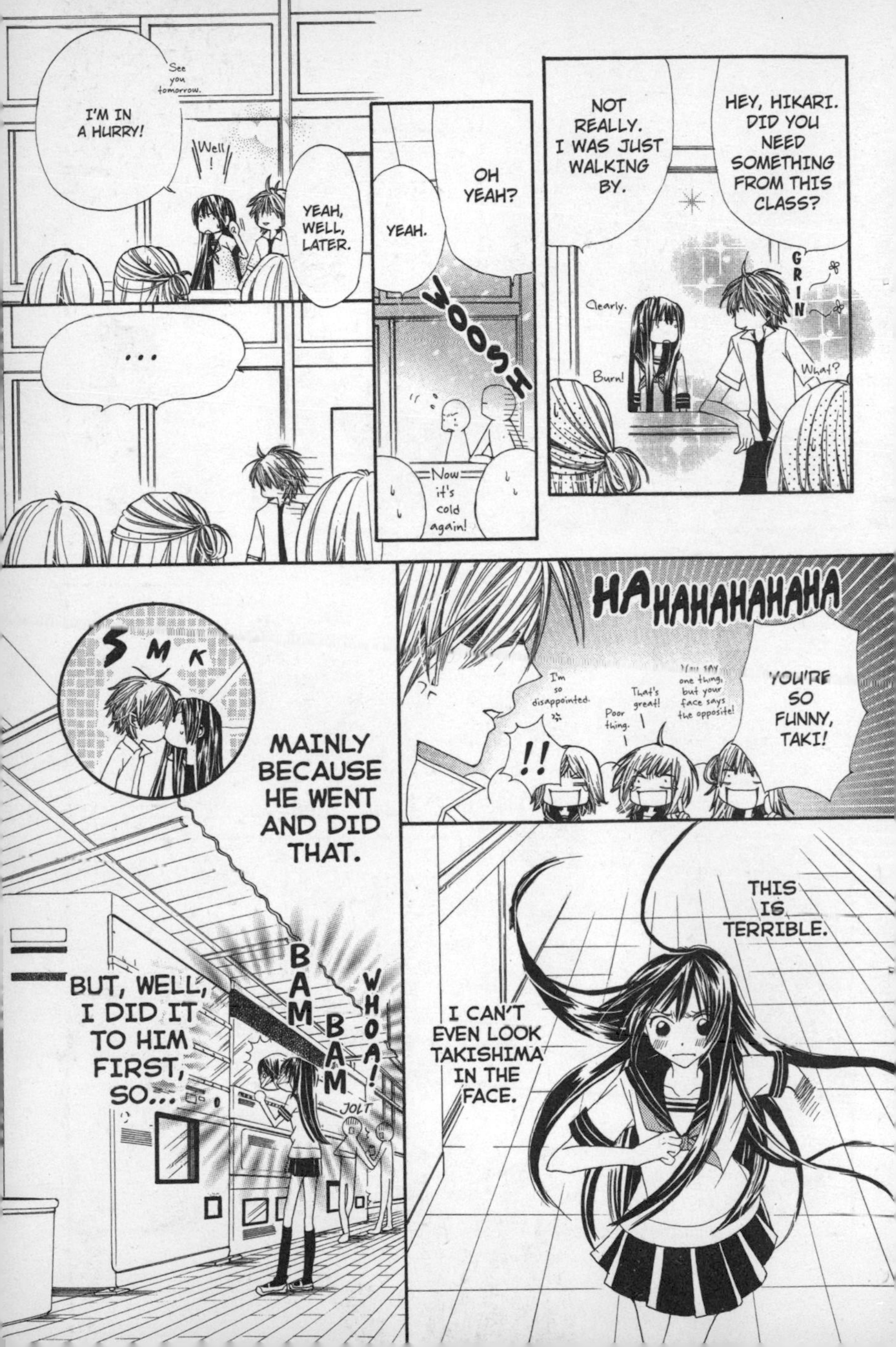
NOT REALLY. I WAS JUST WALKING BY.
HEY, HIKARI. DID YOU NEED SOMETHING FROM THIS CLASS?
GRIN
What?
Clearly.
Burn!
OH YEAH?
YEAH.
WOOSH
Now it's cold again!
I'M IN A HURRY!
See you tomorrow.
Well!
YEAH, WELL, LATER.
...
HAHAHAHAHAHA
YOU'RE SO FUNNY, TAKI!
You say one thing, but your face says the opposite!
That's great!
Poor thing.
I'm so disappointed.
!!
THIS IS TERRIBLE.
I CAN'T EVEN LOOK TAKISHIMA IN THE FACE.
SMK
MAINLY BECAUSE HE WENT AND DID THAT.
BUT, WELL, I DID IT TO HIM FIRST, SO...
WHOA!
BAM
BAM
BAM
JOLT

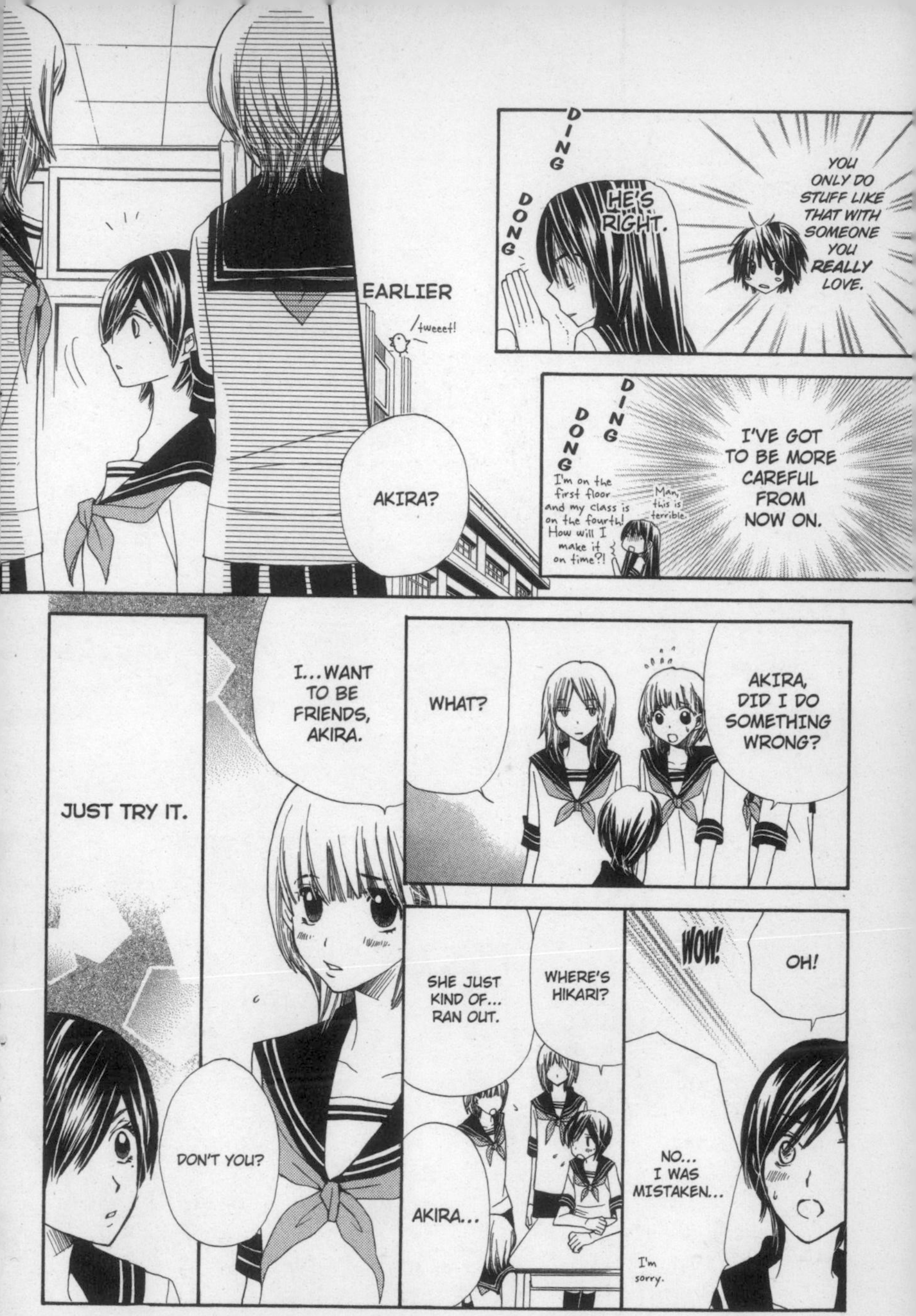
YOU ONLY DO STUFF LIKE THAT WITH SOMEONE YOU REALLY LOVE.
DING DONG
HE'S RIGHT.
I'VE GOT TO BE MORE CAREFUL FROM NOW ON.
Man, this is terrible.
DING DONG
I'm on the first floor and my class is on the fourth! How will I make it on time?!
EARLIER
tweeet!
AKIRA?
AKIRA, DID I DO SOMETHING WRONG?
WHAT?
OH!
WOW!
NO... I WAS MISTAKEN...
I'm sorry.
WHERE'S HIKARI?
SHE JUST KIND OF... RAN OUT.
AKIRA...
I...WANT TO BE FRIENDS, AKIRA.
DON'T YOU?
JUST TRY IT.

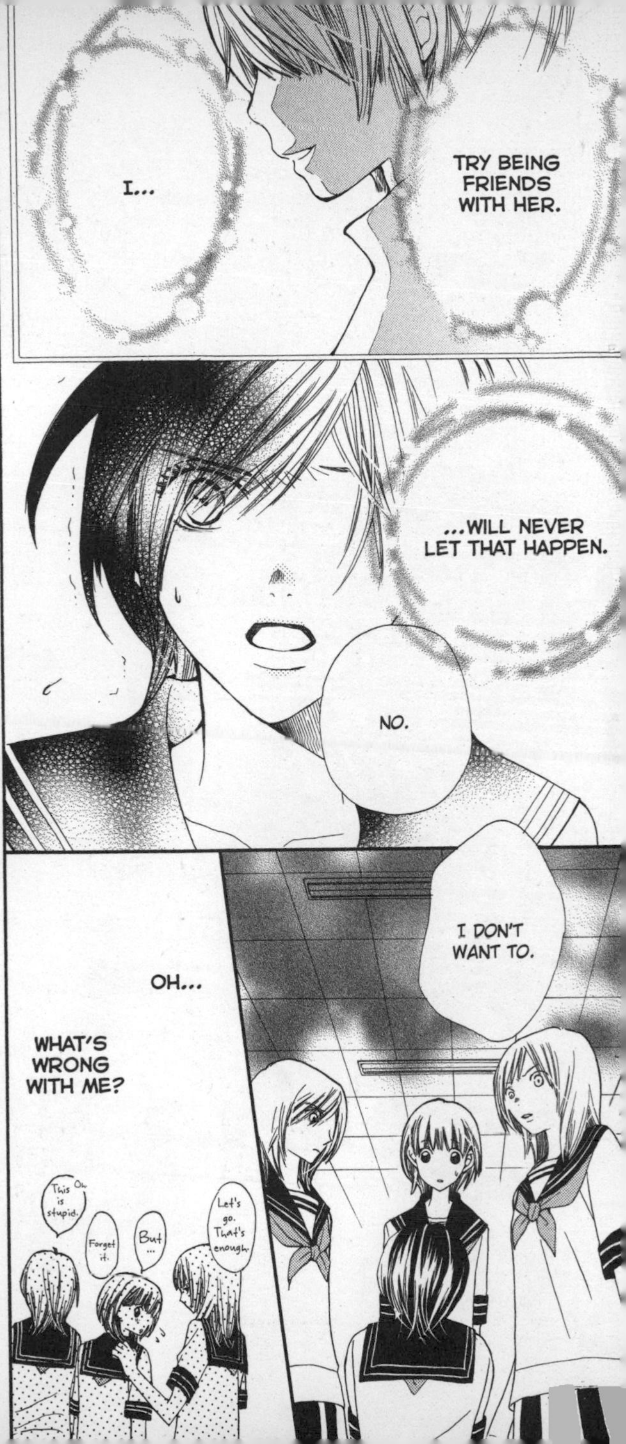
TRY BEING FRIENDS WITH HER.
I...
...WILL NEVER LET THAT HAPPEN.
NO.
I DON'T WANT TO.
OH...
WHAT'S WRONG WITH ME?
Let's go. That's enough.
But ...
Forget it.
This is stupid.
Oh
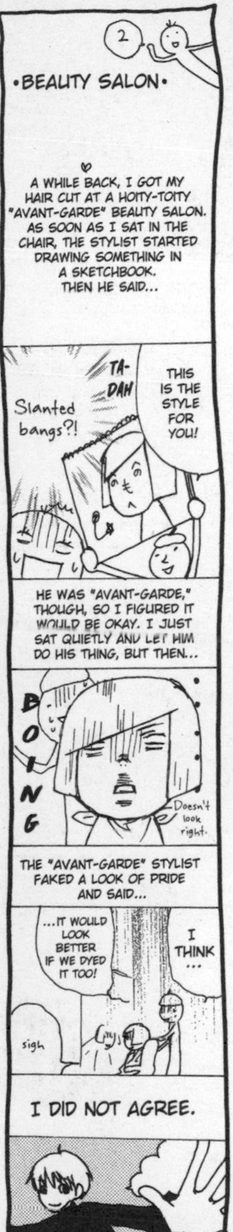
2
•BEAUTY SALON•
A WHILE BACK, I GOT MY HAIR CUT AT A HOITY-TOITY "AVANT-GARDE" BEAUTY SALON. AS SOON AS I SAT IN THE CHAIR, THE STYLIST STARTED DRAWING SOMETHING IN A SKETCHBOOK. THEN HE SAID...
THIS IS THE STYLE FOR YOU!
TA-DAH
Slanted bangs?!
HE WAS "AVANT-GARDE," THOUGH, SO I FIGURED IT WOULD BE OKAY. I JUST SAT QUIETLY AND LET HIM DO HIS THING, BUT THEN...
BOING
Doesn't look right.
THE "AVANT-GARDE" STYLIST FAKED A LOOK OF PRIDE AND SAID...
I THINK ...
...IT WOULD LOOK BETTER IF WE DYED IT TOO!
sigh
I DID NOT AGREE.

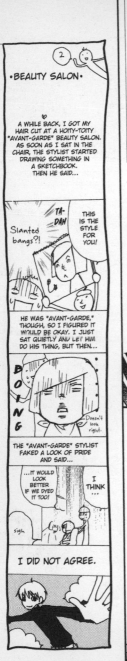

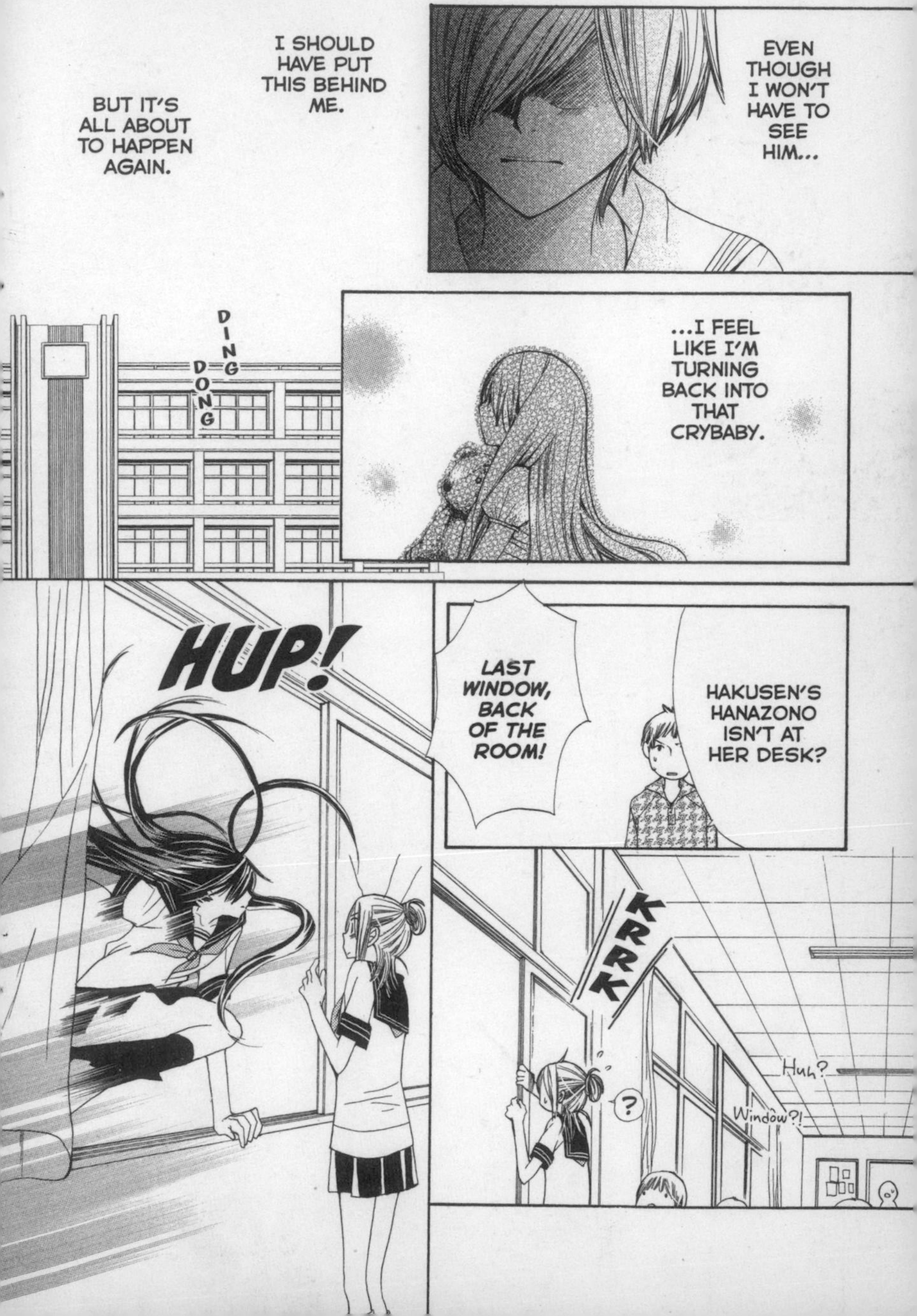
EVEN THOUGH I WON'T HAVE TO SEE HIM...
I SHOULD HAVE PUT THIS BEHIND ME.
BUT IT'S ALL ABOUT TO HAPPEN AGAIN.
...I FEEL LIKE I'M TURNING BACK INTO THAT CRYBABY.
DING DONG
HAKUSEN'S HANAZONO ISN'T AT HER DESK?
LAST WINDOW, BACK OF THE ROOM!
KRRRK
Huh?
Window?!
?
HUP!

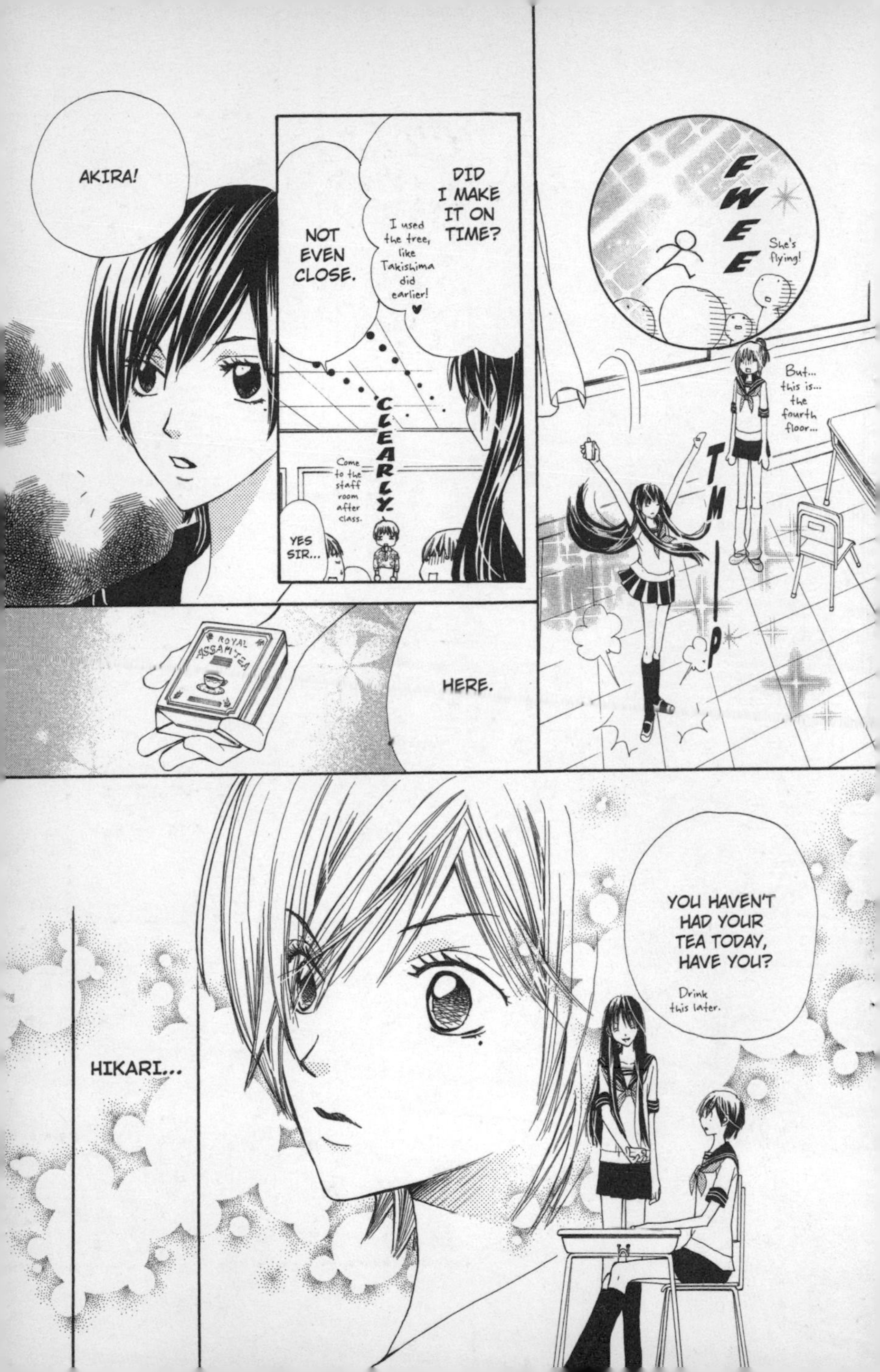
FWEE
She's flying!
But... this is... the fourth floor...
TMP
DID I MAKE IT ON TIME?
NOT EVEN CLOSE.
I used the tree, like Takishima did earlier!
CLEARLY.
Come to the staff room after class.
YES SIR...
AKIRA!
ROYAL ASSAM TEA
HERE.
YOU HAVEN'T HAD YOUR TEA TODAY, HAVE YOU?
Drink this later.
HIKARI...

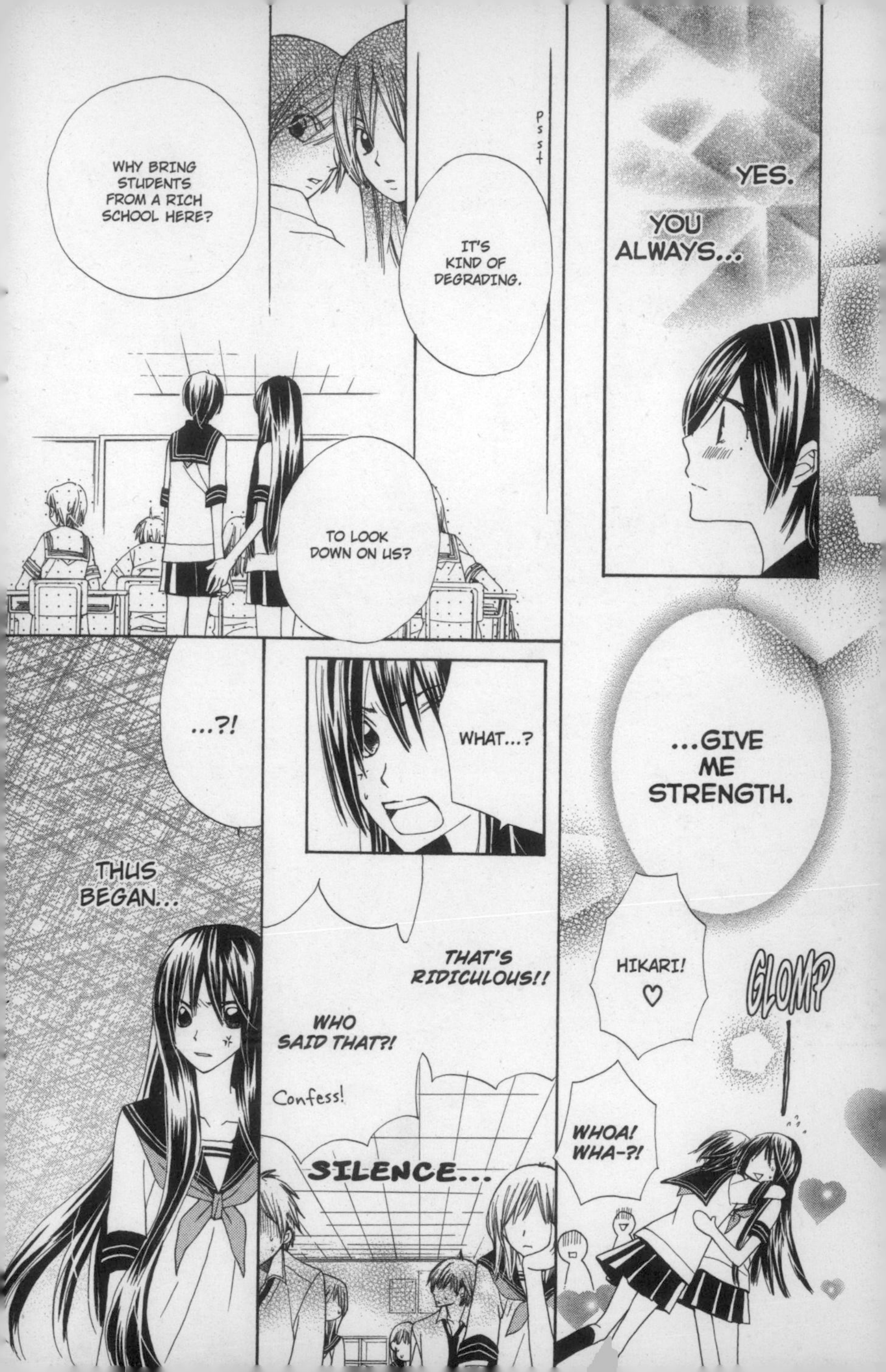
YES.
YOU ALWAYS...
...GIVE ME STRENGTH.
HIKARI! ♡
GLOMP
WHOA! WHA-?!
Psst
IT'S KIND OF DEGRADING.
WHY BRING STUDENTS FROM A RICH SCHOOL HERE?
TO LOOK DOWN ON US?
WHAT...?
...?!
THAT'S RIDICULOUS!!
WHO SAID THAT?!
Confess!
SILENCE...
THUS BEGAN...

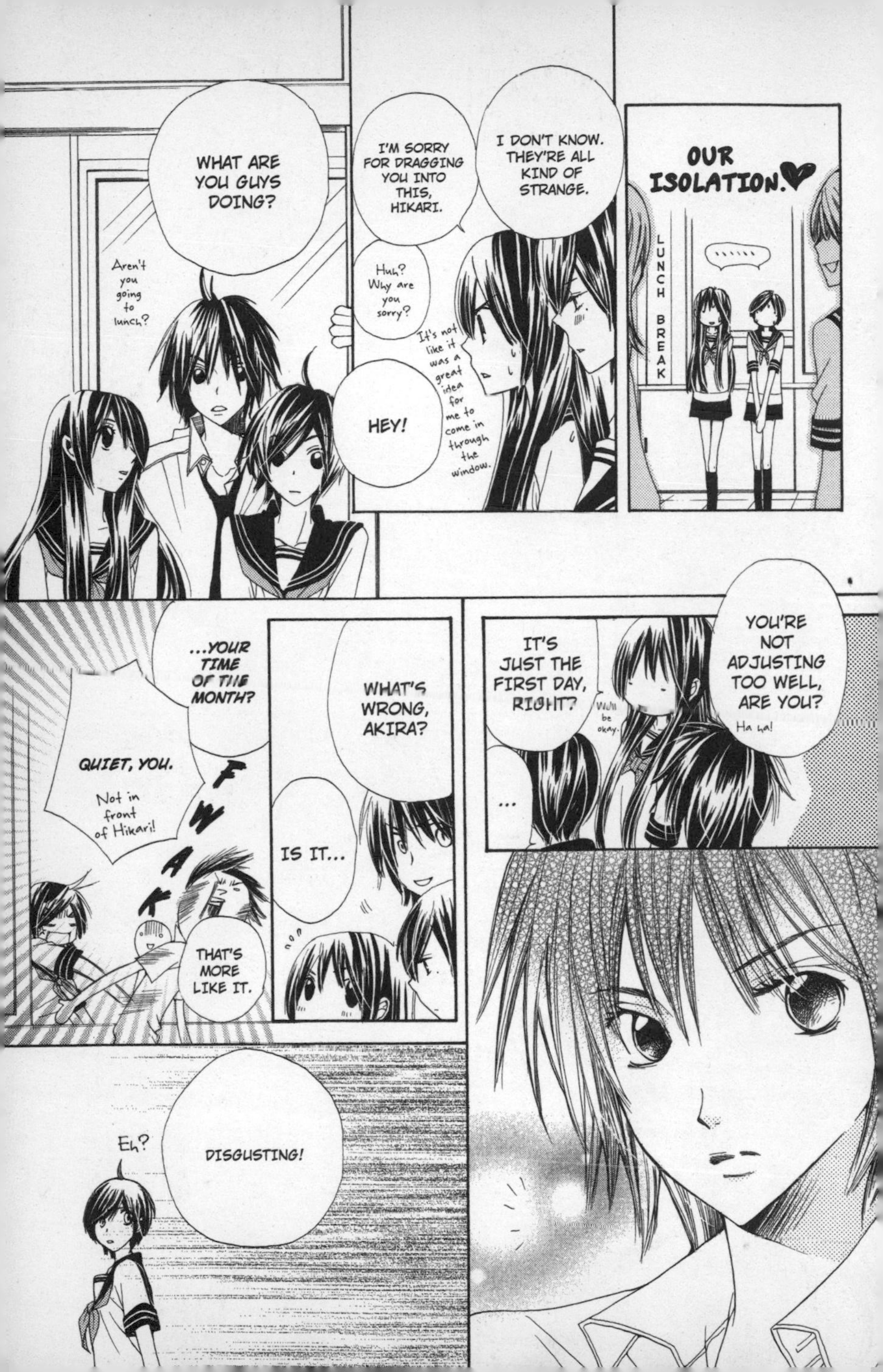
OUR ISOLATION.♥
LUNCH BREAK
......
I DON'T KNOW. THEY'RE ALL KIND OF STRANGE.
I'M SORRY FOR DRAGGING YOU INTO THIS, HIKARI.
Huh? Why are you sorry?
It's not like it was a great idea for me to come in through the window.
HEY!
WHAT ARE YOU GUYS DOING?
Aren't you going to lunch?
YOU'RE NOT ADJUSTING TOO WELL, ARE YOU?
Ha ha!
IT'S JUST THE FIRST DAY, RIGHT?
Will be okay.
...
WHAT'S WRONG, AKIRA?
IS IT...
...YOUR TIME OF THE MONTH?
QUIET, YOU.
Not in front of Hikari!
FWAAK
THAT'S MORE LIKE IT.
DISGUSTING!
Eh?

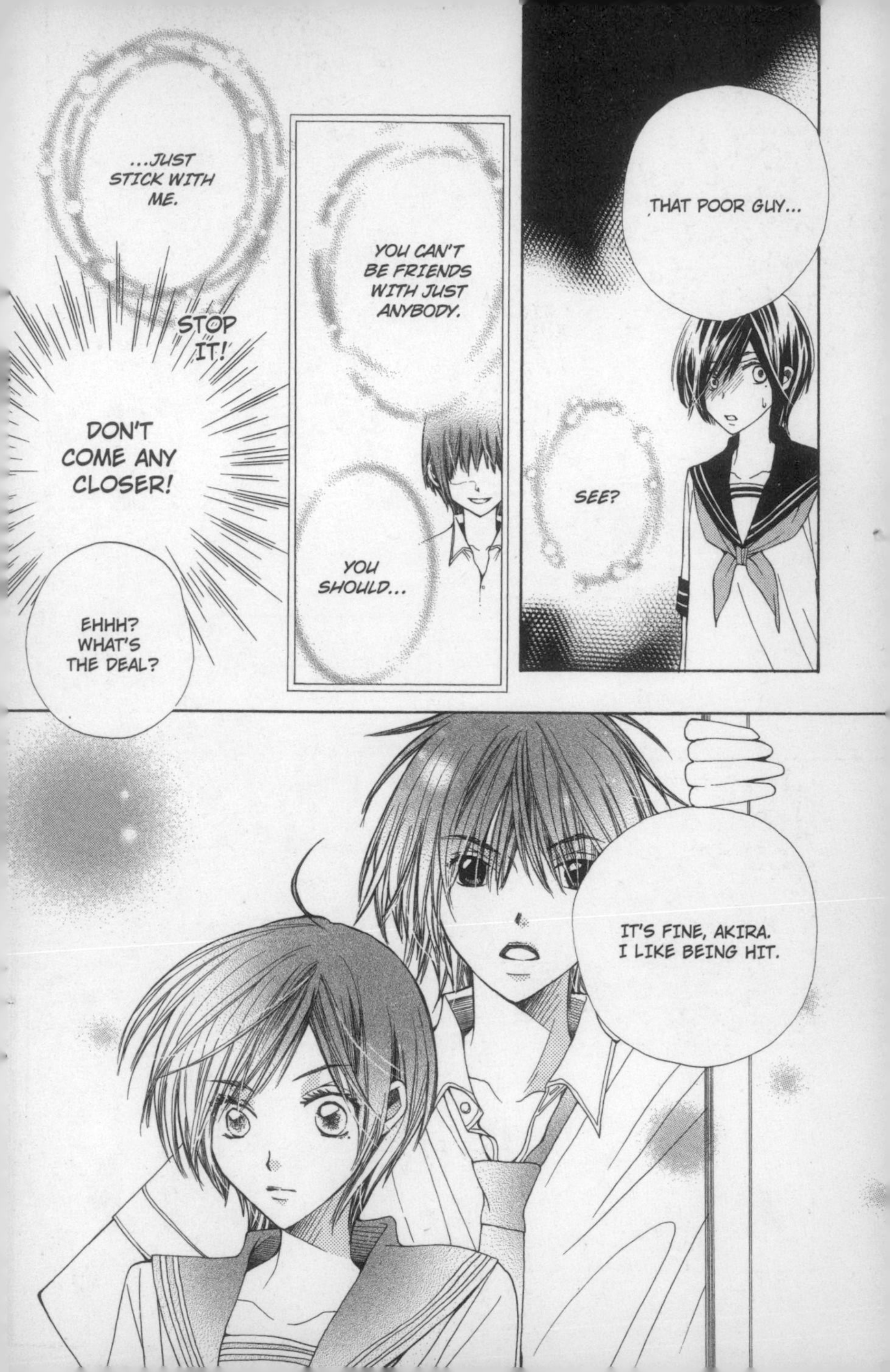
THAT POOR GUY...
SEE?
YOU CAN'T BE FRIENDS WITH JUST ANYBODY.
YOU SHOULD...
...JUST STICK WITH ME.
STOP IT!
DON'T COME ANY CLOSER!
EHHH? WHAT'S THE DEAL?
IT'S FINE, AKIRA. I LIKE BEING HIT.

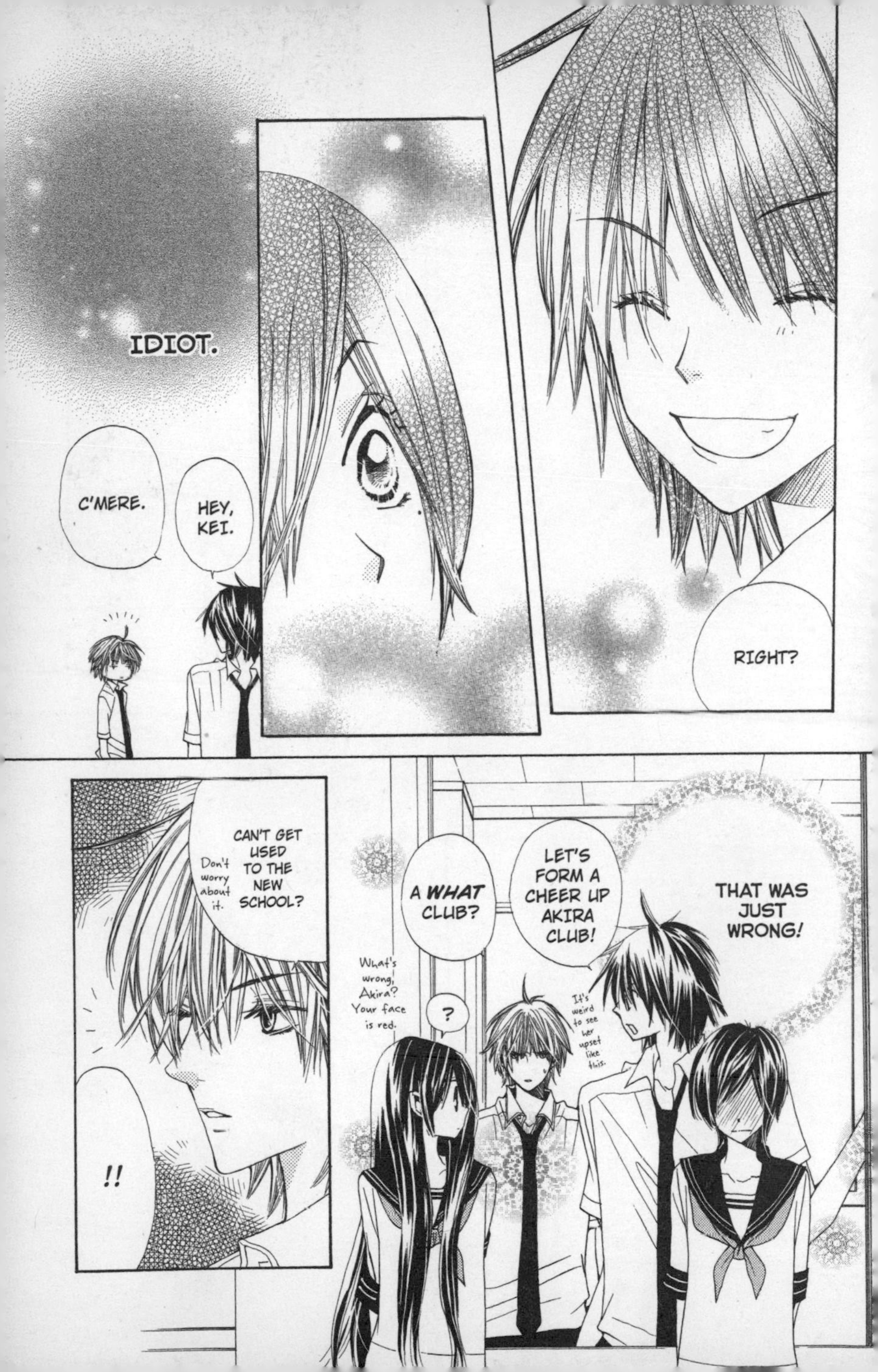
RIGHT?
IDIOT.
HEY, KEI.
C'MERE.
THAT WAS JUST WRONG!
LET'S FORM A CHEER UP AKIRA CLUB!
It's weird to see her upset like this.
A WHAT CLUB?
?
What's wrong, Akira? Your face is red.
CAN'T GET USED TO THE NEW SCHOOL?
Don't worry about it.
!!

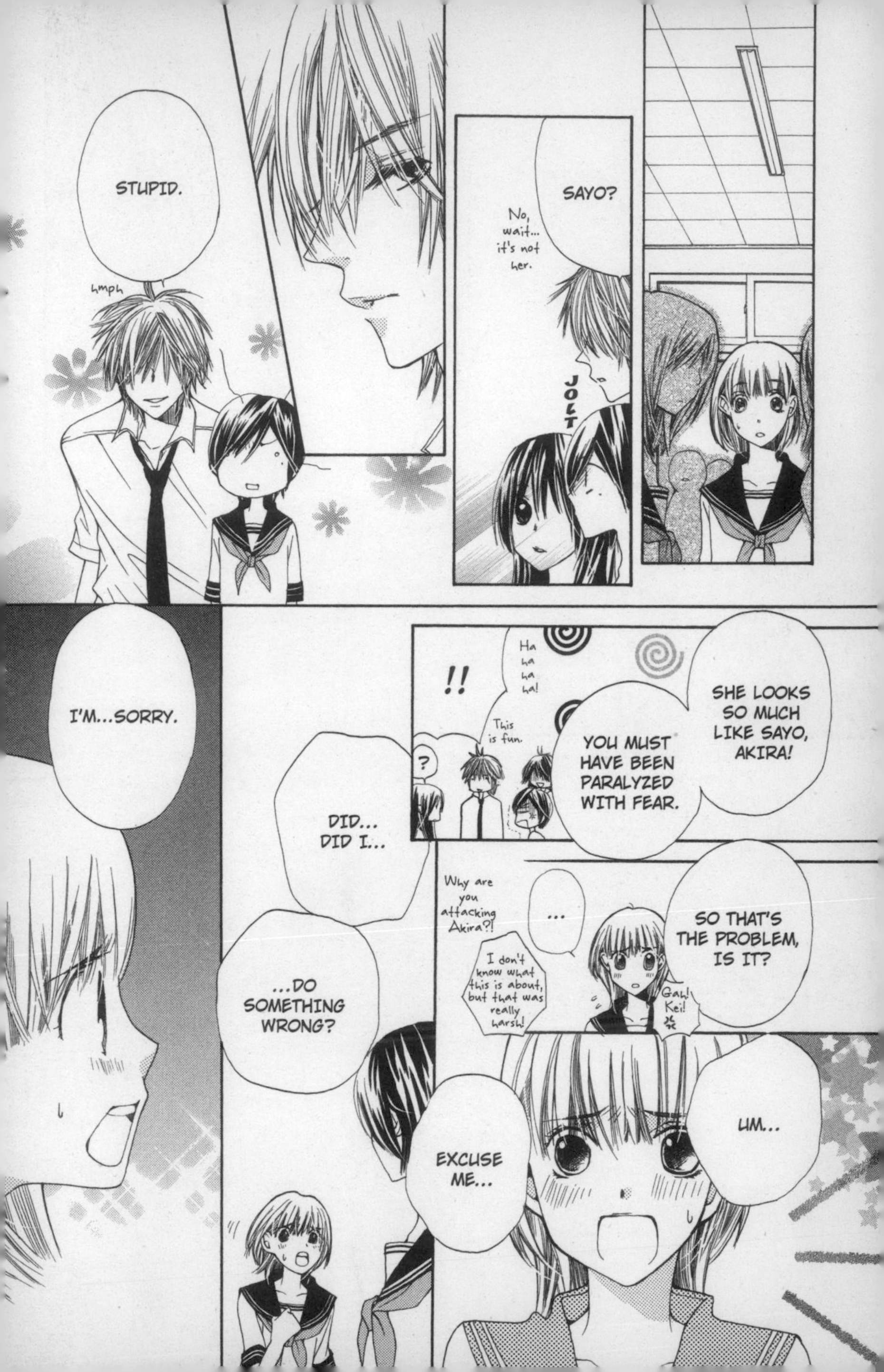
SAYO?
No, wait... it's not her.
JOLT
STUPID.
hmph
SHE LOOKS SO MUCH LIKE SAYO, AKIRA!
YOU MUST HAVE BEEN PARALYZED WITH FEAR.
Ha ha ha ha!
This is fun.
!!
?
SO THAT'S THE PROBLEM, IS IT?
Gah! Kei!
...
Why are you attacking Akira?!
I don't know what this is about, but that was really harsh!
DID... DID I...
...DO SOMETHING WRONG?
UM...
EXCUSE ME...
I'M...SORRY.

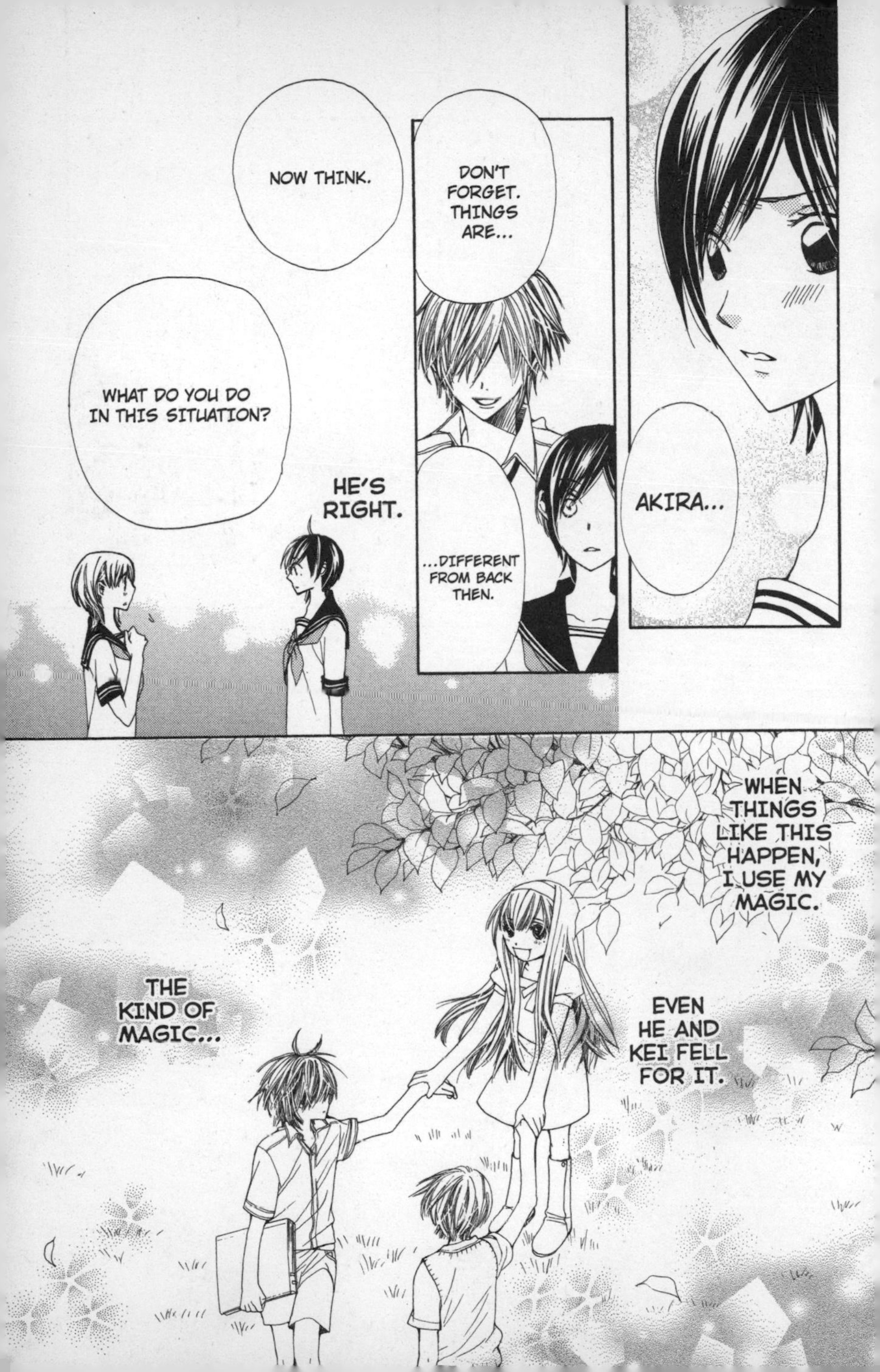
AKIRA...
DON'T FORGET. THINGS ARE...
...DIFFERENT FROM BACK THEN.
NOW THINK.
WHAT DO YOU DO IN THIS SITUATION?
HE'S RIGHT.
WHEN THINGS LIKE THIS HAPPEN, I USE MY MAGIC.
EVEN HE AND KEI FELL FOR IT.
THE KIND OF MAGIC...

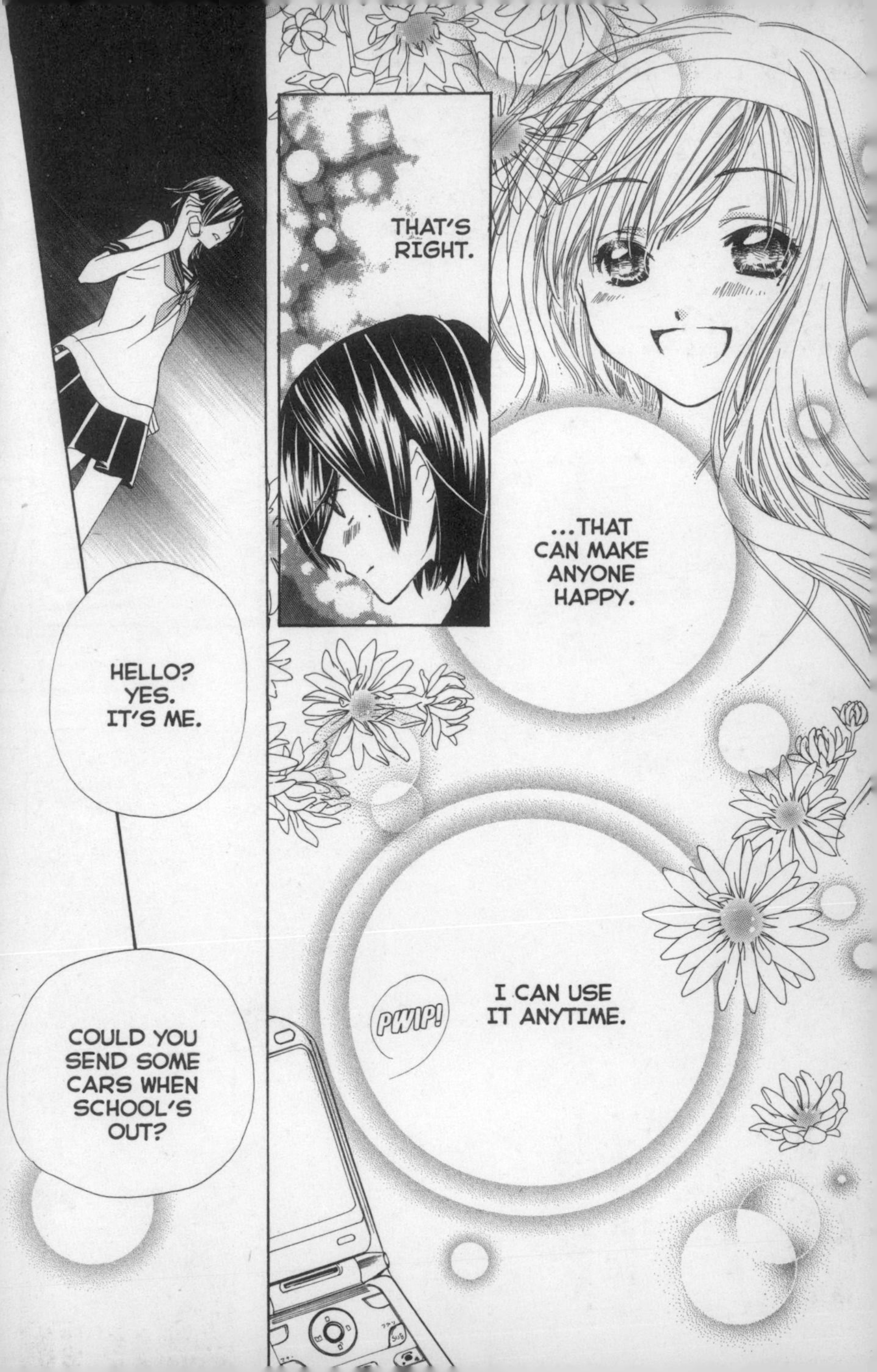
THAT'S RIGHT.
...THAT CAN MAKE ANYONE HAPPY.
PWIP!
I CAN USE IT ANYTIME.
HELLO? YES. IT'S ME.
COULD YOU SEND SOME CARS WHEN SCHOOL'S OUT?

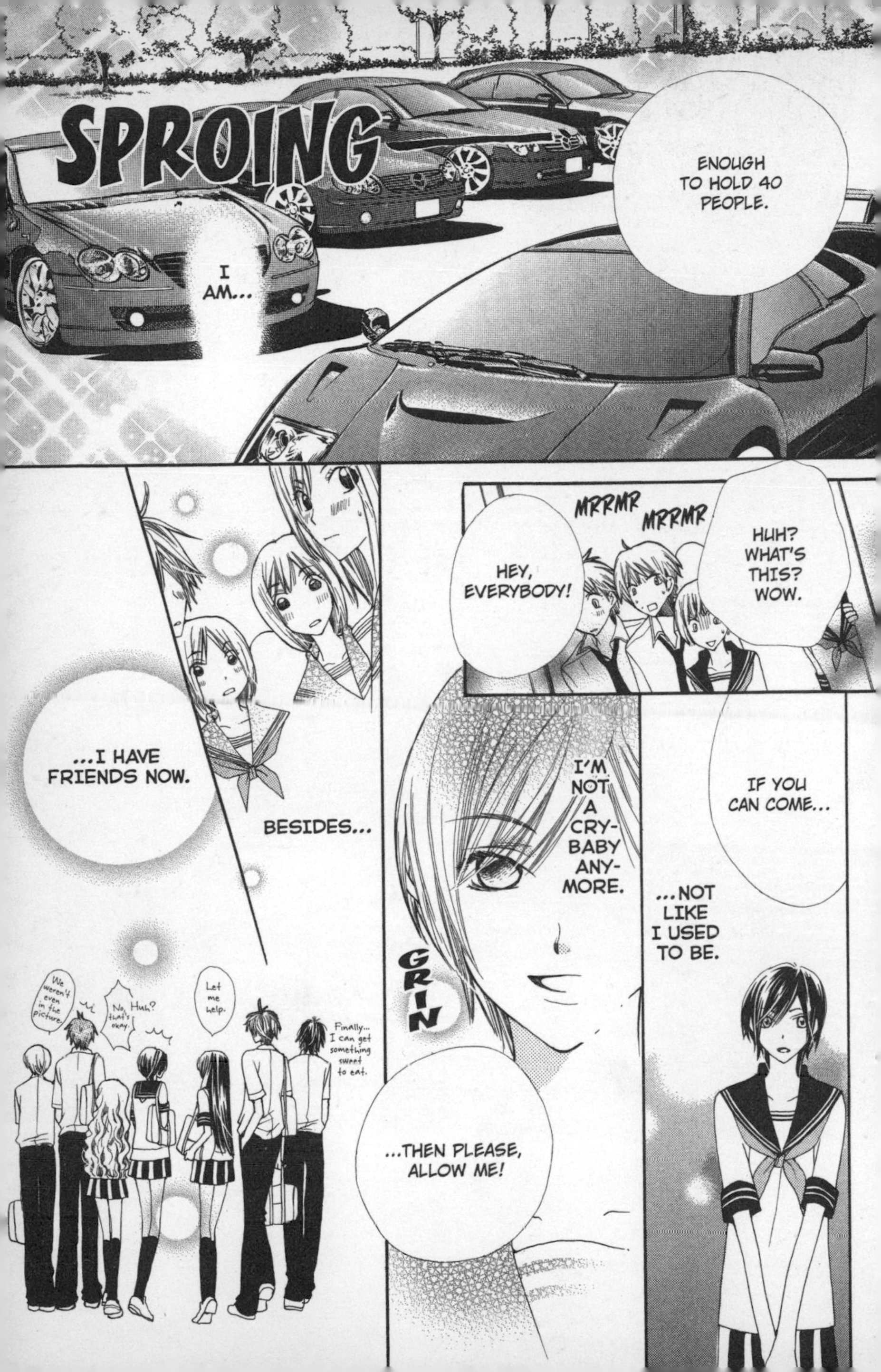
ENOUGH TO HOLD 40 PEOPLE.
SPROING
I AM...
HUH? WHAT'S THIS? WOW.
MRRMR
MRRMR
HEY, EVERYBODY!
IF YOU CAN COME...
...NOT LIKE I USED TO BE.
I'M NOT A CRY-BABY ANY-MORE.
GRIN
...THEN PLEASE, ALLOW ME!
BESIDES...
...I HAVE FRIENDS NOW.
Finally... I can get something sweet to eat.
Let me help.
Huh?
No, that's okay.
We weren't even in the picture.

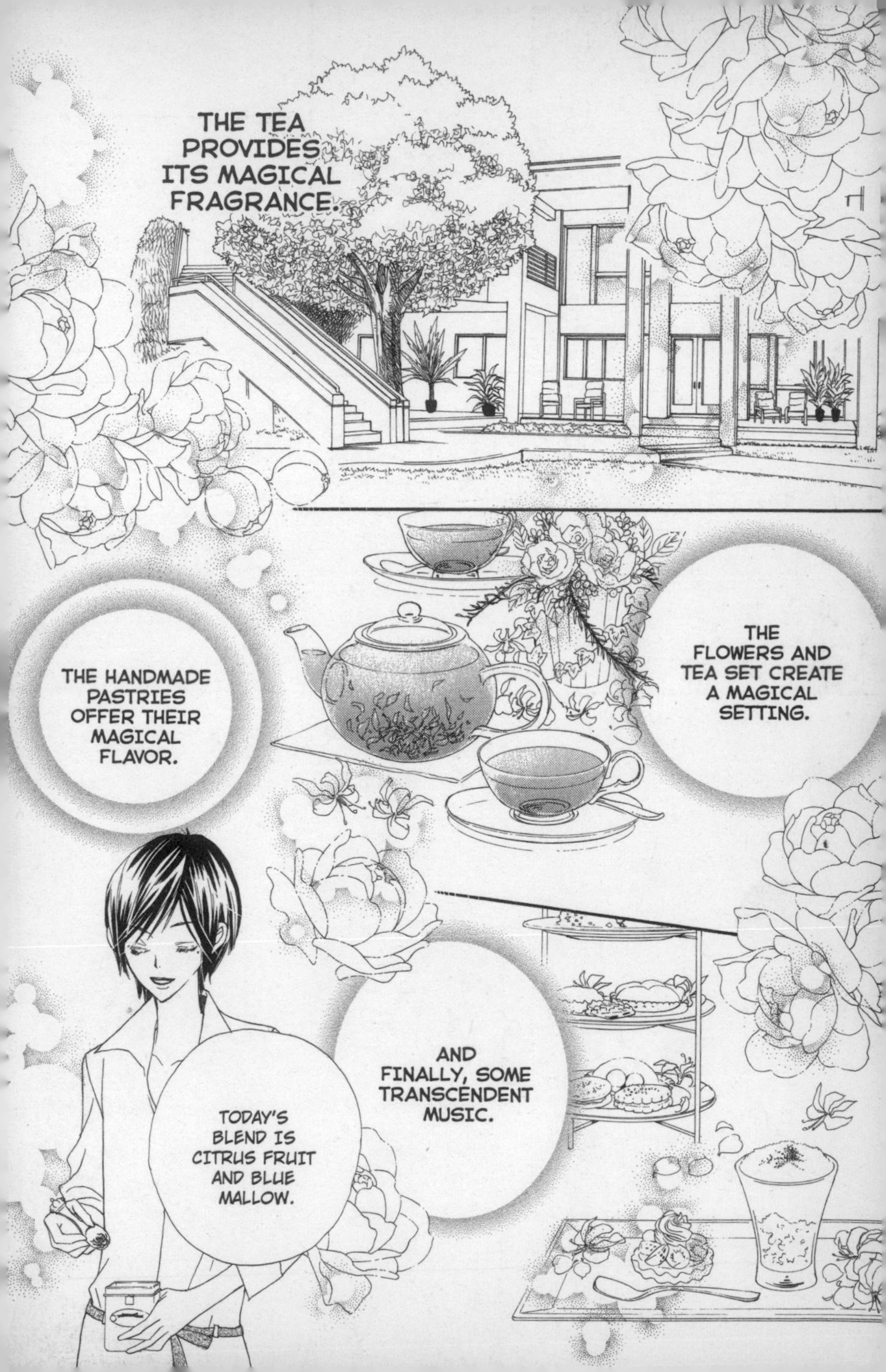
THE TEA PROVIDES ITS MAGICAL FRAGRANCE.
THE FLOWERS AND TEA SET CREATE A MAGICAL SETTING.
THE HANDMADE PASTRIES OFFER THEIR MAGICAL FLAVOR.
AND FINALLY, SOME TRANSCENDENT MUSIC.
TODAY'S BLEND IS CITRUS FRUIT AND BLUE MALLOW.

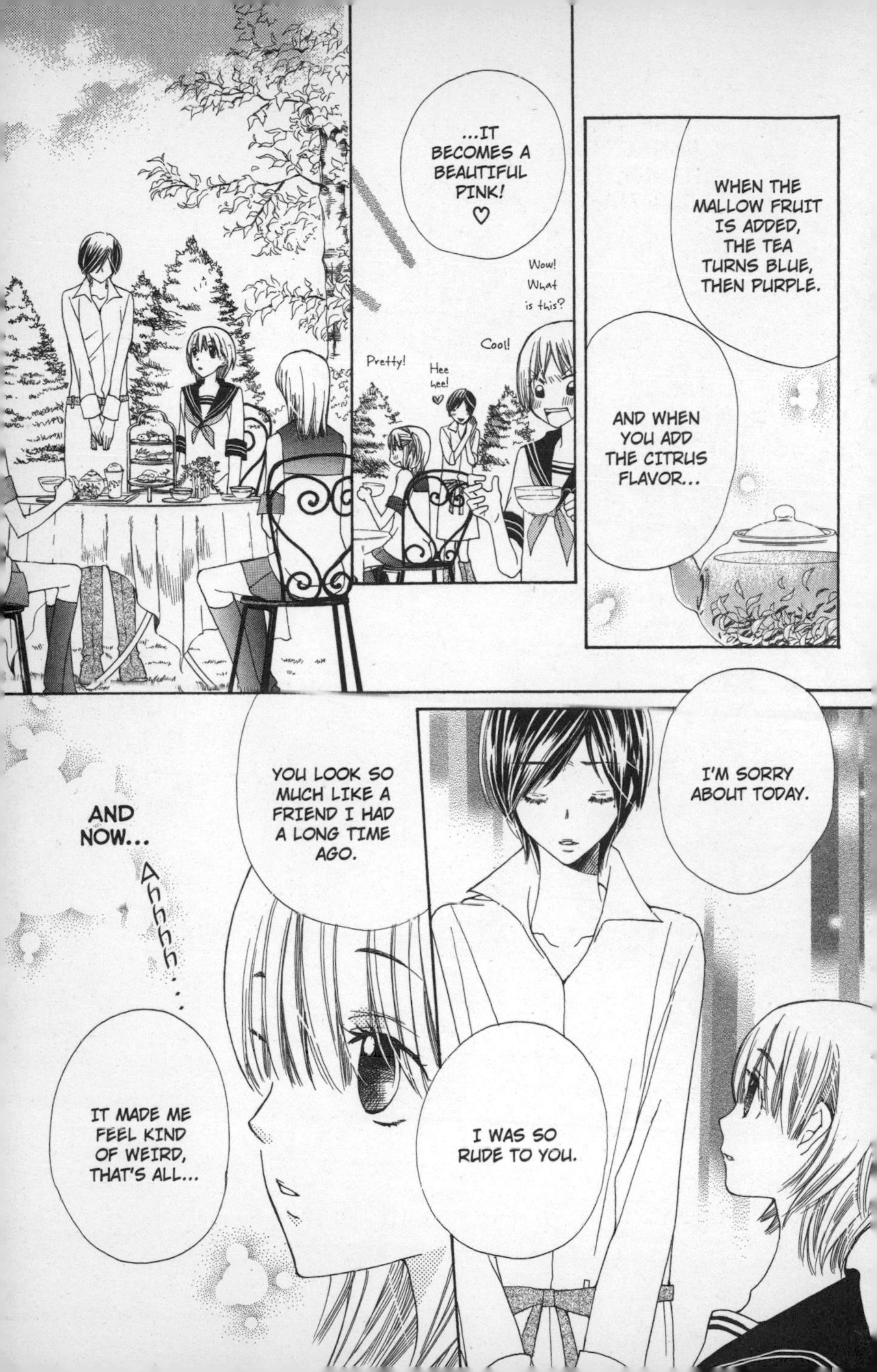
WHEN THE MALLOW FRUIT IS ADDED, THE TEA TURNS BLUE, THEN PURPLE.
AND WHEN YOU ADD THE CITRUS FLAVOR...
...IT BECOMES A BEAUTIFUL PINK! ♡
Wow! What is this?
Cool!
Hee hee! ♡
Pretty!
I'M SORRY ABOUT TODAY.
I WAS SO RUDE TO YOU.
YOU LOOK SO MUCH LIKE A FRIEND I HAD A LONG TIME AGO.
IT MADE ME FEEL KIND OF WEIRD, THAT'S ALL...
AND NOW...
Ahhhh...

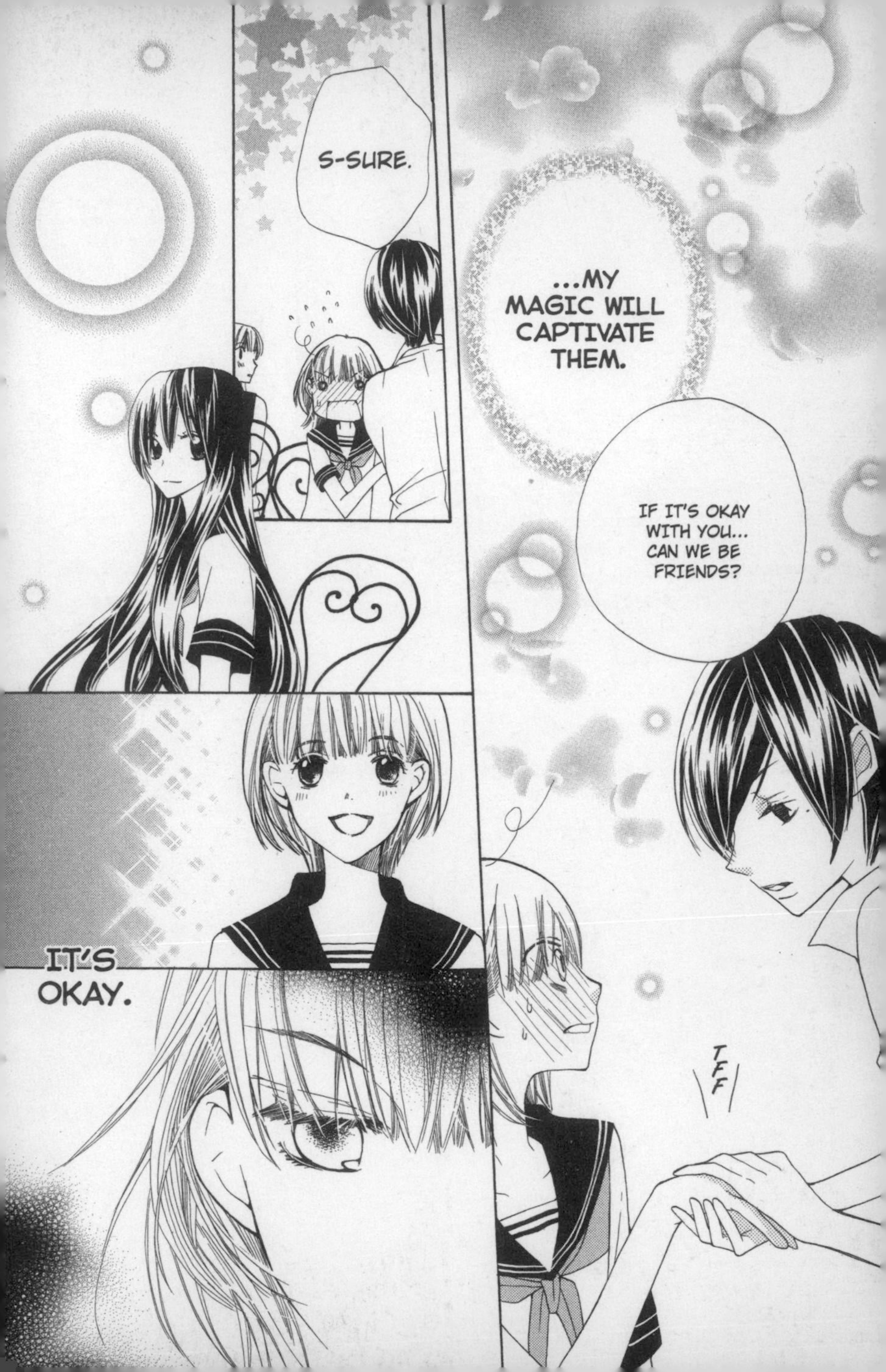
...MY MAGIC WILL CAPTIVATE THEM.
IF IT'S OKAY WITH YOU... CAN WE BE FRIENDS?
TFF
S-SURE.
IT'S OKAY.

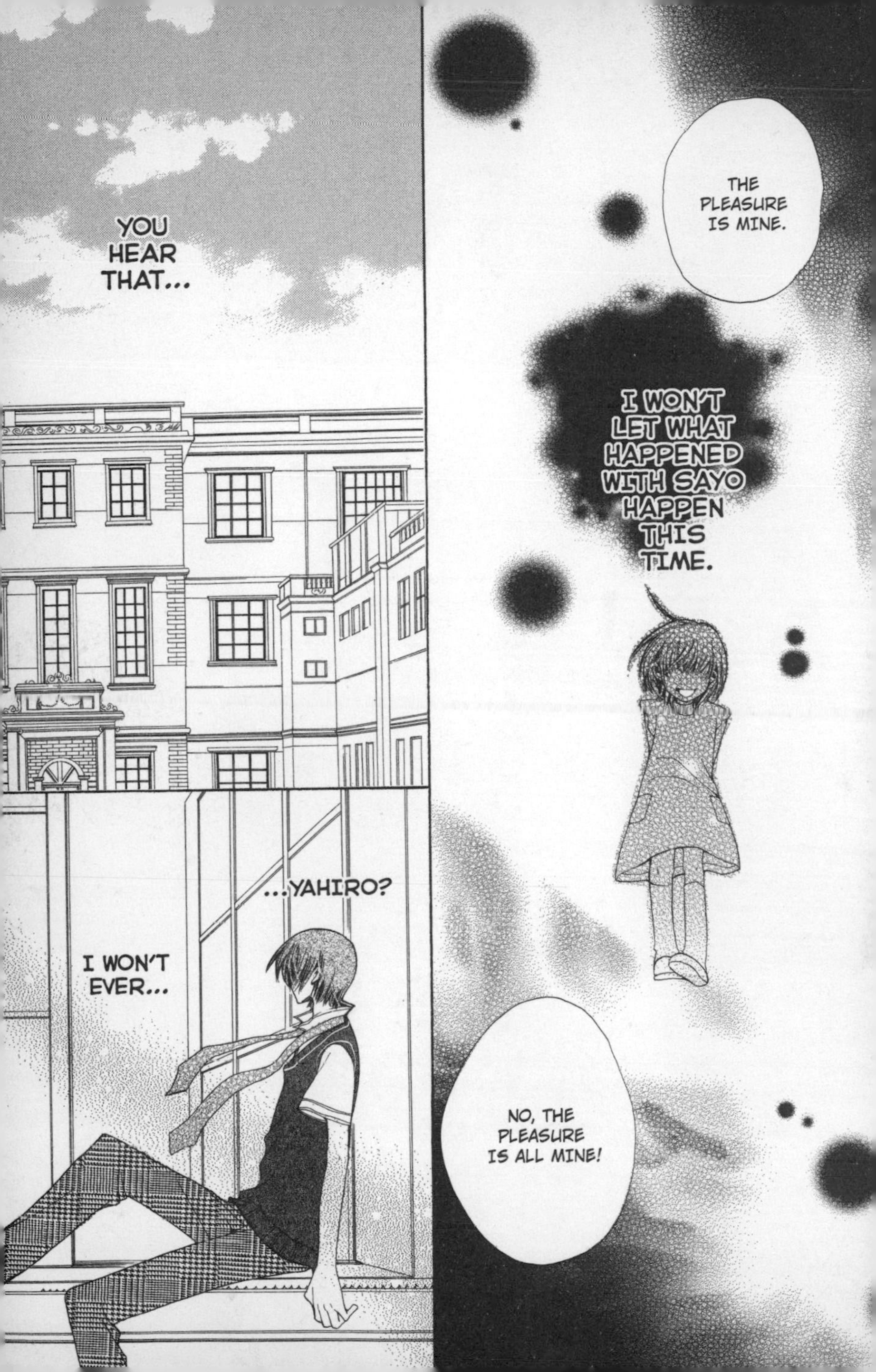
THE PLEASURE IS MINE.
I WON'T LET WHAT HAPPENED WITH SAYO HAPPEN THIS TIME.
NO, THE PLEASURE IS ALL MINE!
YOU HEAR THAT...
...YAHIRO?
I WON'T EVER...

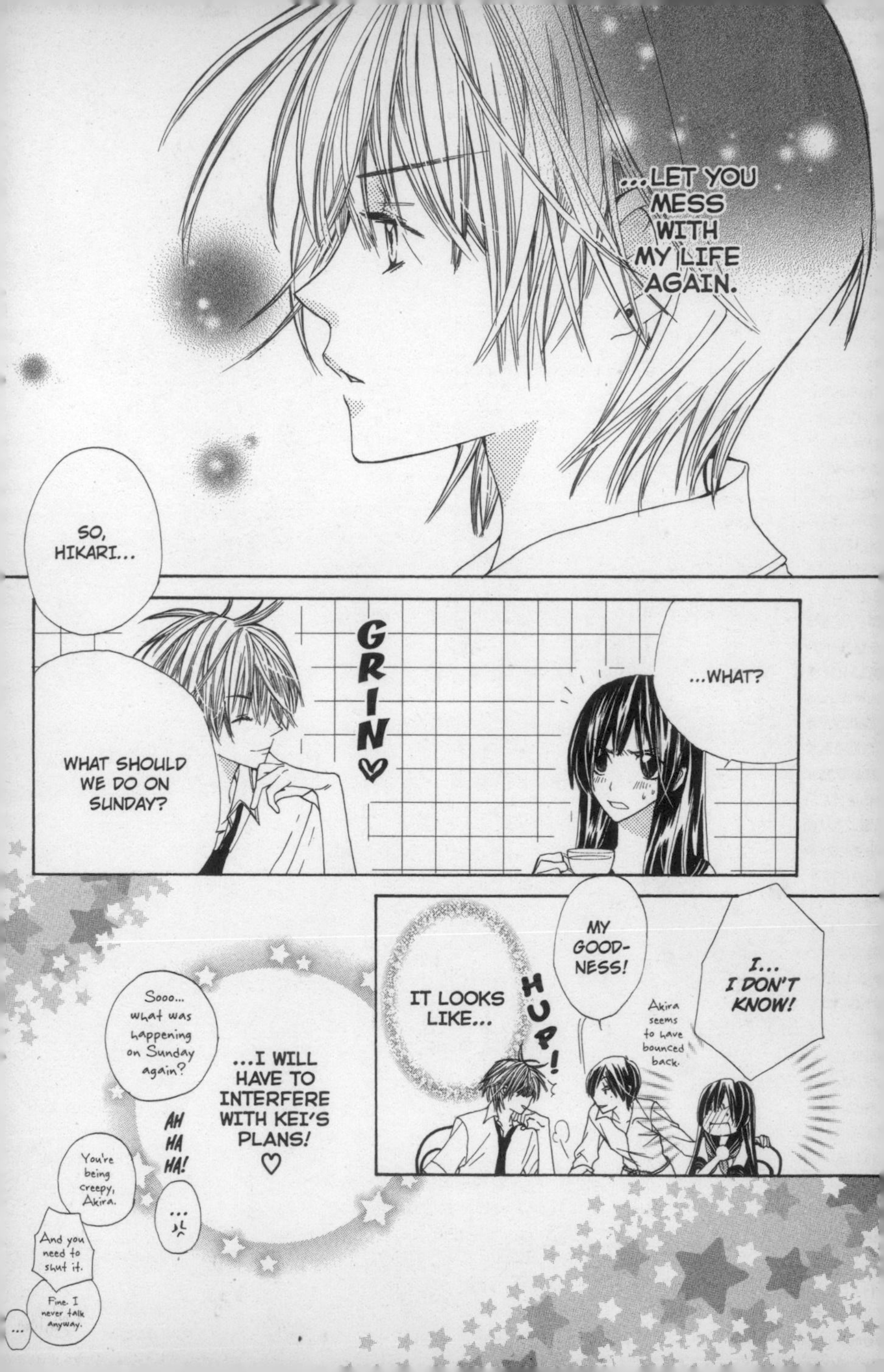
...LET YOU MESS WITH MY LIFE AGAIN.
SO, HIKARI...
...WHAT?
GRIN ♡
WHAT SHOULD WE DO ON SUNDAY?
I... I DON'T KNOW!
MY GOODNESS!
Akira seems to have bounced back.
HUP!
IT LOOKS LIKE...
...I WILL HAVE TO INTERFERE WITH KEI'S PLANS! ♡
Sooo... what was happening on Sunday again?
AH HA HA!
You're being creepy, Akira.
...
And you need to shut it.
Fine. I never talk anyway.
...

Chapter 19

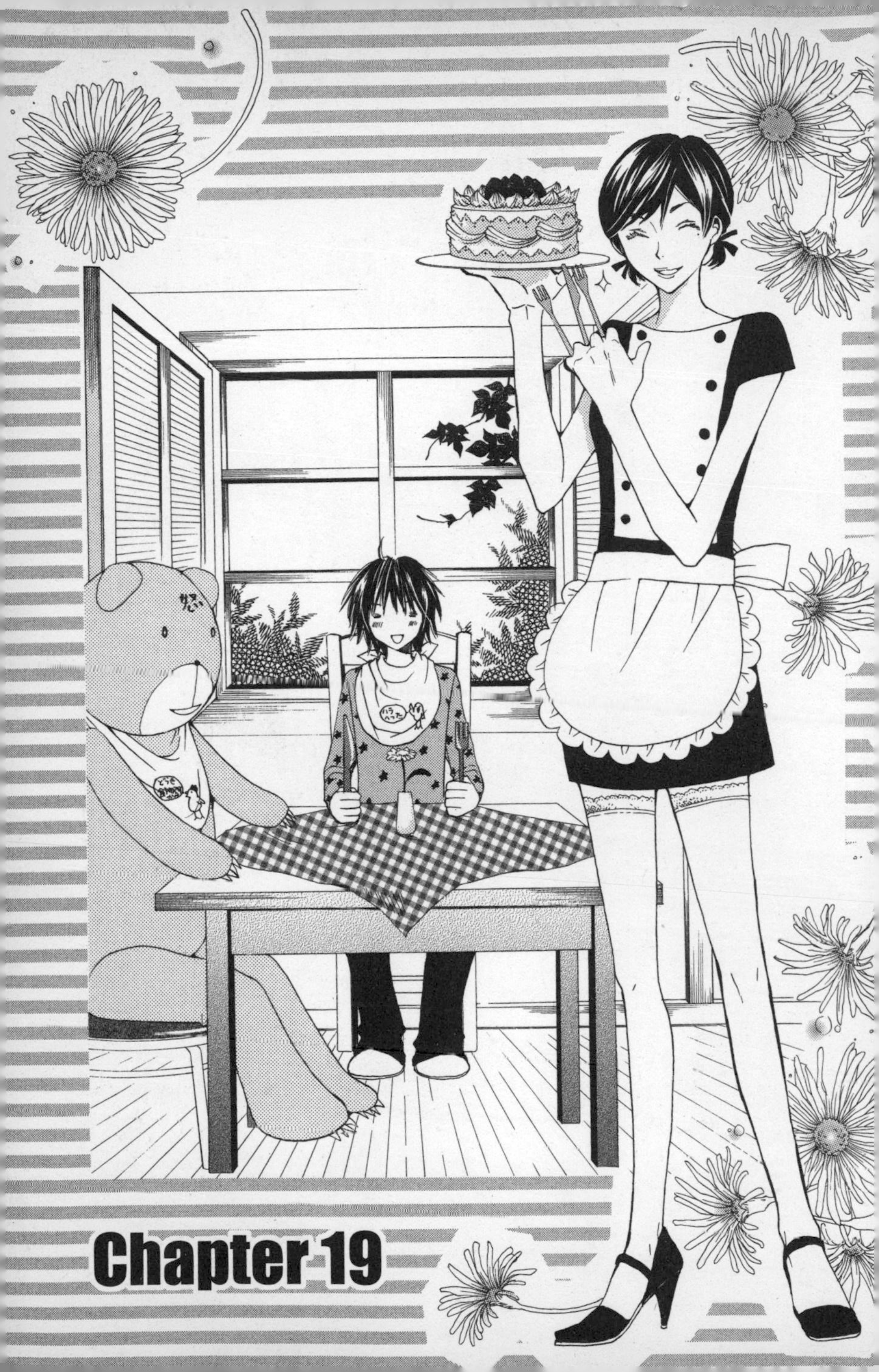

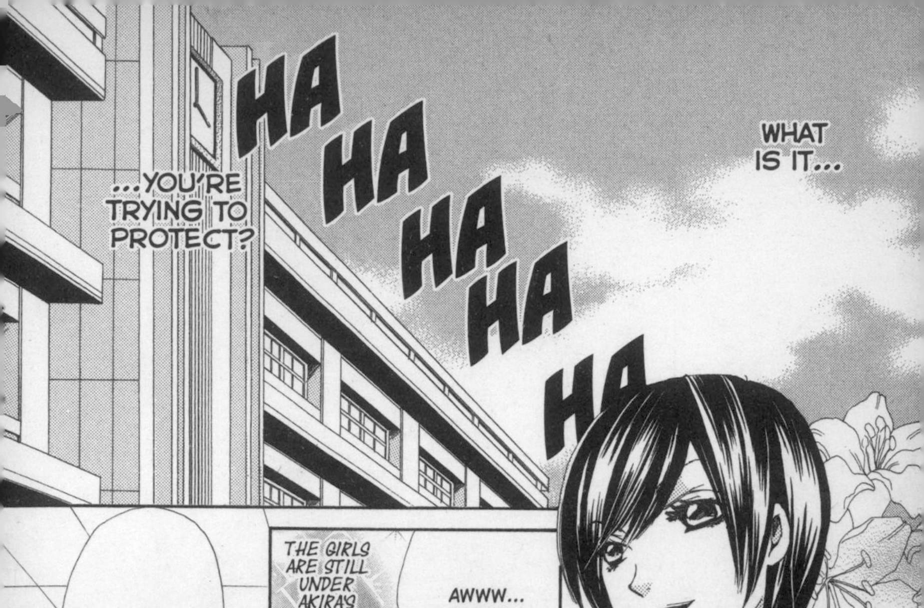
WHAT IS IT...
HA HA HA HA HA HA
...YOU'RE TRYING TO PROTECT?
WHY SO SAD, MY PUSSYCATS?
AWWW... TODAY'S YOUR LAST DAY!
THE GIRLS ARE STILL UNDER AKIRA'S SPELL.
TWINKLE
TWINKLE
PLEASE DON'T GO, MISS AKIRA!
SILLY GIRLS. ♡
POKE
ugh!
Get back! She poked you!!

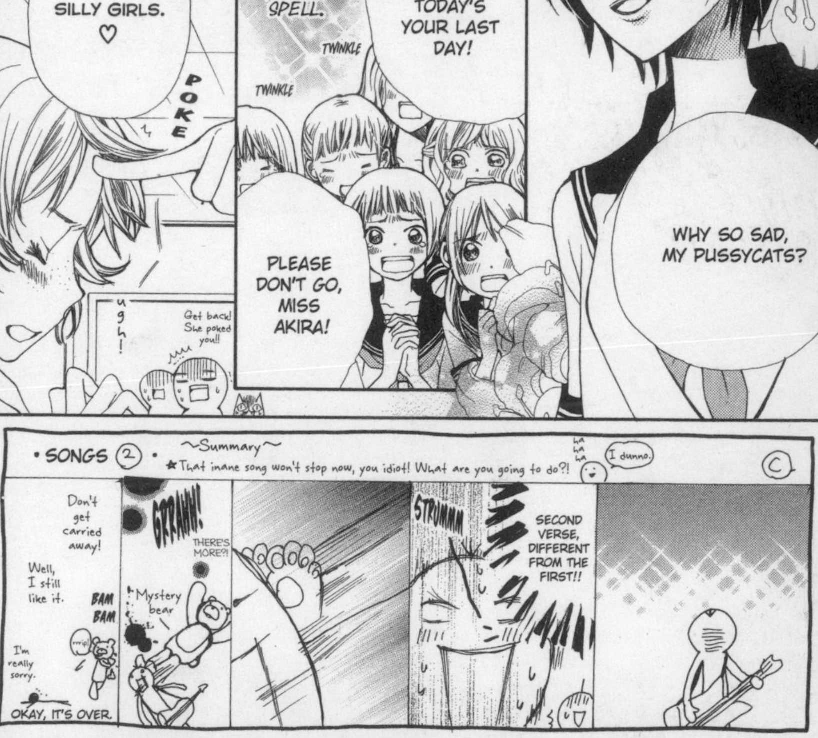
• SONGS ② •
~Summary~
☆That inane song won't stop now, you idiot! What are you going to do?!
ha ha ha
I dunno.
C
STRUMMM
SECOND VERSE, DIFFERENT FROM THE FIRST!!
GRRAHH!
THERE'S MORE?!
Mystery bear
Don't get carried away!
Well, I still like it.
BAM BAM
I'm really sorry.
OKAY, IT'S OVER.

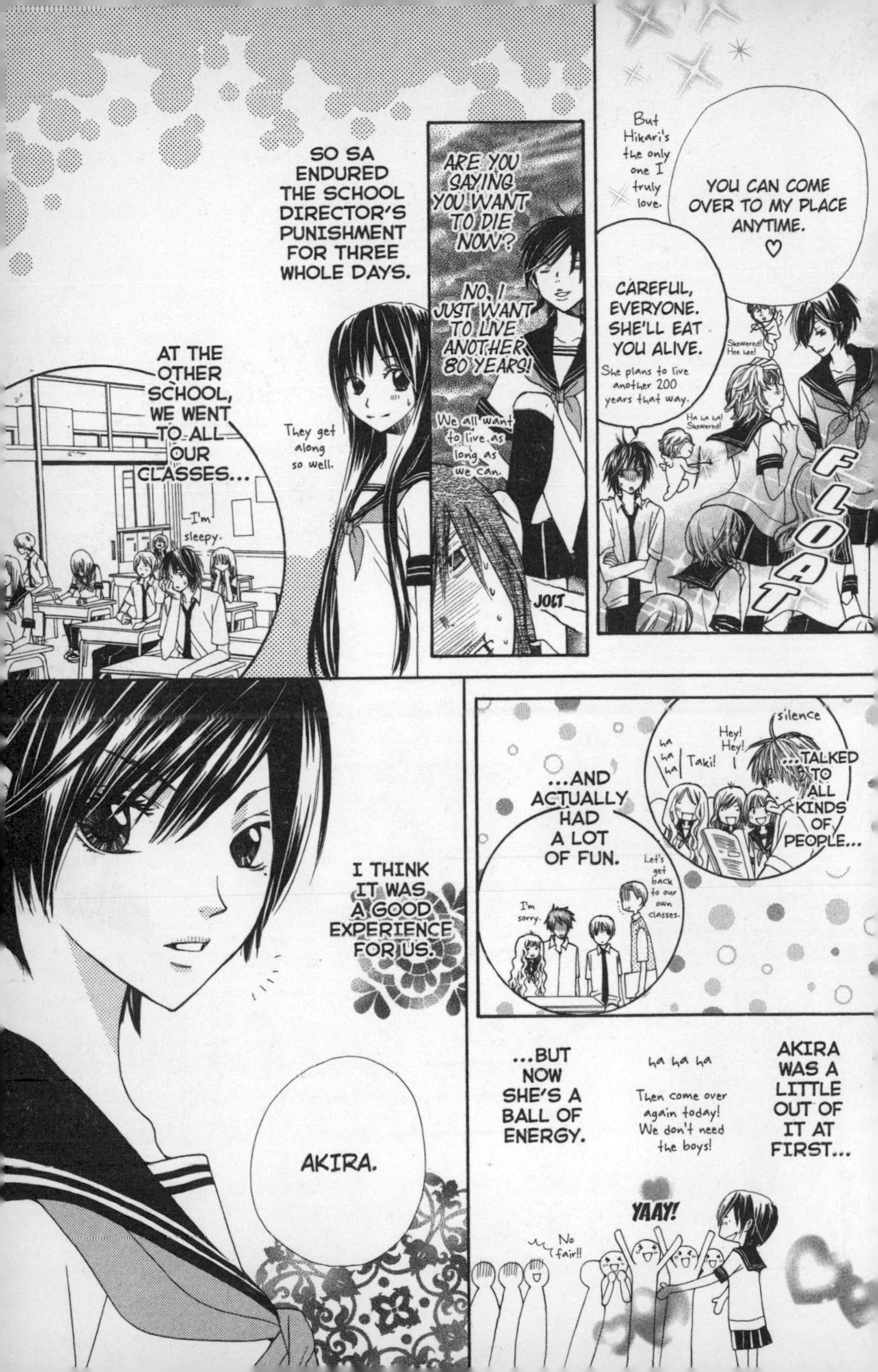
YOU CAN COME OVER TO MY PLACE ANYTIME. ♡
But Hikari's the only one I truly love.
CAREFUL, EVERYONE. SHE'LL EAT YOU ALIVE.
She plans to live another 200 years that way.
Skewered! Hee hee!
Ha ha ha! Skewered!
FLOAT
ARE YOU SAYING YOU WANT TO DIE NOW?
NO, I JUST WANT TO LIVE ANOTHER 80 YEARS!
We all want to live as long as we can.
JOLT
SO SA ENDURED THE SCHOOL DIRECTOR'S PUNISHMENT FOR THREE WHOLE DAYS.
They get along so well.
AT THE OTHER SCHOOL, WE WENT TO ALL OUR CLASSES...
I'm sleepy.
...TALKED TO ALL KINDS OF PEOPLE...
silence
Hey! Hey!
Taki!
ha ha ha
...AND ACTUALLY HAD A LOT OF FUN.
Let's get back to our own classes.
I'm sorry.
AKIRA WAS A LITTLE OUT OF IT AT FIRST...
ha ha ha
Then come over again today! We don't need the boys!
...BUT NOW SHE'S A BALL OF ENERGY.
YAAY!
No fair!!
I THINK IT WAS A GOOD EXPERIENCE FOR US.
AKIRA.

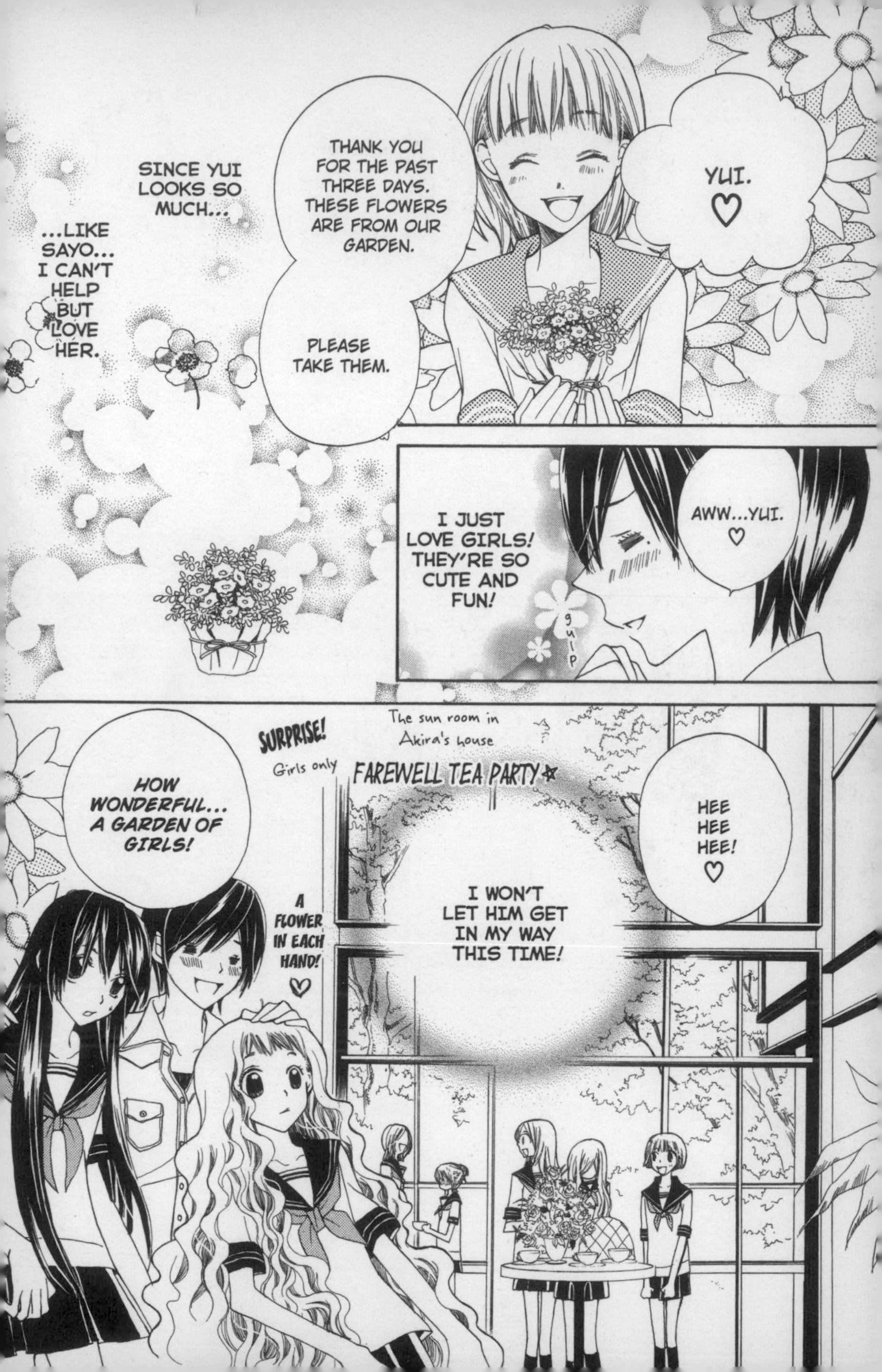
YUI. ♡
THANK YOU FOR THE PAST THREE DAYS. THESE FLOWERS ARE FROM OUR GARDEN.
PLEASE TAKE THEM.
SINCE YUI LOOKS SO MUCH...
...LIKE SAYO... I CAN'T HELP BUT LOVE HER.
AWW...YUI. ♡
I JUST LOVE GIRLS! THEY'RE SO CUTE AND FUN!
gulp
The sun room in Akira's house
SURPRISE!
Girls only
FAREWELL TEA PARTY
HEE HEE HEE! ♡
I WON'T LET HIM GET IN MY WAY THIS TIME!
A FLOWER IN EACH HAND! ♡
HOW WONDERFUL... A GARDEN OF GIRLS!

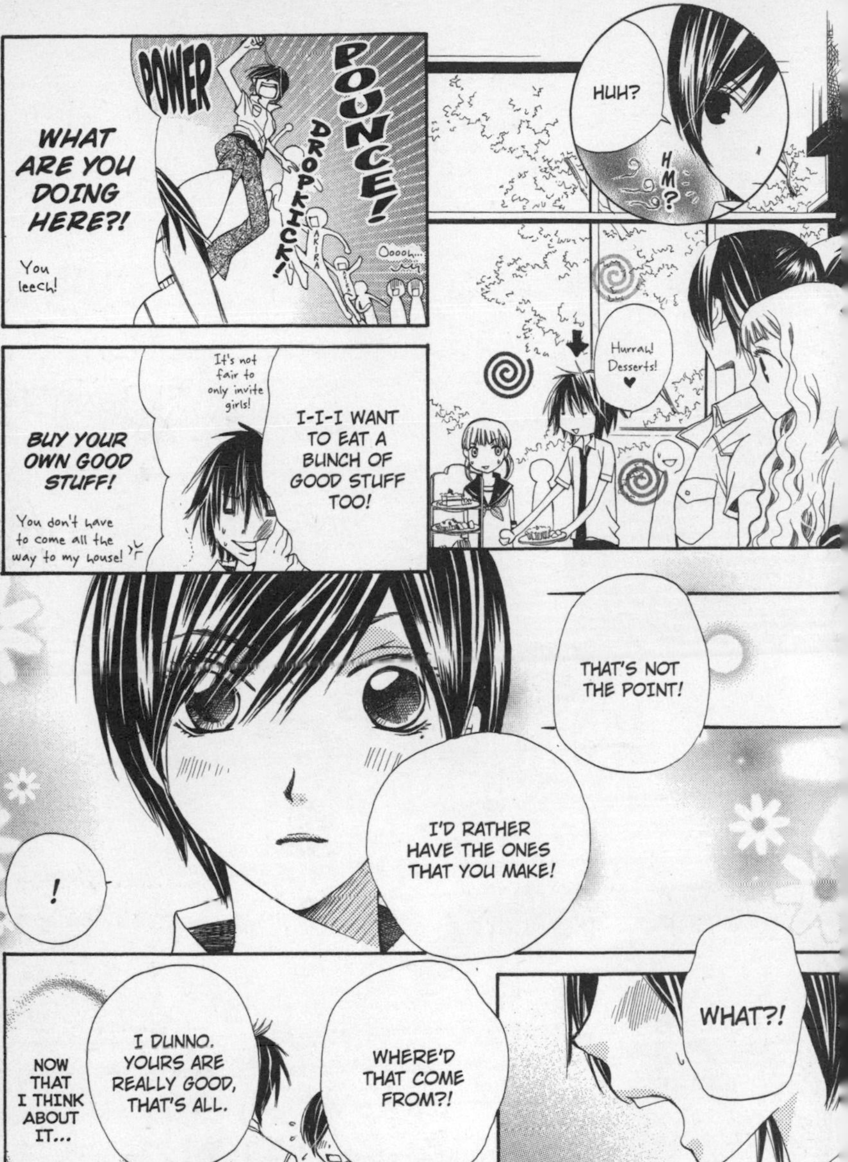
HUH?
HM?
Hurrah! Desserts! ♥
POWER
POUNCE!
DROPKICK!
AKIRA
Ooooh...
WHAT ARE YOU DOING HERE?!
You leech!
I-I-I WANT TO EAT A BUNCH OF GOOD STUFF TOO!
It's not fair to only invite girls!
BUY YOUR OWN GOOD STUFF!
You don't have to come all the way to my house!
THAT'S NOT THE POINT!
I'D RATHER HAVE THE ONES THAT YOU MAKE!
!
WHAT?!
WHERE'D THAT COME FROM?!
I DUNNO. YOURS ARE REALLY GOOD, THAT'S ALL.
NOW THAT I THINK ABOUT IT...

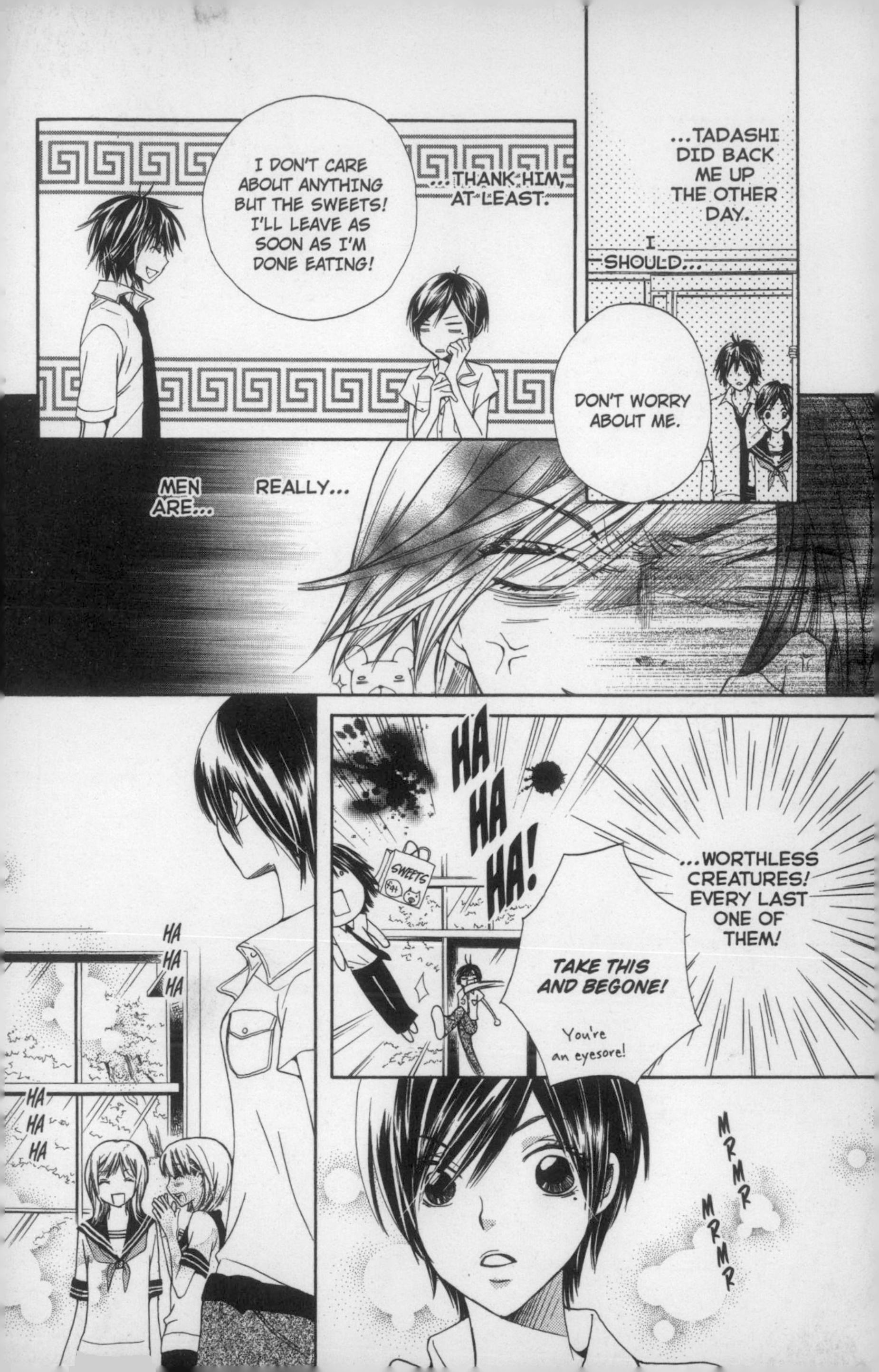
...TADASHI DID BACK ME UP THE OTHER DAY.
I SHOULD...
...THANK HIM, AT LEAST.
I DON'T CARE ABOUT ANYTHING BUT THE SWEETS! I'LL LEAVE AS SOON AS I'M DONE EATING!
DON'T WORRY ABOUT ME.
MEN ARE...
REALLY...
HA HA HA!
SWEETS
...WORTHLESS CREATURES! EVERY LAST ONE OF THEM!
TAKE THIS AND BEGONE!
You're an eyesore!
HA HA HA
HA HA HA
MRMR
MRMR

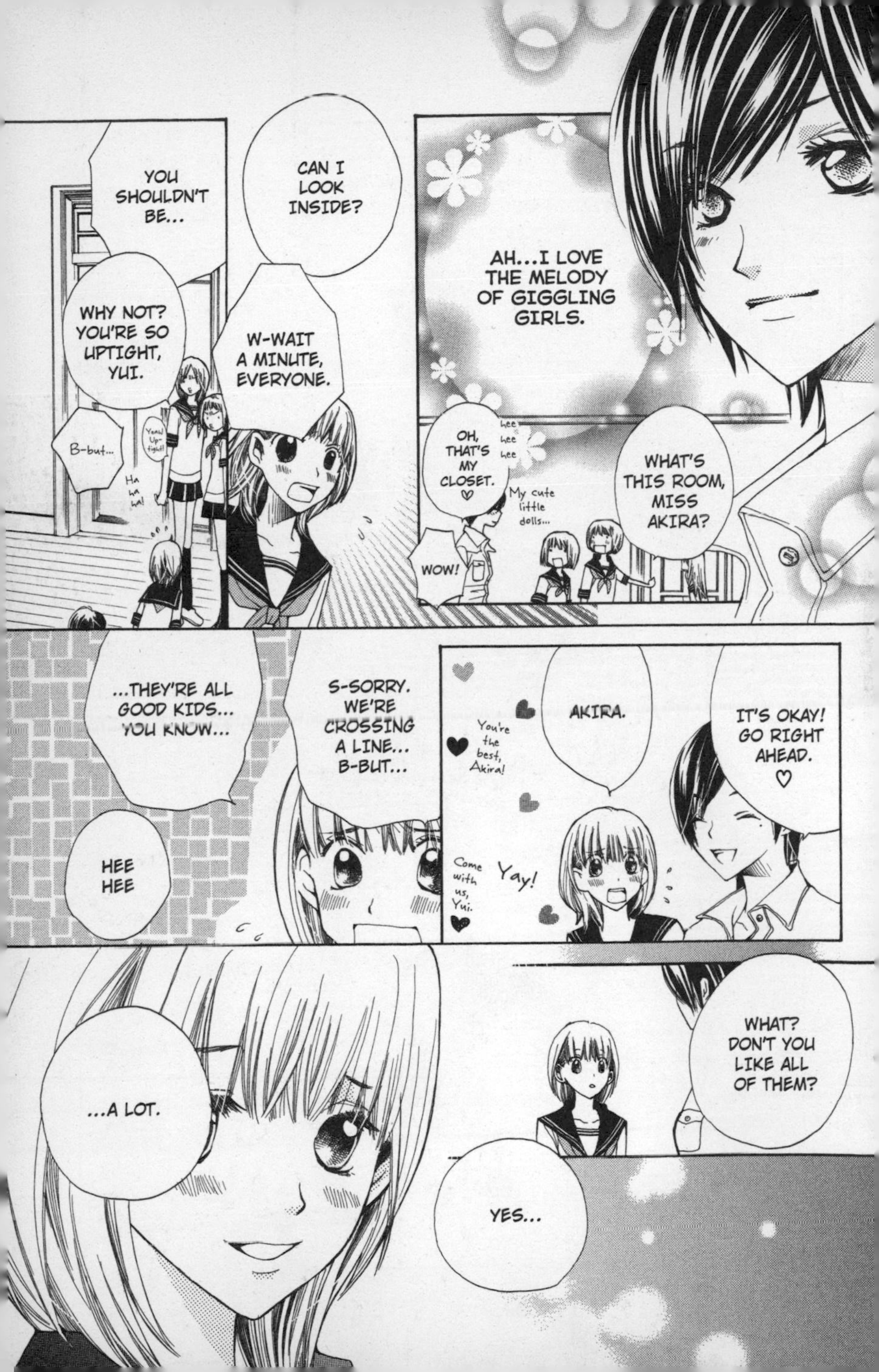
AH...I LOVE THE MELODY OF GIGGLING GIRLS.
WHAT'S THIS ROOM, MISS AKIRA?
OH, THAT'S MY CLOSET. ♡
hee hee hee
My cute little dolls...
WOW!
CAN I LOOK INSIDE?
YOU SHOULDN'T BE...
W-WAIT A MINUTE, EVERYONE.
WHY NOT? YOU'RE SO UPTIGHT, YUI.
Yeah! Up-tight!
B-but...
Ha ha ha!
IT'S OKAY! GO RIGHT AHEAD. ♡
AKIRA.
You're the best, Akira!
Yay!
Come with us, Yui.
S-SORRY. WE'RE CROSSING A LINE... B-BUT...
...THEY'RE ALL GOOD KIDS... YOU KNOW...
HEE HEE
WHAT? DON'T YOU LIKE ALL OF THEM?
YES...
...A LOT.

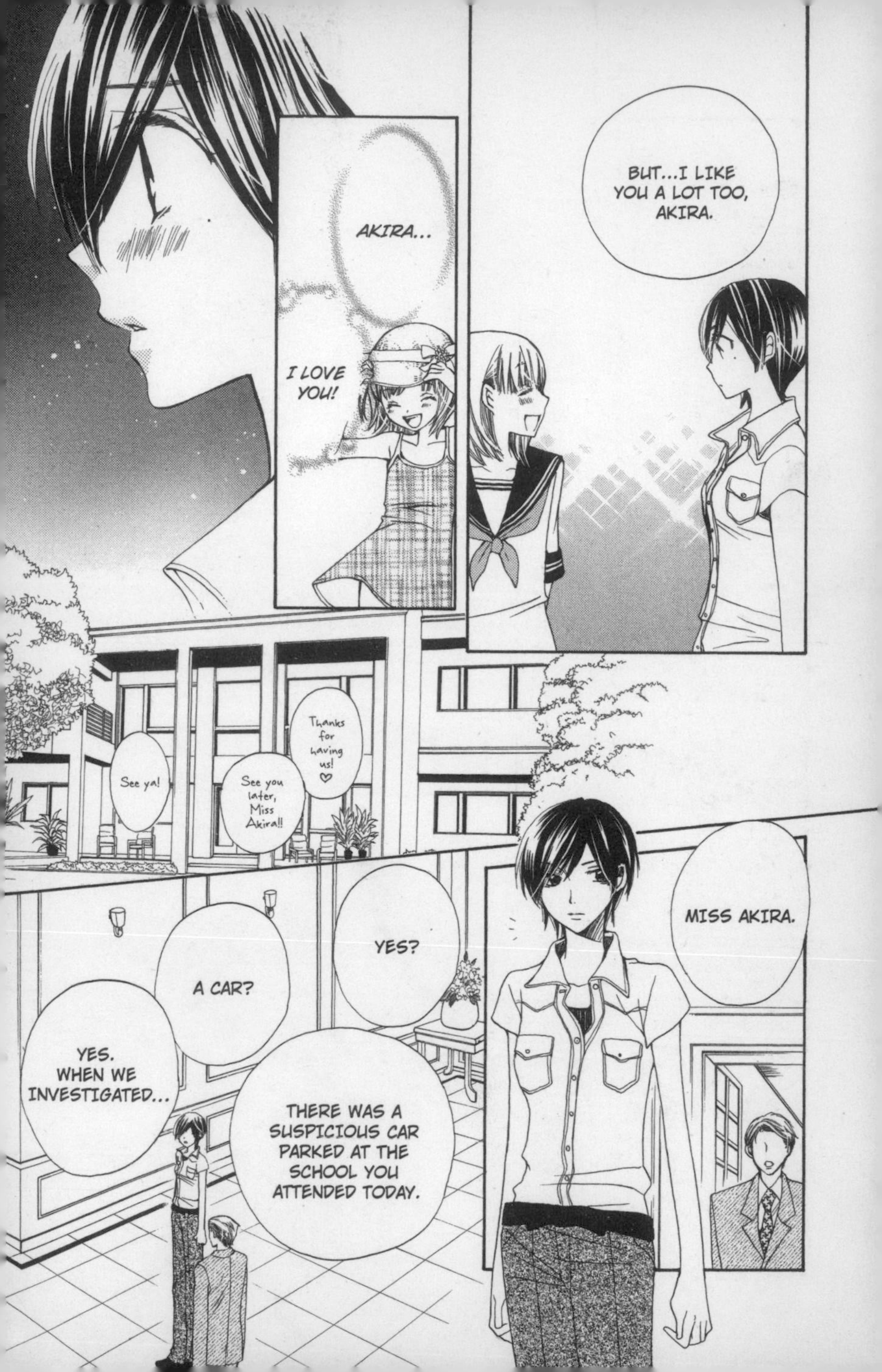
BUT...I LIKE YOU A LOT TOO, AKIRA.
AKIRA...
I LOVE YOU!
Thanks for having us! ♡
See you later, Miss Akira!!
See ya!
MISS AKIRA.
YES?
THERE WAS A SUSPICIOUS CAR PARKED AT THE SCHOOL YOU ATTENDED TODAY.
A CAR?
YES. WHEN WE INVESTIGATED...

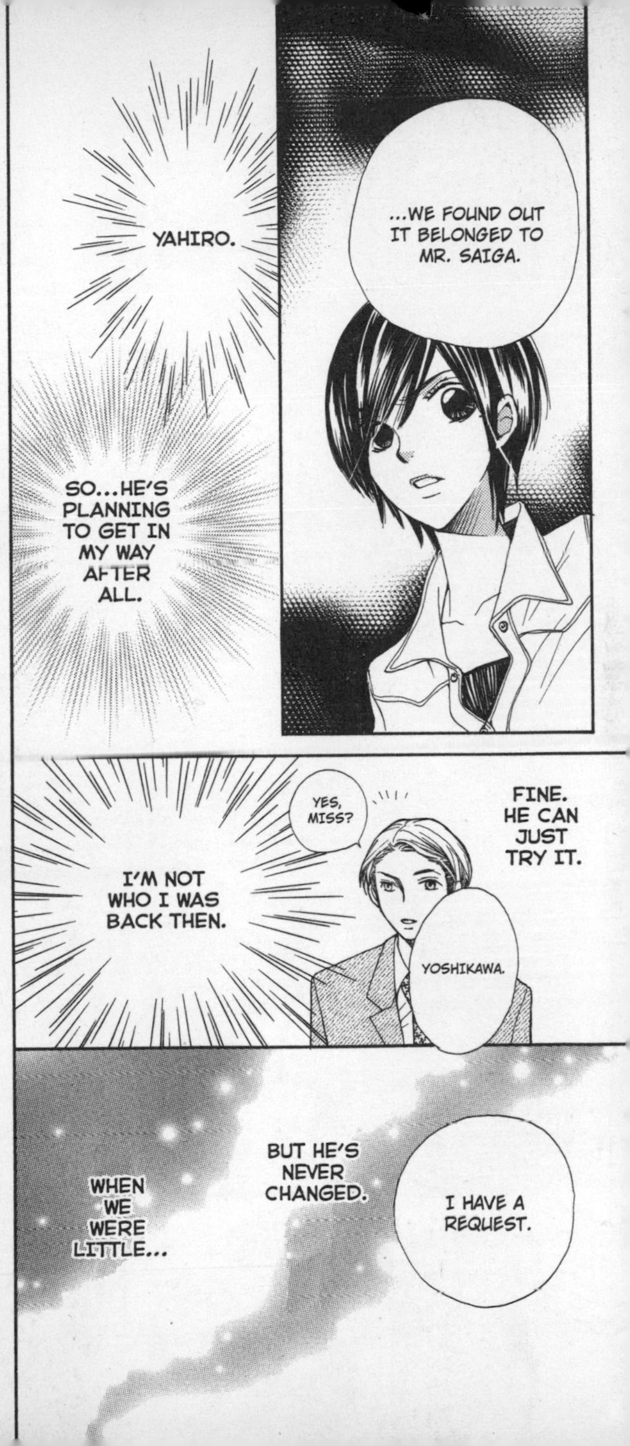
...WE FOUND OUT IT BELONGED TO MR. SAIGA.
YAHIRO.
SO...HE'S PLANNING TO GET IN MY WAY AFTER ALL.
FINE. HE CAN JUST TRY IT.
YES, MISS?
YOSHIKAWA.
I'M NOT WHO I WAS BACK THEN.
I HAVE A REQUEST.
BUT HE'S NEVER CHANGED.
WHEN WE WERE LITTLE...

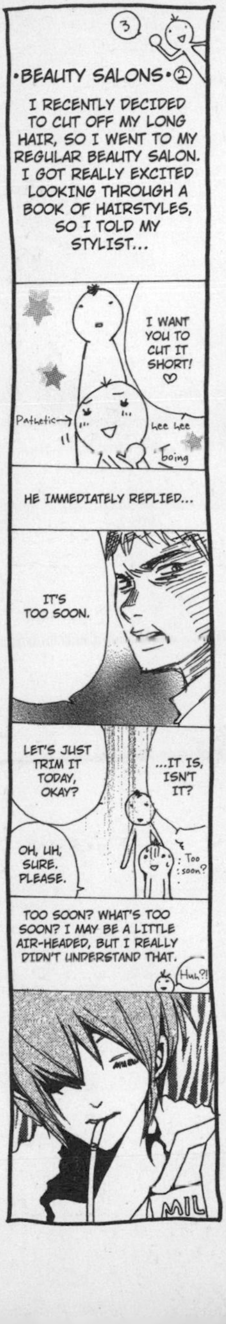
3
•BEAUTY SALONS•②
I RECENTLY DECIDED TO CUT OFF MY LONG HAIR, SO I WENT TO MY REGULAR BEAUTY SALON. I GOT REALLY EXCITED LOOKING THROUGH A BOOK OF HAIRSTYLES, SO I TOLD MY STYLIST...
I WANT YOU TO CUT IT SHORT! ♡
Pathetic
hee hee
boing
HE IMMEDIATELY REPLIED...
IT'S TOO SOON.
...IT IS, ISN'T IT?
LET'S JUST TRIM IT TODAY, OKAY?
OH, UH, SURE. PLEASE.
Too soon?
TOO SOON? WHAT'S TOO SOON? I MAY BE A LITTLE AIR-HEADED, BUT I REALLY DIDN'T UNDERSTAND THAT.
Huh?!
MIL

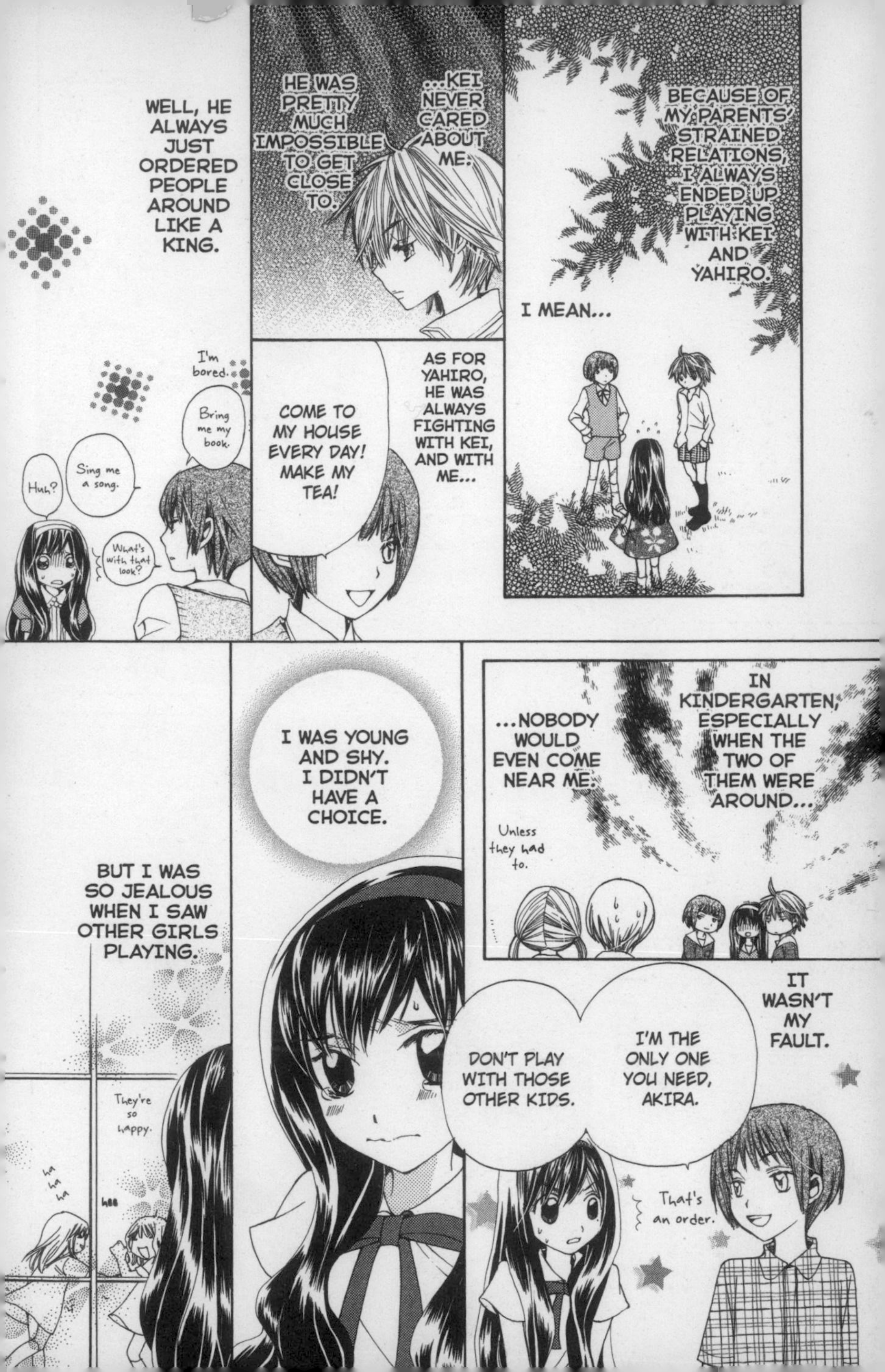
BECAUSE OF MY PARENTS' STRAINED RELATIONS, I ALWAYS ENDED UP PLAYING WITH KEI AND YAHIRO.
I MEAN...
...KEI NEVER CARED ABOUT ME.
HE WAS PRETTY MUCH IMPOSSIBLE TO GET CLOSE TO.
AS FOR YAHIRO, HE WAS ALWAYS FIGHTING WITH KEI, AND WITH ME...
COME TO MY HOUSE EVERY DAY! MAKE MY TEA!
WELL, HE ALWAYS JUST ORDERED PEOPLE AROUND LIKE A KING.
I'm bored.
Bring me my book.
Sing me a song.
Huh?
What's with that look?
IN KINDERGARTEN, ESPECIALLY WHEN THE TWO OF THEM WERE AROUND...
...NOBODY WOULD EVEN COME NEAR ME.
Unless they had to.
IT WASN'T MY FAULT.
I'M THE ONLY ONE YOU NEED, AKIRA.
DON'T PLAY WITH THOSE OTHER KIDS.
That's an order.
I WAS YOUNG AND SHY. I DIDN'T HAVE A CHOICE.
BUT I WAS SO JEALOUS WHEN I SAW OTHER GIRLS PLAYING.
They're so happy.
ha ha ha
hee

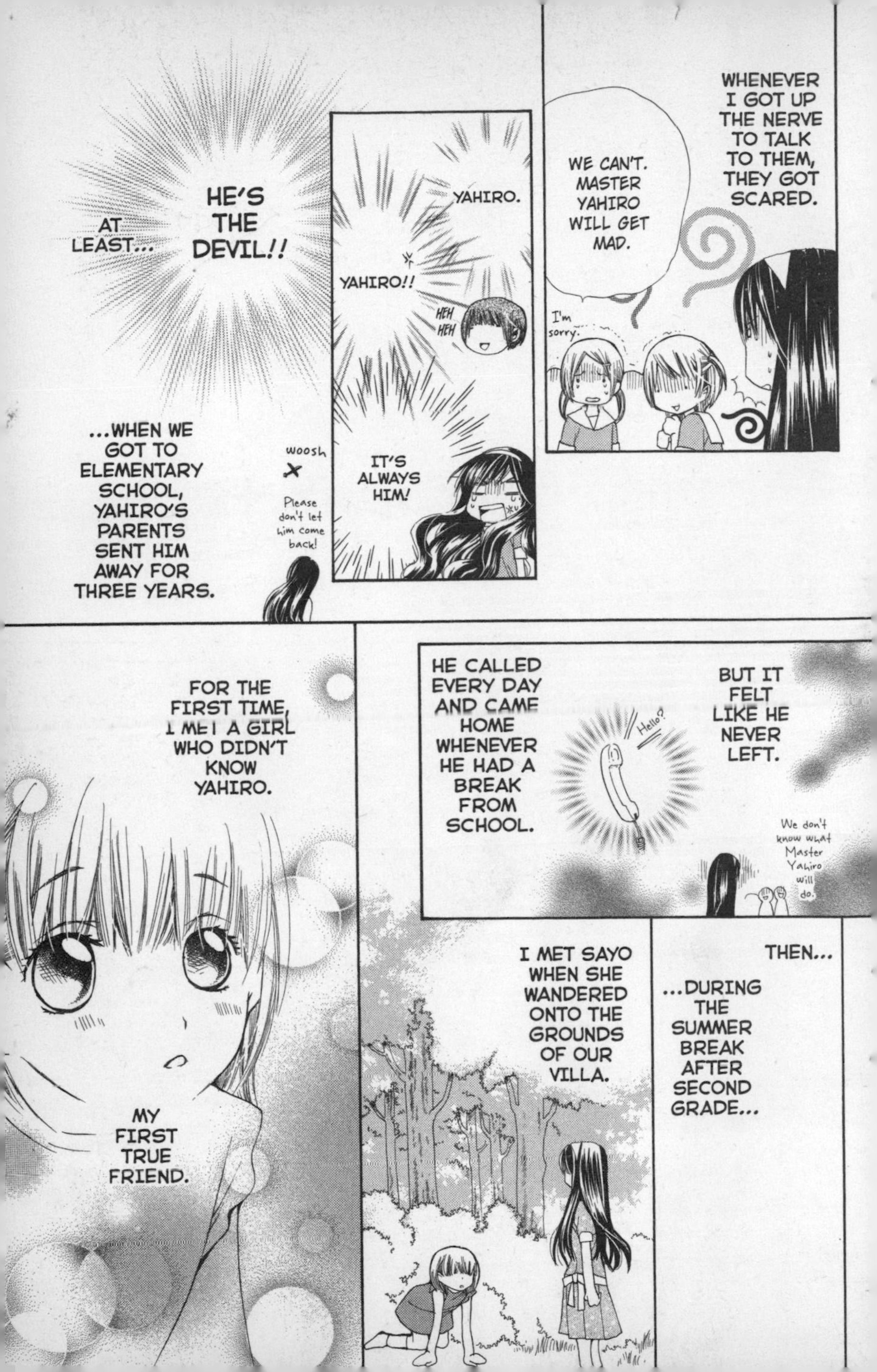
WHENEVER I GOT UP THE NERVE TO TALK TO THEM, THEY GOT SCARED.
WE CAN'T. MASTER YAHIRO WILL GET MAD.
I'm sorry.
YAHIRO.
YAHIRO!!
HEH HEH
IT'S ALWAYS HIM!
HE'S THE DEVIL!!
AT LEAST...
...WHEN WE GOT TO ELEMENTARY SCHOOL, YAHIRO'S PARENTS SENT HIM AWAY FOR THREE YEARS.
woosh
Please don't let him come back!
HE CALLED EVERY DAY AND CAME HOME WHENEVER HE HAD A BREAK FROM SCHOOL.
Hello?
BUT IT FELT LIKE HE NEVER LEFT.
We don't know what Master Yahiro will do.
THEN...
...DURING THE SUMMER BREAK AFTER SECOND GRADE...
I MET SAYO WHEN SHE WANDERED ONTO THE GROUNDS OF OUR VILLA.
FOR THE FIRST TIME, I MET A GIRL WHO DIDN'T KNOW YAHIRO.
MY FIRST TRUE FRIEND.

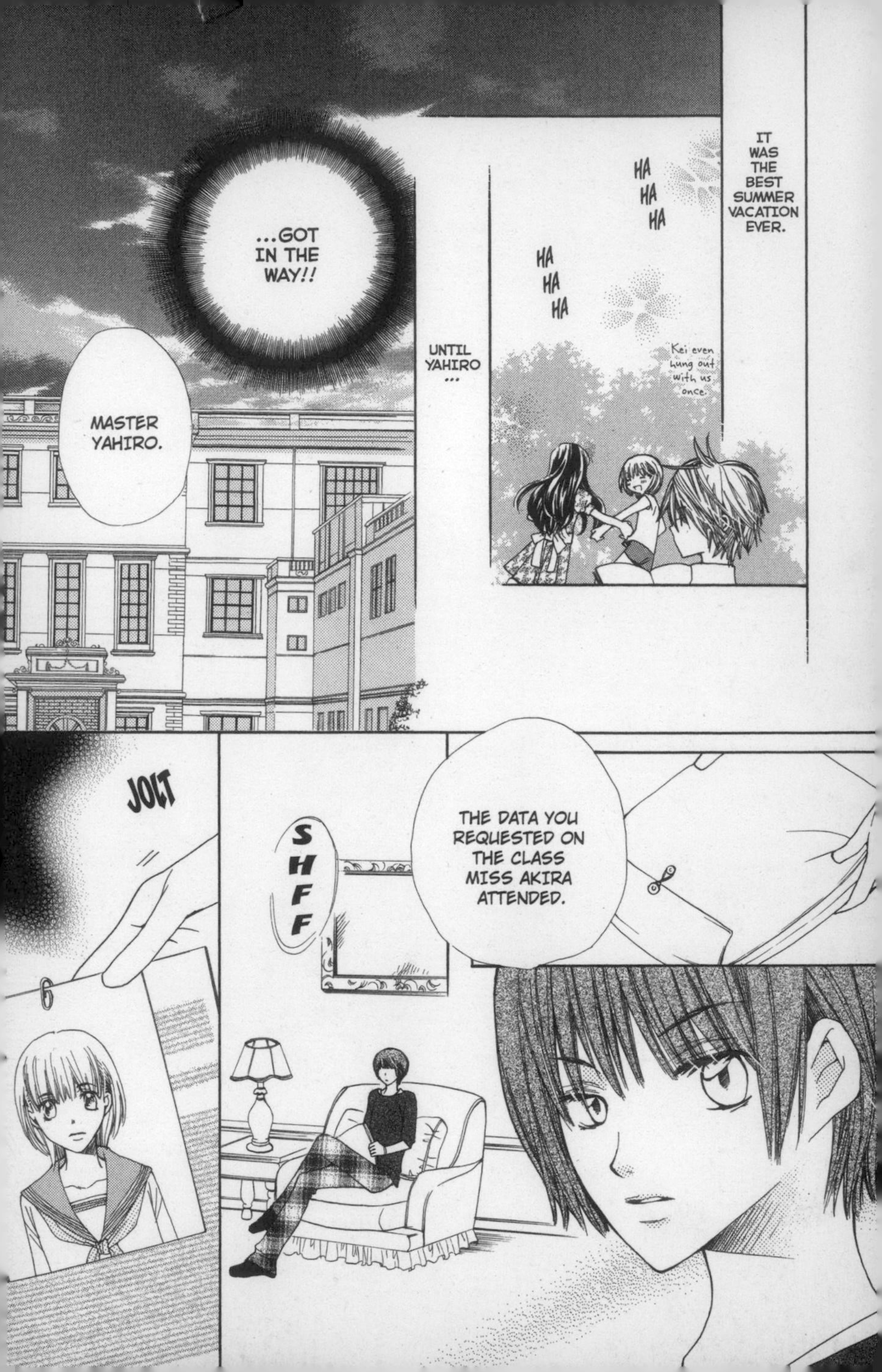
IT WAS THE BEST SUMMER VACATION EVER.
HA HA HA
HA HA HA
Kei even hung out with us once.
UNTIL YAHIRO...
...GOT IN THE WAY!!
MASTER YAHIRO.
THE DATA YOU REQUESTED ON THE CLASS MISS AKIRA ATTENDED.
SHFF
JOLT

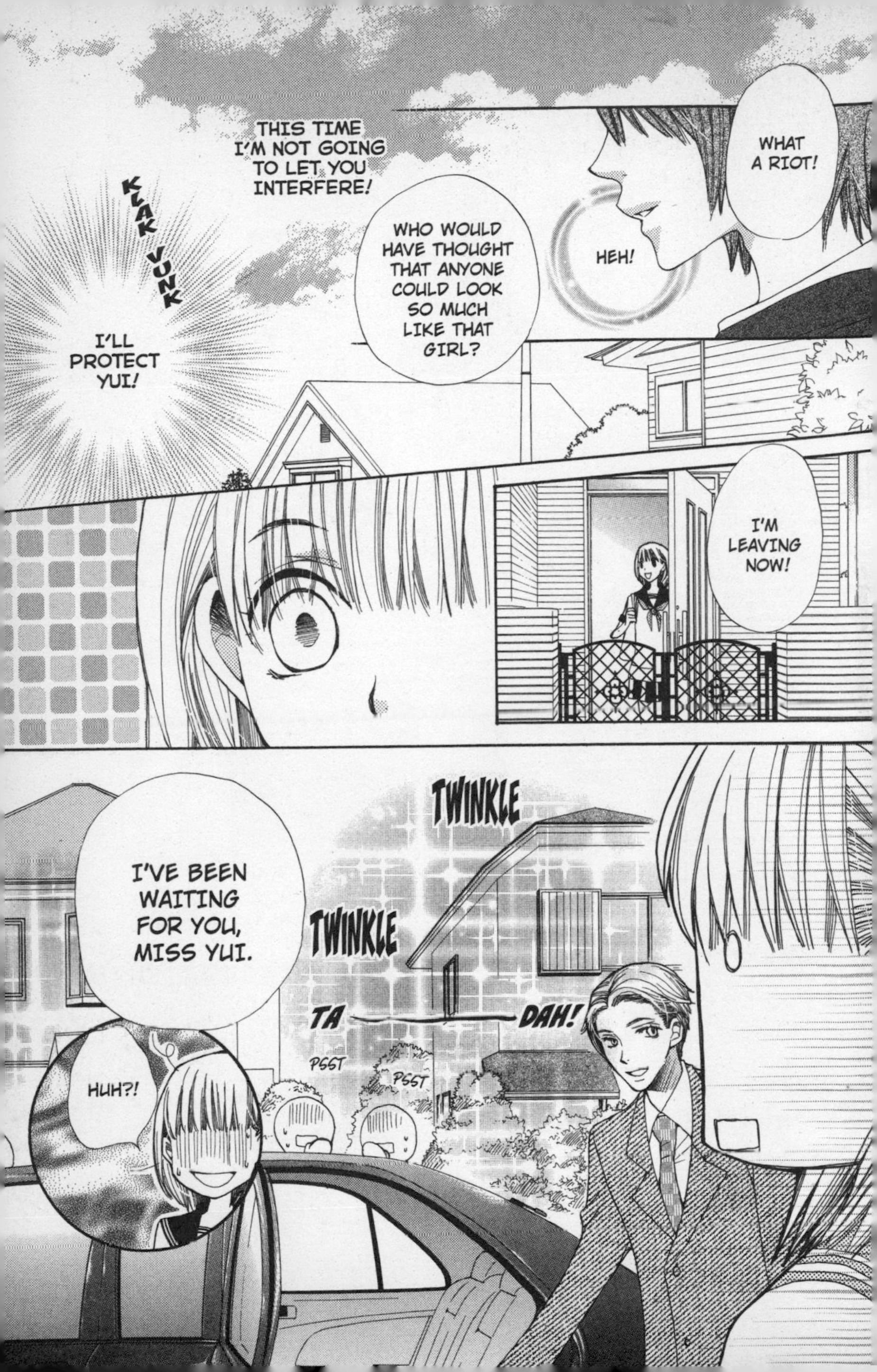
WHAT A RIOT!
HEH!
WHO WOULD HAVE THOUGHT THAT ANYONE COULD LOOK SO MUCH LIKE THAT GIRL?
THIS TIME I'M NOT GOING TO LET YOU INTERFERE!
KLAK VUNK
I'LL PROTECT YUI!
I'M LEAVING NOW!
TWINKLE
I'VE BEEN WAITING FOR YOU, MISS YUI.
TWINKLE
TA—DAH!
PSST
PSST
HUH?!

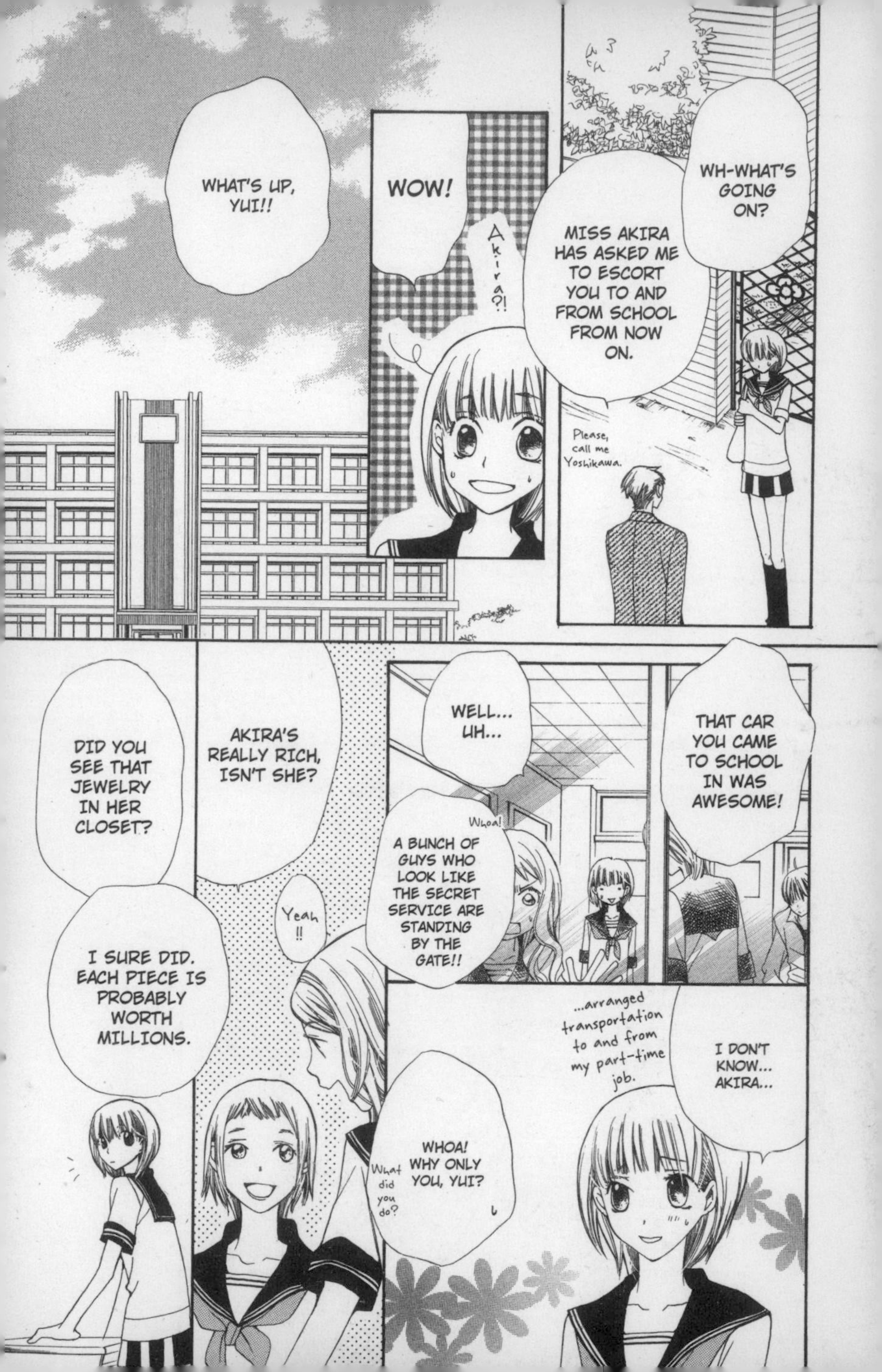
WH-WHAT'S GOING ON?
MISS AKIRA HAS ASKED ME TO ESCORT YOU TO AND FROM SCHOOL FROM NOW ON.
Please, call me Yoshikawa.
WOW!
Akira?!
WHAT'S UP, YUI!!
THAT CAR YOU CAME TO SCHOOL IN WAS AWESOME!
WELL... UH...
Whoa!
A BUNCH OF GUYS WHO LOOK LIKE THE SECRET SERVICE ARE STANDING BY THE GATE!!
I DON'T KNOW... AKIRA...
...arranged transportation to and from my part-time job.
AKIRA'S REALLY RICH, ISN'T SHE?
Yeah!!
WHOA! WHY ONLY YOU, YUI?
What did you do?
DID YOU SEE THAT JEWELRY IN HER CLOSET?
I SURE DID. EACH PIECE IS PROBABLY WORTH MILLIONS.

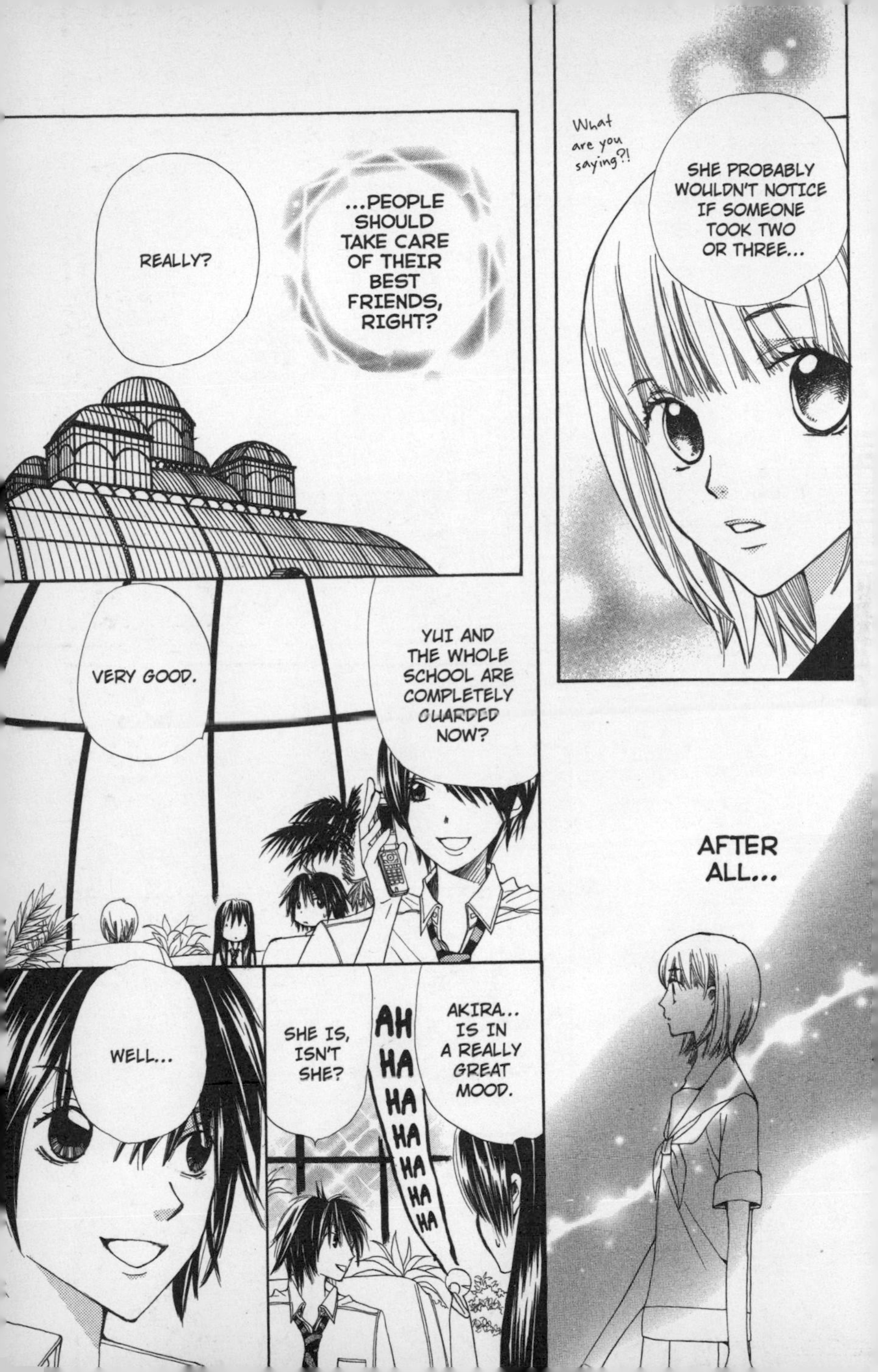
What are you saying?!
SHE PROBABLY WOULDN'T NOTICE IF SOMEONE TOOK TWO OR THREE...
...PEOPLE SHOULD TAKE CARE OF THEIR BEST FRIENDS, RIGHT?
REALLY?
YUI AND THE WHOLE SCHOOL ARE COMPLETELY GUARDED NOW?
VERY GOOD.
AKIRA... IS IN A REALLY GREAT MOOD.
AH HA HA HA HA HA HA HA
SHE IS, ISN'T SHE?
WELL...
AFTER ALL...

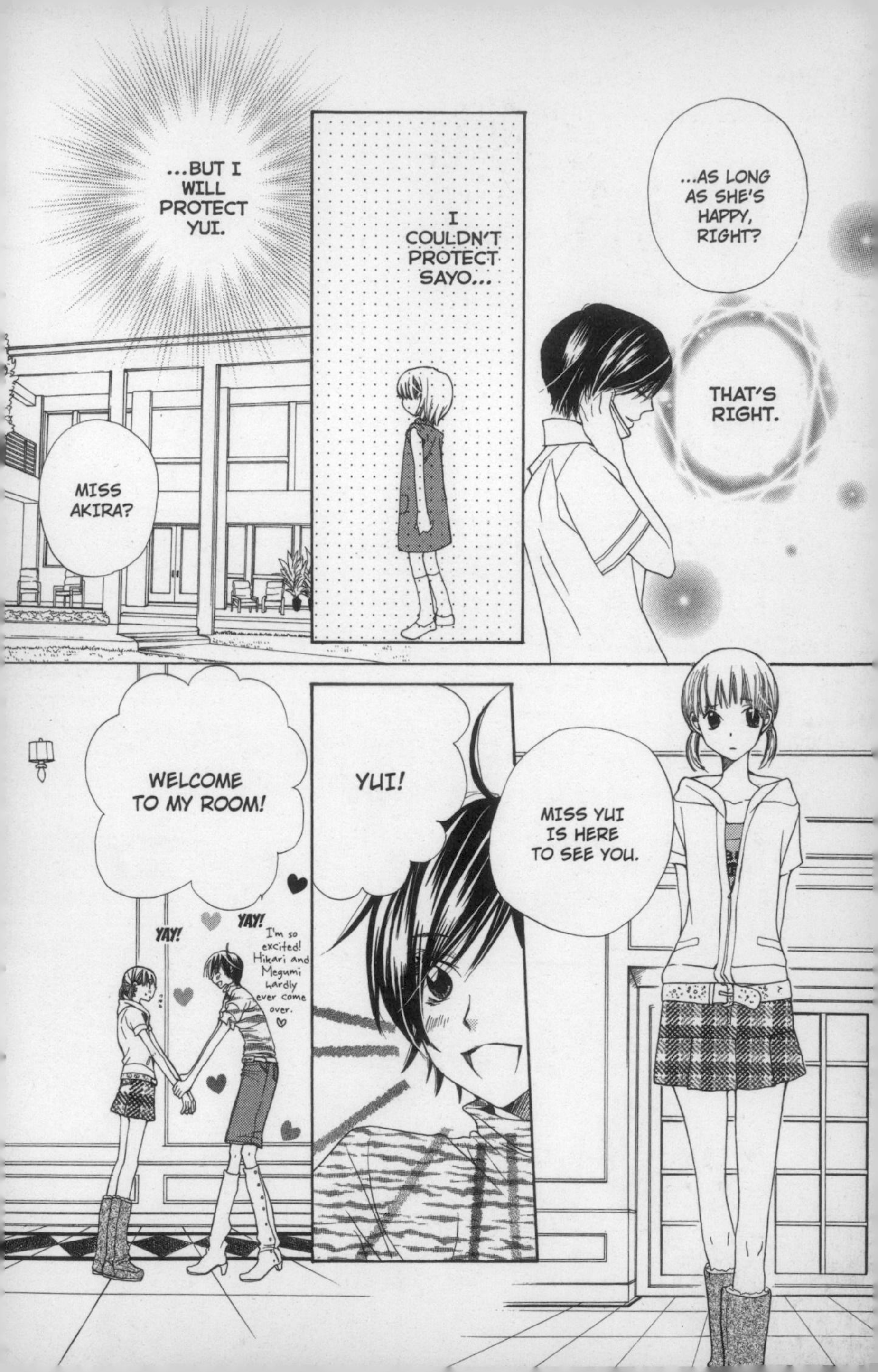
...AS LONG AS SHE'S HAPPY, RIGHT?
THAT'S RIGHT.
I COULDN'T PROTECT SAYO...
...BUT I WILL PROTECT YUI.
MISS AKIRA?
MISS YUI IS HERE TO SEE YOU.
YUI!
WELCOME TO MY ROOM!
YAY!
YAY!
I'm so excited! Hikari and Megumi hardly ever come over.

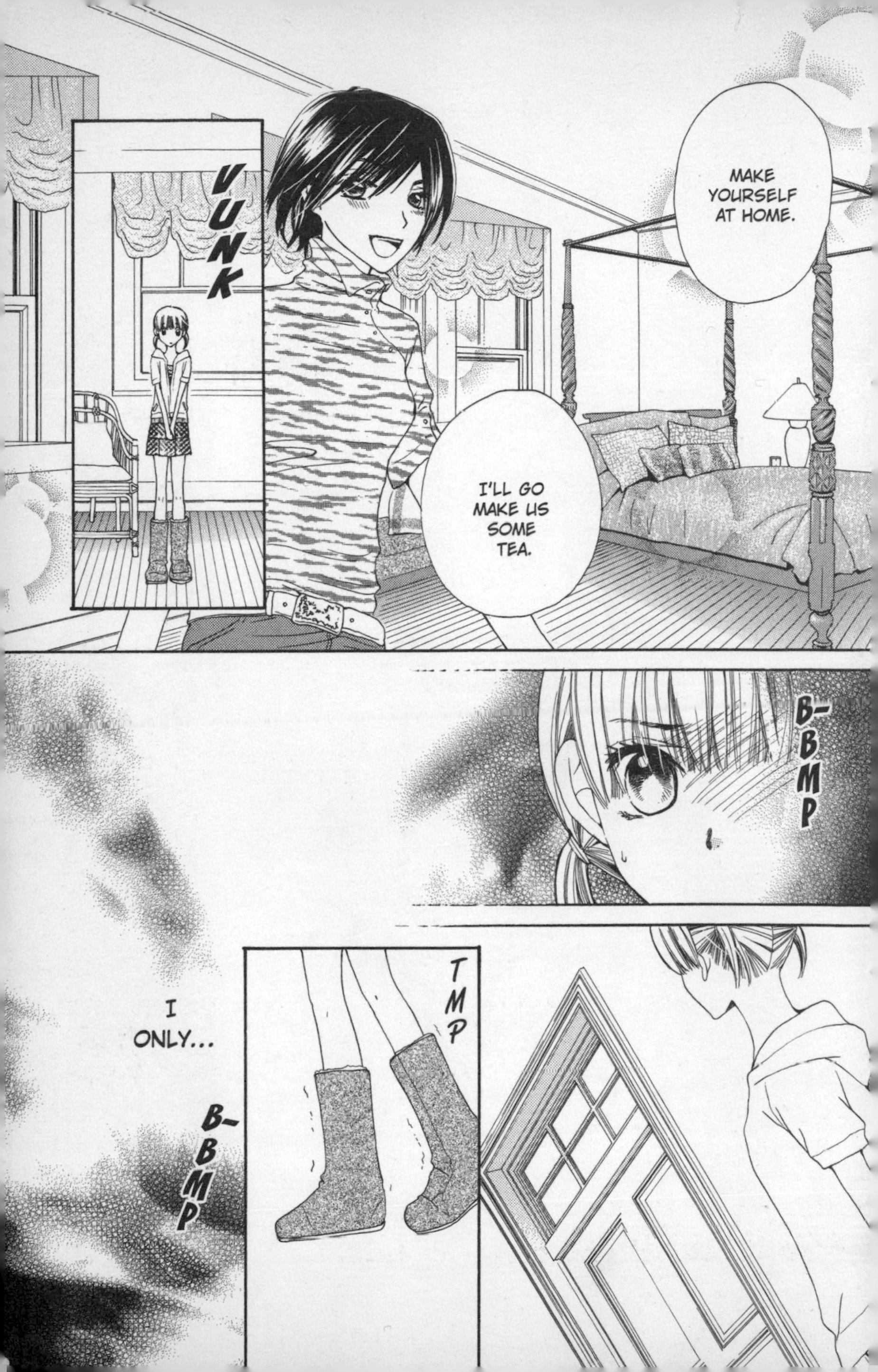
MAKE YOURSELF AT HOME.
I'LL GO MAKE US SOME TEA.
VUNK
B-BMP
TMP
I ONLY...
B-BMP

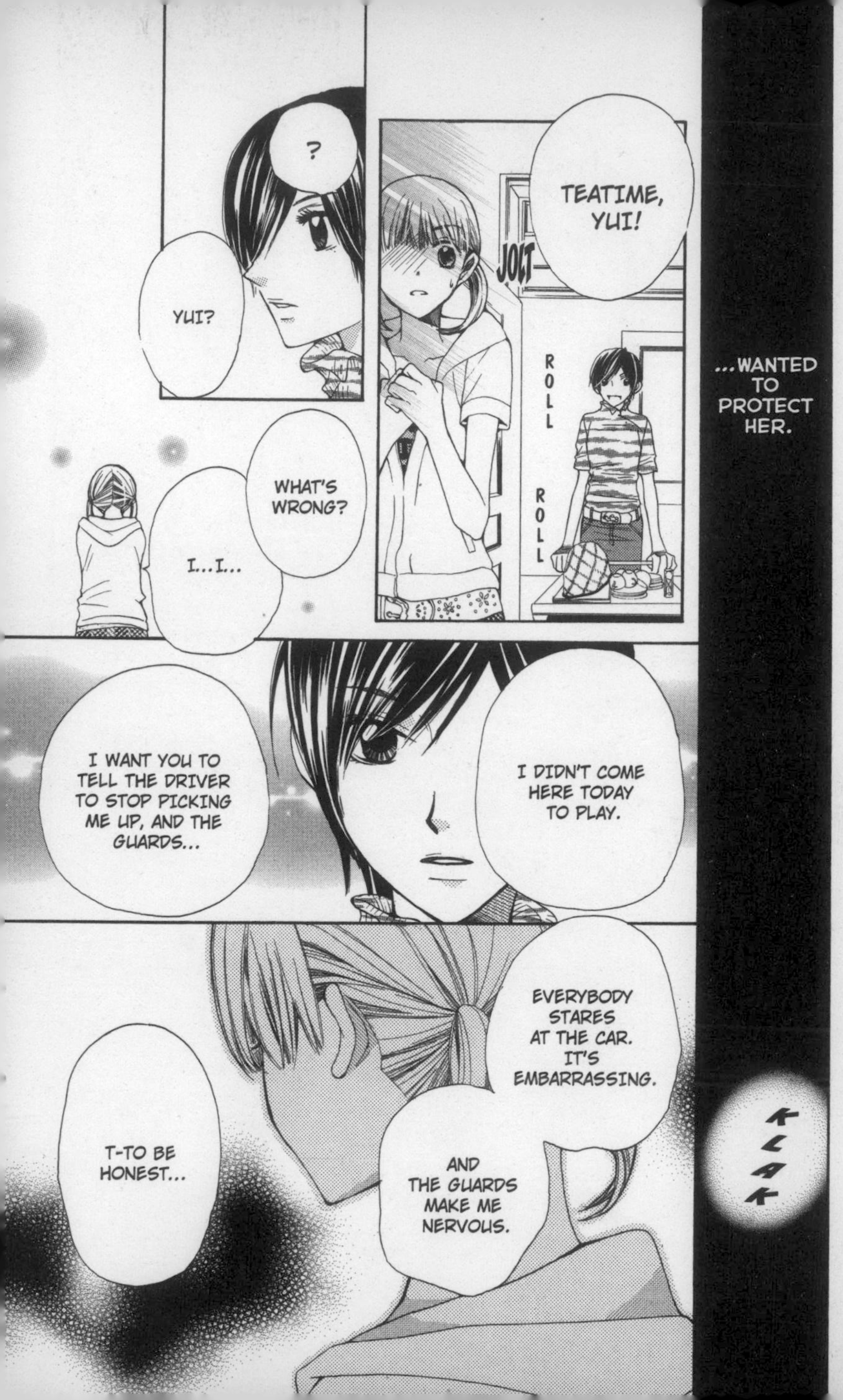
...WANTED TO PROTECT HER.
KLAK
TEATIME, YUI!
JOLT
ROLL ROLL
?
YUI?
WHAT'S WRONG?
I...I...
I DIDN'T COME HERE TODAY TO PLAY.
I WANT YOU TO TELL THE DRIVER TO STOP PICKING ME UP, AND THE GUARDS...
EVERYBODY STARES AT THE CAR. IT'S EMBARRASSING.
AND THE GUARDS MAKE ME NERVOUS.
T-TO BE HONEST...

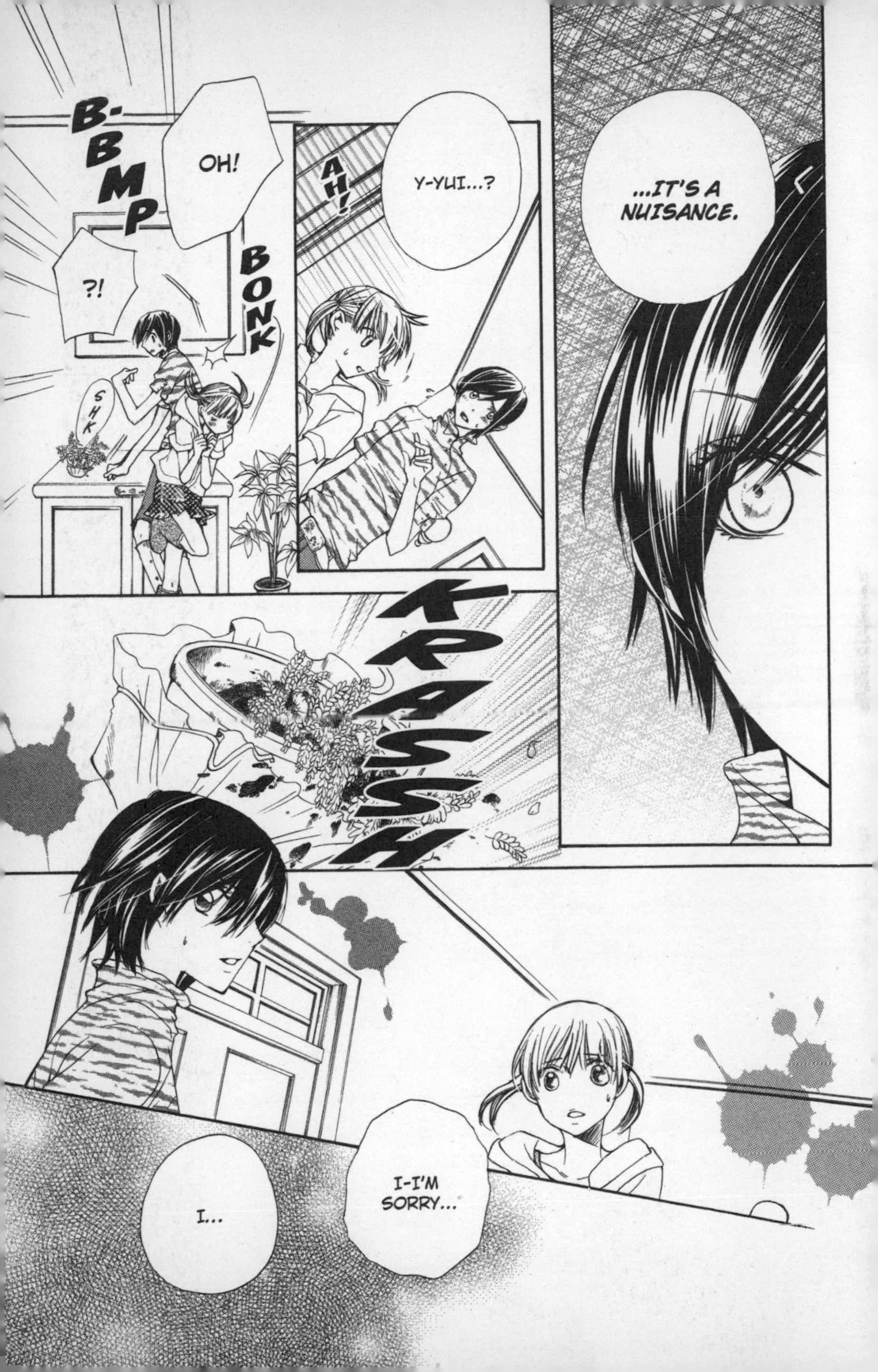

...IT'S A NUISANCE.
Y-YUI...?
AH!
B-BMP
OH!
BONK
?!
SHK
KRASH
I-I'M SORRY...
I...

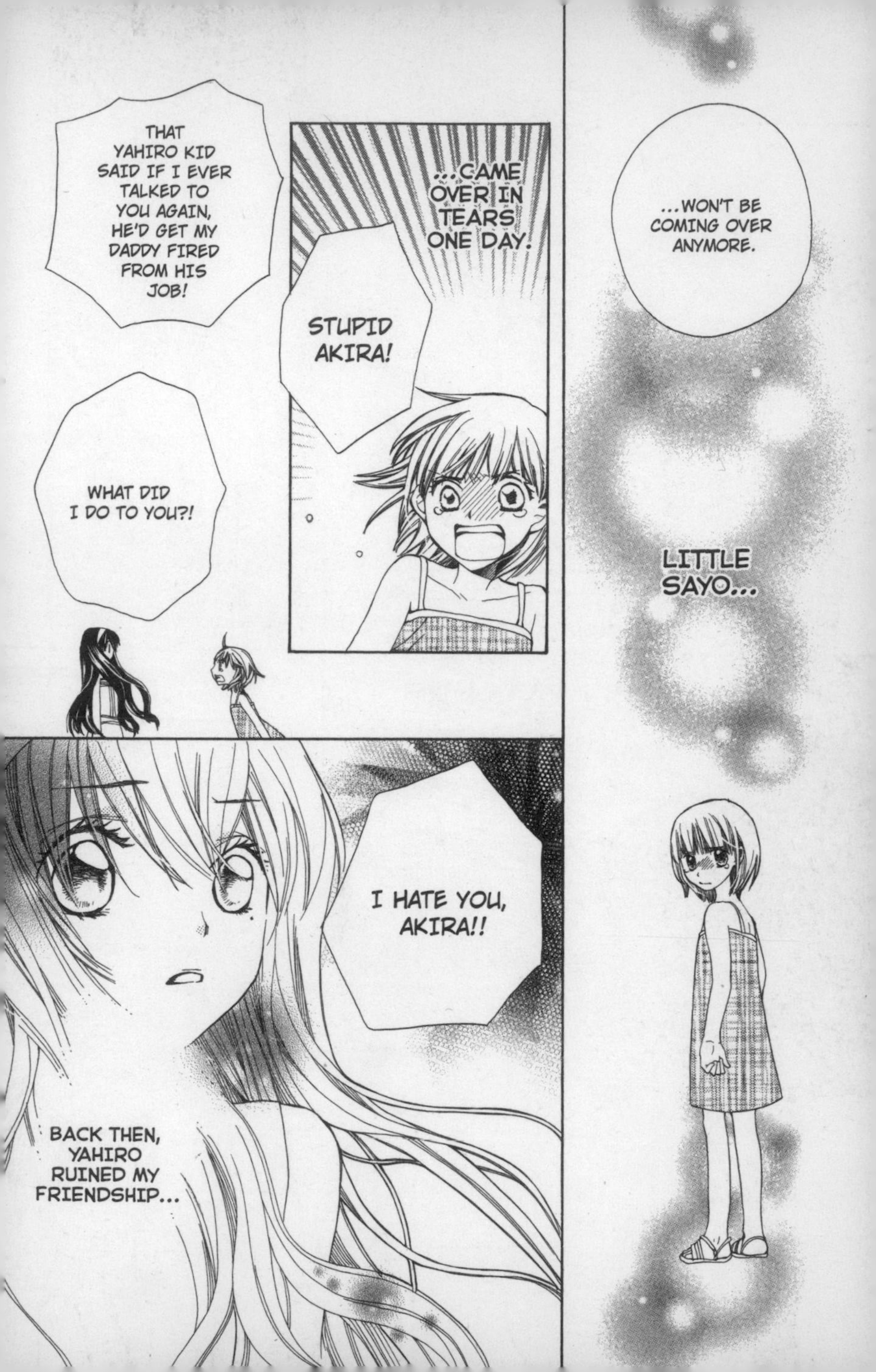
...WON'T BE COMING OVER ANYMORE.
LITTLE SAYO...
...CAME OVER IN TEARS ONE DAY.
STUPID AKIRA!
THAT YAHIRO KID SAID IF I EVER TALKED TO YOU AGAIN, HE'D GET MY DADDY FIRED FROM HIS JOB!
WHAT DID I DO TO YOU?!
I HATE YOU, AKIRA!!
BACK THEN, YAHIRO RUINED MY FRIENDSHIP...

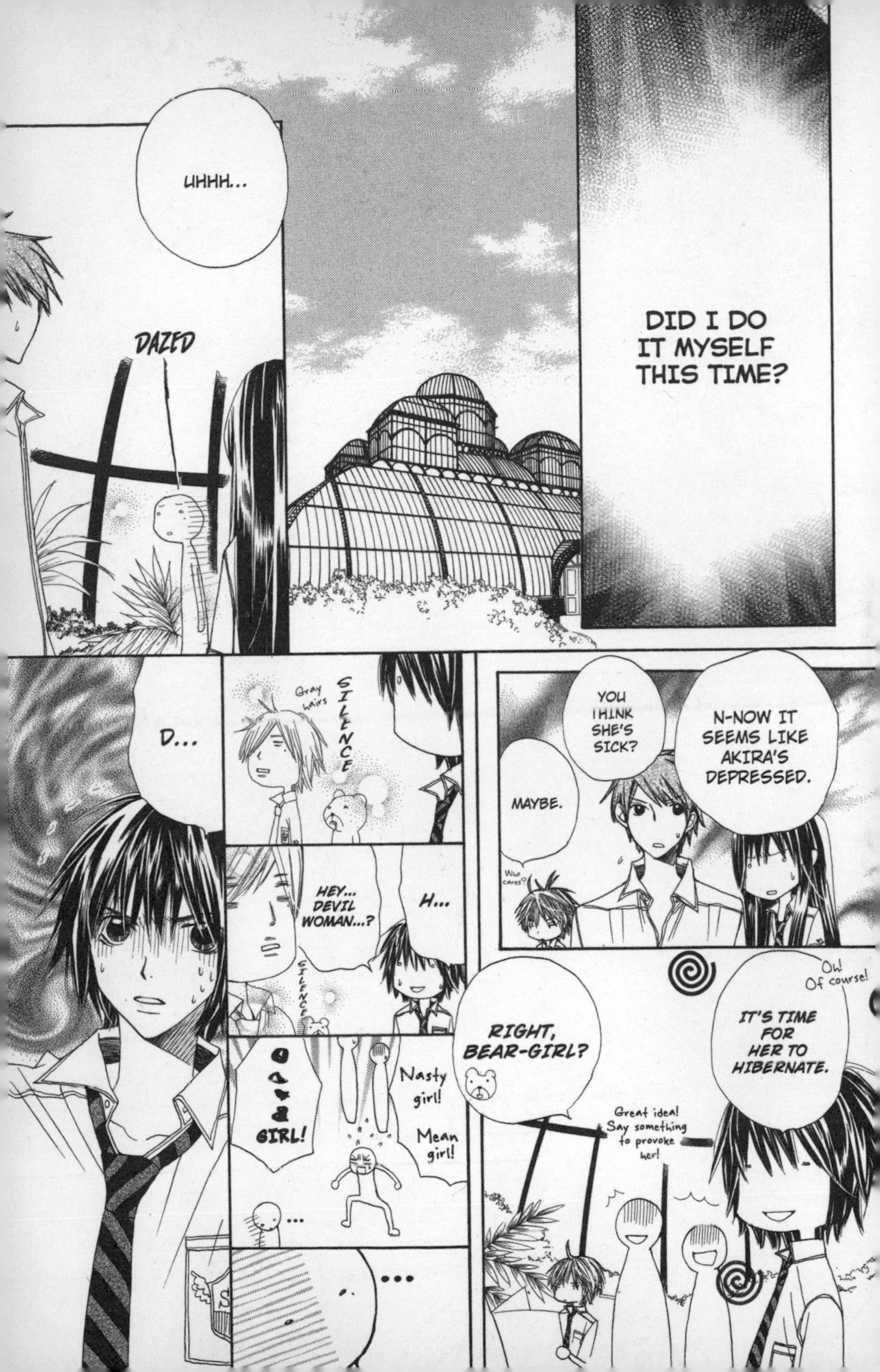
DID I DO IT MYSELF THIS TIME?
UHHH...
DAZED
N-NOW IT SEEMS LIKE AKIRA'S DEPRESSED.
YOU THINK SHE'S SICK?
MAYBE.
Who cares?
Oh! Of course!
IT'S TIME FOR HER TO HIBERNATE.
RIGHT, BEAR-GIRL?
Great idea! Say something to provoke her!
Gray hairs
SILENCE
H...
HEY... DEVIL WOMAN...?
SILENCE
Nasty girl!
Mean girl!
○△□ GIRL!
...
...
D...

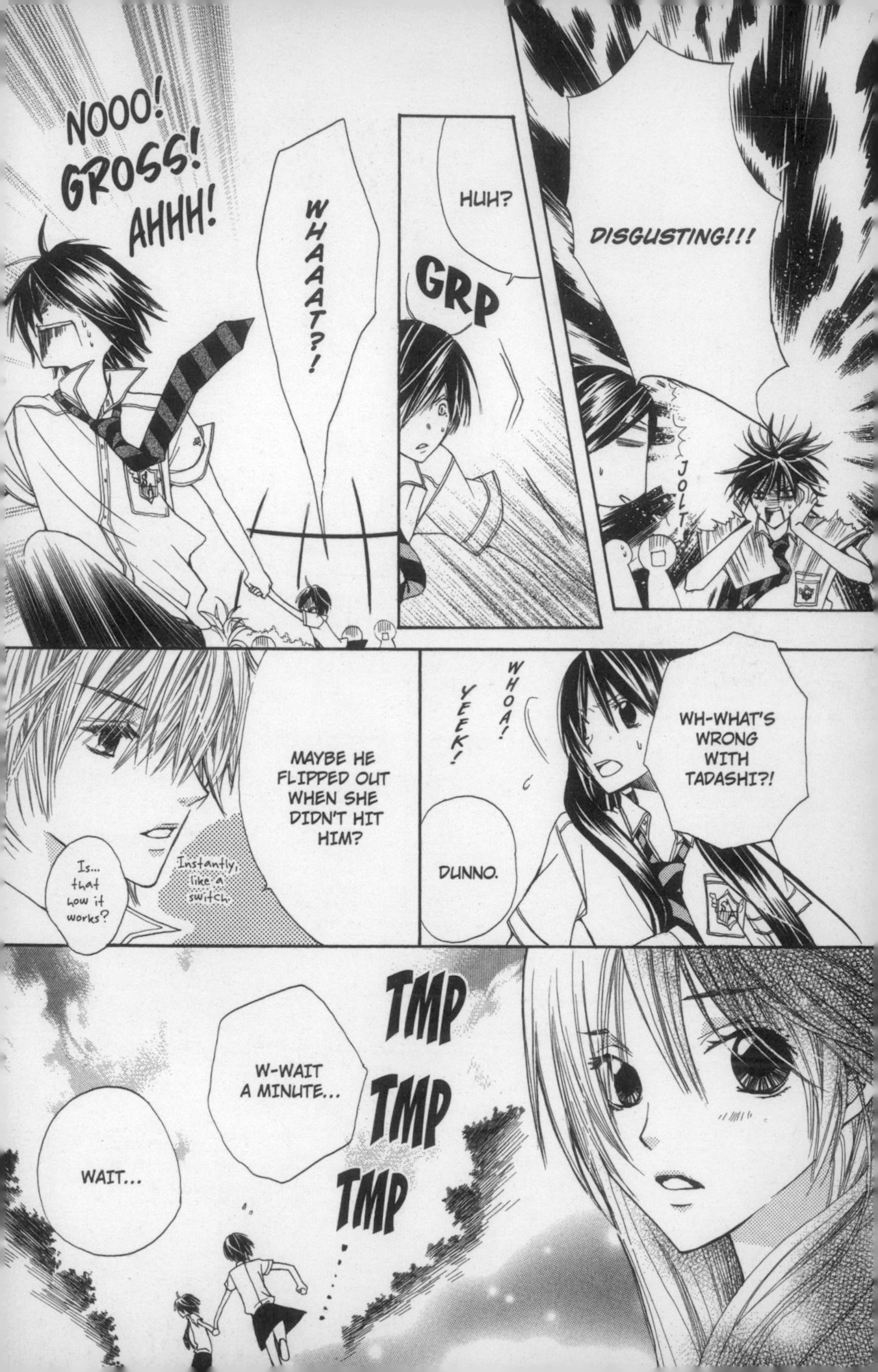
DISGUSTING!!!
JOLT
HUH?
GRP
WHAAAT?!
NOOO! GROSS! AHHH!
WH-WHAT'S WRONG WITH TADASHI?!
WHOA!
YEEK!
DUNNO.
MAYBE HE FLIPPED OUT WHEN SHE DIDN'T HIT HIM?
Instantly, like a switch.
Is... that how it works?
WH-WHAT
TMP TMP TMP
W-WAIT A MINUTE...
WAIT...

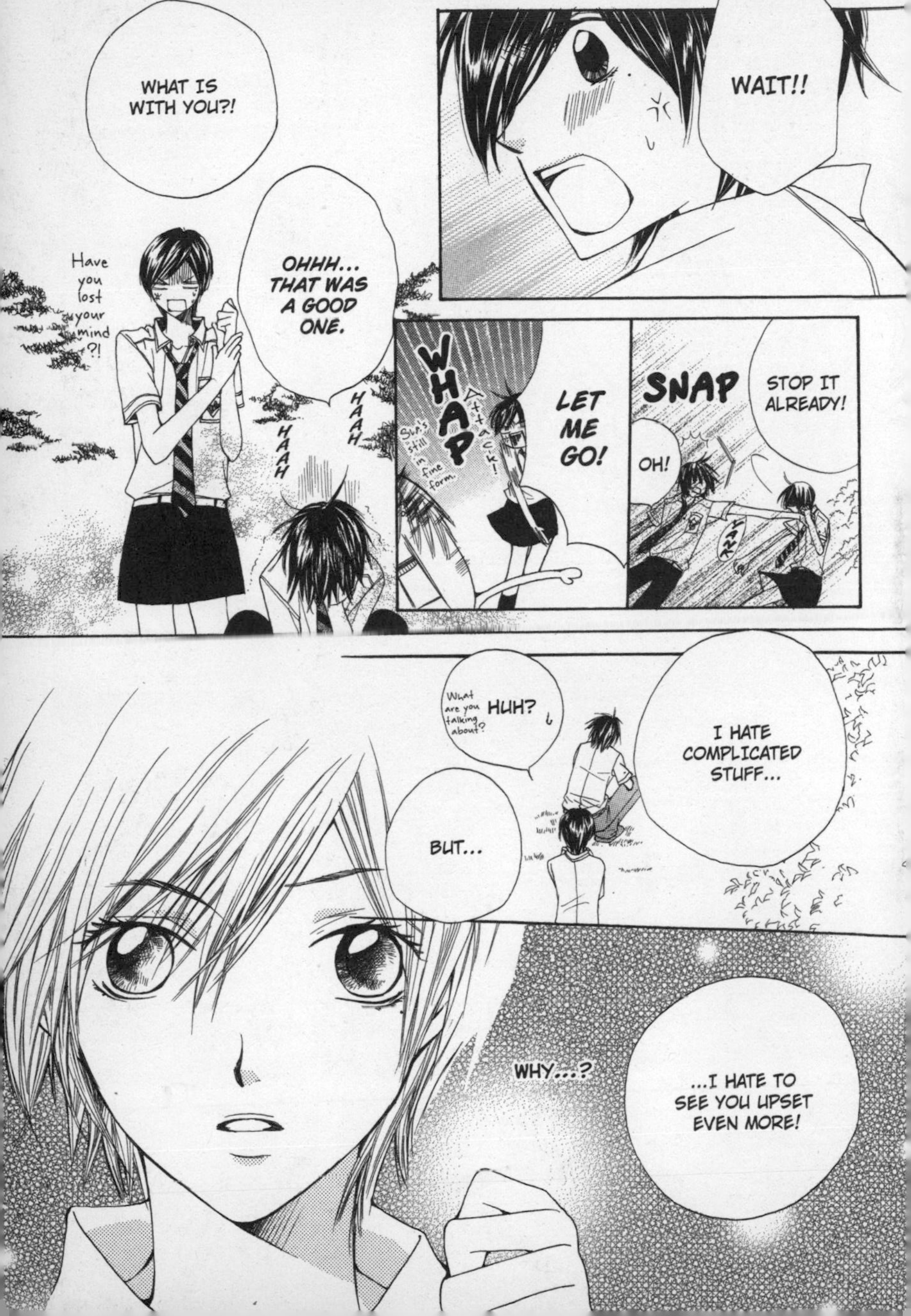
WAIT!!
STOP IT ALREADY!
SNAP
OH!
YANK
LET ME GO!
WHAP
Attack!
Sun's still in fine form.
WHAT IS WITH YOU?!
OHHH... THAT WAS A GOOD ONE.
Have you lost your mind?!
HAAH HAAH
I HATE COMPLICATED STUFF...
HUH?
What are you talking about?
BUT...
...I HATE TO SEE YOU UPSET EVEN MORE!
WHY...?

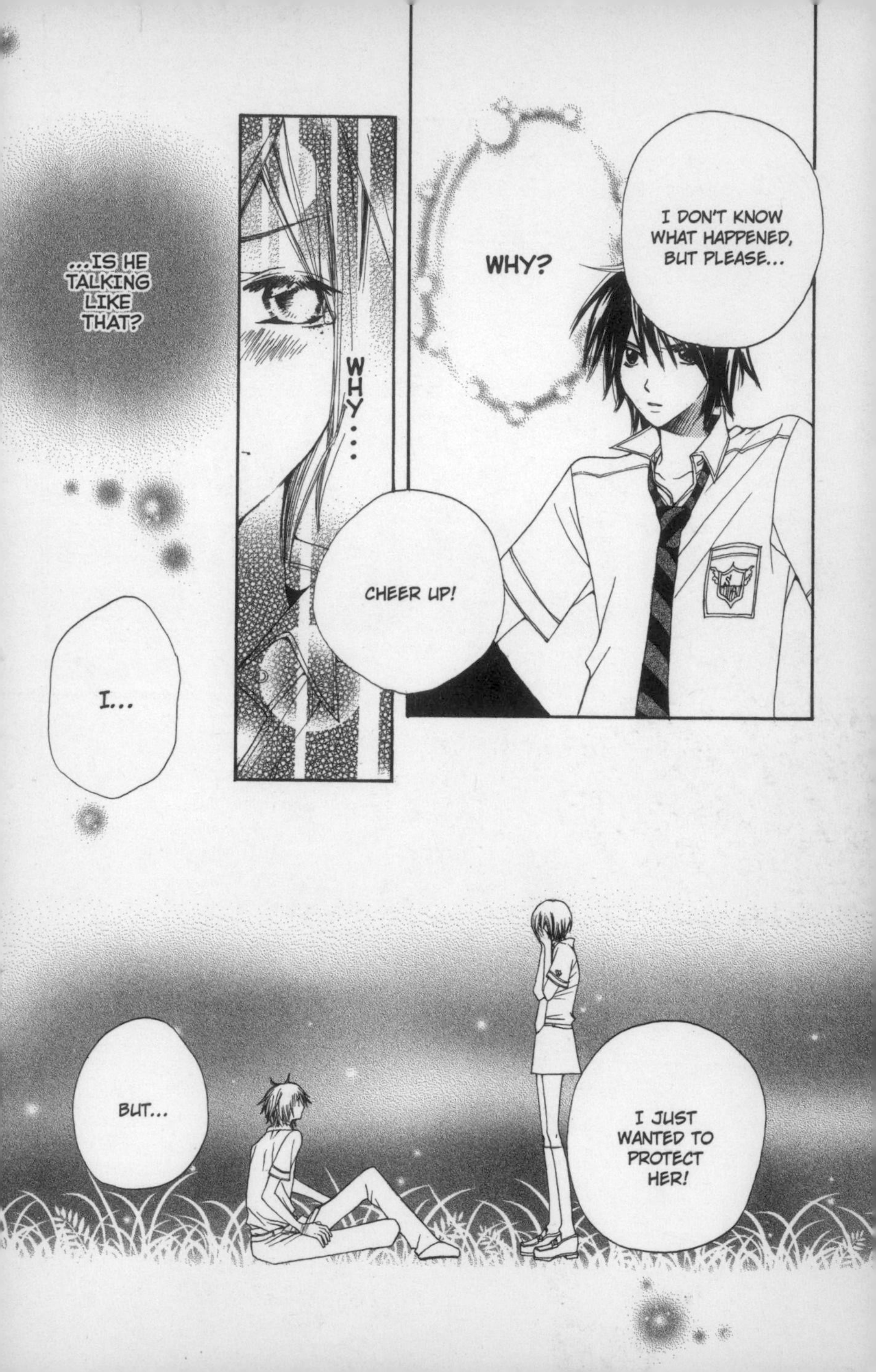
I DON'T KNOW WHAT HAPPENED, BUT PLEASE...
WHY?
CHEER UP!
WHY...
...IS HE TALKING LIKE THAT?
I...
I JUST WANTED TO PROTECT HER!
BUT...

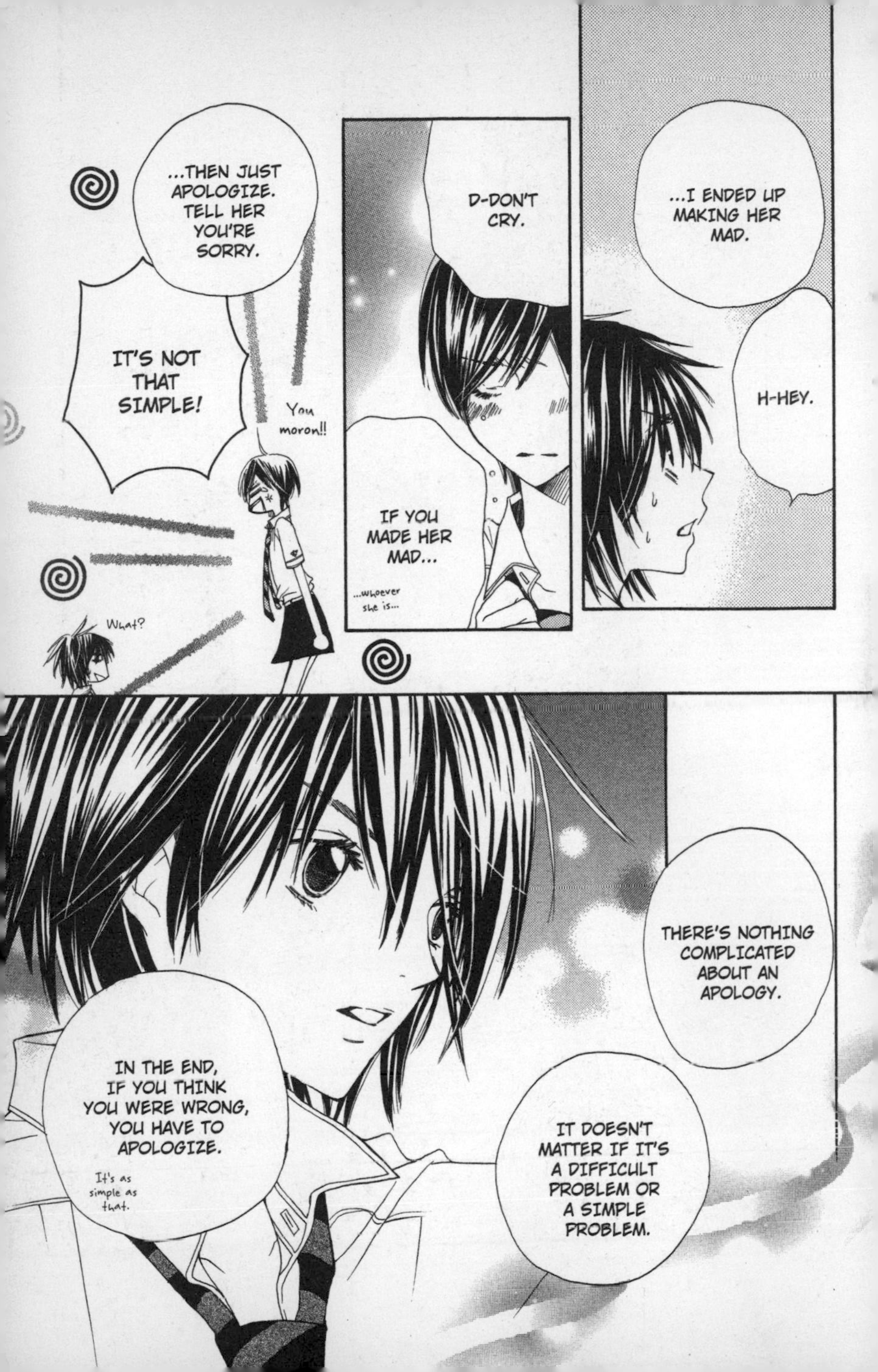
...I ENDED UP MAKING HER MAD.
H-HEY.
D-DON'T CRY.
IF YOU MADE HER MAD...
...whoever she is...
...THEN JUST APOLOGIZE. TELL HER YOU'RE SORRY.
IT'S NOT THAT SIMPLE!
You moron!!
What?
THERE'S NOTHING COMPLICATED ABOUT AN APOLOGY.
IT DOESN'T MATTER IF IT'S A DIFFICULT PROBLEM OR A SIMPLE PROBLEM.
IN THE END, IF YOU THINK YOU WERE WRONG, YOU HAVE TO APOLOGIZE.
It's as simple as that.

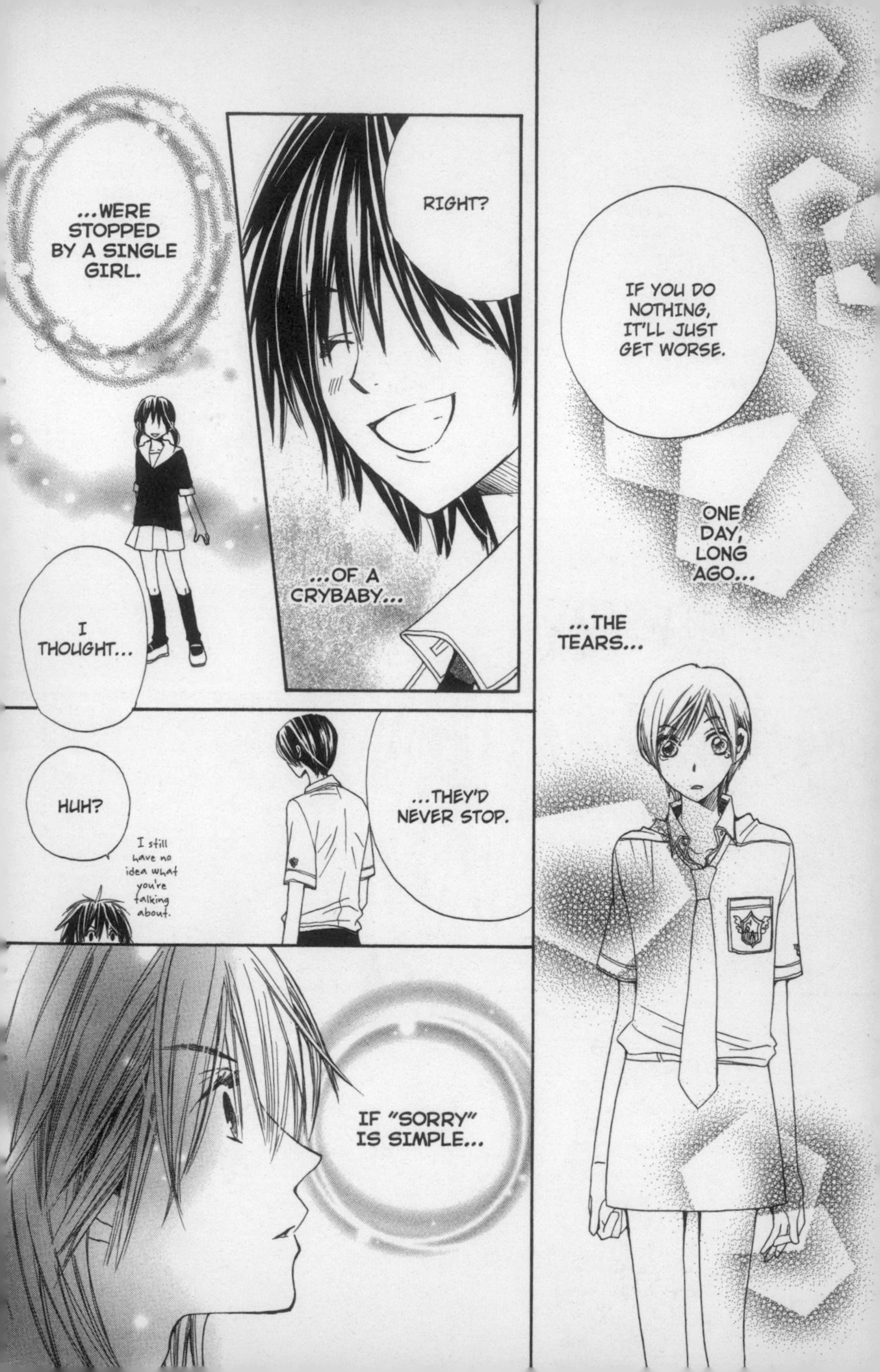
IF YOU DO NOTHING, IT'LL JUST GET WORSE.
ONE DAY, LONG AGO...
...THE TEARS...
RIGHT?
...OF A CRYBABY...
...WERE STOPPED BY A SINGLE GIRL.
I THOUGHT...
...THEY'D NEVER STOP.
HUH?
I still have no idea what you're talking about.
IF "SORRY" IS SIMPLE...

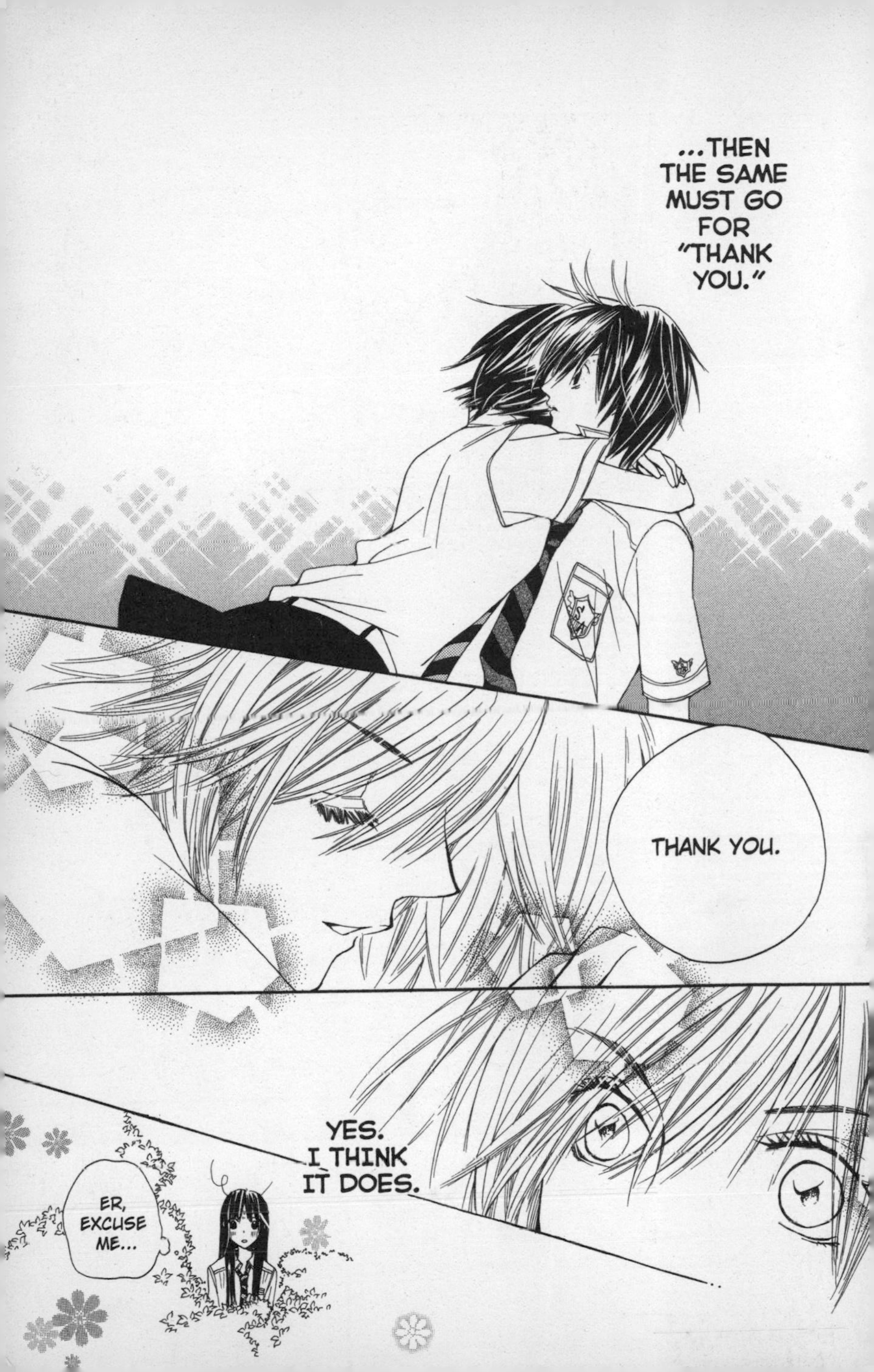
...THEN THE SAME MUST GO FOR "THANK YOU."
THANK YOU.
YES. I THINK IT DOES.
ER, EXCUSE ME...

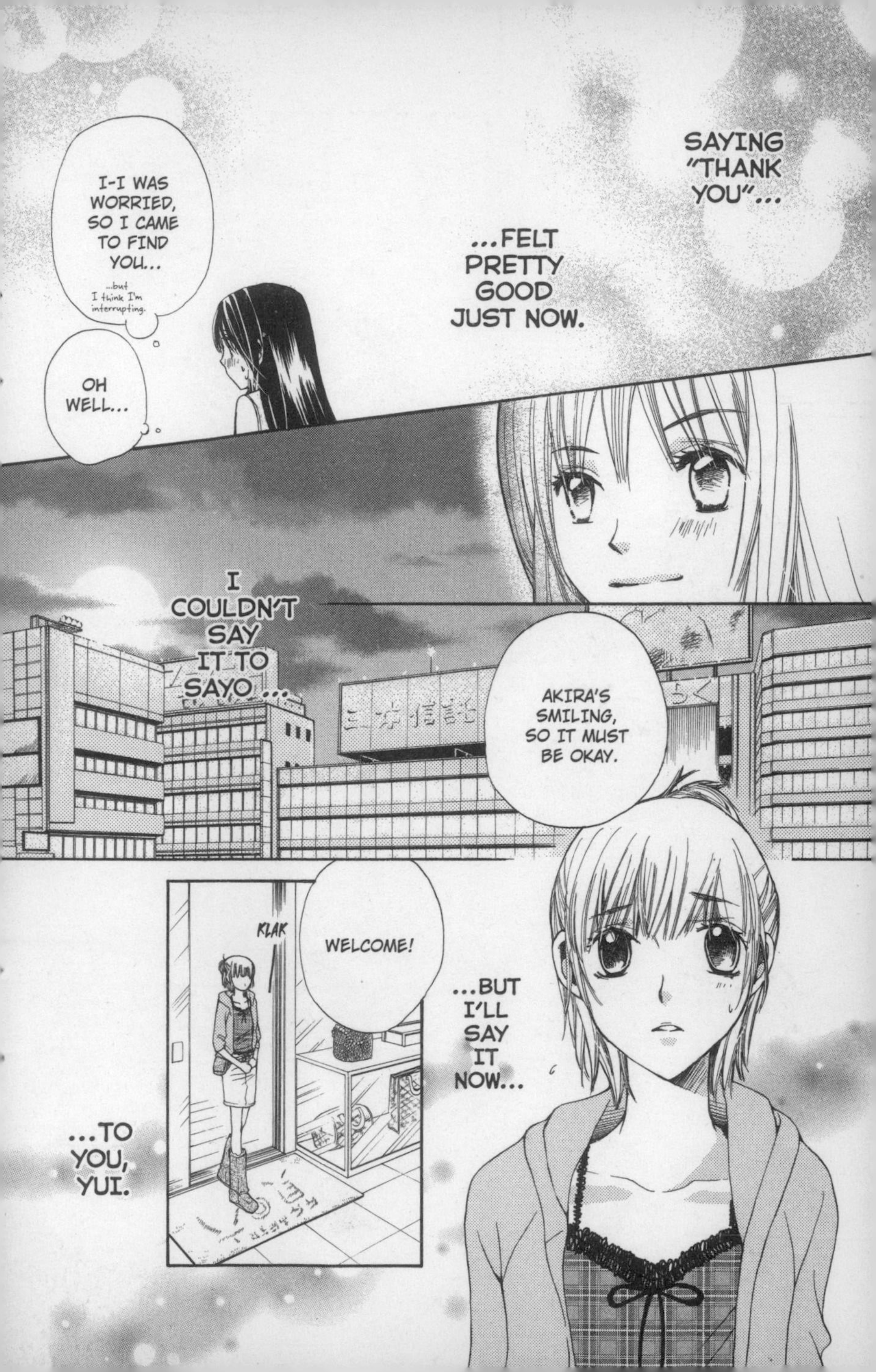
SAYING "THANK YOU"...
...FELT PRETTY GOOD JUST NOW.
I-I WAS WORRIED, SO I CAME TO FIND YOU...
...but I think I'm interrupting.
OH WELL...
AKIRA'S SMILING, SO IT MUST BE OKAY.
I COULDN'T SAY IT TO SAYO...
...BUT I'LL SAY IT NOW...
WELCOME!
KLAK
...TO YOU, YUI.

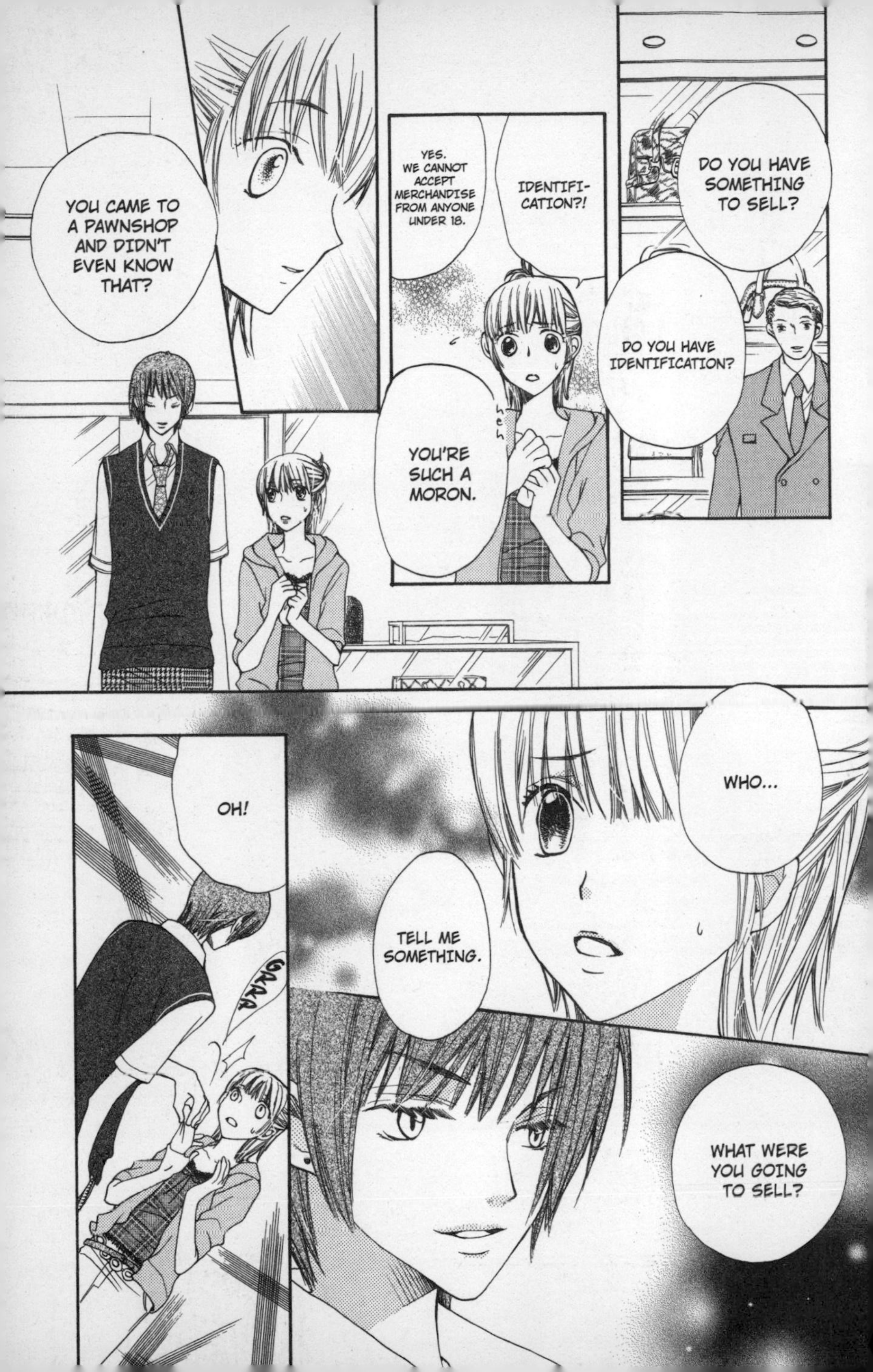
DO YOU HAVE SOMETHING TO SELL?
DO YOU HAVE IDENTIFICATION?
IDENTIFICATION?!
YES. WE CANNOT ACCEPT MERCHANDISE FROM ANYONE UNDER 18.
heh
YOU'RE SUCH A MORON.
YOU CAME TO A PAWNSHOP AND DIDN'T EVEN KNOW THAT?
WHO...
TELL ME SOMETHING.
WHAT WERE YOU GOING TO SELL?
OH!
GRRR

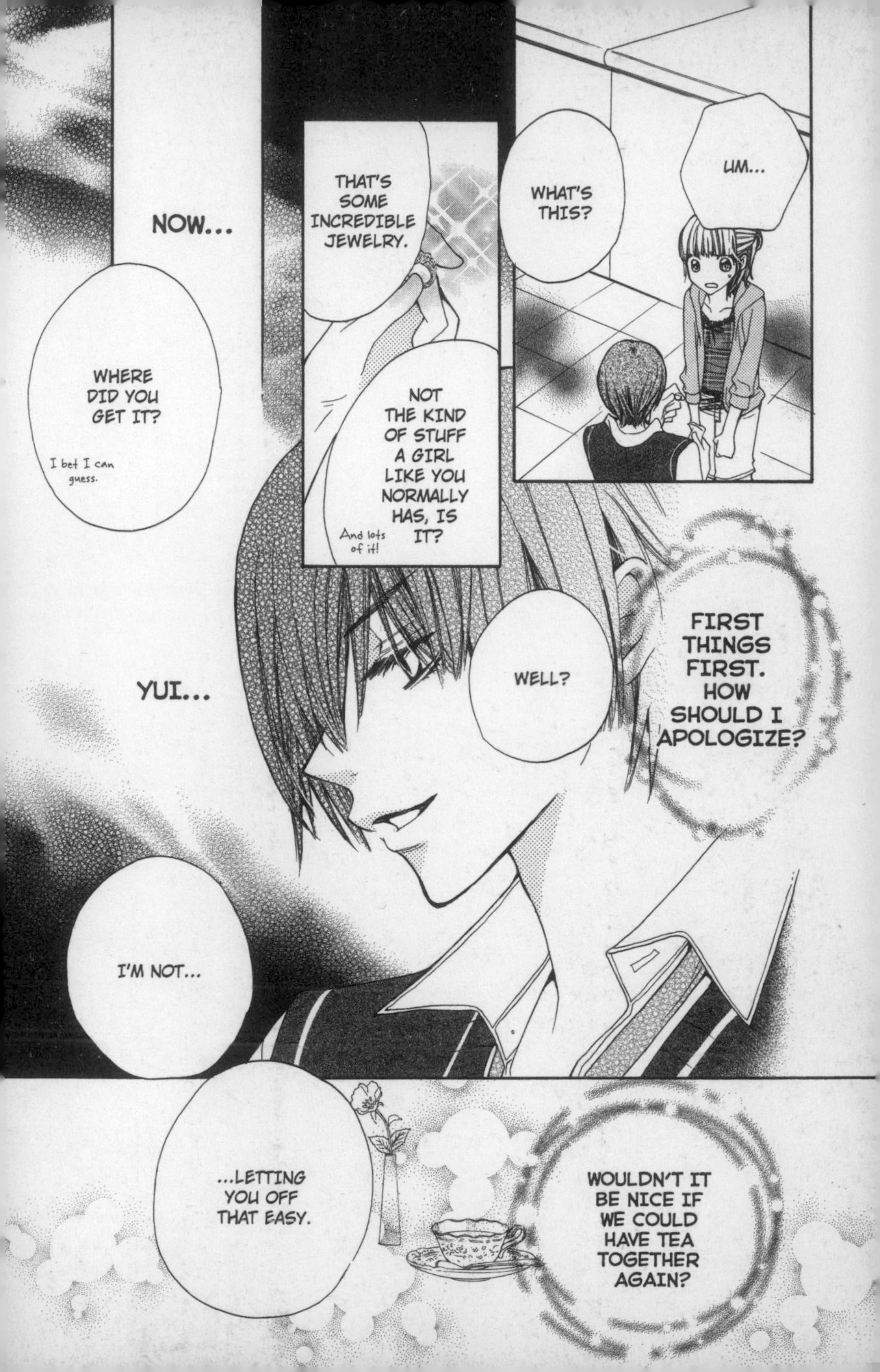
UM...
WHAT'S THIS?
THAT'S SOME INCREDIBLE JEWELRY.
NOT THE KIND OF STUFF A GIRL LIKE YOU NORMALLY HAS, IS IT?
And lots of it!
NOW...
WHERE DID YOU GET IT?
I bet I can guess.
FIRST THINGS FIRST. HOW SHOULD I APOLOGIZE?
WELL?
YUI...
I'M NOT...
WOULDN'T IT BE NICE IF WE COULD HAVE TEA TOGETHER AGAIN?
...LETTING YOU OFF THAT EASY.

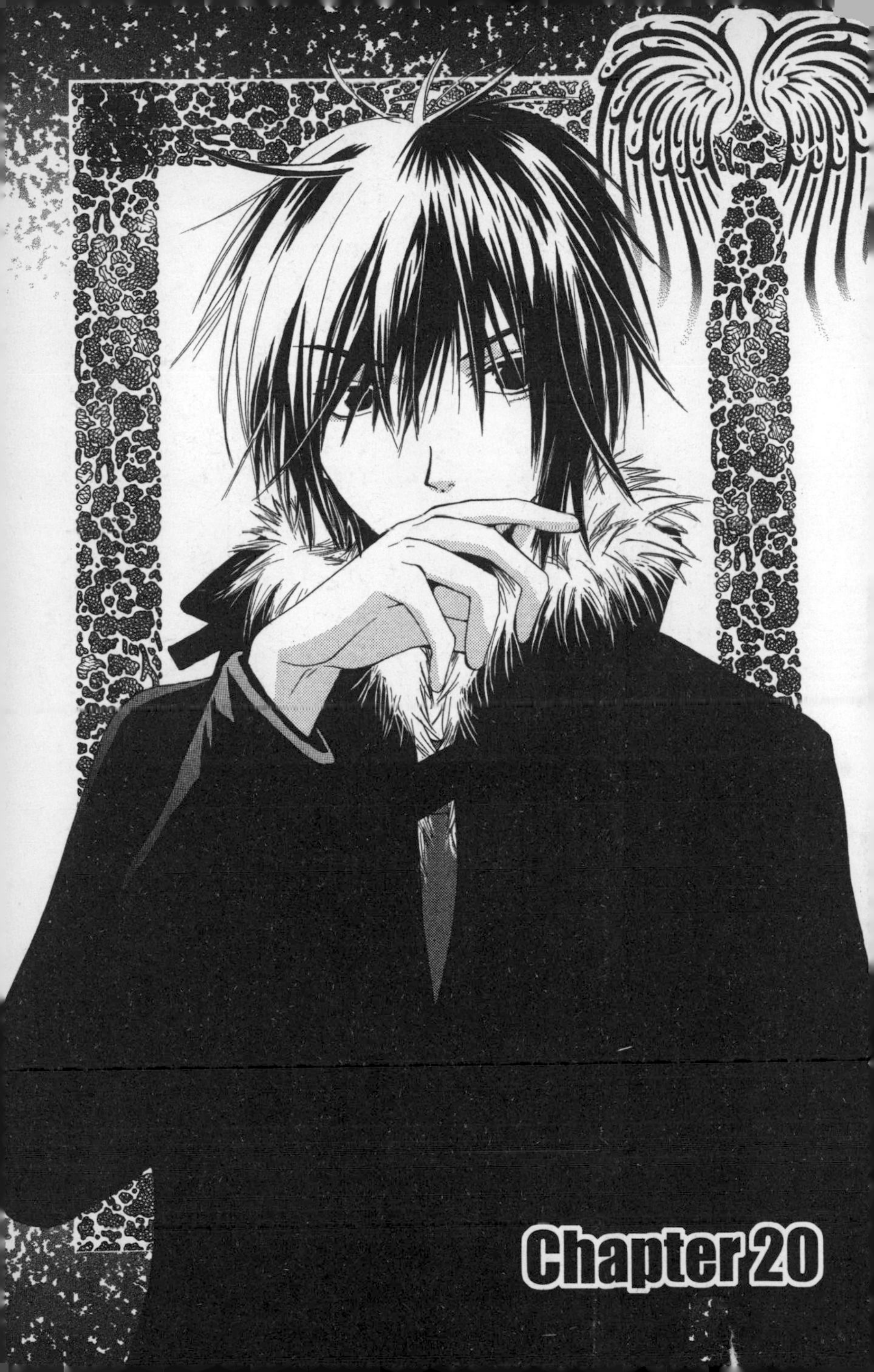
Chapter 20

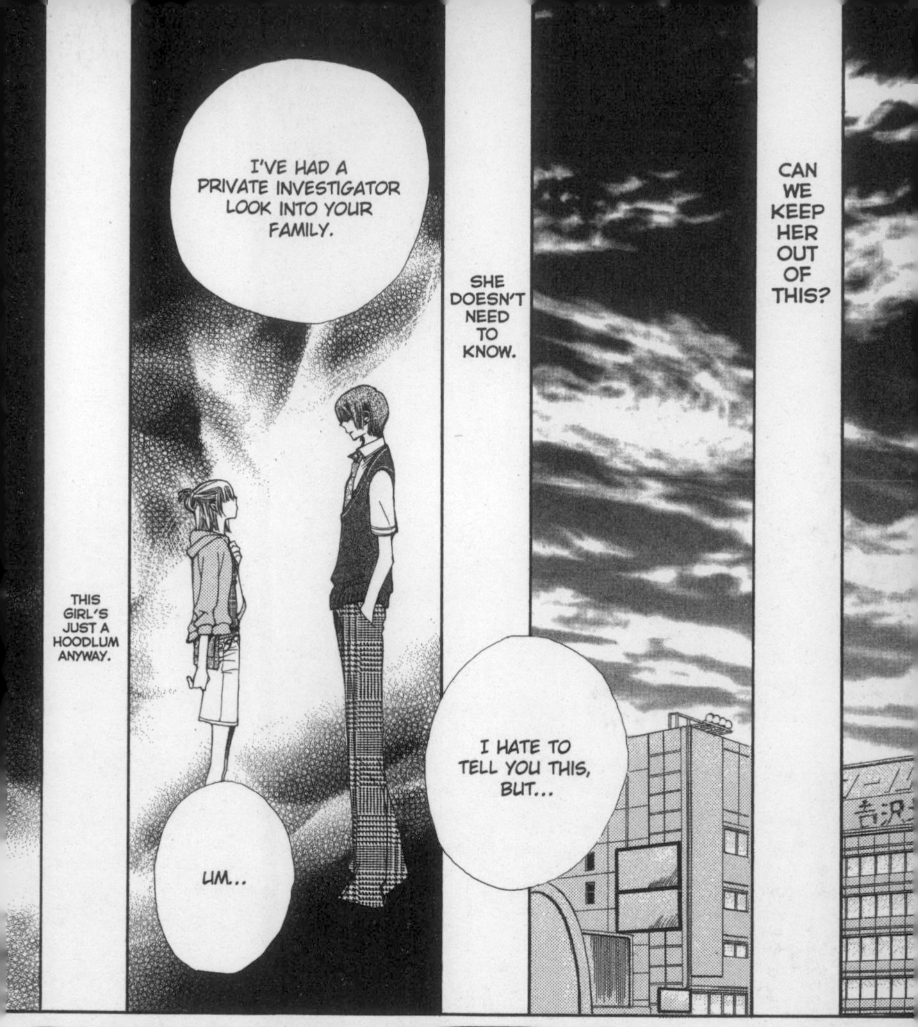
CAN WE KEEP HER OUT OF THIS?
I HATE TO TELL YOU THIS, BUT...
SHE DOESN'T NEED TO KNOW.
I'VE HAD A PRIVATE INVESTIGATOR LOOK INTO YOUR FAMILY.
UM...
THIS GIRL'S JUST A HOODLUM ANYWAY.

•QUESTION ①•

I WANT TO USE THIS SPACE TO ANSWER SOME COMMON QUESTIONS FROM THE LETTERS YOU WRITE ME (THANK YOU SO MUCH!!). ♡

Q: Why did you become a cartoonist?

A: Um... → Let's see... → ... →

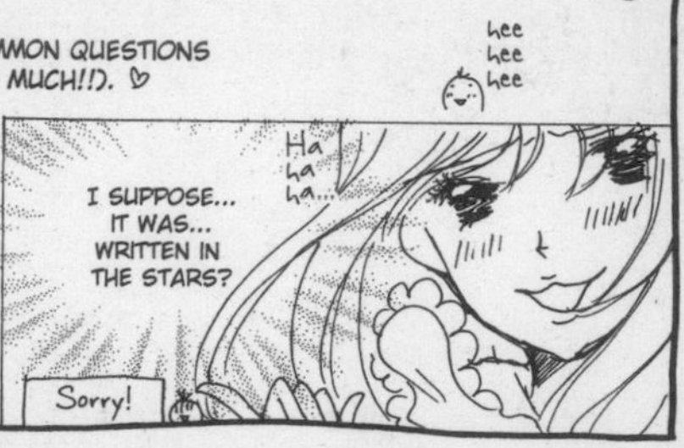
hee hee hee
Ha ha ha...
I SUPPOSE... IT WAS... WRITTEN IN THE STARS?
Sorry!

Real answer:
A: BECAUSE I'VE ALWAYS LOVED TO DRAW.

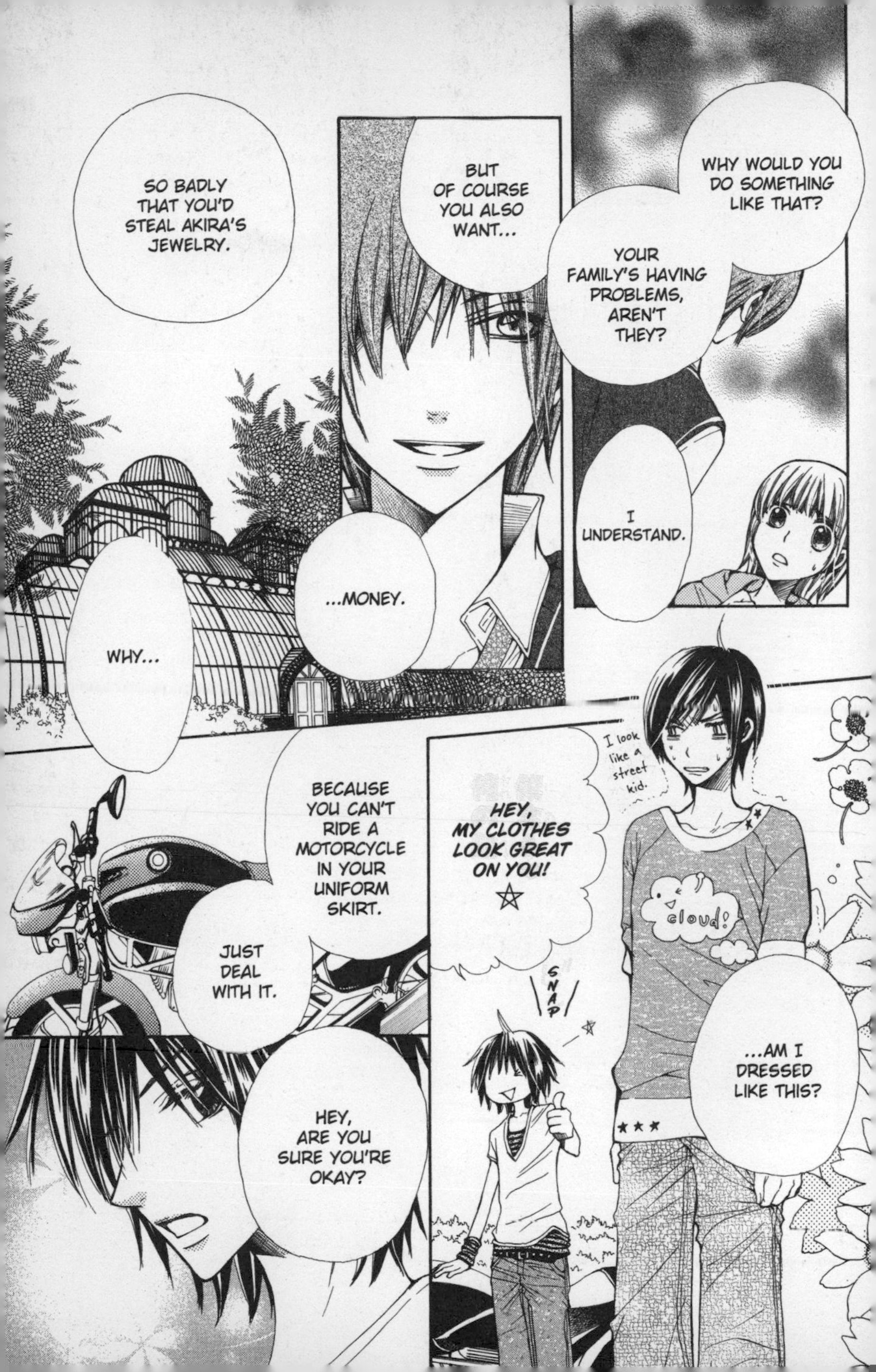
WHY WOULD YOU DO SOMETHING LIKE THAT?
YOUR FAMILY'S HAVING PROBLEMS, AREN'T THEY?
I UNDERSTAND.
BUT OF COURSE YOU ALSO WANT...
...MONEY.
SO BADLY THAT YOU'D STEAL AKIRA'S JEWELRY.
WHY...
...AM I DRESSED LIKE THIS?
I look like a street kid.
HEY, MY CLOTHES LOOK GREAT ON YOU! ☆
SNAP
BECAUSE YOU CAN'T RIDE A MOTORCYCLE IN YOUR UNIFORM SKIRT.
JUST DEAL WITH IT.
HEY, ARE YOU SURE YOU'RE OKAY?

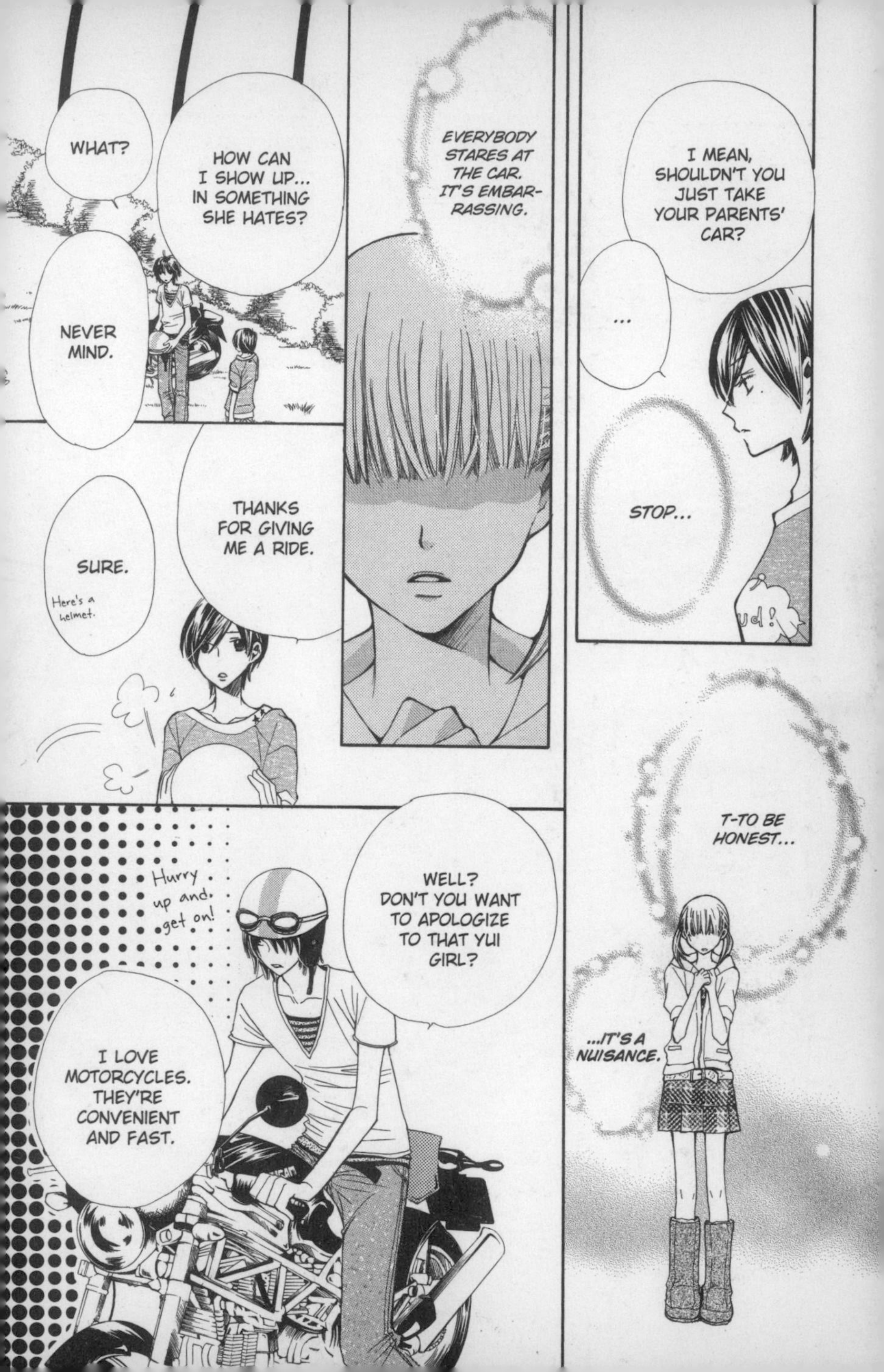
I MEAN, SHOULDN'T YOU JUST TAKE YOUR PARENTS' CAR?
...
STOP...
T-TO BE HONEST...
...IT'S A NUISANCE.
EVERYBODY STARES AT THE CAR. IT'S EMBAR-RASSING.
HOW CAN I SHOW UP... IN SOMETHING SHE HATES?
WHAT?
NEVER MIND.
THANKS FOR GIVING ME A RIDE.
SURE.
Here's a helmet.
WELL? DON'T YOU WANT TO APOLOGIZE TO THAT YUI GIRL?
Hurry up and get on!
I LOVE MOTORCYCLES. THEY'RE CONVENIENT AND FAST.

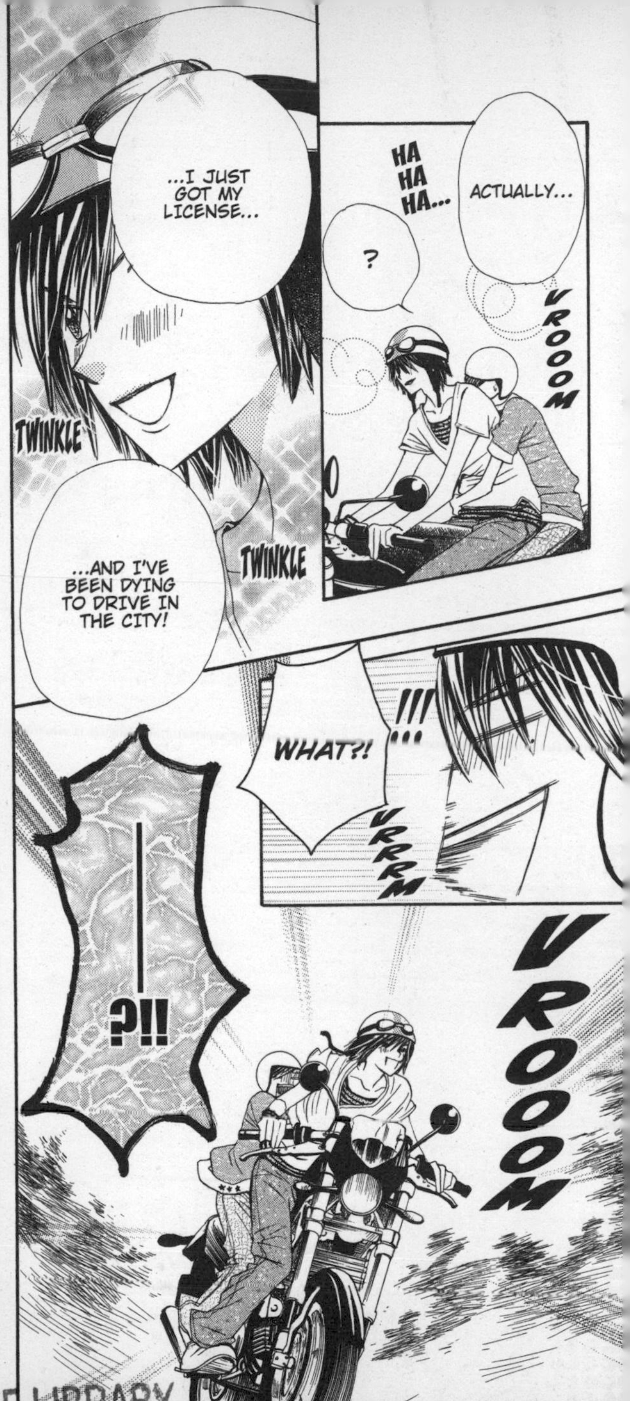
HA HA HA...
ACTUALLY...
?
VROOOM
...I JUST GOT MY LICENSE...
TWINKLE
TWINKLE
...AND I'VE BEEN DYING TO DRIVE IN THE CITY!
!!!
WHAT?!
URRRM
?!!
VROOOM

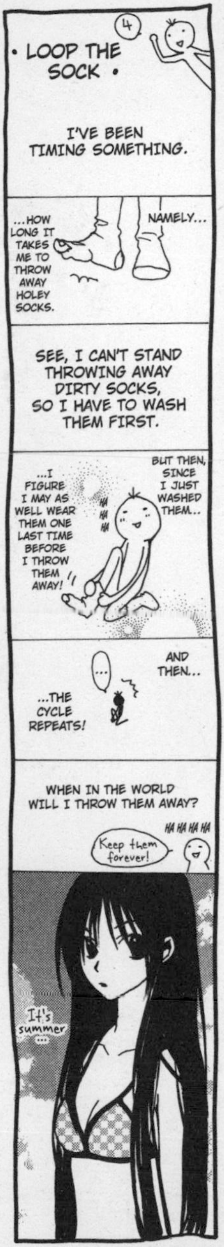
4
• LOOP THE SOCK •
I'VE BEEN TIMING SOMETHING.
NAMELY...
...HOW LONG IT TAKES ME TO THROW AWAY HOLEY SOCKS.
SEE, I CAN'T STAND THROWING AWAY DIRTY SOCKS, SO I HAVE TO WASH THEM FIRST.
BUT THEN, SINCE I JUST WASHED THEM...
HA HA HA
...I FIGURE I MAY AS WELL WEAR THEM ONE LAST TIME BEFORE I THROW THEM AWAY!
AND THEN...
...
...THE CYCLE REPEATS!
WHEN IN THE WORLD WILL I THROW THEM AWAY?
HA HA HA HA
Keep them forever!
It's summer...

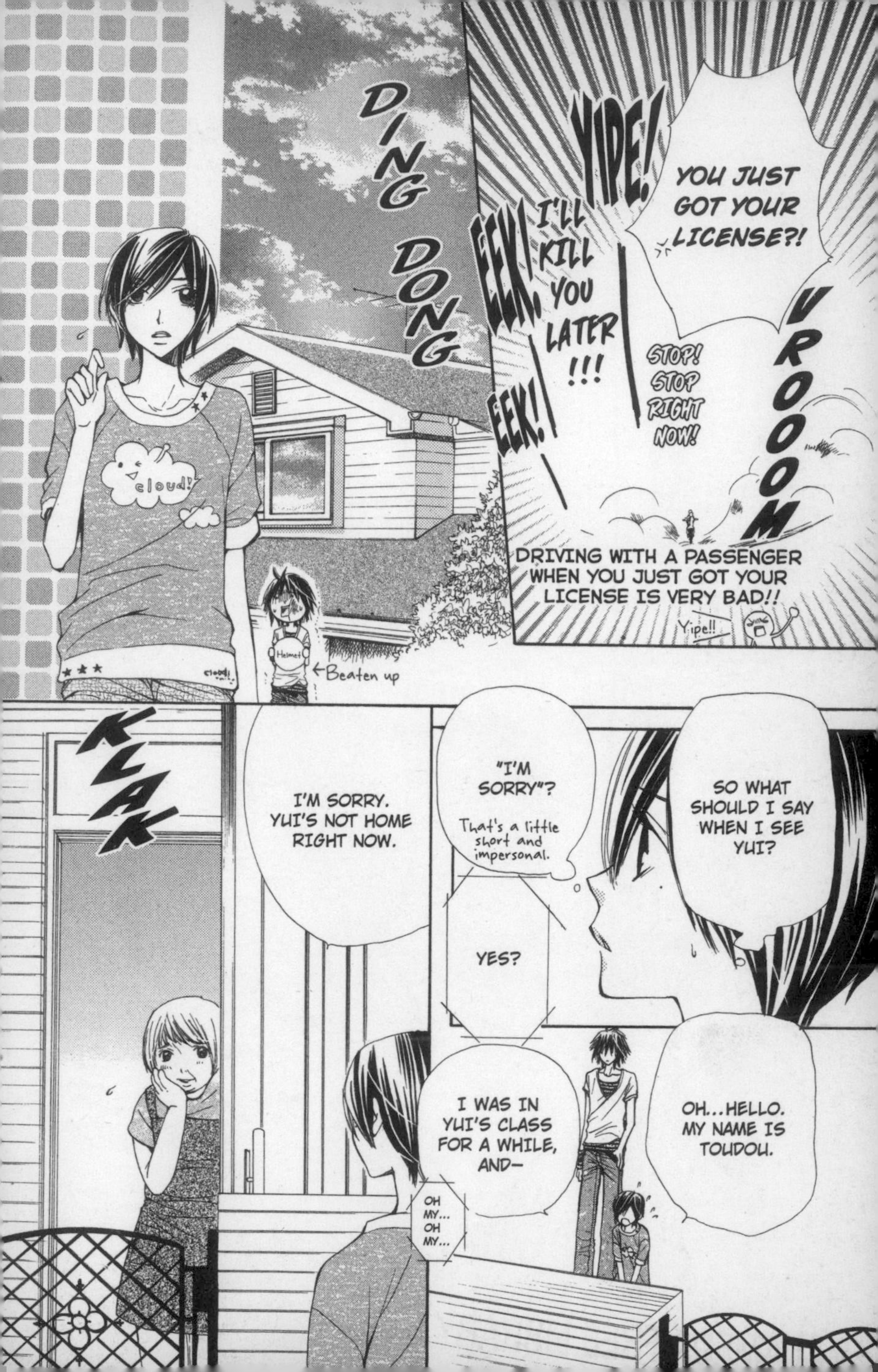
YOU JUST GOT YOUR LICENSE?!
YIPE!
I'LL KILL YOU LATER!!!
EEK!
EEK!
STOP! STOP RIGHT NOW!
VROOOOM
DRIVING WITH A PASSENGER WHEN YOU JUST GOT YOUR LICENSE IS VERY BAD!!
Yipe!!
DING DONG
cloud!
Helmet
←Beaten up
SO WHAT SHOULD I SAY WHEN I SEE YUI?
"I'M SORRY"?
That's a little short and impersonal.
YES?
OH...HELLO. MY NAME IS TOUDOU.
I WAS IN YUI'S CLASS FOR A WHILE, AND—
OH MY... OH MY...
KLAK
I'M SORRY. YUI'S NOT HOME RIGHT NOW.

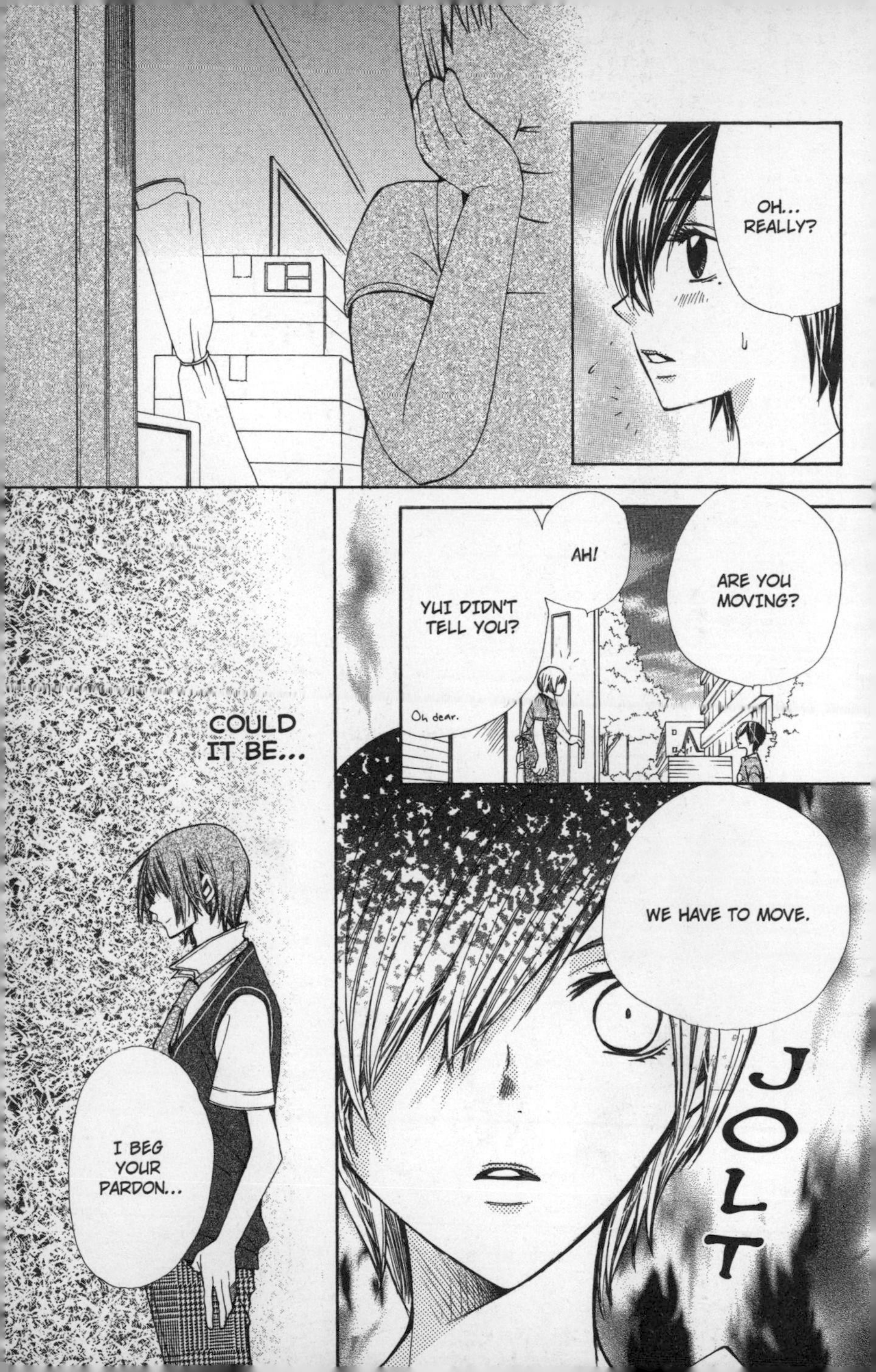
OH... REALLY?
ARE YOU MOVING?
AH!
YUI DIDN'T TELL YOU?
Oh dear.
WE HAVE TO MOVE.
JOLT
COULD IT BE...
I BEG YOUR PARDON...

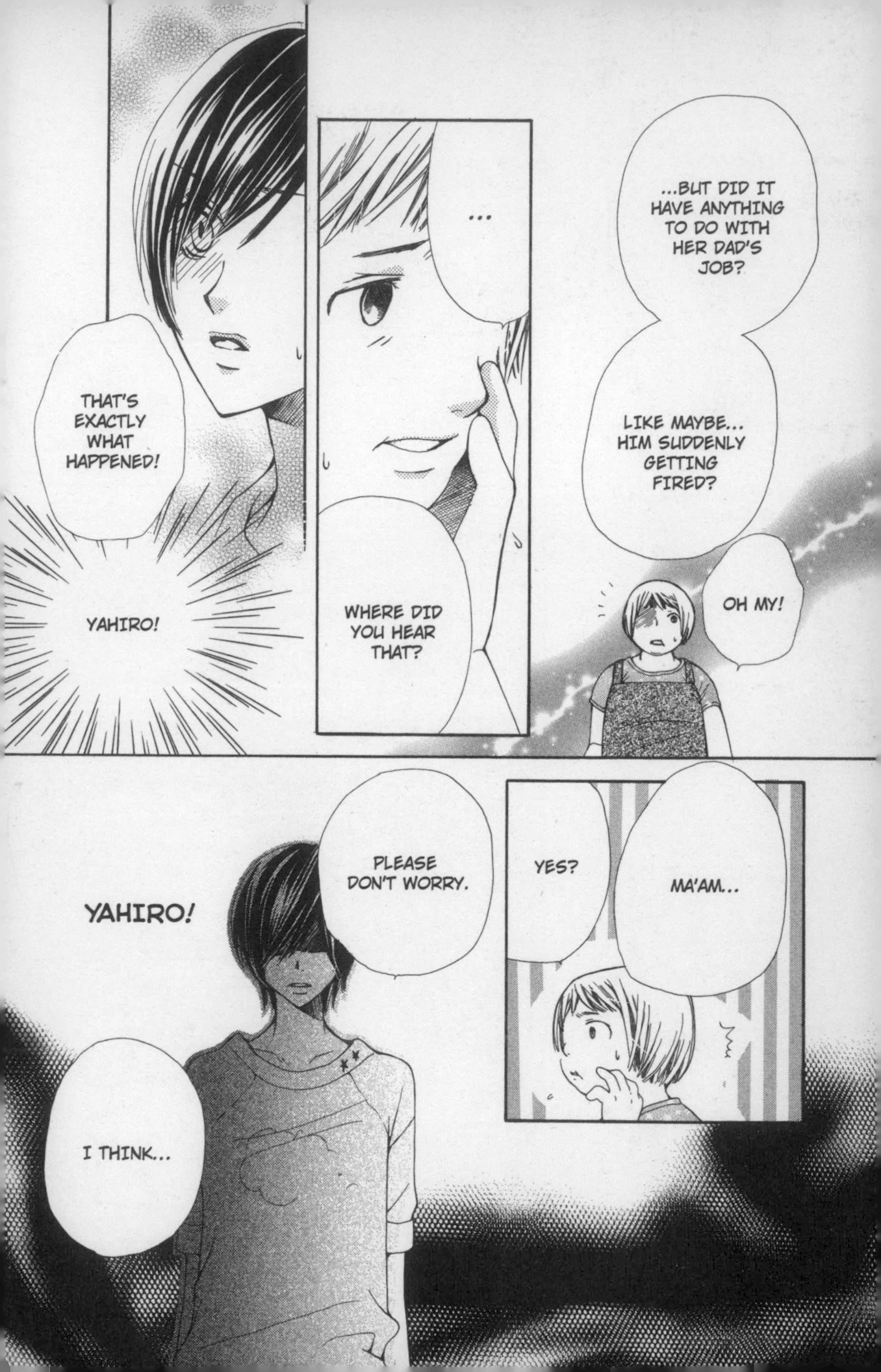
...BUT DID IT HAVE ANYTHING TO DO WITH HER DAD'S JOB?
LIKE MAYBE... HIM SUDDENLY GETTING FIRED?
OH MY!
...
WHERE DID YOU HEAR THAT?
THAT'S EXACTLY WHAT HAPPENED!
YAHIRO!
MA'AM...
YES?
PLEASE DON'T WORRY.
YAHIRO!
I THINK...

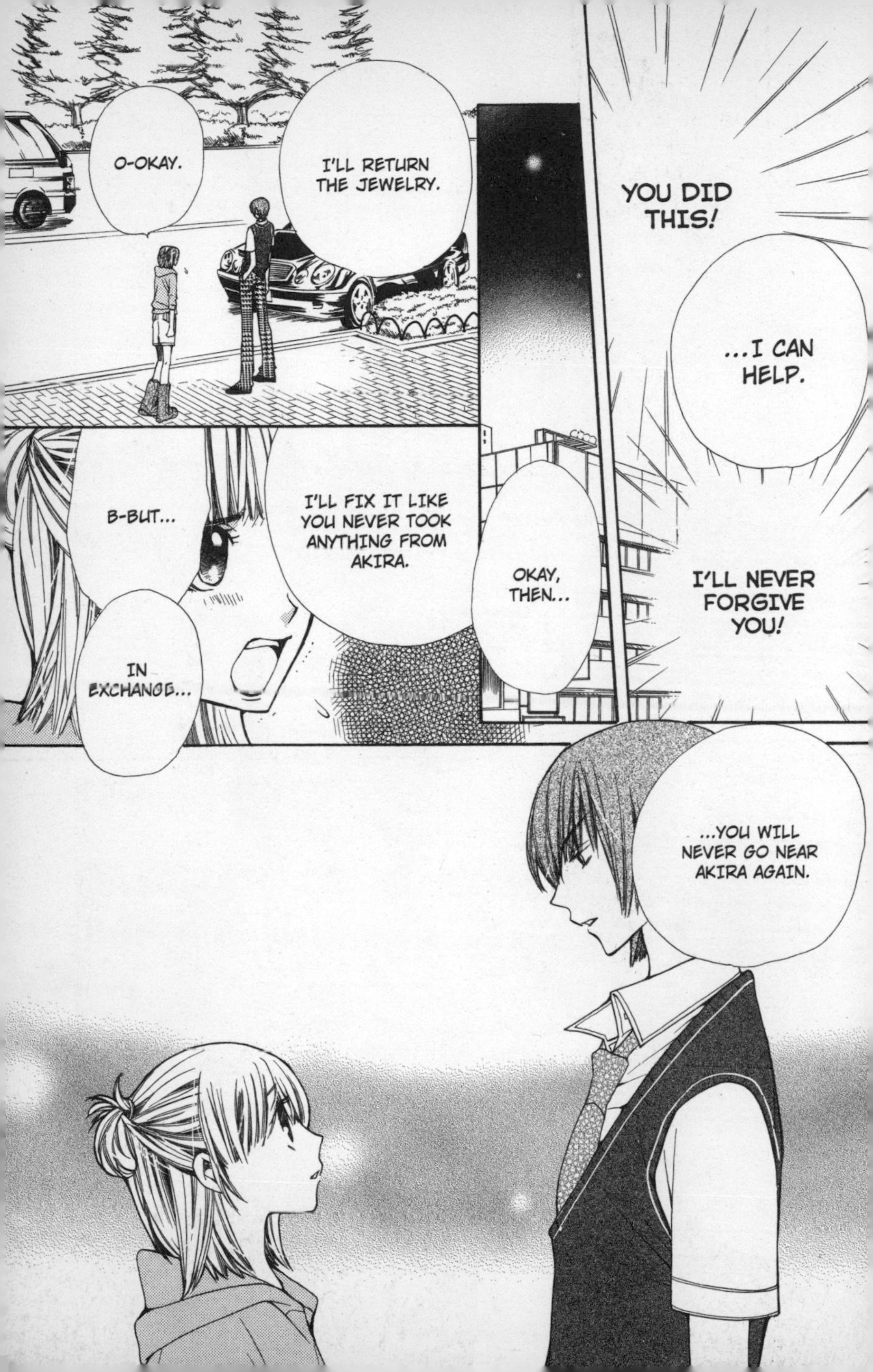
YOU DID THIS!
...I CAN HELP.
I'LL NEVER FORGIVE YOU!
OKAY, THEN...
I'LL RETURN THE JEWELRY.
O-OKAY.
I'LL FIX IT LIKE YOU NEVER TOOK ANYTHING FROM AKIRA.
B-BUT...
IN EXCHANGE...
...YOU WILL NEVER GO NEAR AKIRA AGAIN.

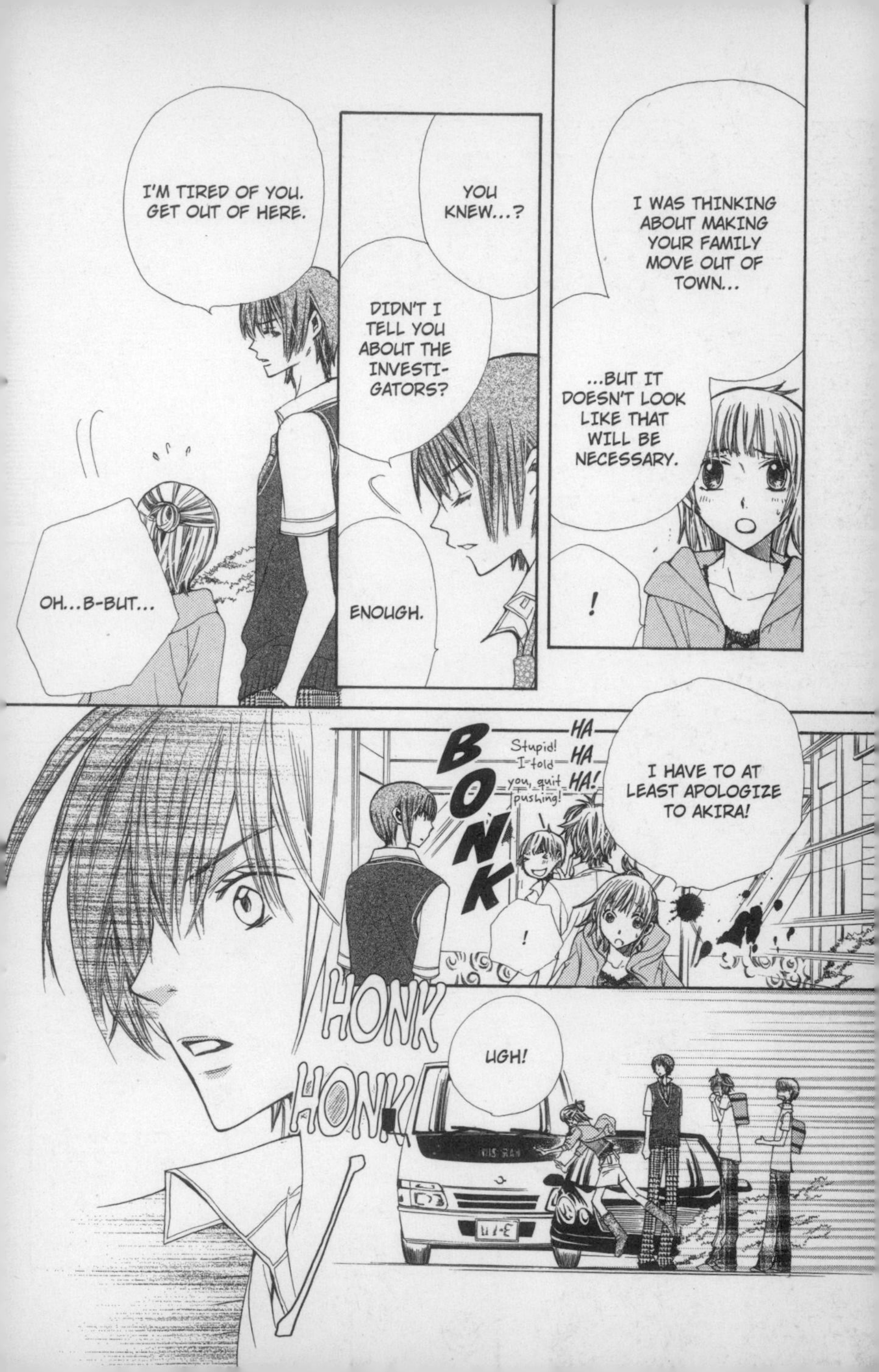
I WAS THINKING ABOUT MAKING YOUR FAMILY MOVE OUT OF TOWN...
...BUT IT DOESN'T LOOK LIKE THAT WILL BE NECESSARY.
!
YOU KNEW...?
DIDN'T I TELL YOU ABOUT THE INVESTIGATORS?
ENOUGH.
I'M TIRED OF YOU. GET OUT OF HERE.
OH...B-BUT...
I HAVE TO AT LEAST APOLOGIZE TO AKIRA!
HA HA HA!
Stupid! I told you, quit pushing!
BONK
!
UGH!
HONK
HONK

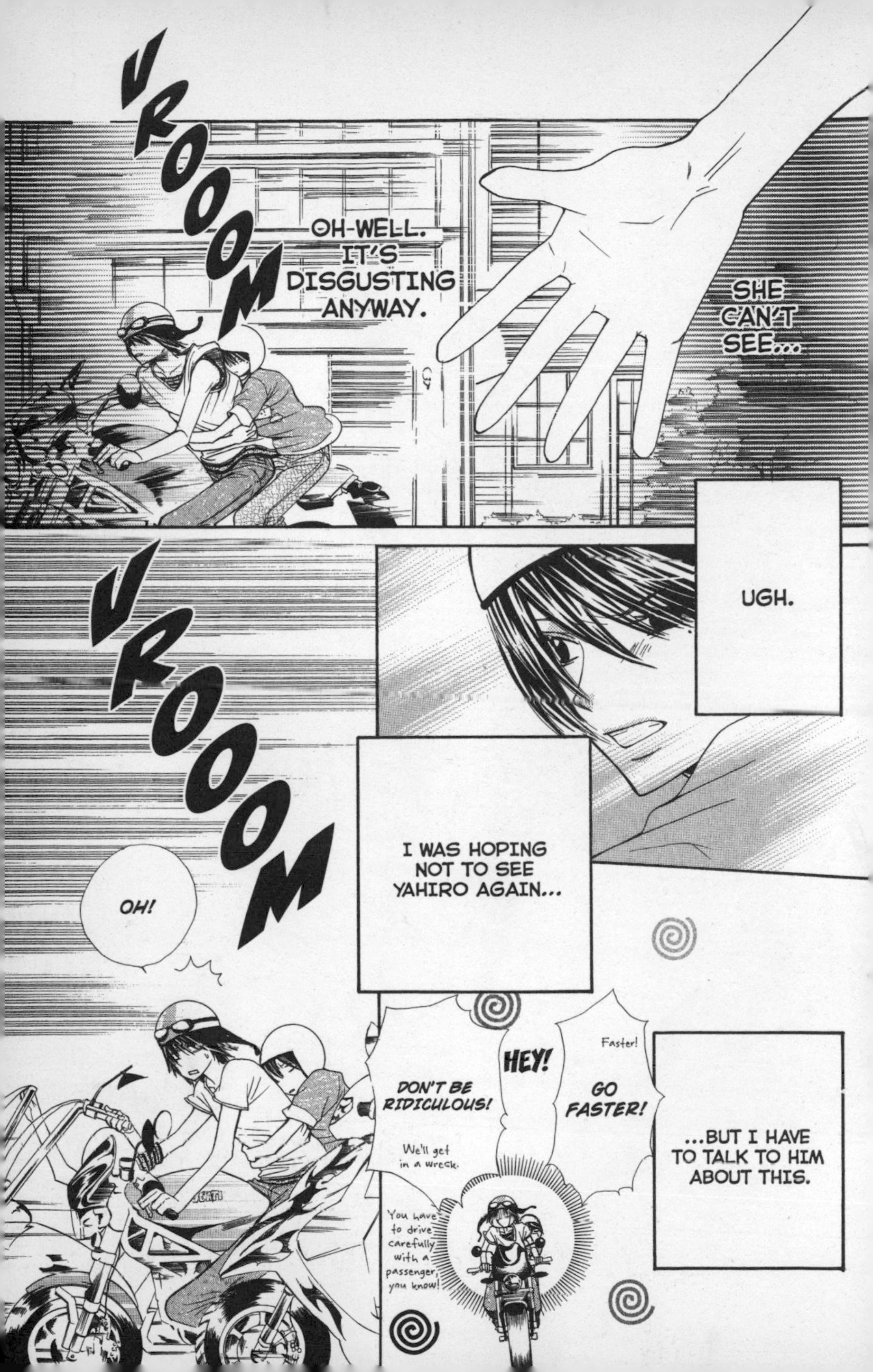
SHE CAN'T SEE...
OH-WELL. IT'S DISGUSTING ANYWAY.
VROOOM
UGH.
I WAS HOPING NOT TO SEE YAHIRO AGAIN...
VROOOOM
OH!
...BUT I HAVE TO TALK TO HIM ABOUT THIS.
Faster!
HEY! GO FASTER!
DON'T BE RIDICULOUS!
We'll get in a wreck.
You have to drive carefully with a passenger, you know!

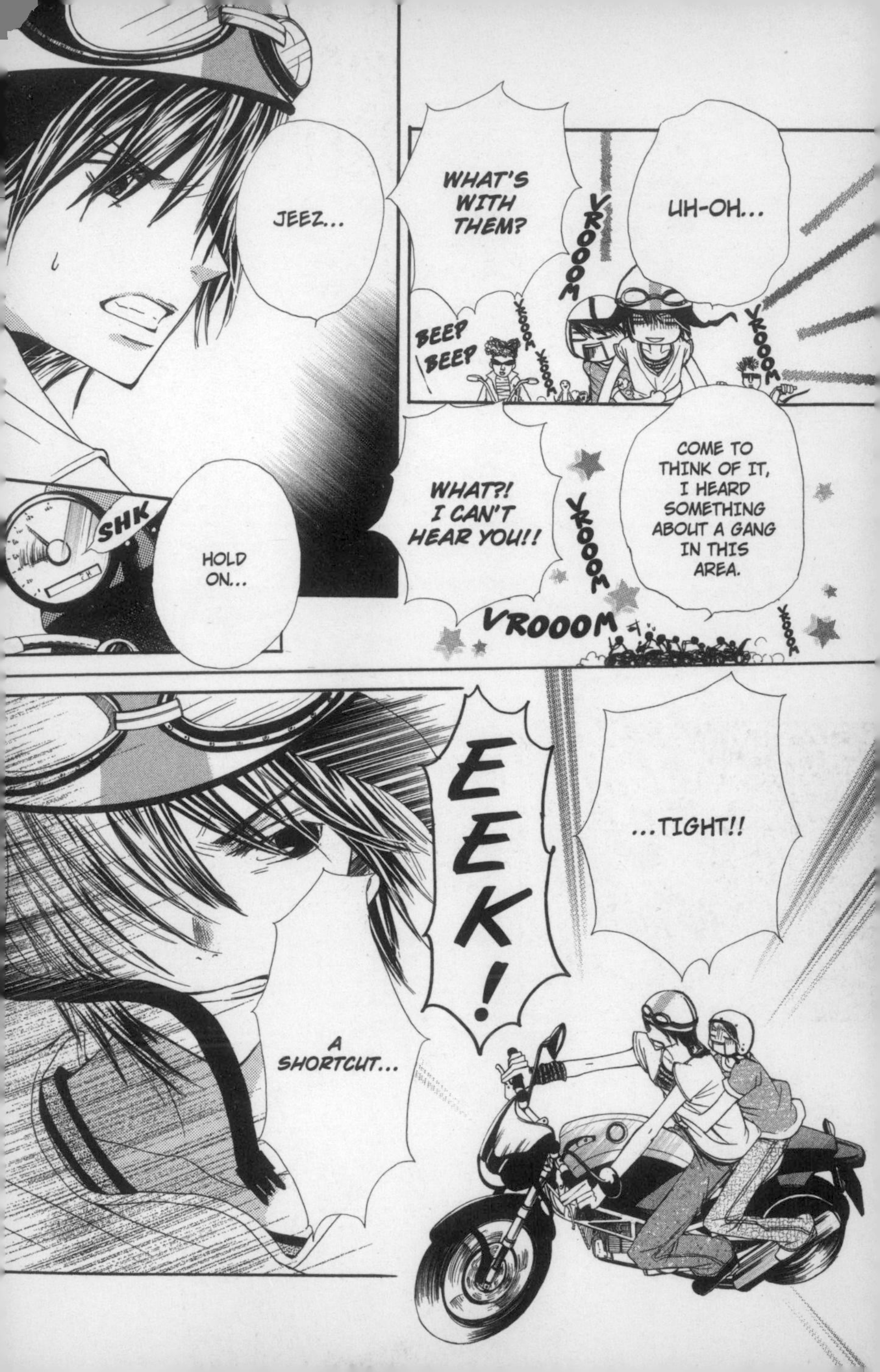
UH-OH...
VROOOM
WHAT'S WITH THEM?
VROOOM
BEEP BEEP
COME TO THINK OF IT, I HEARD SOMETHING ABOUT A GANG IN THIS AREA.
VROOOM
VROOOM
WHAT?! I CAN'T HEAR YOU!!
VROOOM
JEEZ...
SHK
HOLD ON...
...TIGHT!!
EEK!
A SHORTCUT...

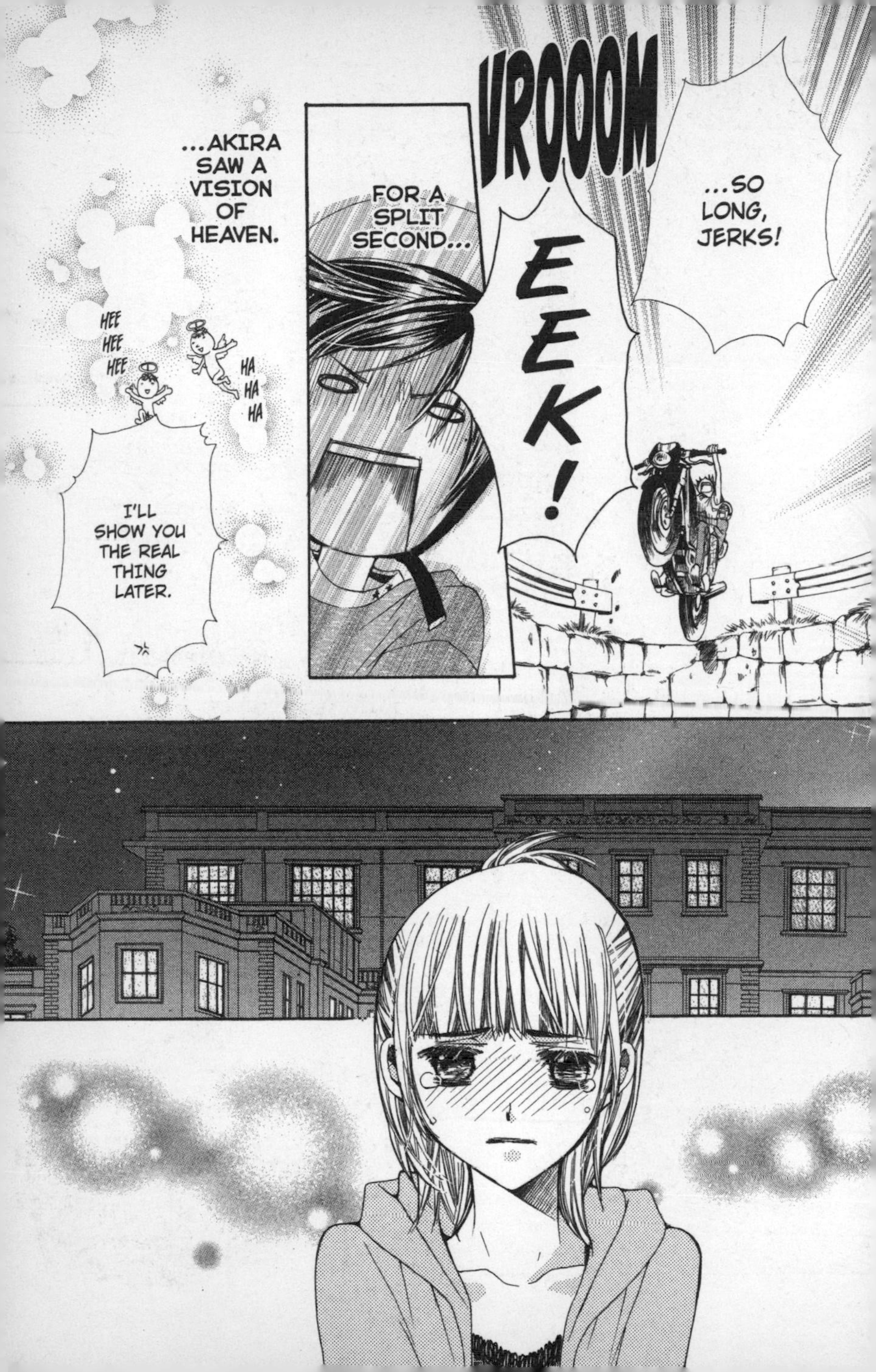
VROOOM
...SO LONG, JERKS!
EEK!
FOR A SPLIT SECOND...
...AKIRA SAW A VISION OF HEAVEN.
HEE HEE HEE
HA HA HA
I'LL SHOW YOU THE REAL THING LATER.

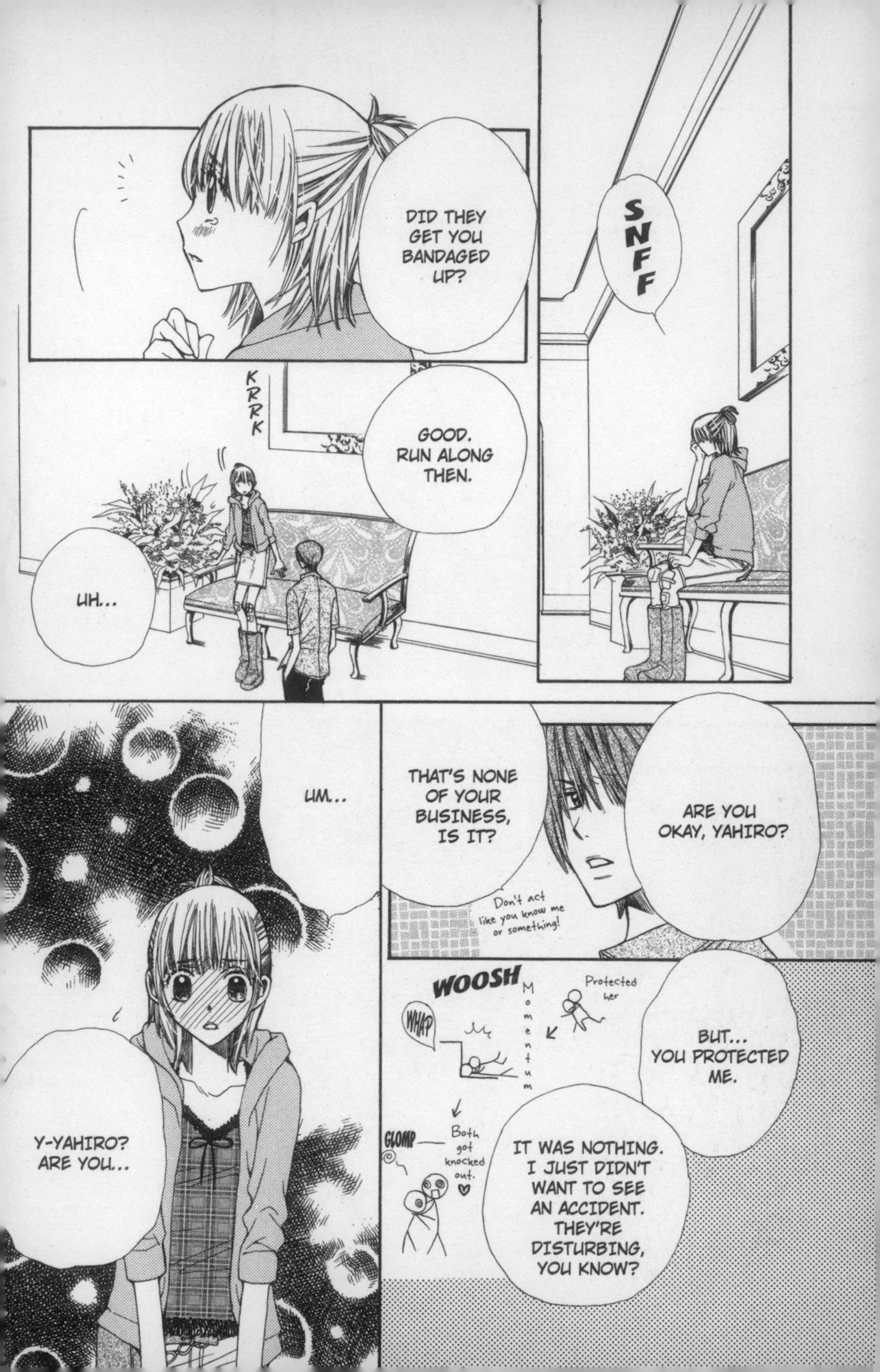
SNFF
DID THEY GET YOU BANDAGED UP?
KRRK
GOOD. RUN ALONG THEN.
UH...
ARE YOU OKAY, YAHIRO?
THAT'S NONE OF YOUR BUSINESS, IS IT?
Don't act like you know me or something!
BUT... YOU PROTECTED ME.
IT WAS NOTHING. I JUST DIDN'T WANT TO SEE AN ACCIDENT. THEY'RE DISTURBING, YOU KNOW?
Protected her
WOOSH
Momentum
WHAP
Both got knocked out.
GLOMP
UM...
Y-YAHIRO? ARE YOU...

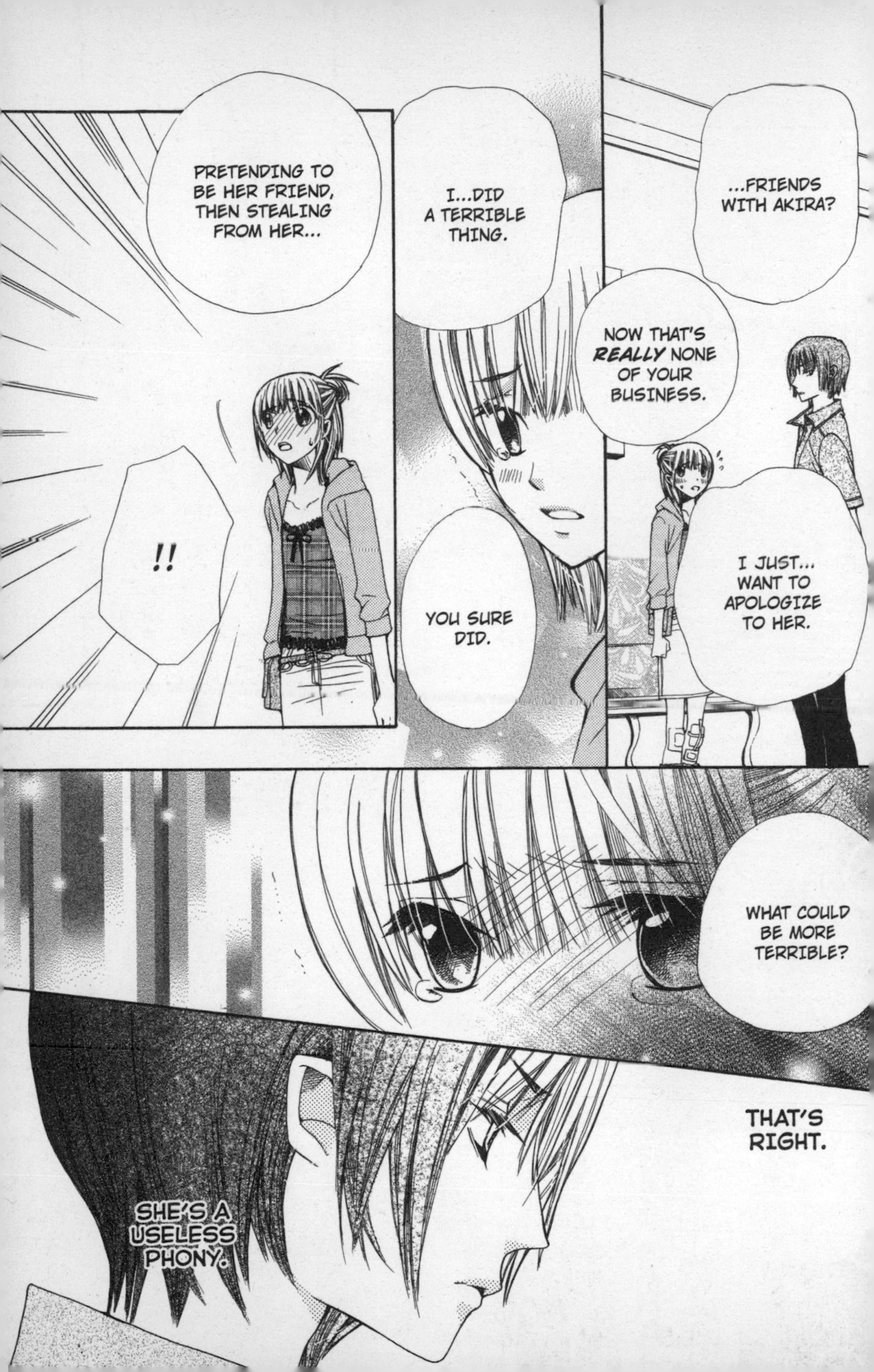
...FRIENDS WITH AKIRA?
NOW THAT'S *REALLY* NONE OF YOUR BUSINESS.
I JUST... WANT TO APOLOGIZE TO HER.
I...DID A TERRIBLE THING.
YOU SURE DID.
PRETENDING TO BE HER FRIEND, THEN STEALING FROM HER...
!!
WHAT COULD BE MORE TERRIBLE?
THAT'S RIGHT.
SHE'S A USELESS PHONY.

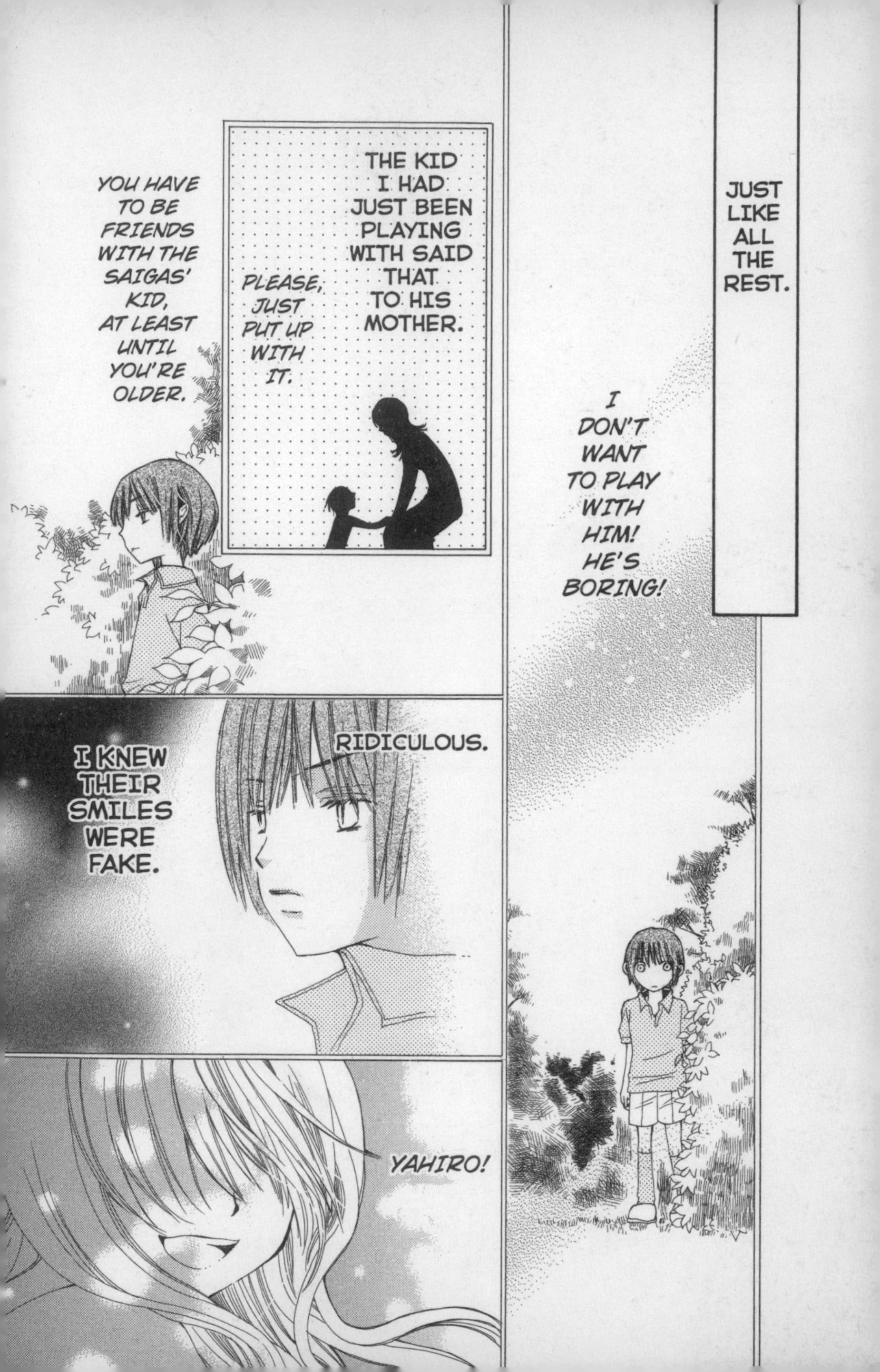
JUST LIKE ALL THE REST.
I DON'T WANT TO PLAY WITH HIM! HE'S BORING!
THE KID I HAD JUST BEEN PLAYING WITH SAID THAT TO HIS MOTHER.
PLEASE, JUST PUT UP WITH IT.
YOU HAVE TO BE FRIENDS WITH THE SAIGAS' KID, AT LEAST UNTIL YOU'RE OLDER.
RIDICULOUS.
I KNEW THEIR SMILES WERE FAKE.
YAHIRO!

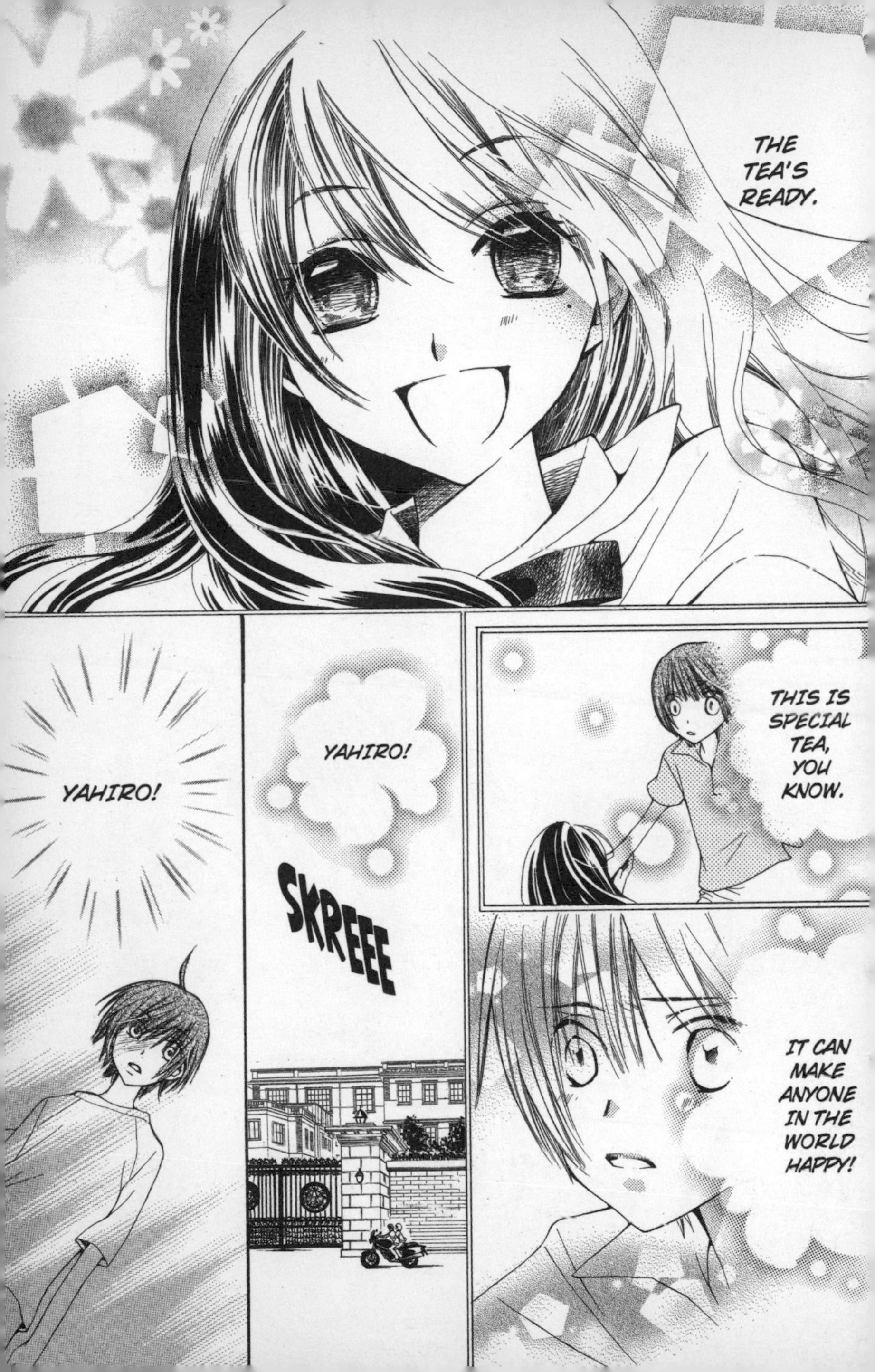
THE TEA'S READY.
THIS IS SPECIAL TEA, YOU KNOW.
IT CAN MAKE ANYONE IN THE WORLD HAPPY!
YAHIRO!
SKREEE
YAHIRO!

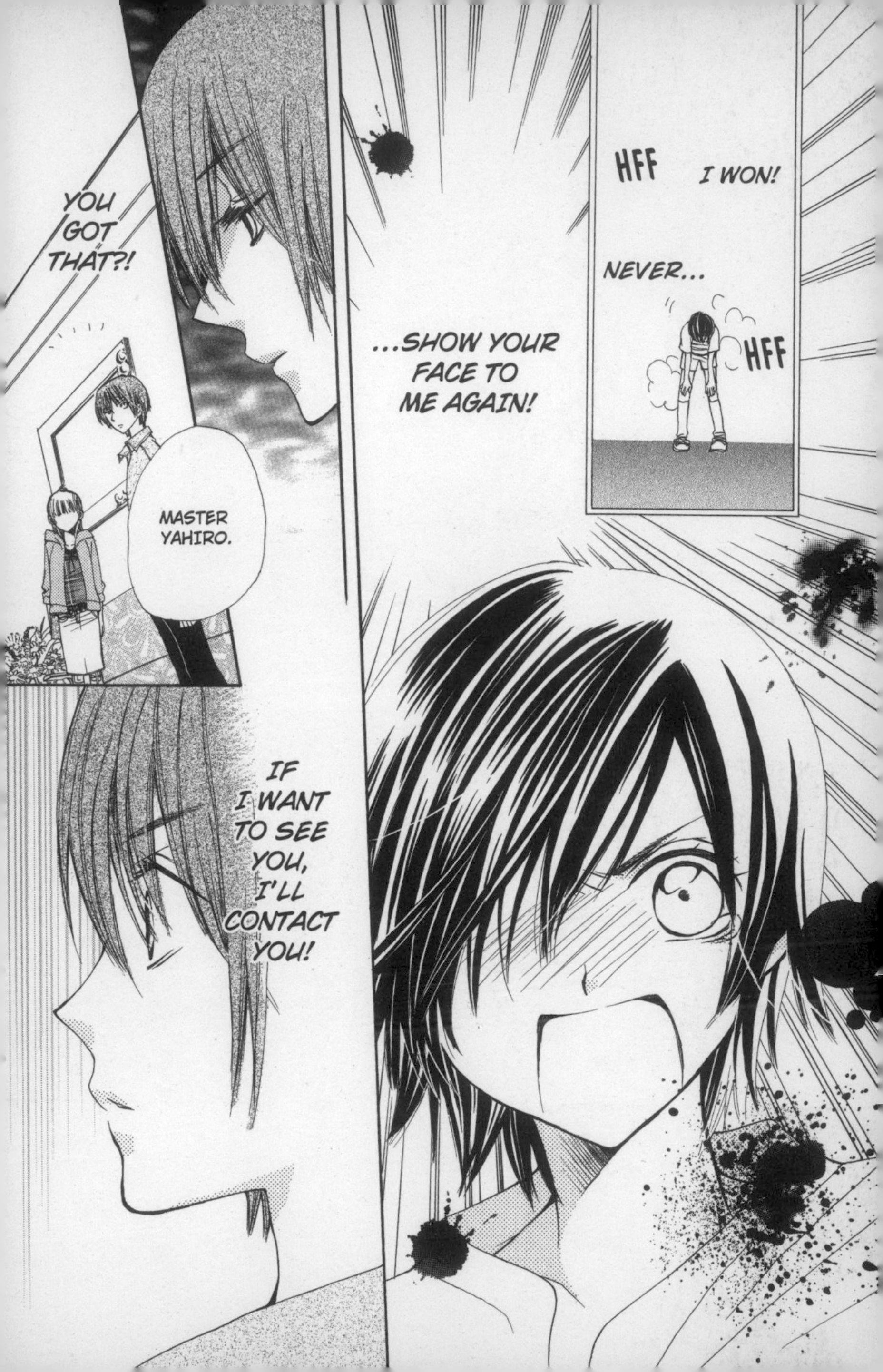
HFF
I WON!
NEVER...
HFF
...SHOW YOUR FACE TO ME AGAIN!
YOU GOT THAT?!
MASTER YAHIRO.
IF I WANT TO SEE YOU, I'LL CONTACT YOU!

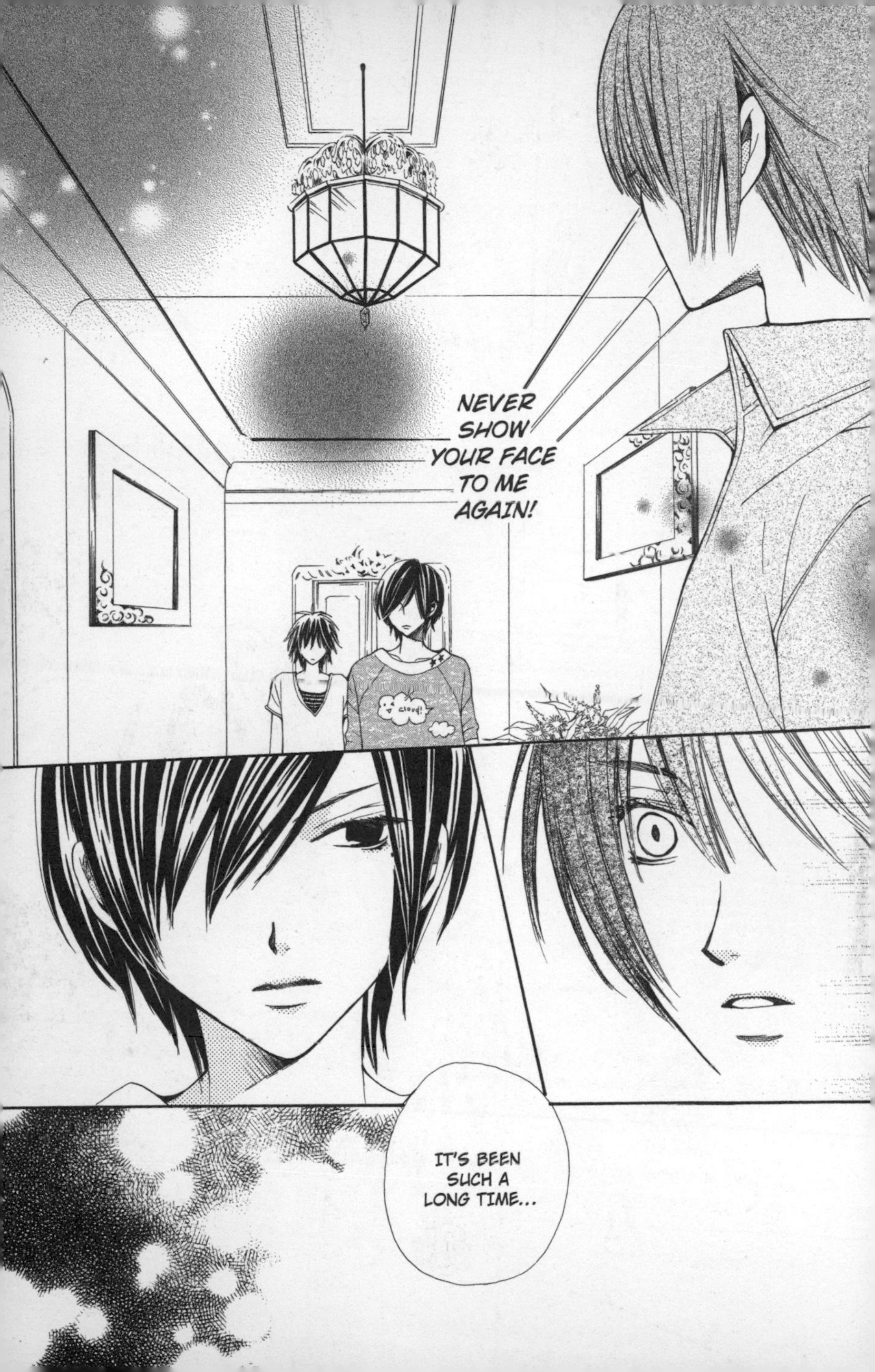
NEVER SHOW YOUR FACE TO ME AGAIN!
IT'S BEEN SUCH A LONG TIME...

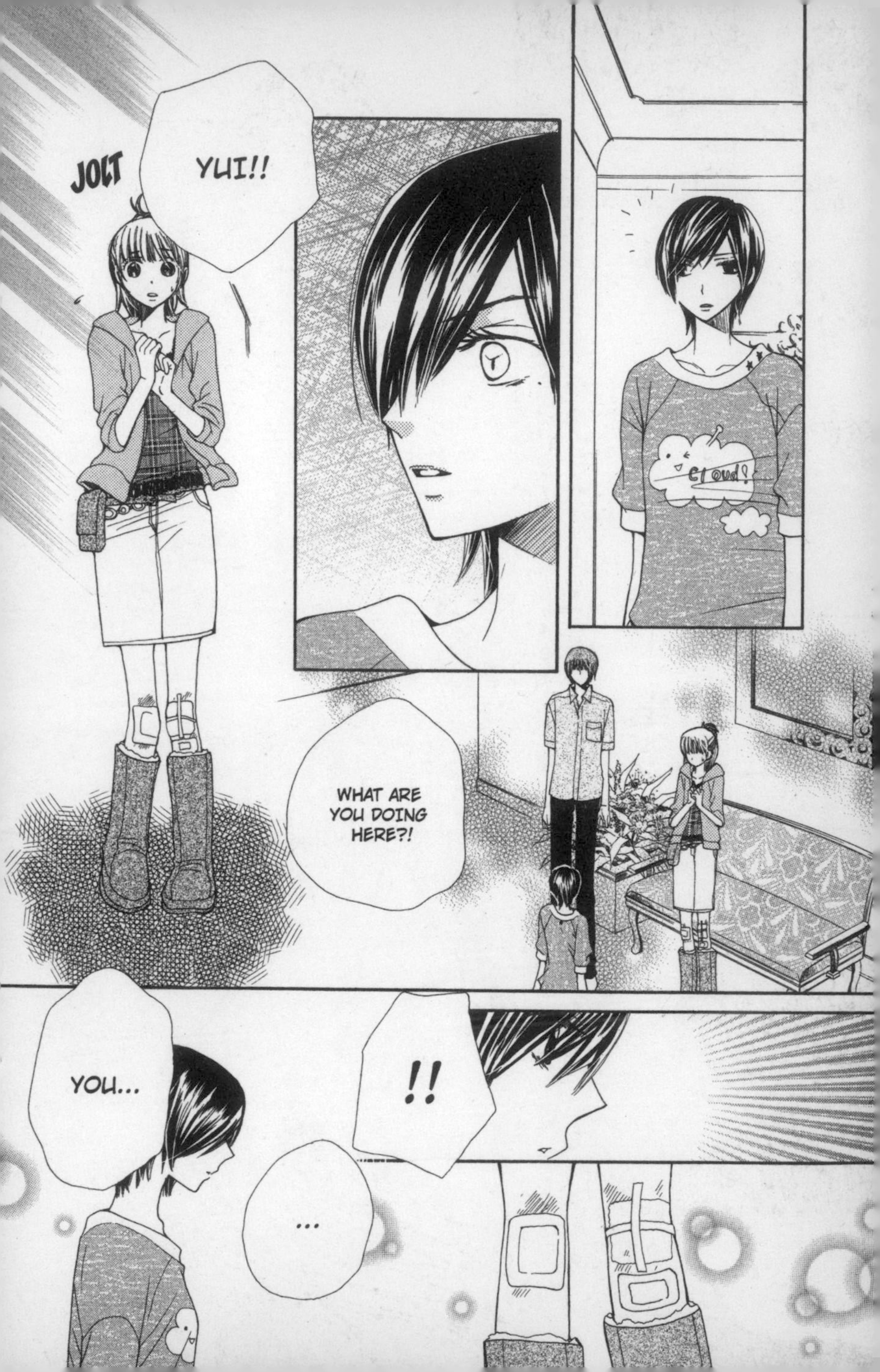
Cloud!
WHAT ARE YOU DOING HERE?!
YUI!!
JOLT
!!
...
YOU...

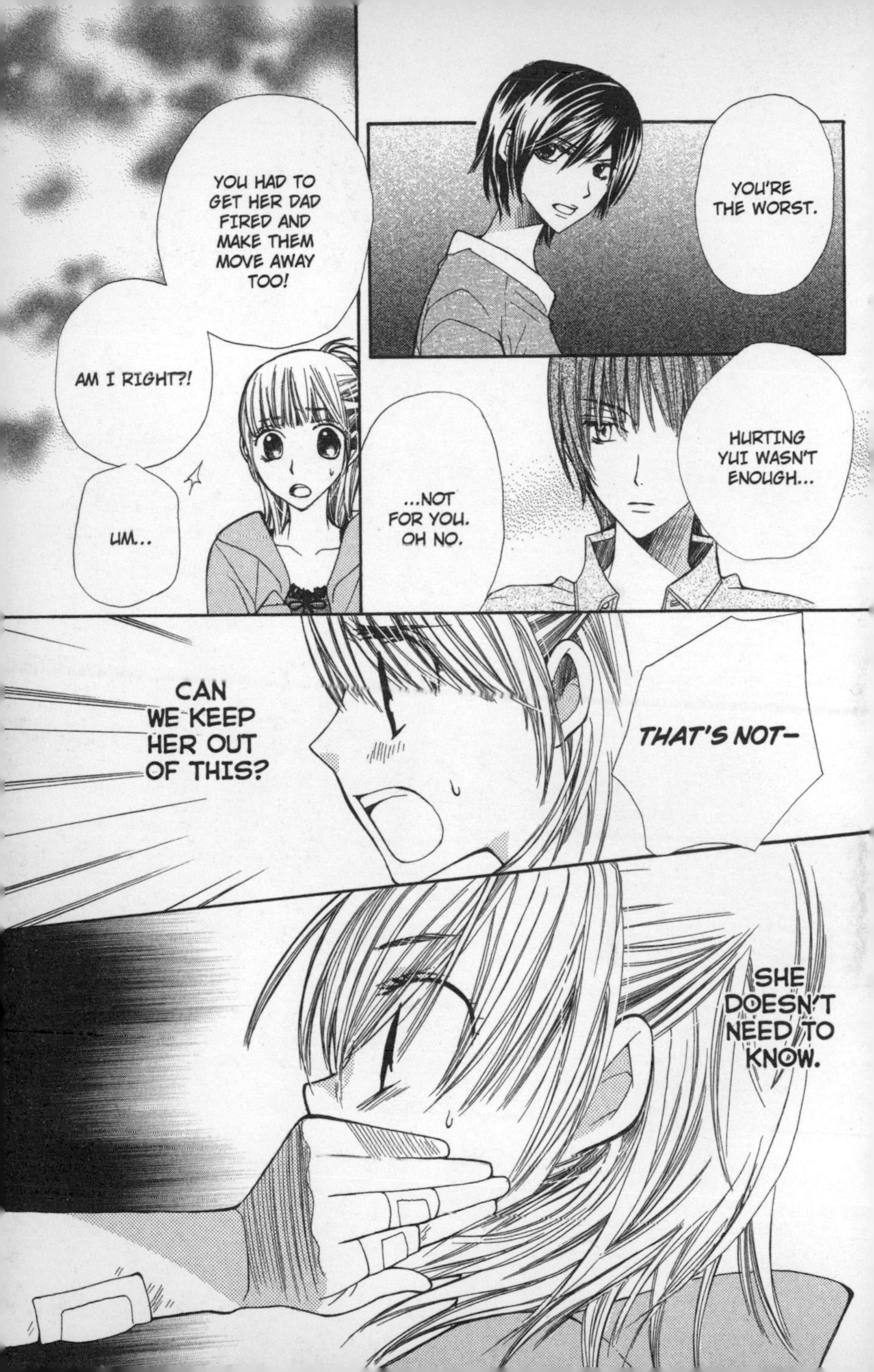
YOU'RE THE WORST.
HURTING YUI WASN'T ENOUGH...
...NOT FOR YOU. OH NO.
YOU HAD TO GET HER DAD FIRED AND MAKE THEM MOVE AWAY TOO!
AM I RIGHT?!
UM...
THAT'S NOT–
CAN WE KEEP HER OUT OF THIS?
SHE DOESN'T NEED TO KNOW.

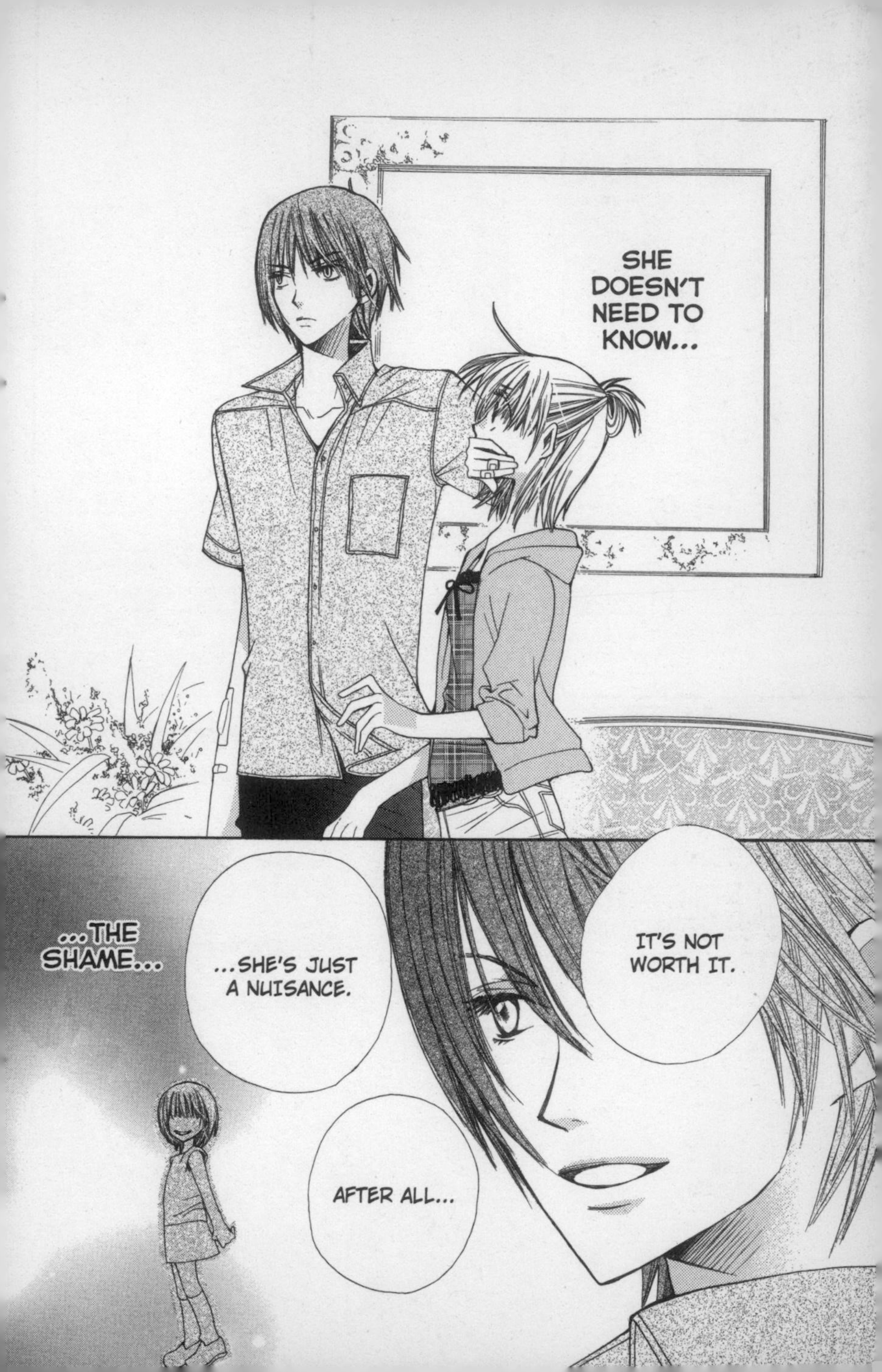

SHE DOESN'T NEED TO KNOW...
IT'S NOT WORTH IT.
AFTER ALL...
...SHE'S JUST A NUISANCE.
...THE SHAME...

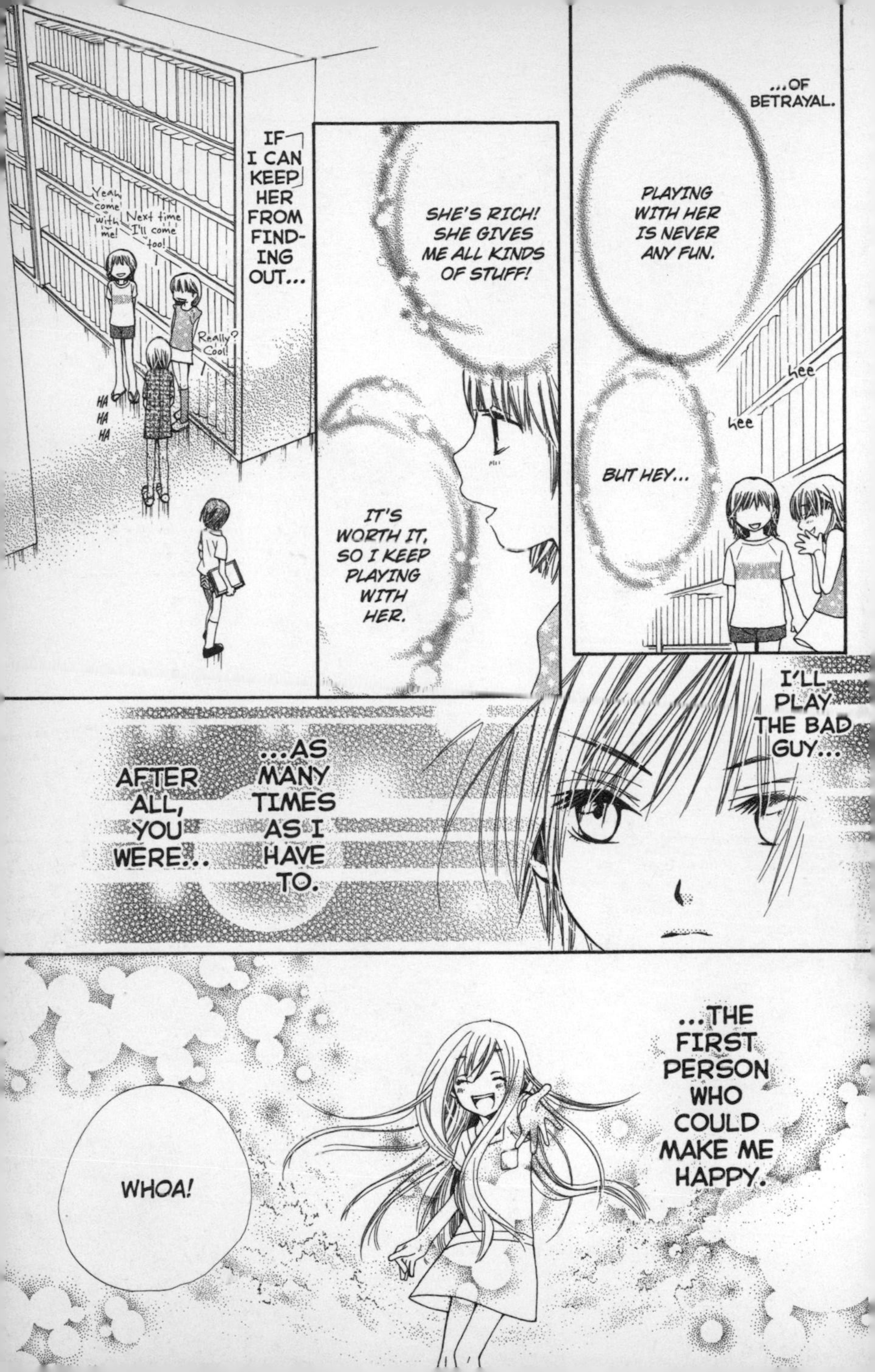
...OF BETRAYAL.
PLAYING WITH HER IS NEVER ANY FUN.
BUT HEY...
Hee
Hee
SHE'S RICH! SHE GIVES ME ALL KINDS OF STUFF!
IT'S WORTH IT, SO I KEEP PLAYING WITH HER.
IF I CAN KEEP HER FROM FINDING OUT...
Next time I'll come too!
Yeah come with me!
Really? Cool!
HA HA HA
I'LL PLAY THE BAD GUY...
...AS MANY TIMES AS I HAVE TO.
AFTER ALL, YOU WERE...
...THE FIRST PERSON WHO COULD MAKE ME HAPPY.
WHOA!

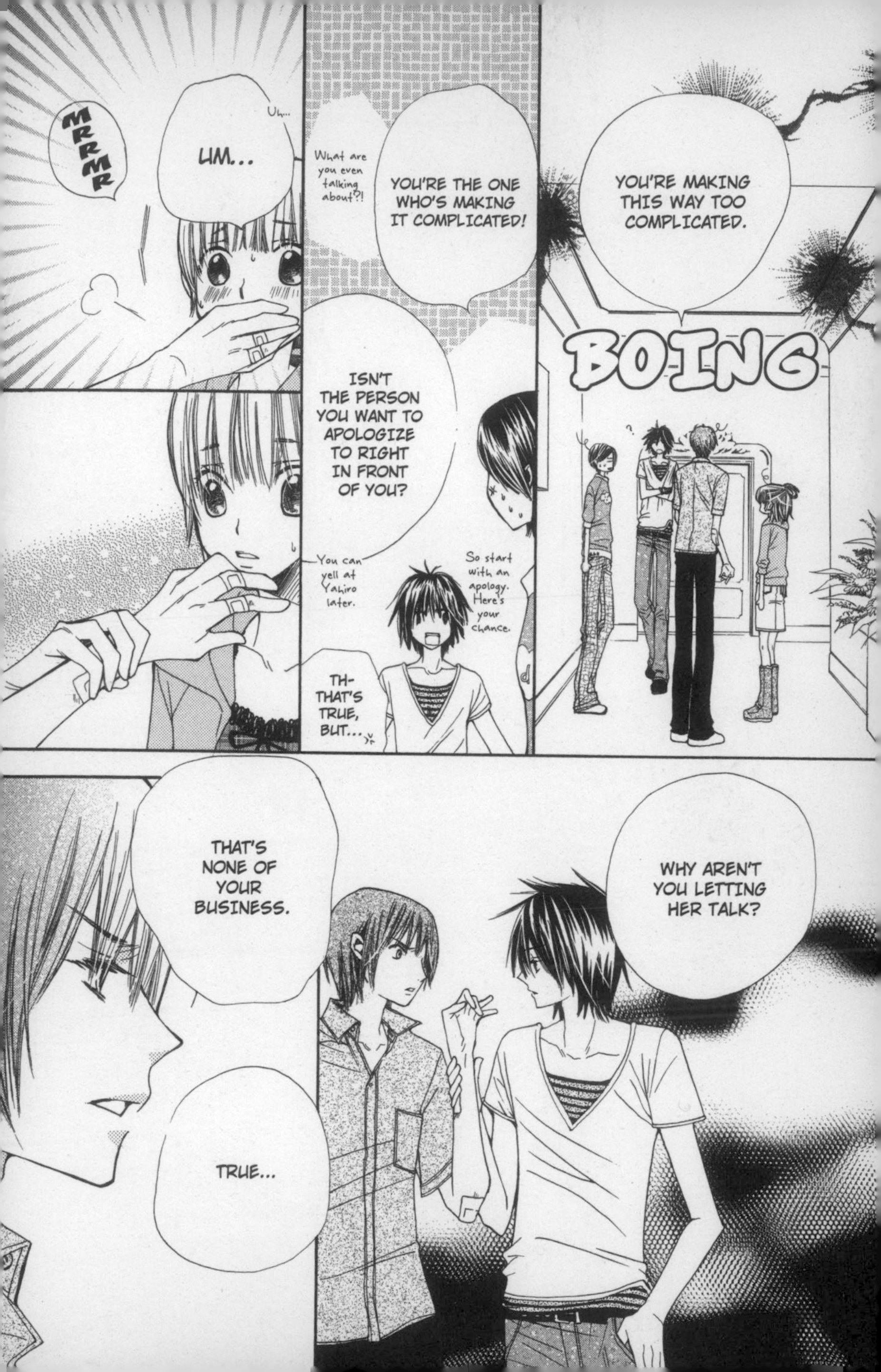
YOU'RE MAKING THIS WAY TOO COMPLICATED.
BOING
YOU'RE THE ONE WHO'S MAKING IT COMPLICATED!
What are you even talking about?!
ISN'T THE PERSON YOU WANT TO APOLOGIZE TO RIGHT IN FRONT OF YOU?
So start with an apology. Here's your chance.
You can yell at Yahiro later.
TH- THAT'S TRUE, BUT...
MRRMR
UM...
Uh...
WHY AREN'T YOU LETTING HER TALK?
THAT'S NONE OF YOUR BUSINESS.
TRUE...

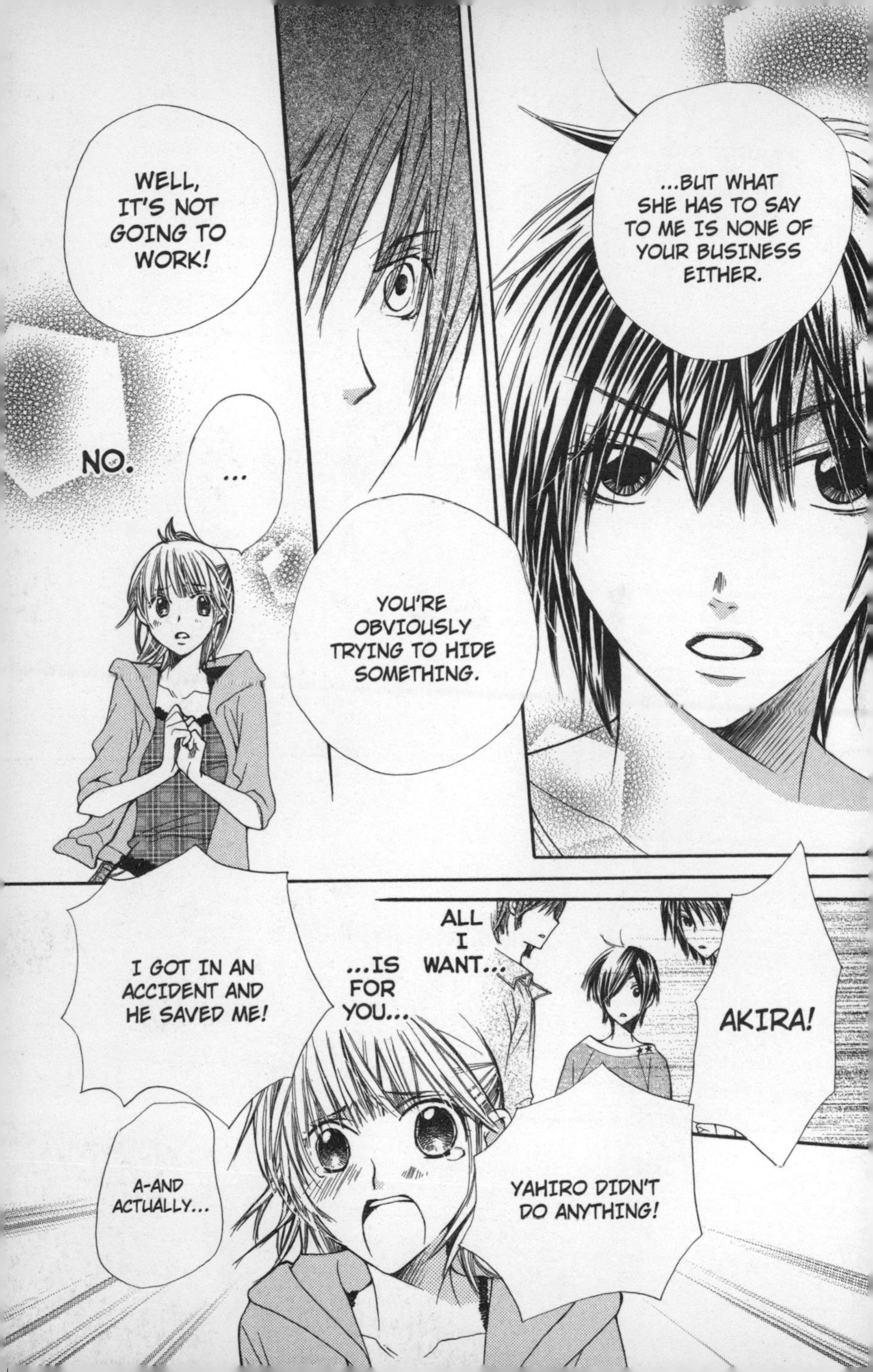
...BUT WHAT SHE HAS TO SAY TO ME IS NONE OF YOUR BUSINESS EITHER.
YOU'RE OBVIOUSLY TRYING TO HIDE SOMETHING.
WELL, IT'S NOT GOING TO WORK!
...
NO.
AKIRA!
ALL I WANT...
...IS FOR YOU...
YAHIRO DIDN'T DO ANYTHING!
I GOT IN AN ACCIDENT AND HE SAVED ME!
A-AND ACTUALLY...

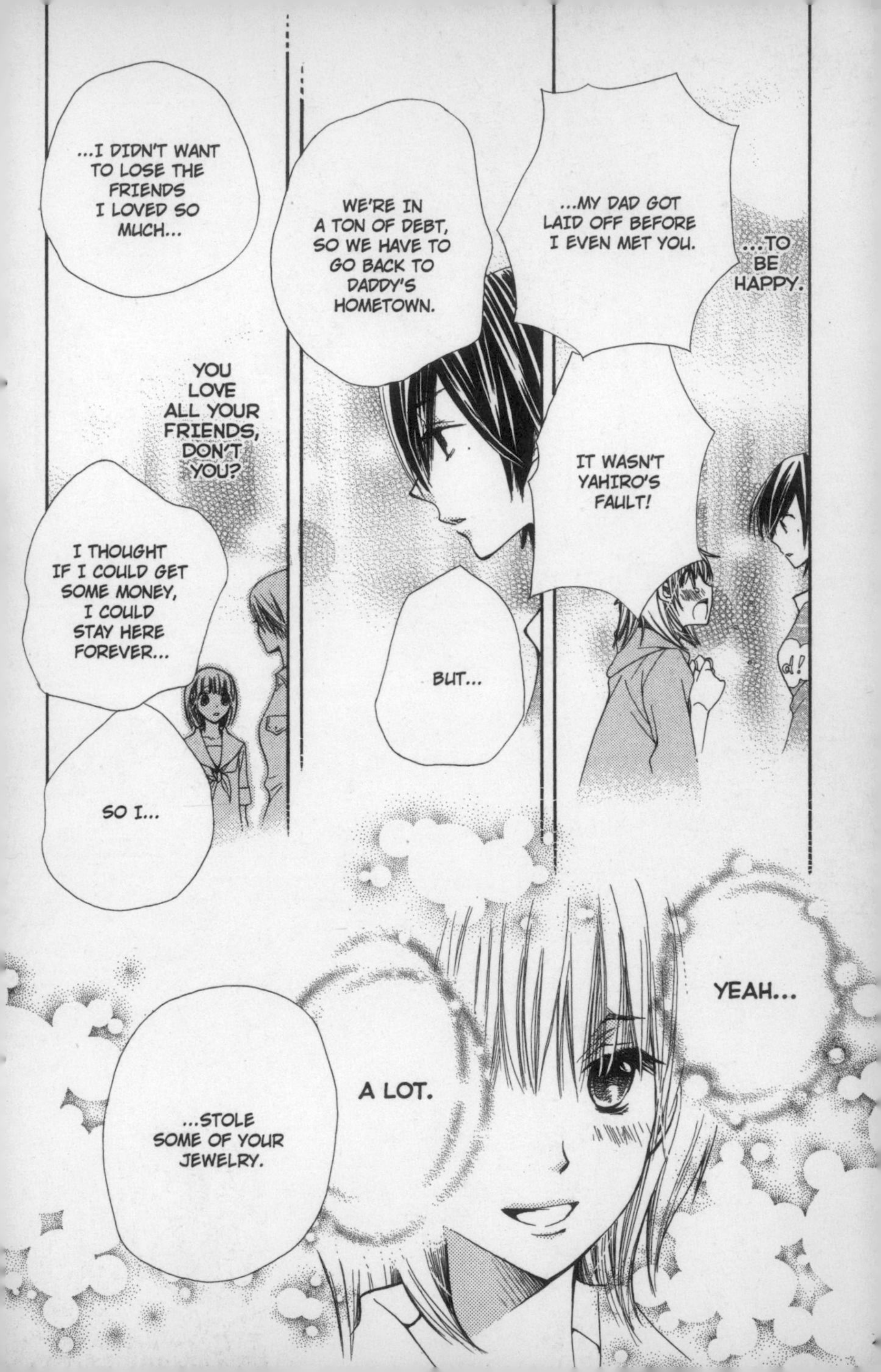
...MY DAD GOT LAID OFF BEFORE I EVEN MET YOU.
...TO BE HAPPY.
IT WASN'T YAHIRO'S FAULT!
WE'RE IN A TON OF DEBT, SO WE HAVE TO GO BACK TO DADDY'S HOMETOWN.
BUT...
...I DIDN'T WANT TO LOSE THE FRIENDS I LOVED SO MUCH...
YOU LOVE ALL YOUR FRIENDS, DON'T YOU?
I THOUGHT IF I COULD GET SOME MONEY, I COULD STAY HERE FOREVER...
SO I...
YEAH...
A LOT.
...STOLE SOME OF YOUR JEWELRY.

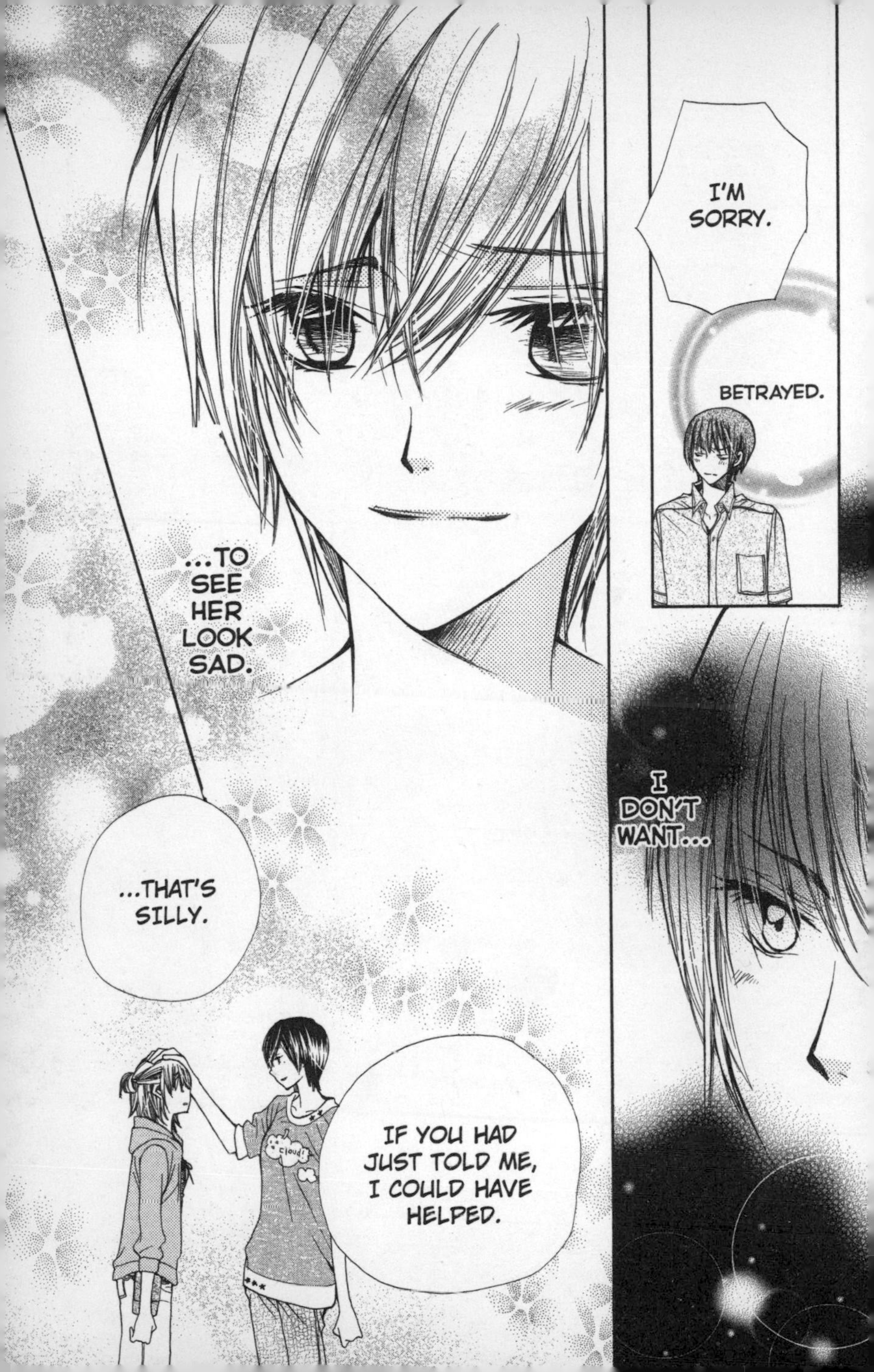

I'M SORRY.
BETRAYED.
I DON'T WANT...
...TO SEE HER LOOK SAD.
...THAT'S SILLY.
IF YOU HAD JUST TOLD ME, I COULD HAVE HELPED.

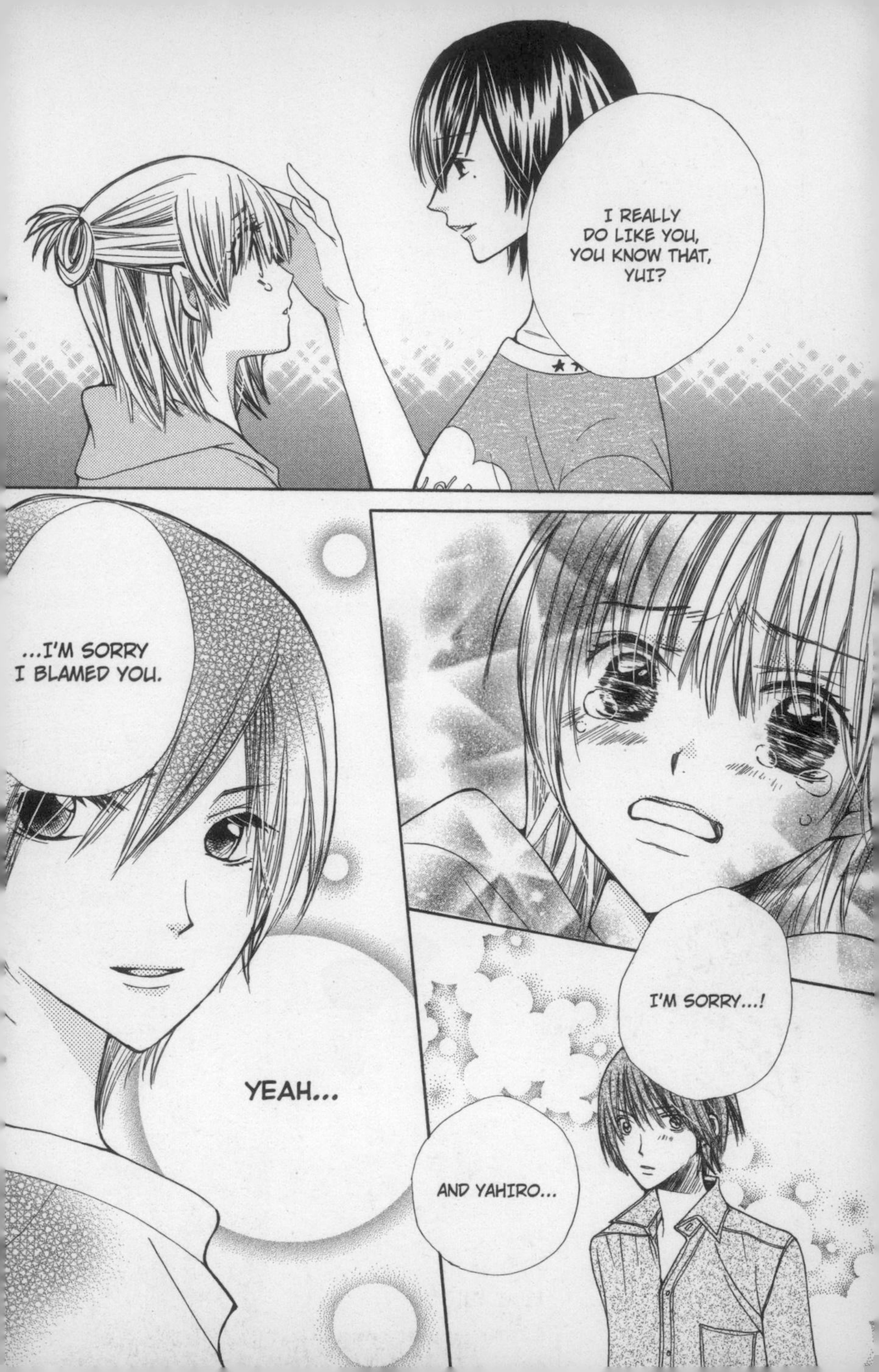
I REALLY DO LIKE YOU, YOU KNOW THAT, YUI?
I'M SORRY...!
AND YAHIRO...
...I'M SORRY I BLAMED YOU.
YEAH...

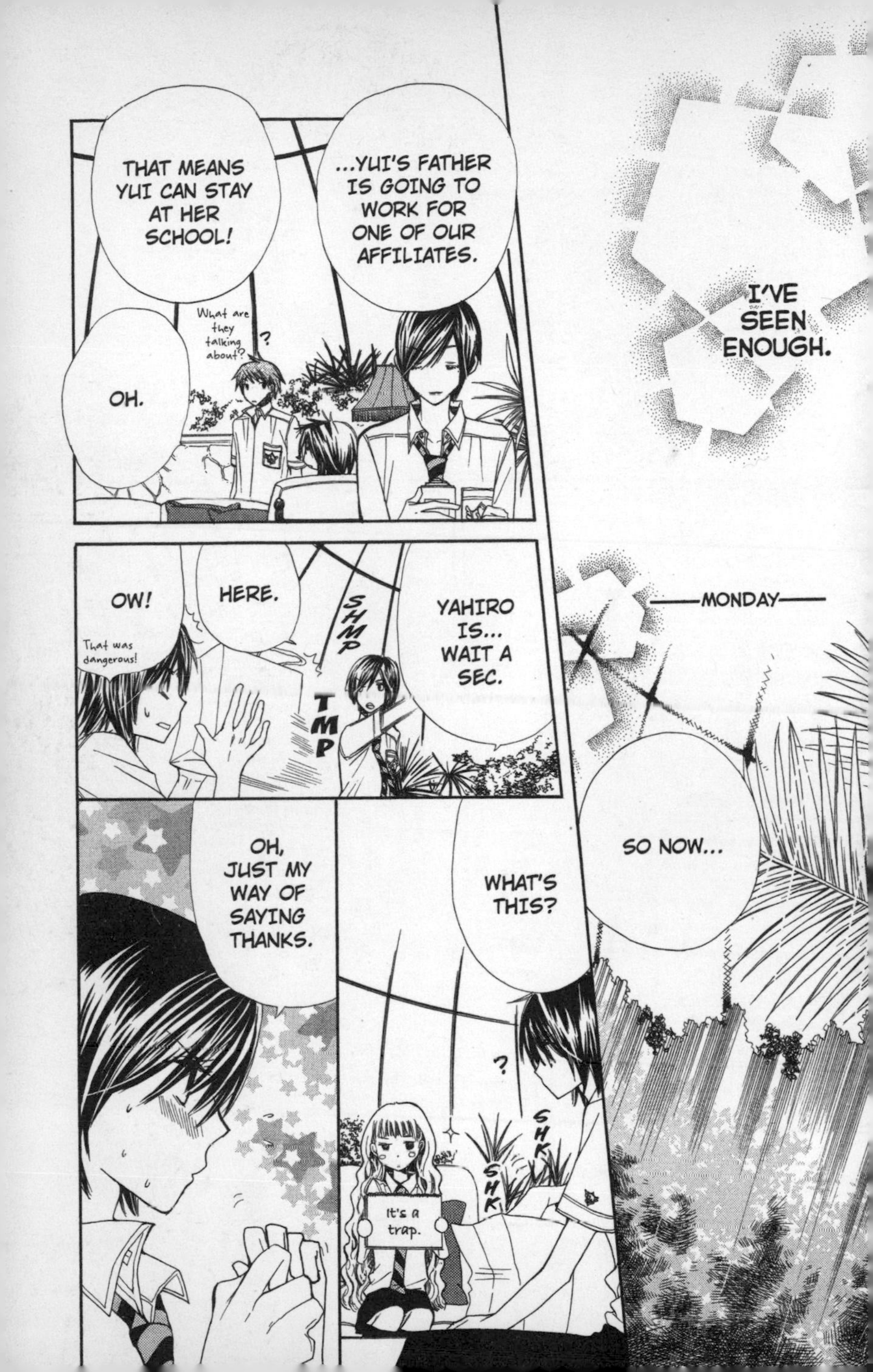
I'VE SEEN ENOUGH.
—MONDAY—
SO NOW...
...YUI'S FATHER IS GOING TO WORK FOR ONE OF OUR AFFILIATES.
THAT MEANS YUI CAN STAY AT HER SCHOOL!
?
What are they talking about?
OH.
YAHIRO IS... WAIT A SEC.
SHMP
TMP
HERE.
OW!
That was dangerous!
WHAT'S THIS?
?
SHK
SHK
It's a trap.
OH, JUST MY WAY OF SAYING THANKS.

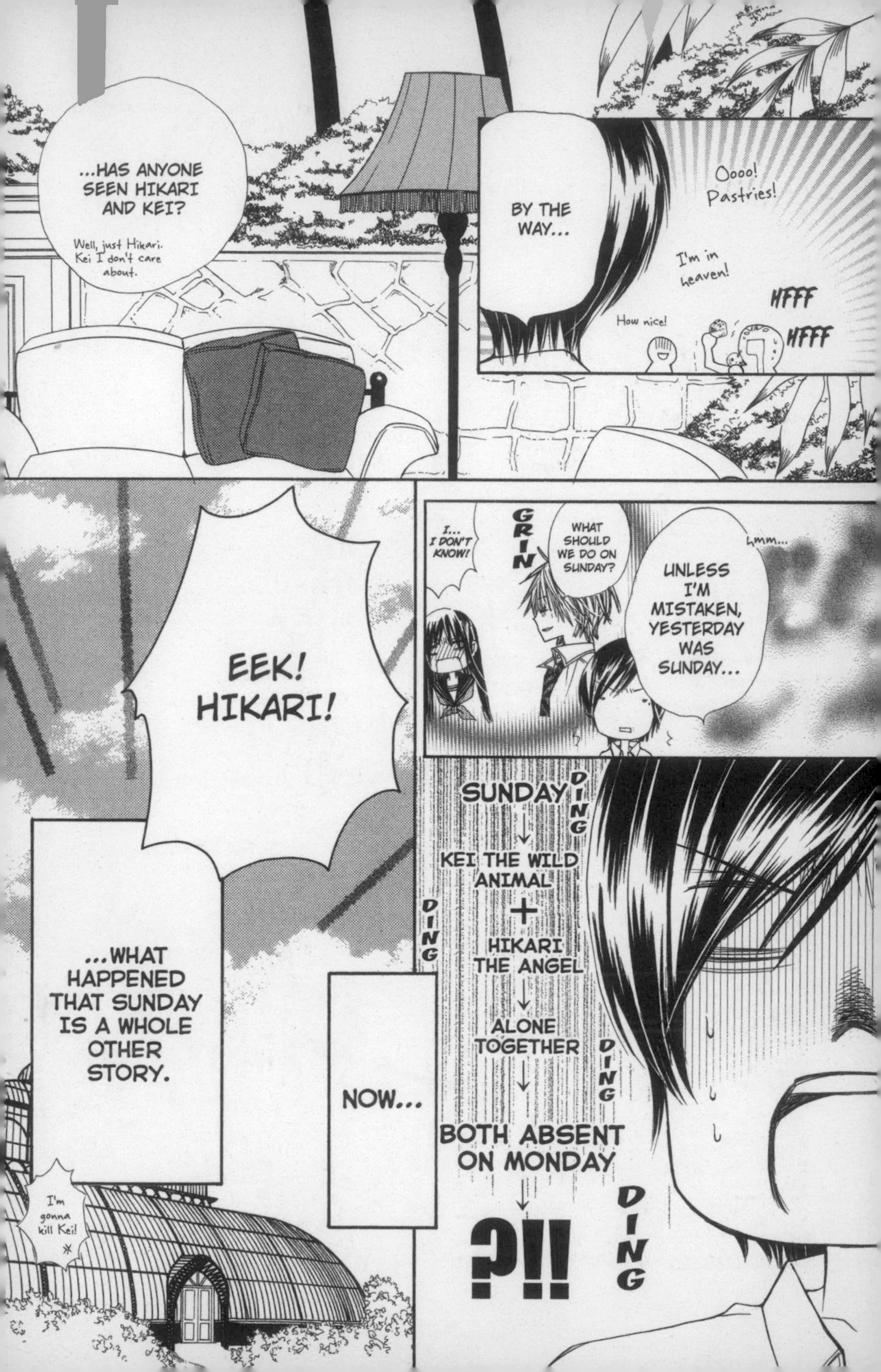
BY THE WAY...
Oooo! Pastries!
I'm in heaven!
HFFF
HFFF
How nice!
...HAS ANYONE SEEN HIKARI AND KEI?
Well, just Hikari. Kei I don't care about.
hmm...
UNLESS I'M MISTAKEN, YESTERDAY WAS SUNDAY...
GRIN
WHAT SHOULD WE DO ON SUNDAY?
I... I DON'T KNOW!
SUNDAY
DING
DING
KEI THE WILD ANIMAL
+
HIKARI THE ANGEL
ALONE TOGETHER
DING
DING
BOTH ABSENT ON MONDAY
DING
?!!
DING
EEK! HIKARI!
...WHAT HAPPENED THAT SUNDAY IS A WHOLE OTHER STORY.
NOW...
I'm gonna kill Kei!

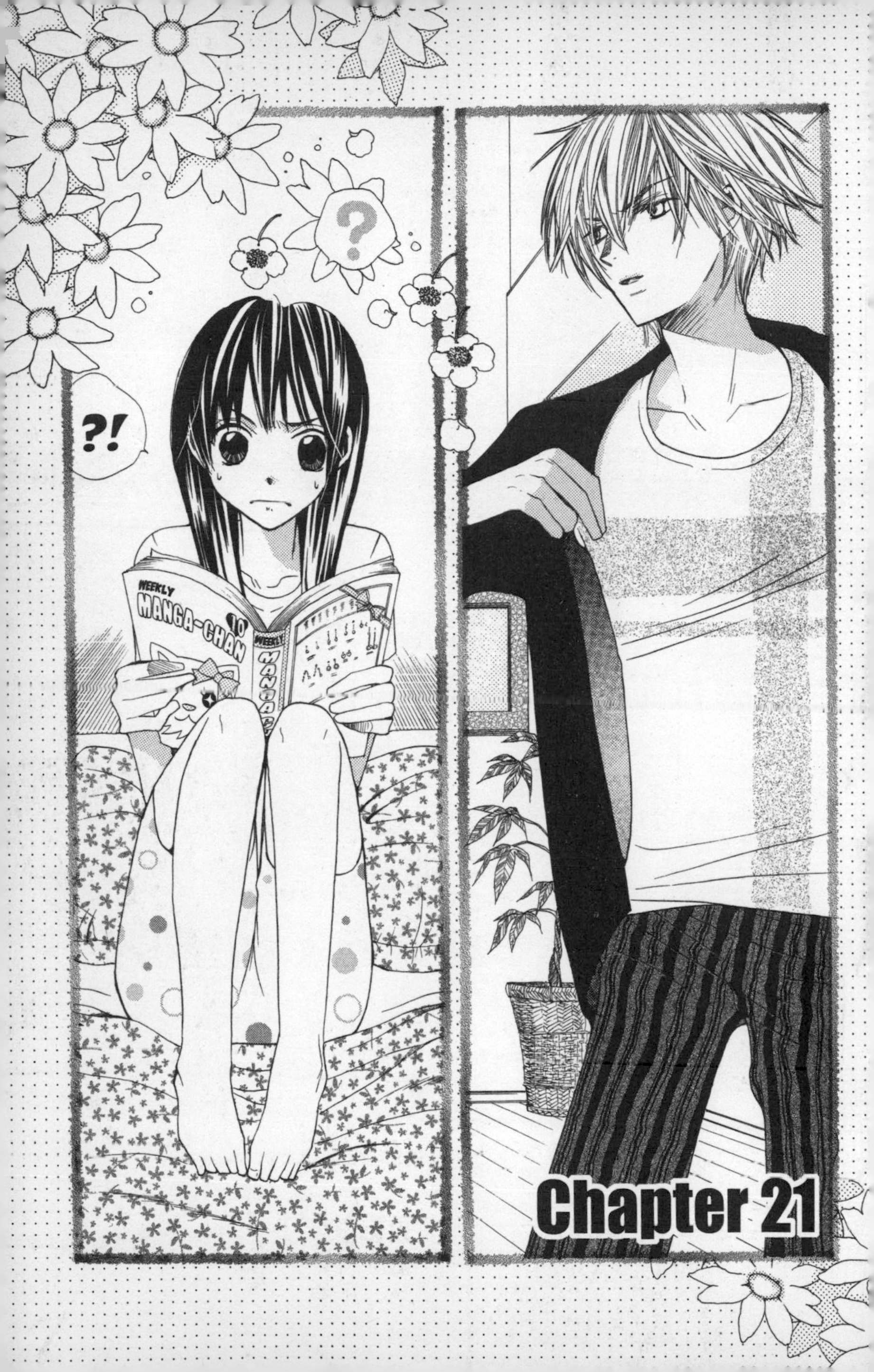
Chapter 21
?!
WEEKLY MANGA-CHAN 10

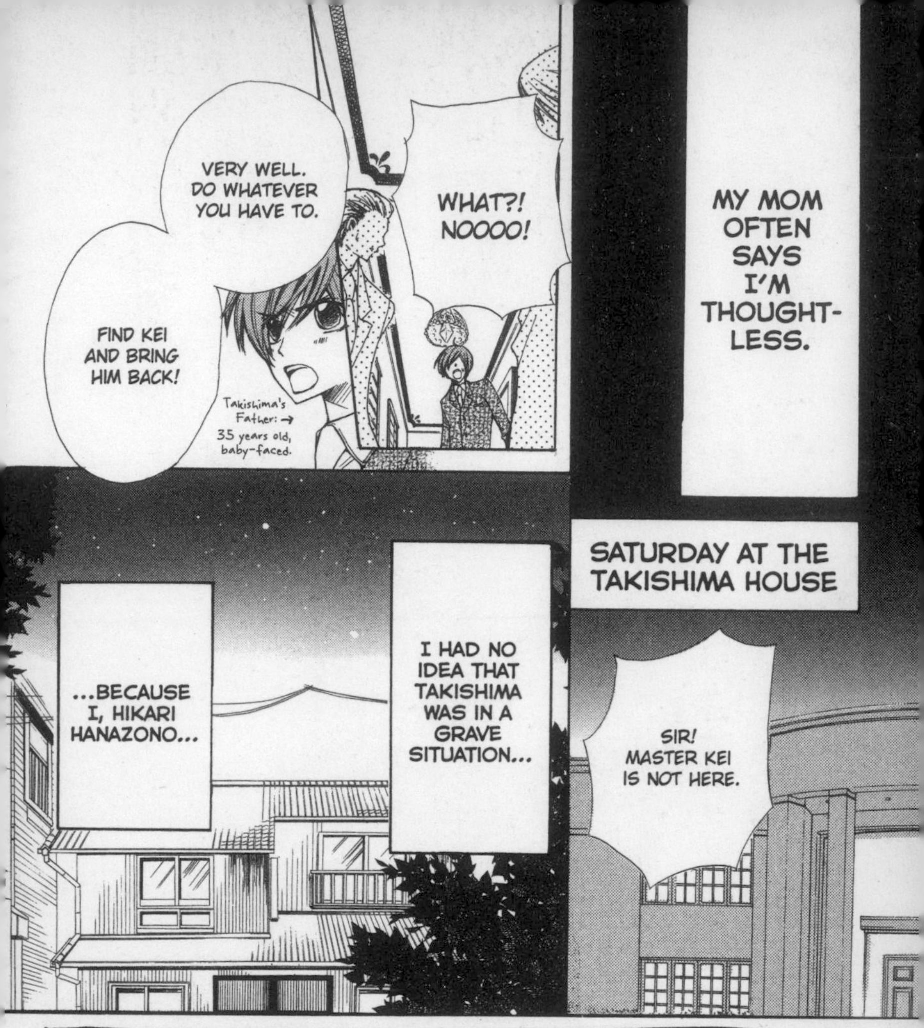
MY MOM OFTEN SAYS I'M THOUGHTLESS.
WHAT?! NOOOO!
VERY WELL. DO WHATEVER YOU HAVE TO.
FIND KEI AND BRING HIM BACK!
Takishima's Father: → 35 years old, baby-faced.
SATURDAY AT THE TAKISHIMA HOUSE
SIR! MASTER KEI IS NOT HERE.
I HAD NO IDEA THAT TAKISHIMA WAS IN A GRAVE SITUATION...
...BECAUSE I, HIKARI HANAZONO...

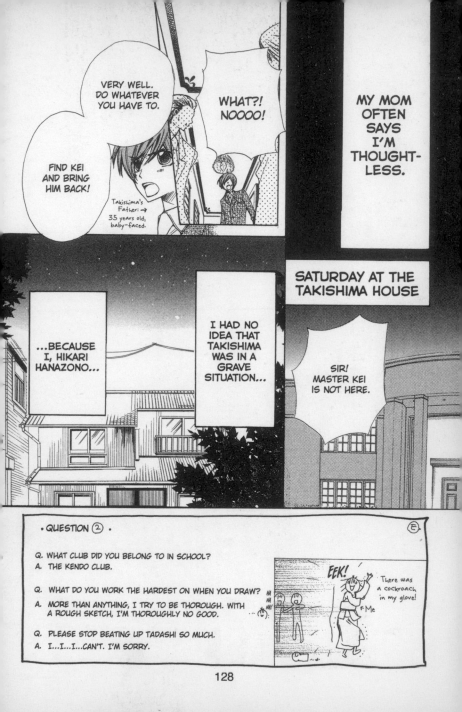

• QUESTION ② •

Q. WHAT CLUB DID YOU BELONG TO IN SCHOOL?
A. THE KENDO CLUB.

Q. WHAT DO YOU WORK THE HARDEST ON WHEN YOU DRAW?
A. MORE THAN ANYTHING, I TRY TO BE THOROUGH. WITH A ROUGH SKETCH, I'M THOROUGHLY NO GOOD.

Q. PLEASE STOP BEATING UP TADASHI SO MUCH.
A. I...I...I...CAN'T. I'M SORRY.

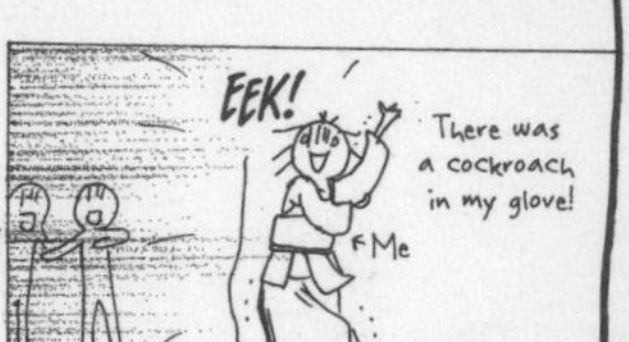
EEK!
HA HA HA!
There was a cockroach in my glove!
← Me

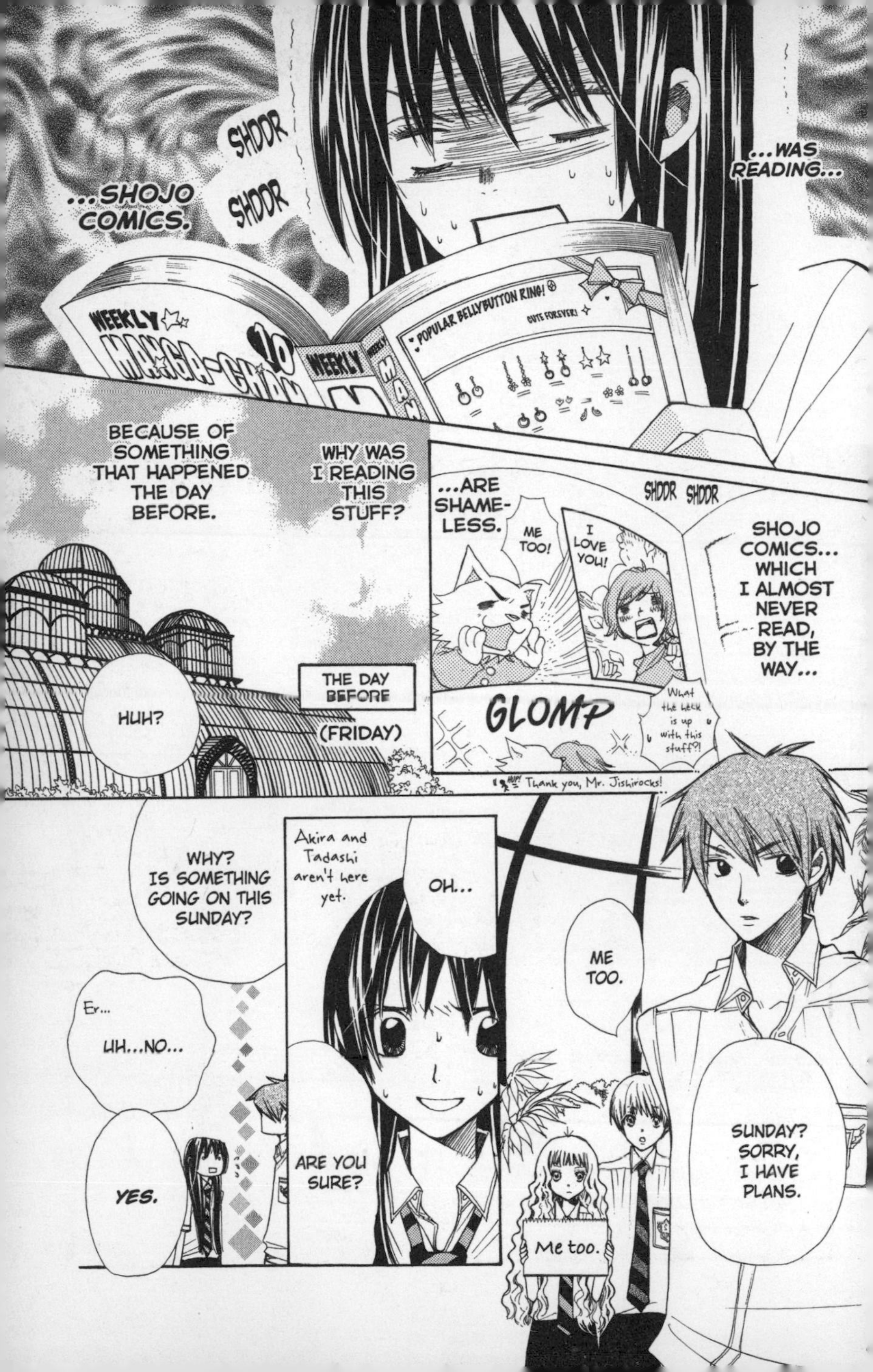
...WAS READING...
SHDDR
SHDDR
...SHOJO COMICS.
POPULAR BELLYBUTTON RING!
CUTE FOREVER!
WEEKLY
10
SHOJO COMICS... WHICH I ALMOST NEVER READ, BY THE WAY...
SHDDR SHDDR
...ARE SHAMELESS.
I LOVE YOU!
ME TOO!
GLOMP
What the heck is up with this stuff?!
Thank you, Mr. Jishirocks!
WHY WAS I READING THIS STUFF?
BECAUSE OF SOMETHING THAT HAPPENED THE DAY BEFORE.
THE DAY BEFORE
(FRIDAY)
HUH?
SUNDAY? SORRY, I HAVE PLANS.
ME TOO.
Me too.
OH...
Akira and Tadashi aren't here yet.
ARE YOU SURE?
WHY? IS SOMETHING GOING ON THIS SUNDAY?
Er...
UH...NO...
YES.

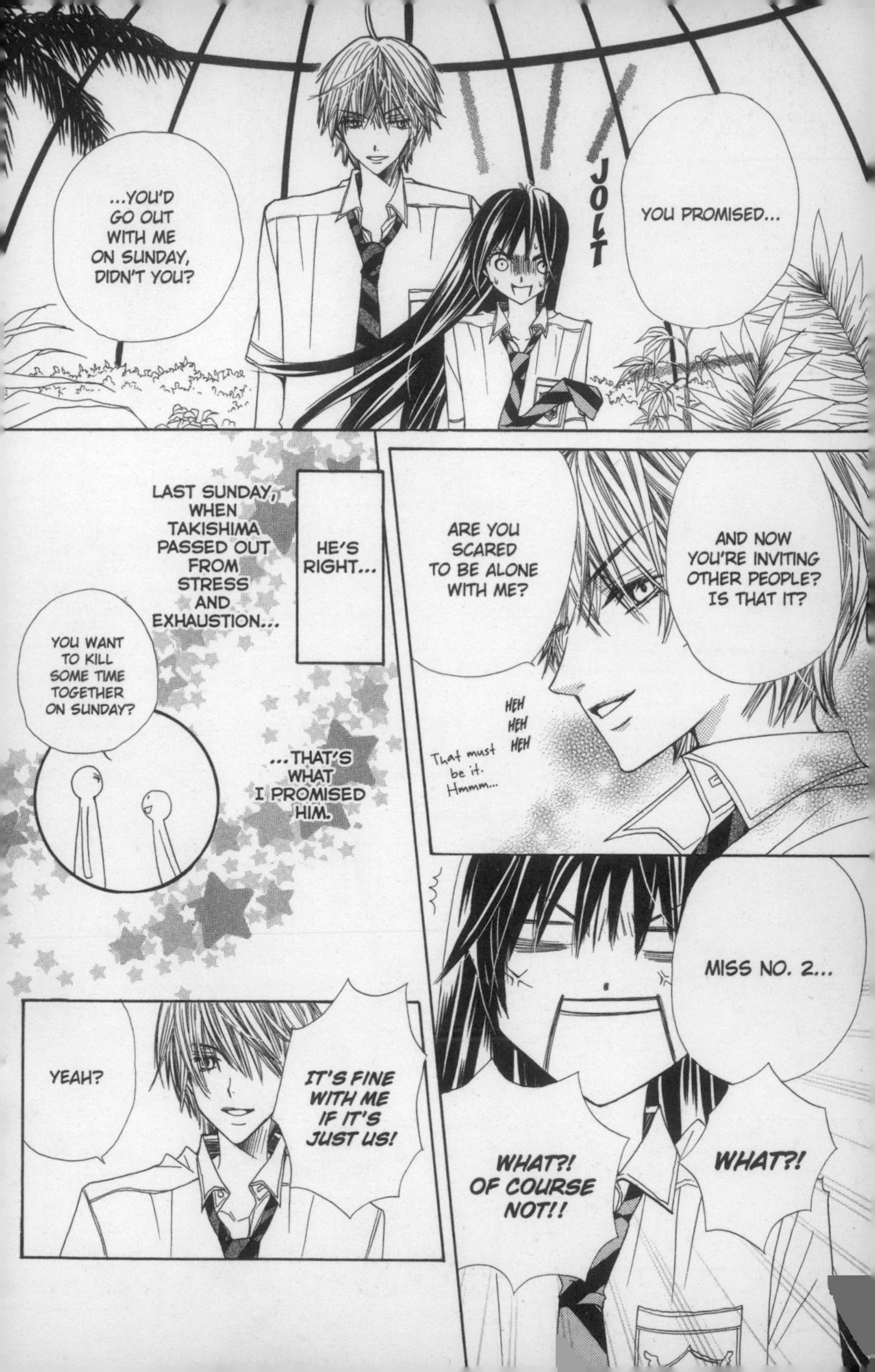
YOU PROMISED...
JOLT
...YOU'D GO OUT WITH ME ON SUNDAY, DIDN'T YOU?
AND NOW YOU'RE INVITING OTHER PEOPLE? IS THAT IT?
ARE YOU SCARED TO BE ALONE WITH ME?
HEH HEH HEH
That must be it. Hmmm...
HE'S RIGHT...
LAST SUNDAY, WHEN TAKISHIMA PASSED OUT FROM STRESS AND EXHAUSTION...
YOU WANT TO KILL SOME TIME TOGETHER ON SUNDAY?
...THAT'S WHAT I PROMISED HIM.
MISS NO. 2...
WHAT?!
WHAT?! OF COURSE NOT!!
IT'S FINE WITH ME IF IT'S JUST US!
YEAH?

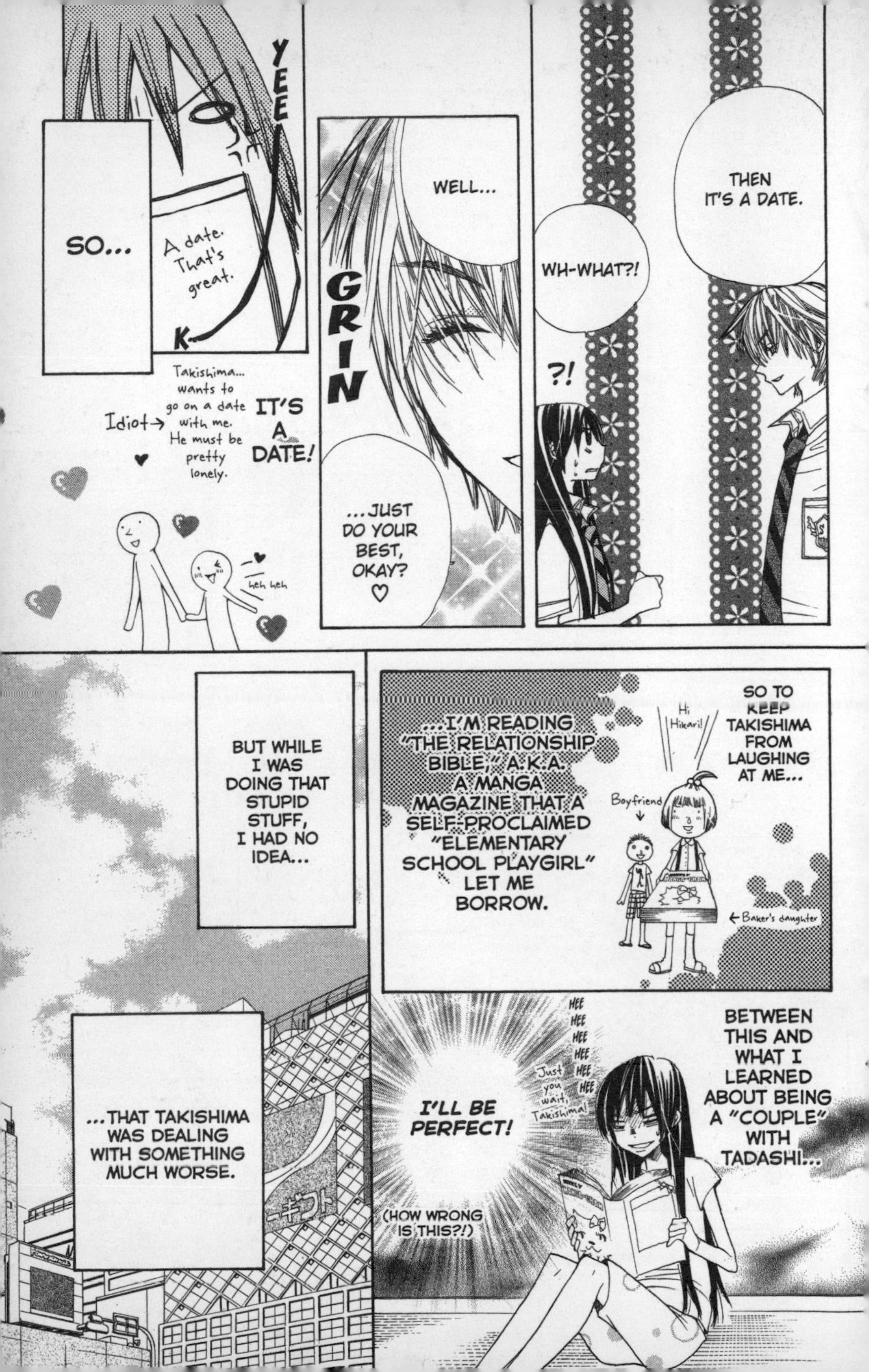
THEN IT'S A DATE.
WH-WHAT?!
?!
WELL...
GRIN
...JUST DO YOUR BEST, OKAY? ♡
YEEK
SO...
A date. That's great.
Takishima... wants to go on a date with me. He must be pretty lonely.
Idiot→
IT'S A DATE!
heh heh
SO TO KEEP TAKISHIMA FROM LAUGHING AT ME...
...I'M READING "THE RELATIONSHIP BIBLE," A.K.A. A MANGA MAGAZINE THAT A SELF-PROCLAIMED "ELEMENTARY SCHOOL PLAYGIRL" LET ME BORROW.
Hi Hikari!
Boyfriend
← Baker's daughter
BETWEEN THIS AND WHAT I LEARNED ABOUT BEING A "COUPLE" WITH TADASHI...
HEE HEE HEE HEE HEE HEE
Just you wait, Takishima!
I'LL BE PERFECT!
(HOW WRONG IS THIS?!)
BUT WHILE I WAS DOING THAT STUPID STUFF, I HAD NO IDEA...
...THAT TAKISHIMA WAS DEALING WITH SOMETHING MUCH WORSE.

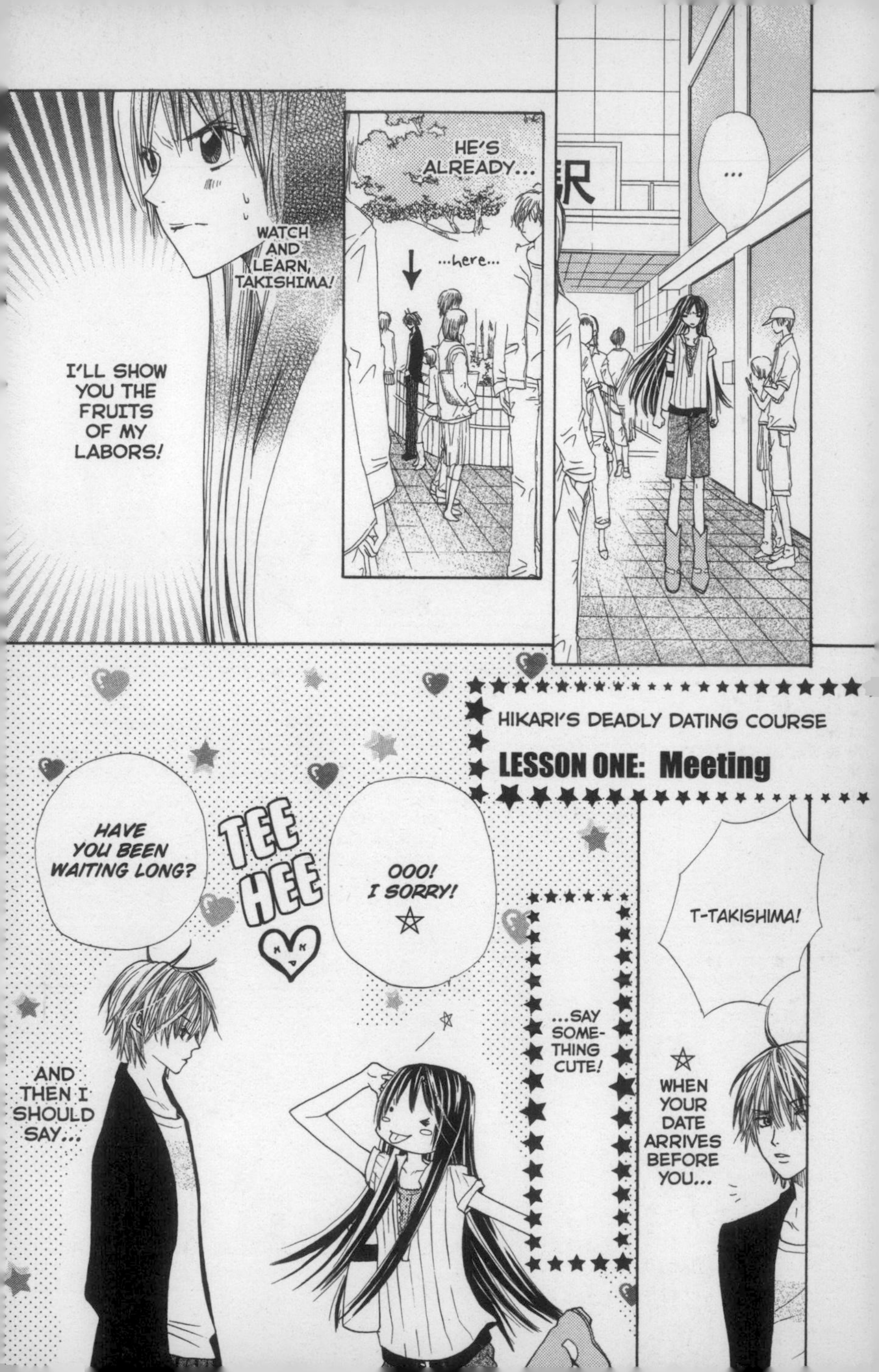
...
HE'S ALREADY...
...here...
WATCH AND LEARN, TAKISHIMA!
I'LL SHOW YOU THE FRUITS OF MY LABORS!
HIKARI'S DEADLY DATING COURSE
LESSON ONE: Meeting
T-TAKISHIMA!
☆ WHEN YOUR DATE ARRIVES BEFORE YOU...
...SAY SOMETHING CUTE!
OOO! I SORRY! ☆
TEE HEE
HAVE YOU BEEN WAITING LONG?
AND THEN I SHOULD SAY...

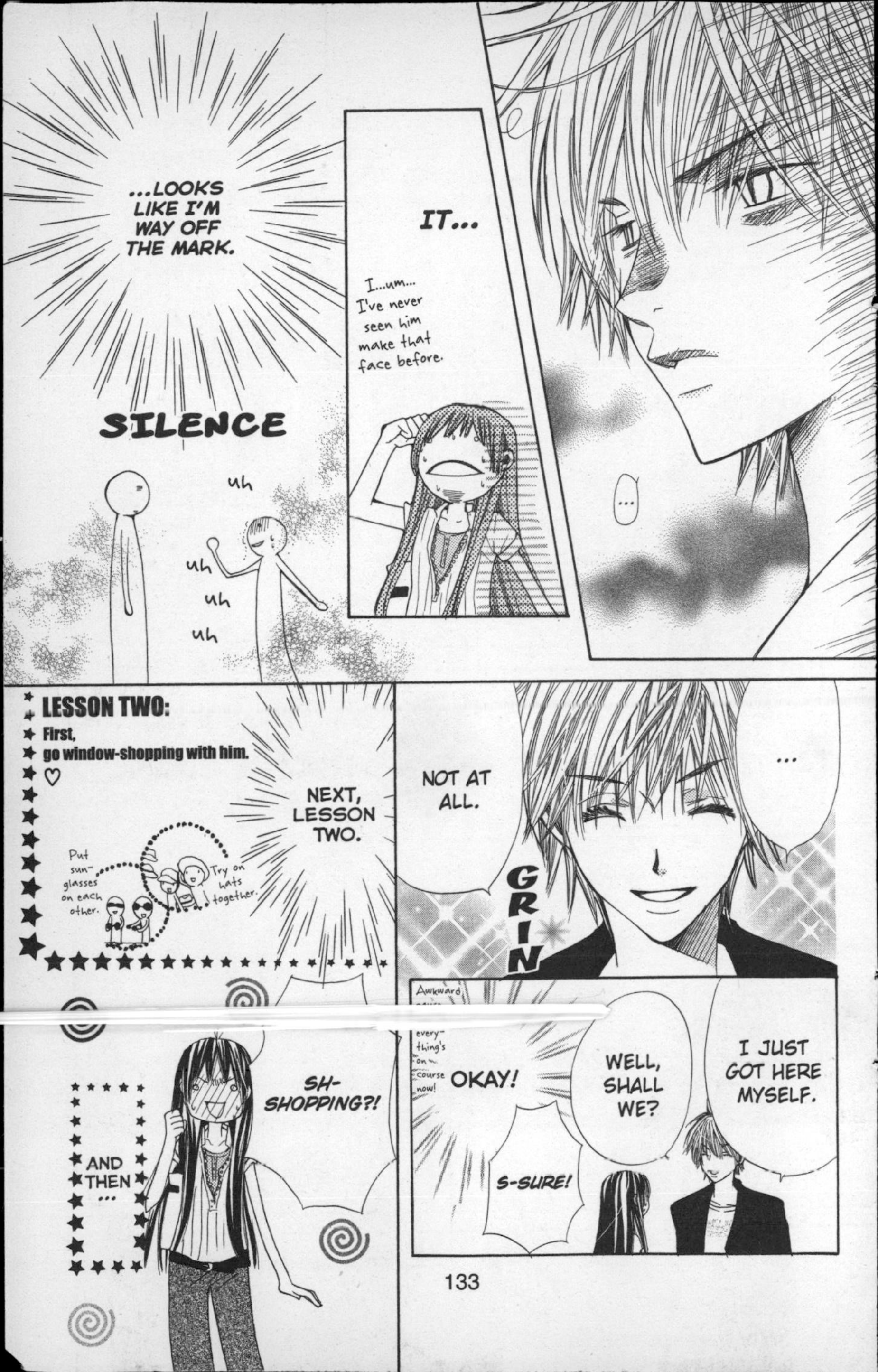
...
IT...
I...um... I've never seen him make that face before.
...LOOKS LIKE I'M WAY OFF THE MARK.
SILENCE
uh
uh
uh
uh
...
NOT AT ALL.
GRIN
I JUST GOT HERE MYSELF.
WELL, SHALL WE?
OKAY!
S-SURE!
Awkward
every-thing's on course now!
LESSON TWO:
First, go window-shopping with him. ♡
Put sun-glasses on each other.
Try on hats together.
NEXT, LESSON TWO.
SH-SHOPPING?!
AND THEN ...

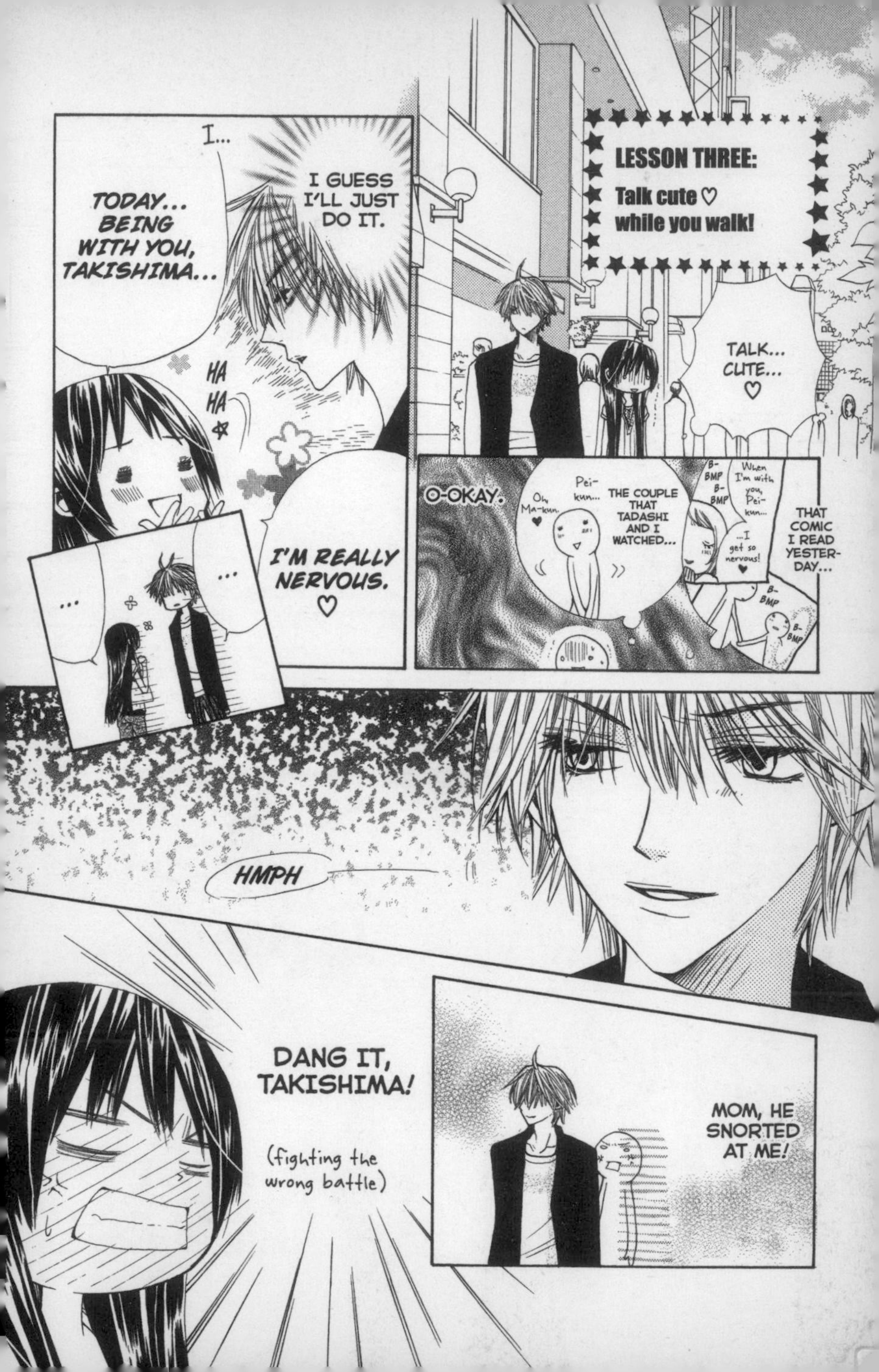

LESSON THREE:
Talk cute ♡ while you walk!
TALK... CUTE... ♡
THAT COMIC I READ YESTERDAY...
B-BMP B-BMP
When I'm with you, Pei-kun...
...I get so nervous! ♥
B-BMP
B-BMP
THE COUPLE THAT TADASHI AND I WATCHED...
Pei-kun...
Oh, Ma-kun. ♥
O-OKAY.
I...
I GUESS I'LL JUST DO IT.
TODAY... BEING WITH YOU, TAKISHIMA...
HA HA
I'M REALLY NERVOUS. ♡
...
...
HMPH
MOM, HE SNORTED AT ME!
DANG IT, TAKISHIMA!
(fighting the wrong battle)

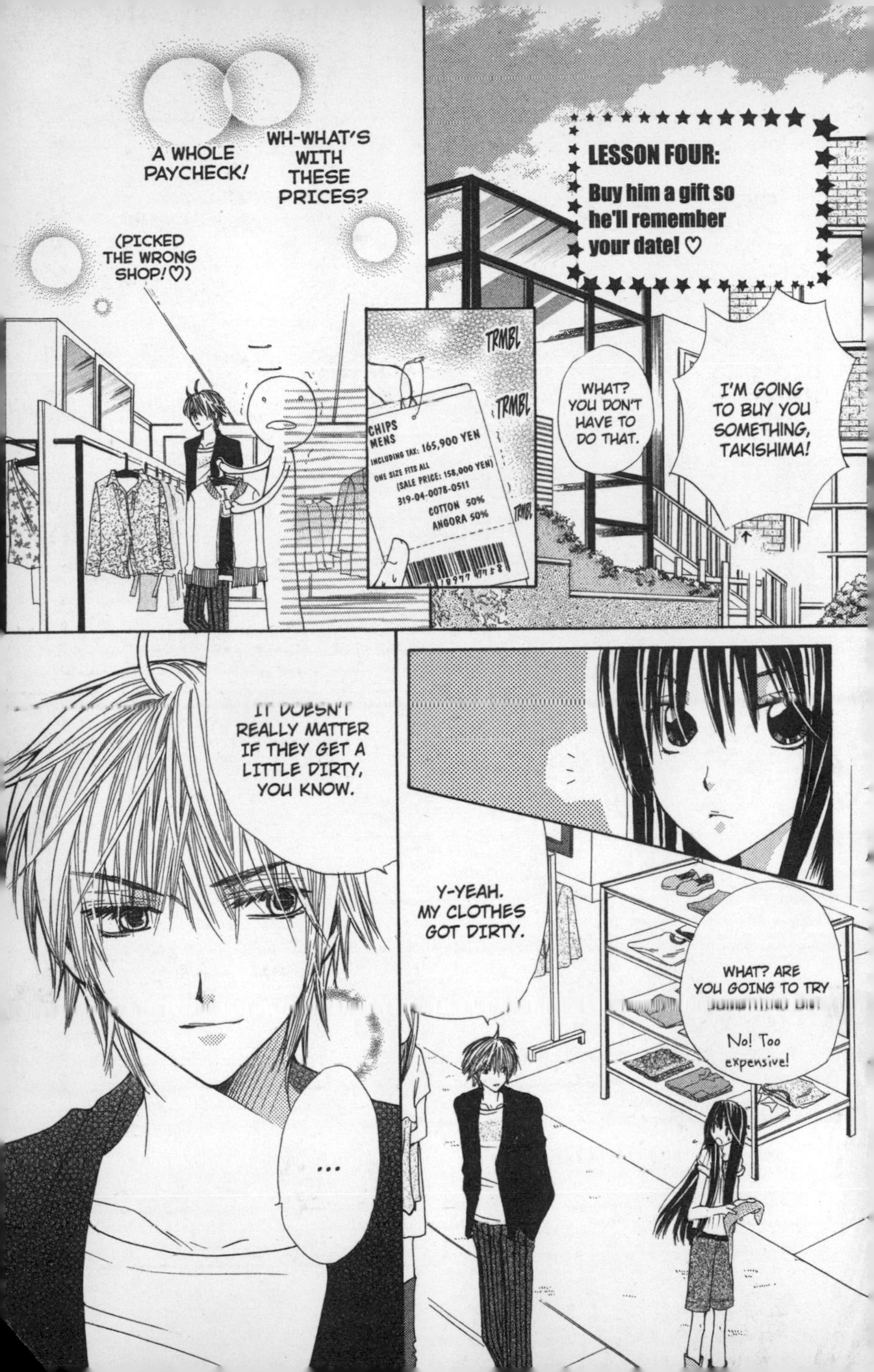
LESSON FOUR:
Buy him a gift so he'll remember your date! ♡
I'M GOING TO BUY YOU SOMETHING, TAKISHIMA!
WHAT? YOU DON'T HAVE TO DO THAT.
TRMBL
TRMBL
TRMBL
CHIPS MENS
INCLUDING TAX: 165,900 YEN
ONE SIZE FITS ALL
(SALE PRICE: 158,000 YEN)
319-04-0078-0511
COTTON 50%
ANGORA 50%
WH-WHAT'S WITH THESE PRICES?
A WHOLE PAYCHECK!
(PICKED THE WRONG SHOP!♡)
WHAT? ARE YOU GOING TO TRY
No! Too expensive!
Y-YEAH. MY CLOTHES GOT DIRTY.
IT DOESN'T REALLY MATTER IF THEY GET A LITTLE DIRTY, YOU KNOW.
...

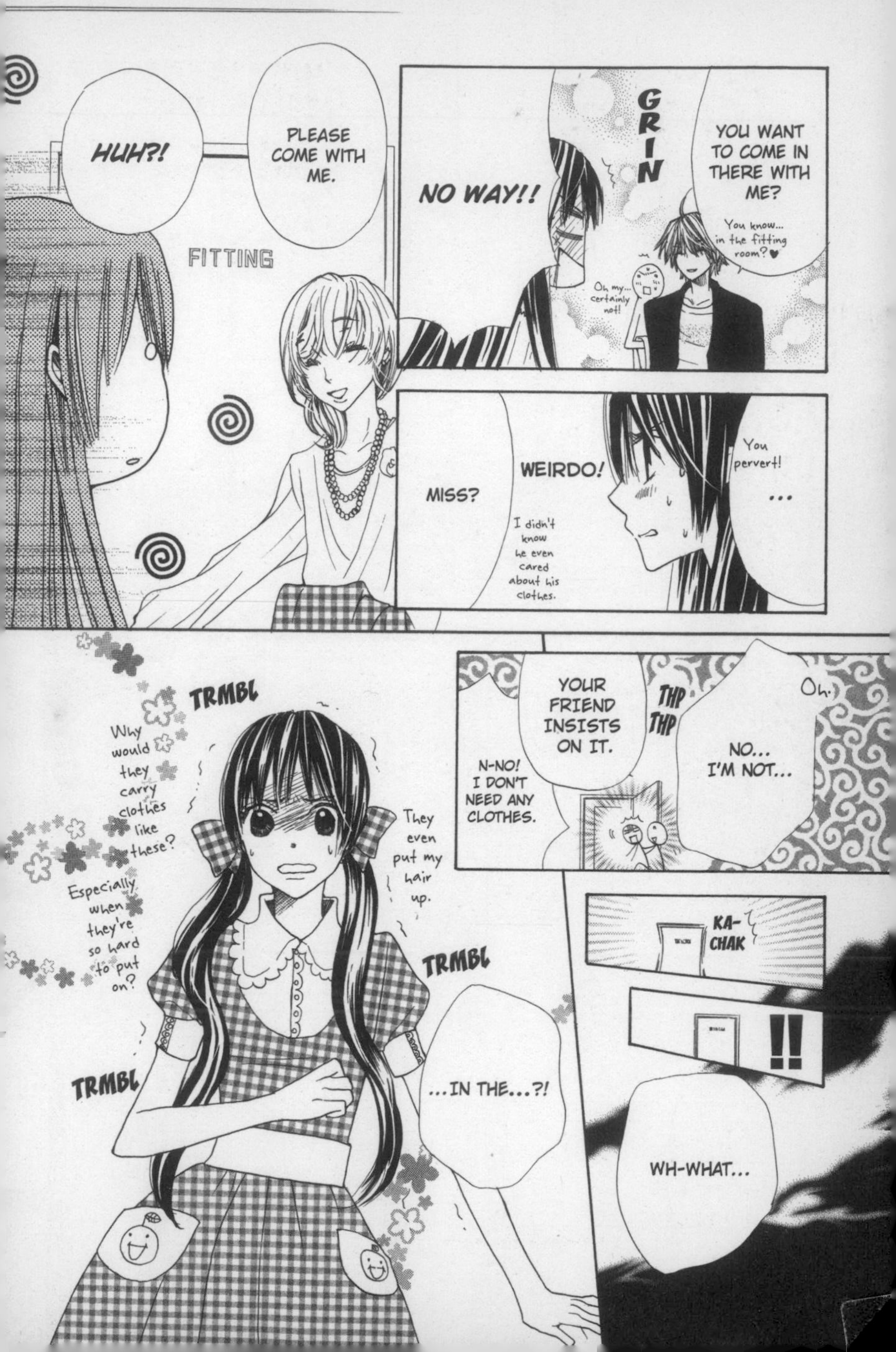
YOU WANT TO COME IN THERE WITH ME?
You know... in the fitting room?♥
GRIN
NO WAY!!
Oh my... certainly not!
You pervert!
...
WEIRDO!
I didn't know he even cared about his clothes.
MISS?
PLEASE COME WITH ME.
HUH?!
FITTING
Oh.
NO... I'M NOT...
THP THP
YOUR FRIEND INSISTS ON IT.
N-NO! I DON'T NEED ANY CLOTHES.
KA-CHAK
!!
WH-WHAT...
...IN THE...?!
TRMBL
They even put my hair up.
TRMBL
Why would they carry clothes like these?
Especially when they're so hard to put on?
TRMBL

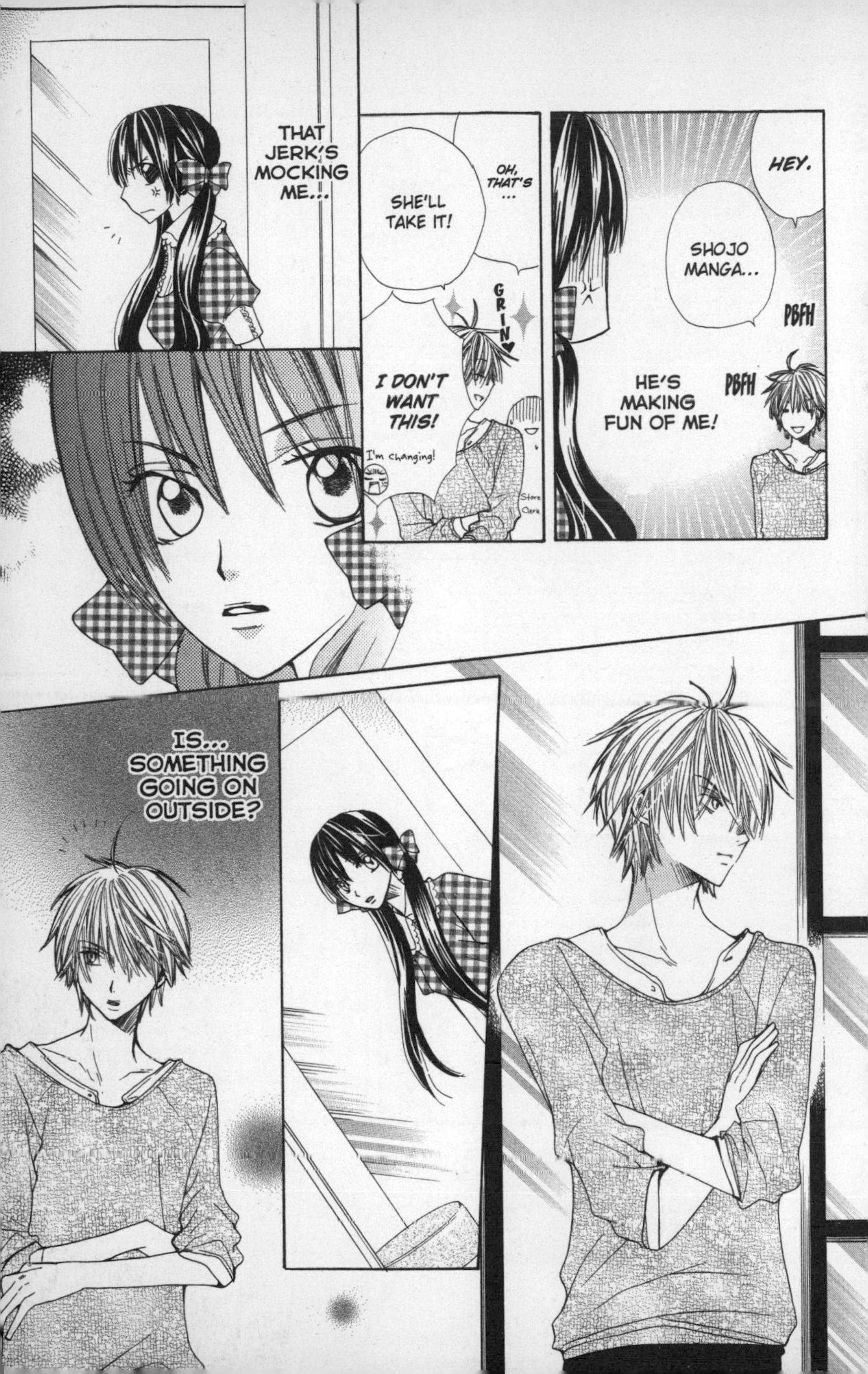
HEY.
SHOJO MANGA...
PBFH
PBFH
HE'S MAKING FUN OF ME!
OH, THAT'S...
SHE'LL TAKE IT!
GRIN
I DON'T WANT THIS!
I'm changing!
Store Clerk
THAT JERK'S MOCKING ME...
IS... SOMETHING GOING ON OUTSIDE?

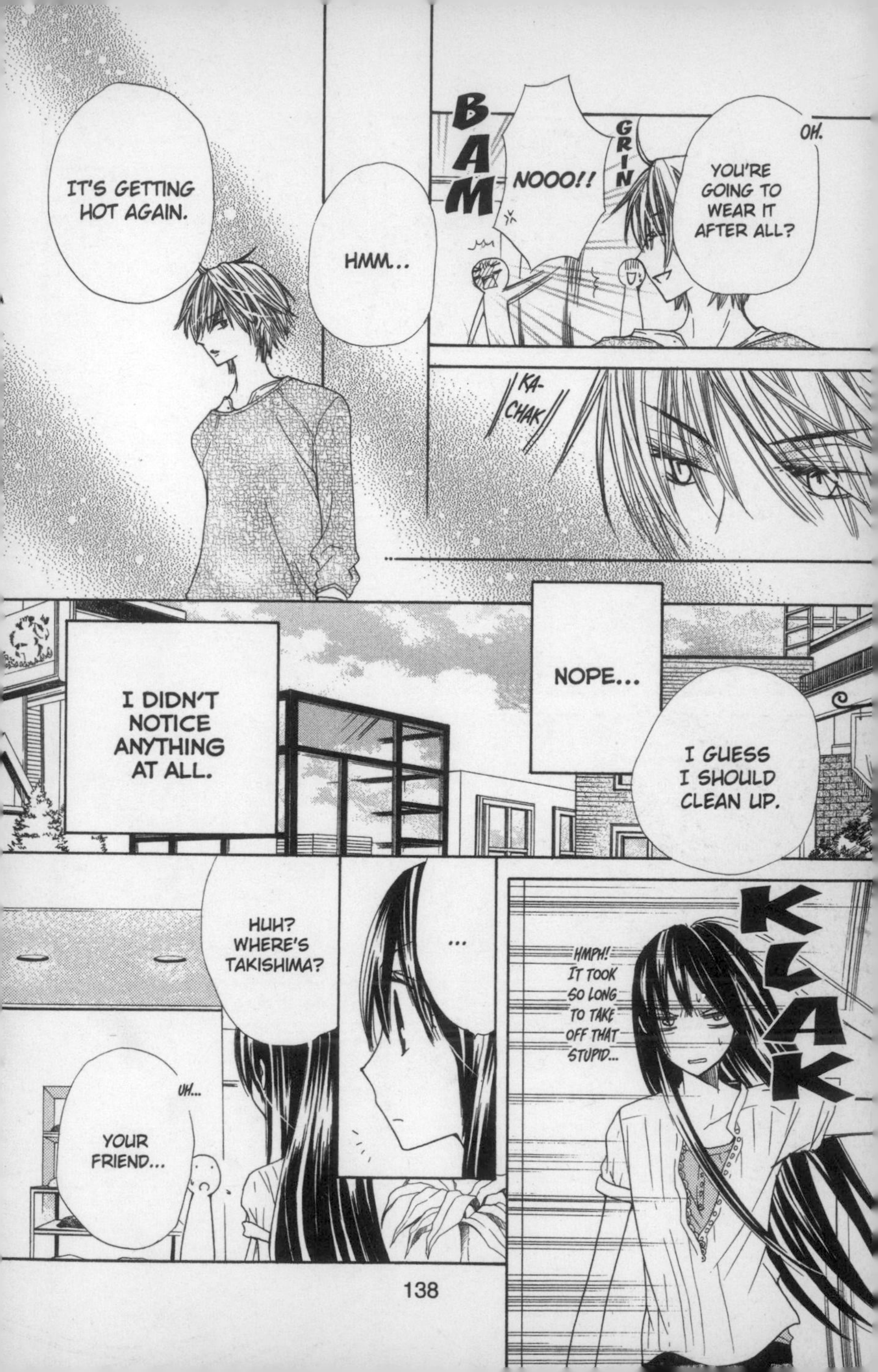
OH.
YOU'RE GOING TO WEAR IT AFTER ALL?
GRIN
NOOO!!
BAM
KA-CHAK
HMM..
IT'S GETTING HOT AGAIN.
NOPE...
I GUESS I SHOULD CLEAN UP.
I DIDN'T NOTICE ANYTHING AT ALL.
KLAK
HMPH! IT TOOK SO LONG TO TAKE OFF THAT STUPID...
...
HUH? WHERE'S TAKISHIMA?
UH...
YOUR FRIEND...

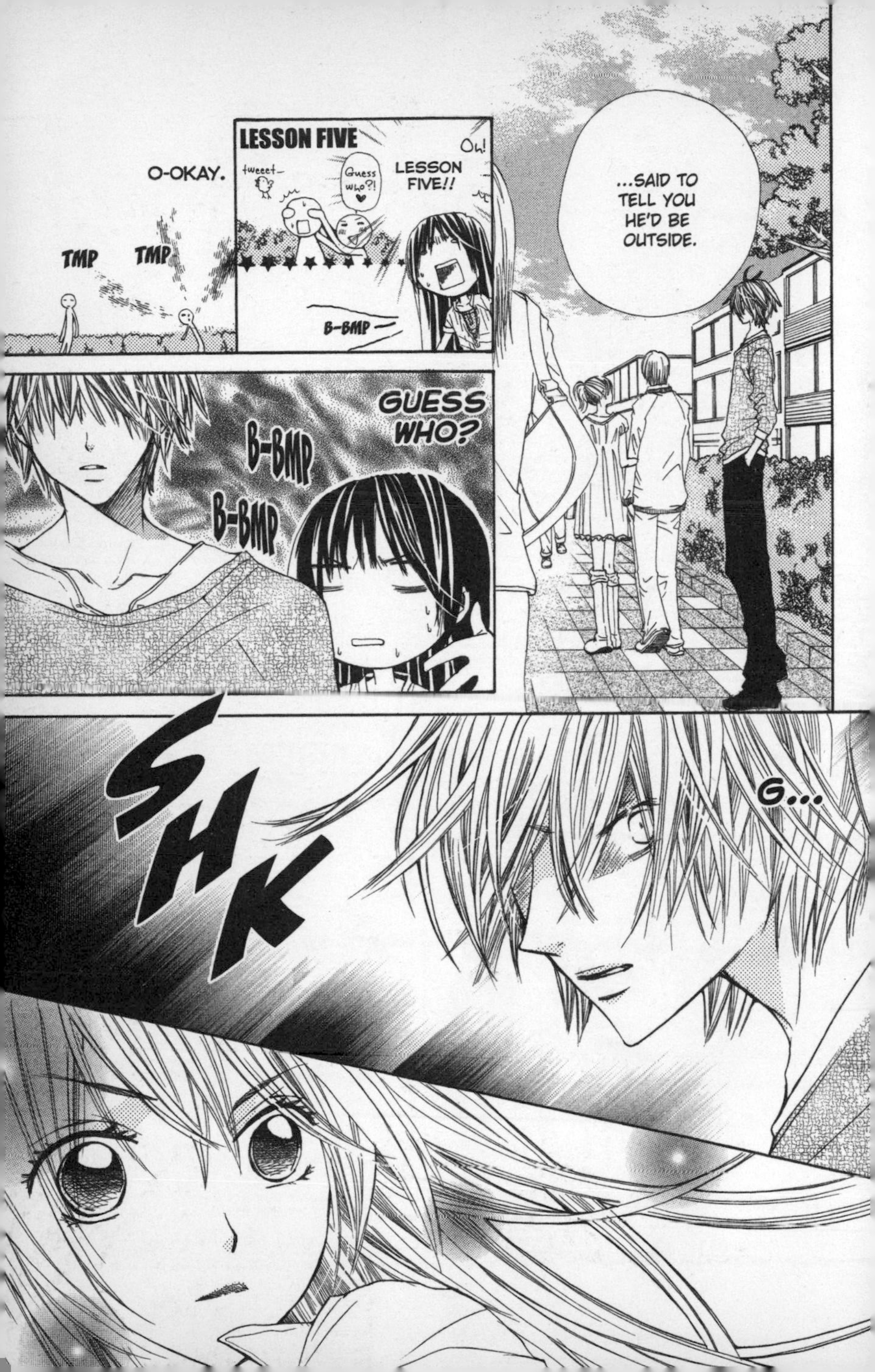
...SAID TO TELL YOU HE'D BE OUTSIDE.
LESSON FIVE
Oh!
LESSON FIVE!!
Guess who?!
tweeet
B-BMP
O-OKAY.
TMP
TMP
GUESS WHO?
B-BMP
B-BMP
G...
SHK

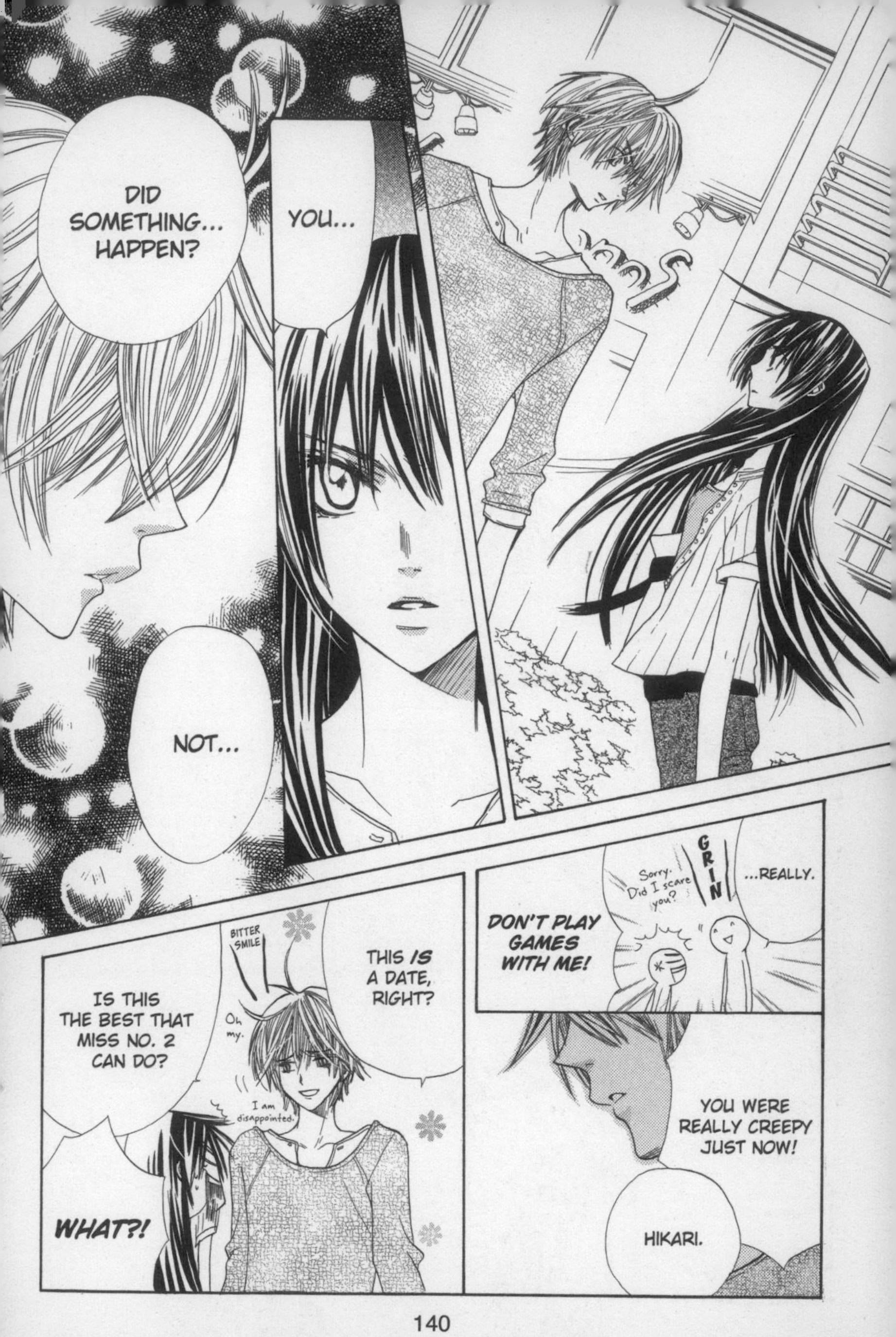
YOU...
DID SOMETHING... HAPPEN?
NOT...
...REALLY.
GRIN
Sorry. Did I scare you?
DON'T PLAY GAMES WITH ME!
YOU WERE REALLY CREEPY JUST NOW!
HIKARI.
THIS *IS* A DATE, RIGHT?
BITTER SMILE
Oh my.
IS THIS THE BEST THAT MISS NO. 2 CAN DO?
I am disappointed.
WHAT?!

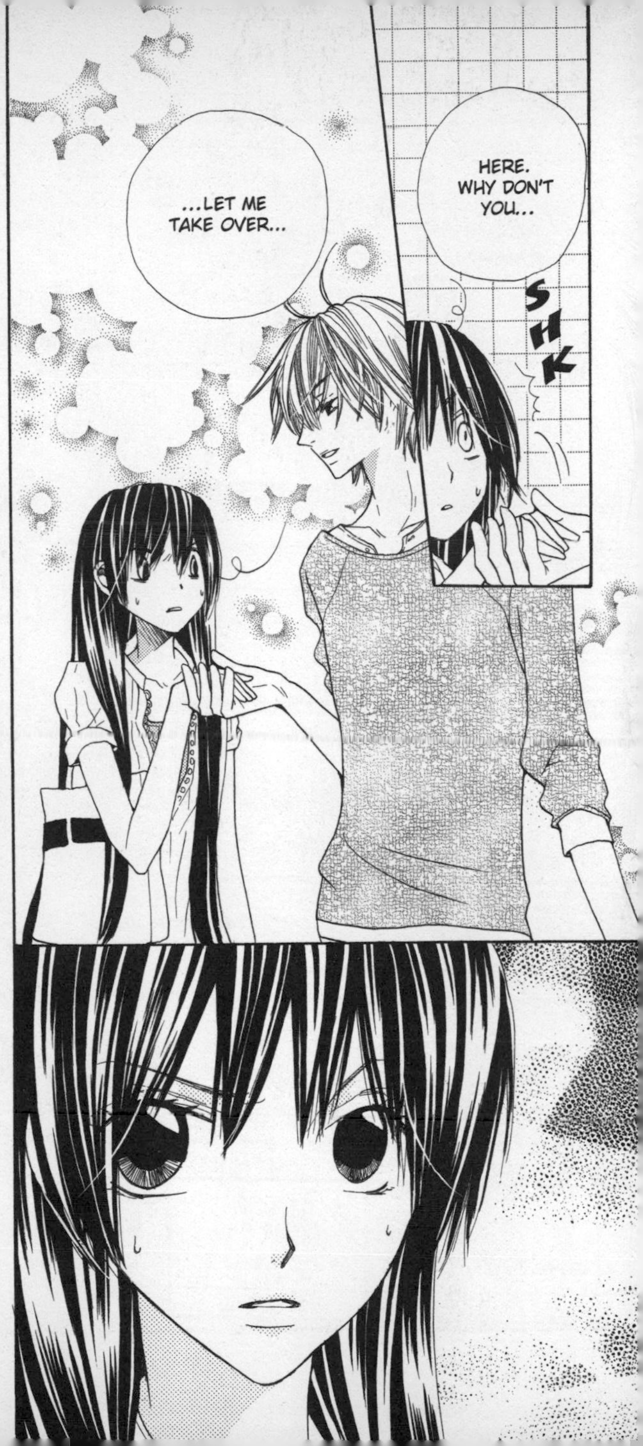
HERE. WHY DON'T YOU...
SHK
...LET ME TAKE OVER...

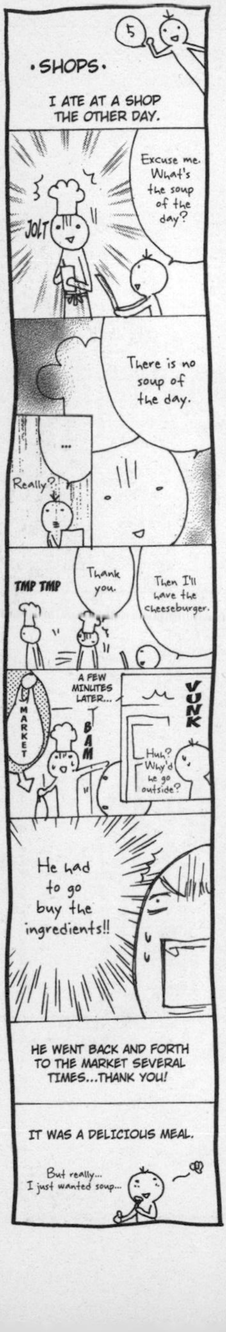
5
•SHOPS•
I ATE AT A SHOP THE OTHER DAY.
Excuse me. What's the soup of the day?
JOLT
There is no soup of the day.
...
Really?
Thank you.
Then I'll have the cheeseburger.
TMP TMP
A FEW MINUTES LATER...
VUNK
BAM
MARKET
Huh? Why'd he go outside?
He had to go buy the ingredients!!
HE WENT BACK AND FORTH TO THE MARKET SEVERAL TIMES...THANK YOU!
IT WAS A DELICIOUS MEAL.
But really... I just wanted soup...

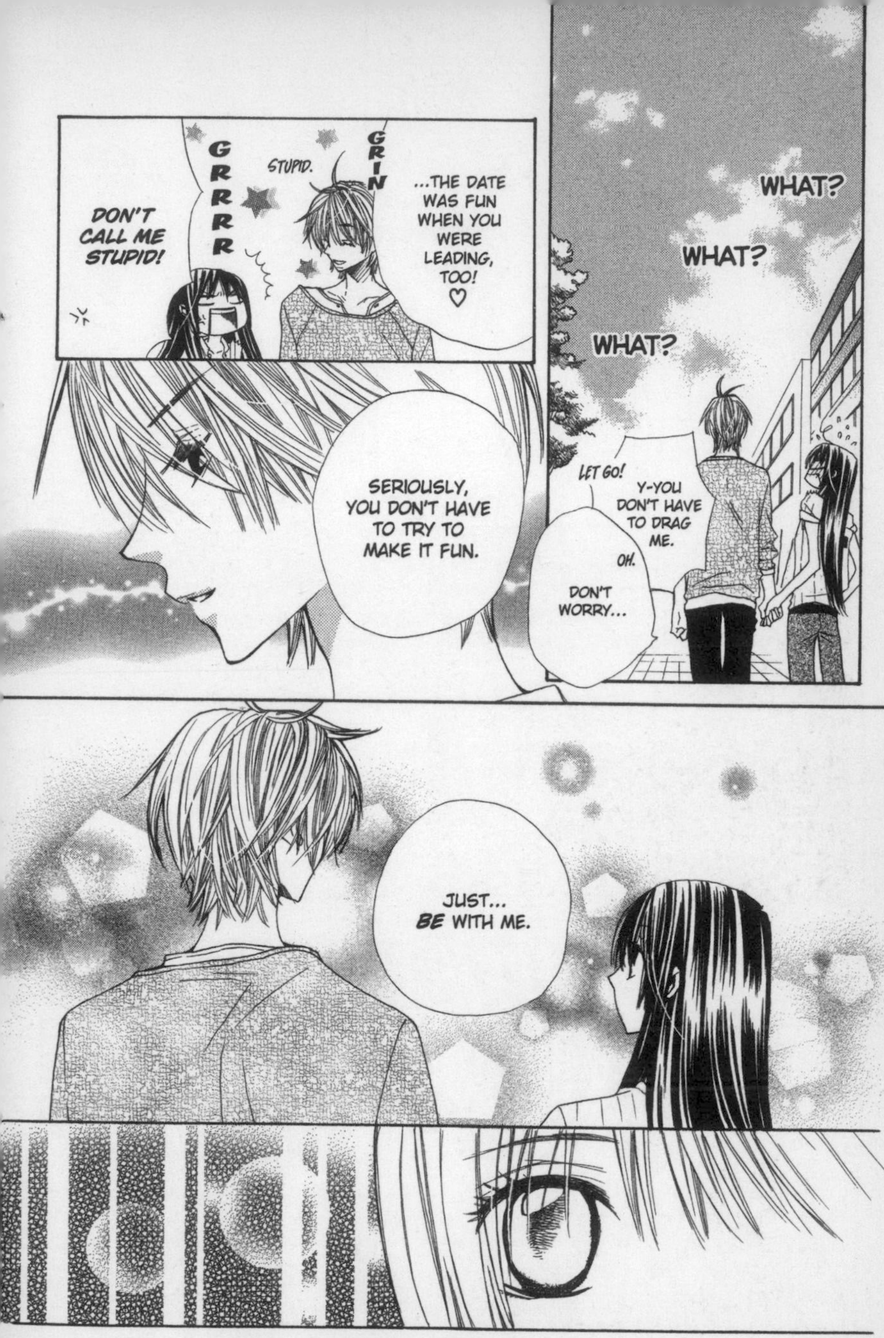
WHAT?
WHAT?
WHAT?
LET GO!
Y-YOU DON'T HAVE TO DRAG ME.
OH.
DON'T WORRY...
GRIN
...THE DATE WAS FUN WHEN YOU WERE LEADING, TOO! ♡
STUPID.
GRRRR
DON'T CALL ME STUPID!
SERIOUSLY, YOU DON'T HAVE TO TRY TO MAKE IT FUN.
JUST... *BE* WITH ME.

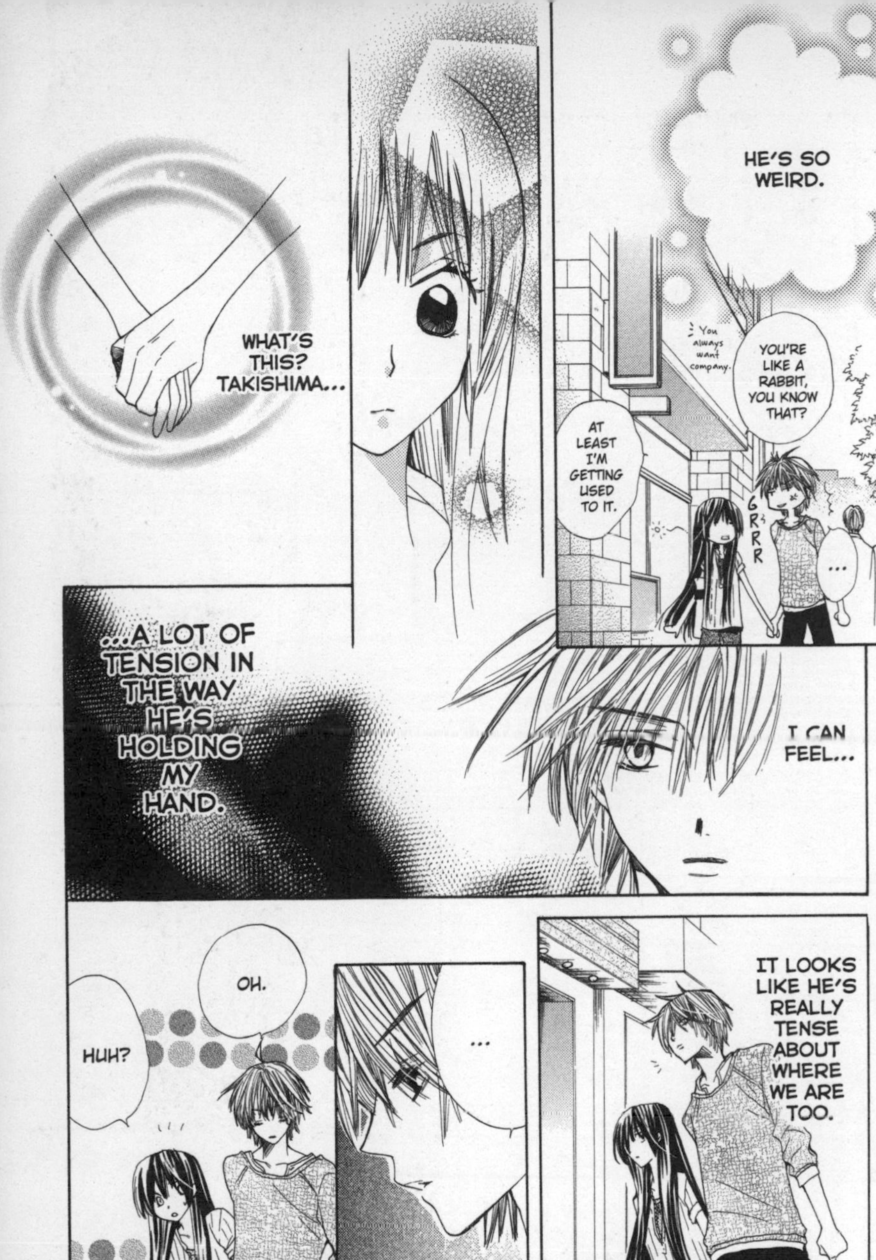
HE'S SO WEIRD.
YOU'RE LIKE A RABBIT, YOU KNOW THAT?
You always want company.
AT LEAST I'M GETTING USED TO IT.
GRRR
...
WHAT'S THIS? TAKISHIMA...
I CAN FEEL...
...A LOT OF TENSION IN THE WAY HE'S HOLDING MY HAND.
IT LOOKS LIKE HE'S REALLY TENSE ABOUT WHERE WE ARE TOO.
...
OH.
HUH?

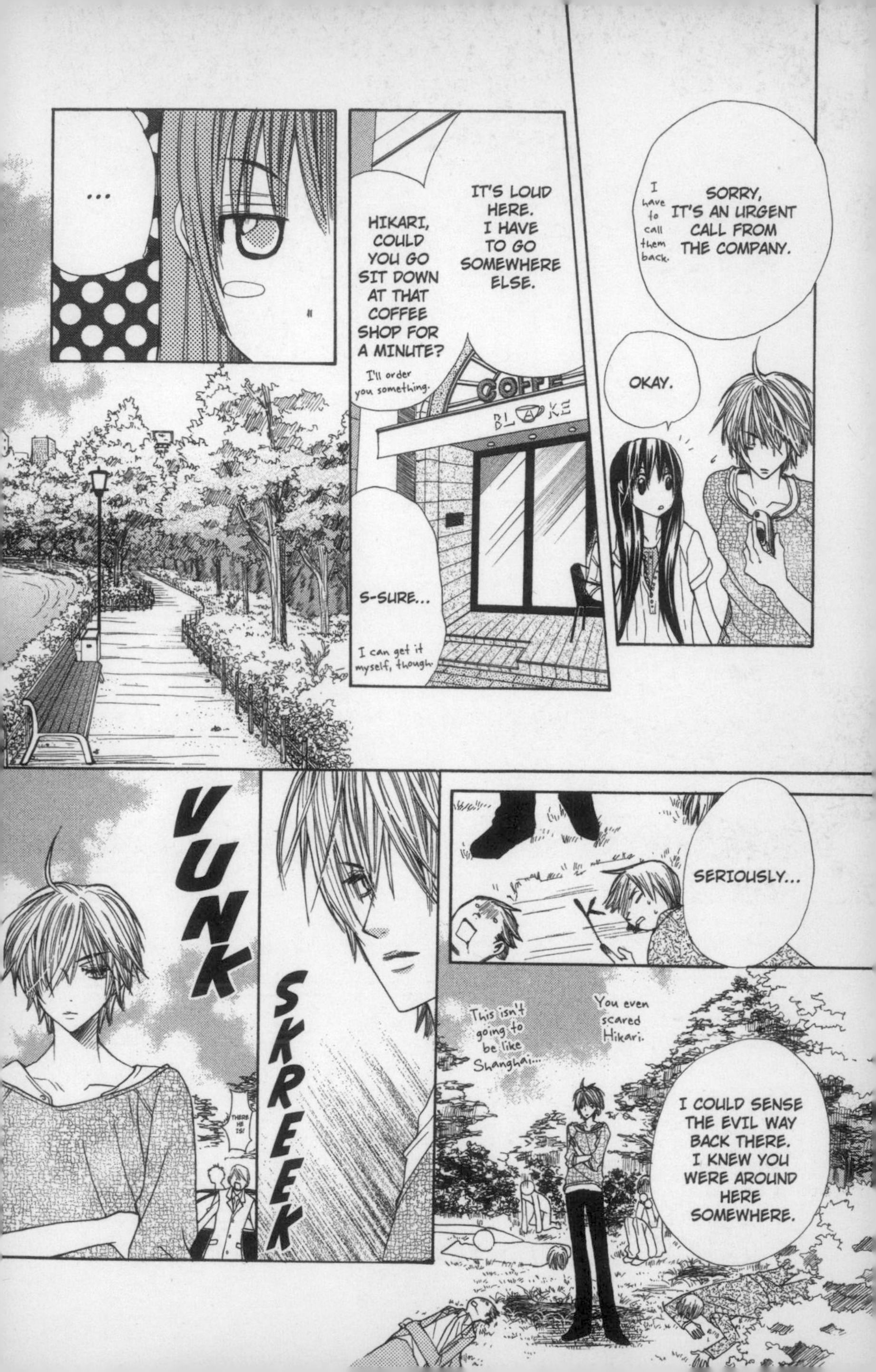
SORRY, IT'S AN URGENT CALL FROM THE COMPANY.
I have to call them back.
OKAY.
IT'S LOUD HERE. I HAVE TO GO SOMEWHERE ELSE.
HIKARI, COULD YOU GO SIT DOWN AT THAT COFFEE SHOP FOR A MINUTE?
I'll order you something.
S-SURE...
I can get it myself, though.
...
SERIOUSLY...
You even scared Hikari.
This isn't going to be like Shanghai...
I COULD SENSE THE EVIL WAY BACK THERE. I KNEW YOU WERE AROUND HERE SOMEWHERE.
SKREEK
VUNK
THERE HE IS!

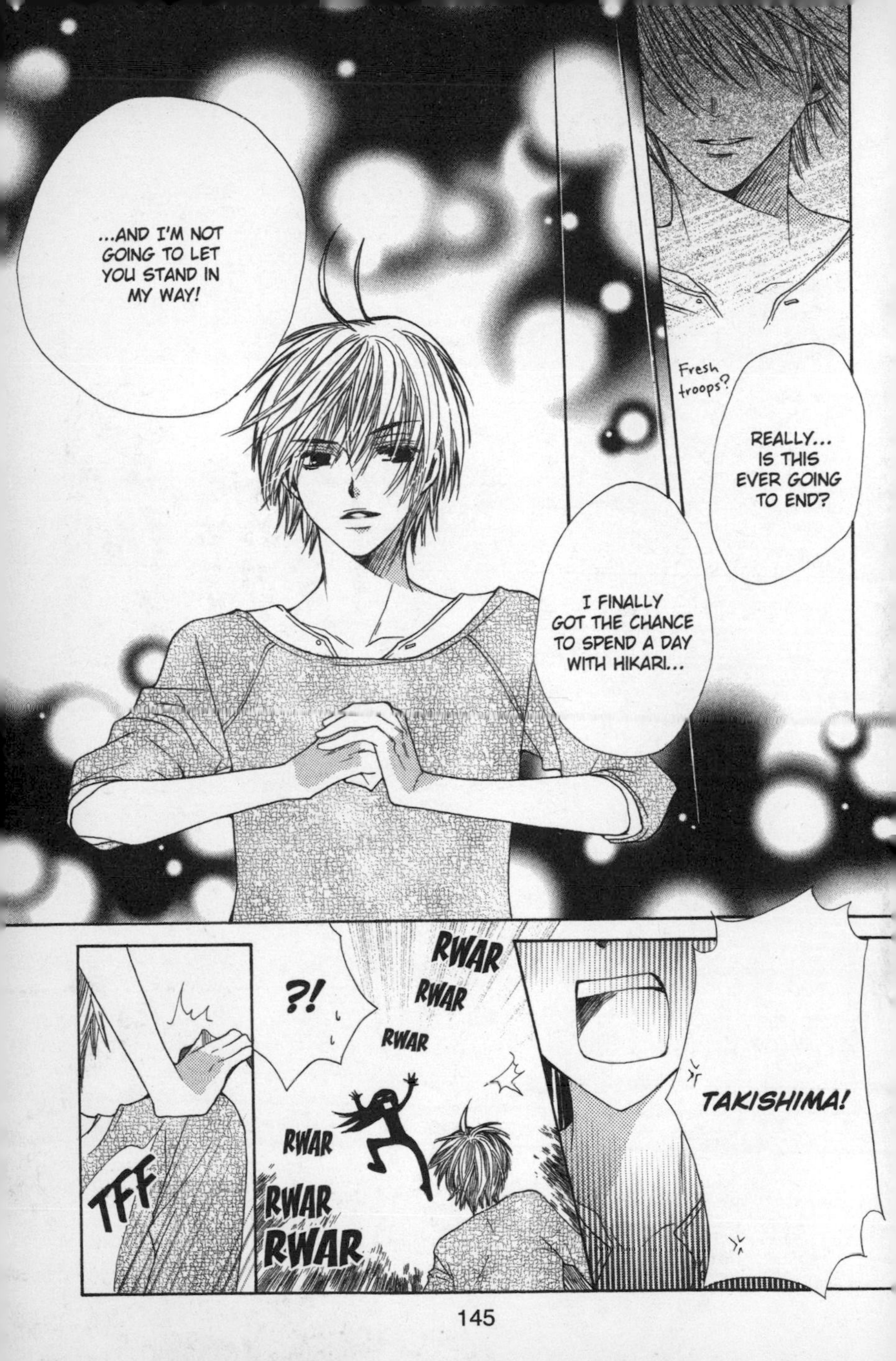
Fresh troops?
REALLY... IS THIS EVER GOING TO END?
I FINALLY GOT THE CHANCE TO SPEND A DAY WITH HIKARI...
...AND I'M NOT GOING TO LET YOU STAND IN MY WAY!
TAKISHIMA!
RWAR
RWAR
RWAR
?!
RWAR
RWAR
RWAR
TFF

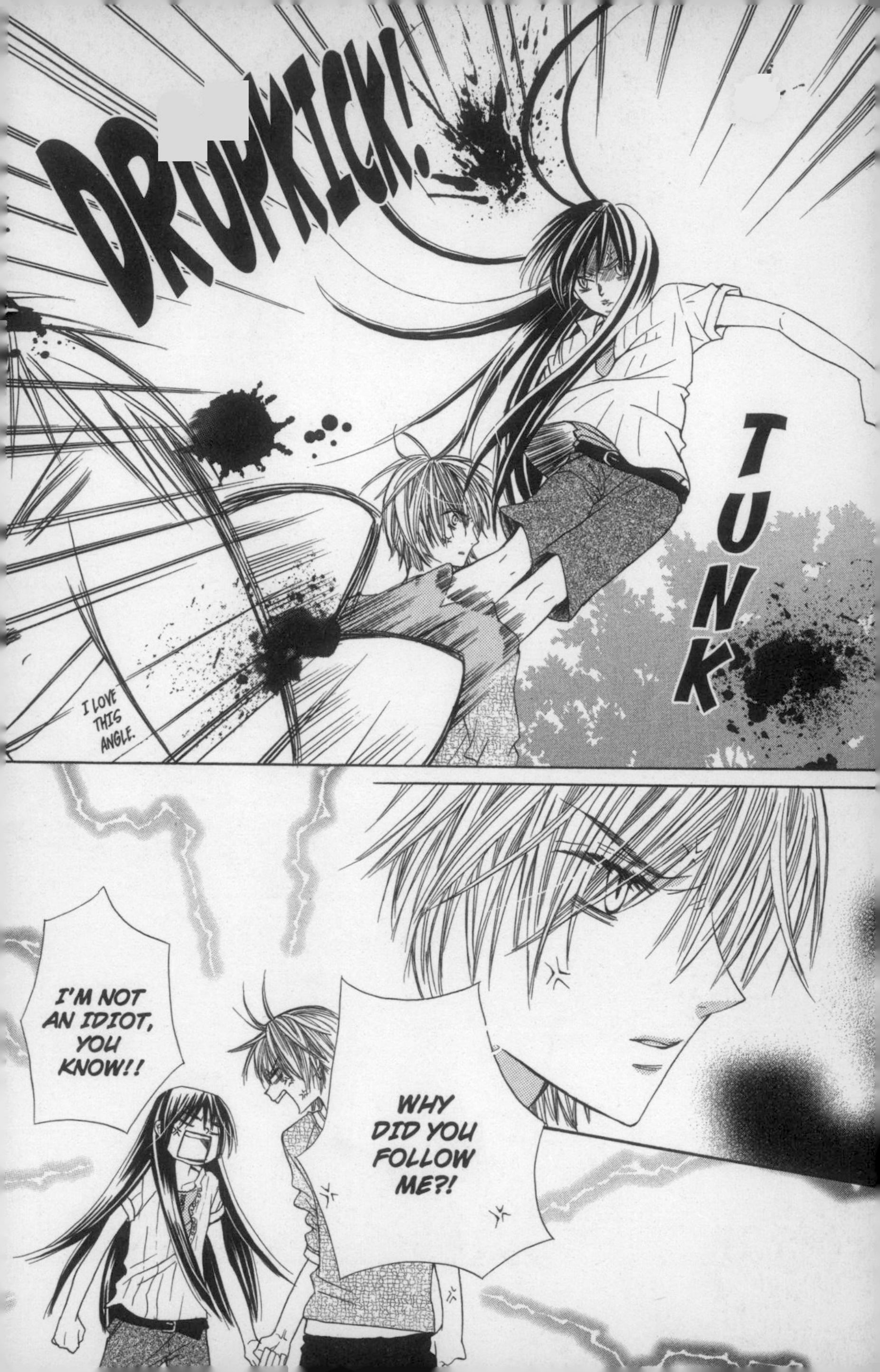
DROPKICK!
TUNK
I LOVE THIS ANGLE.
WHY DID YOU FOLLOW ME?!
I'M NOT AN IDIOT, YOU KNOW!!

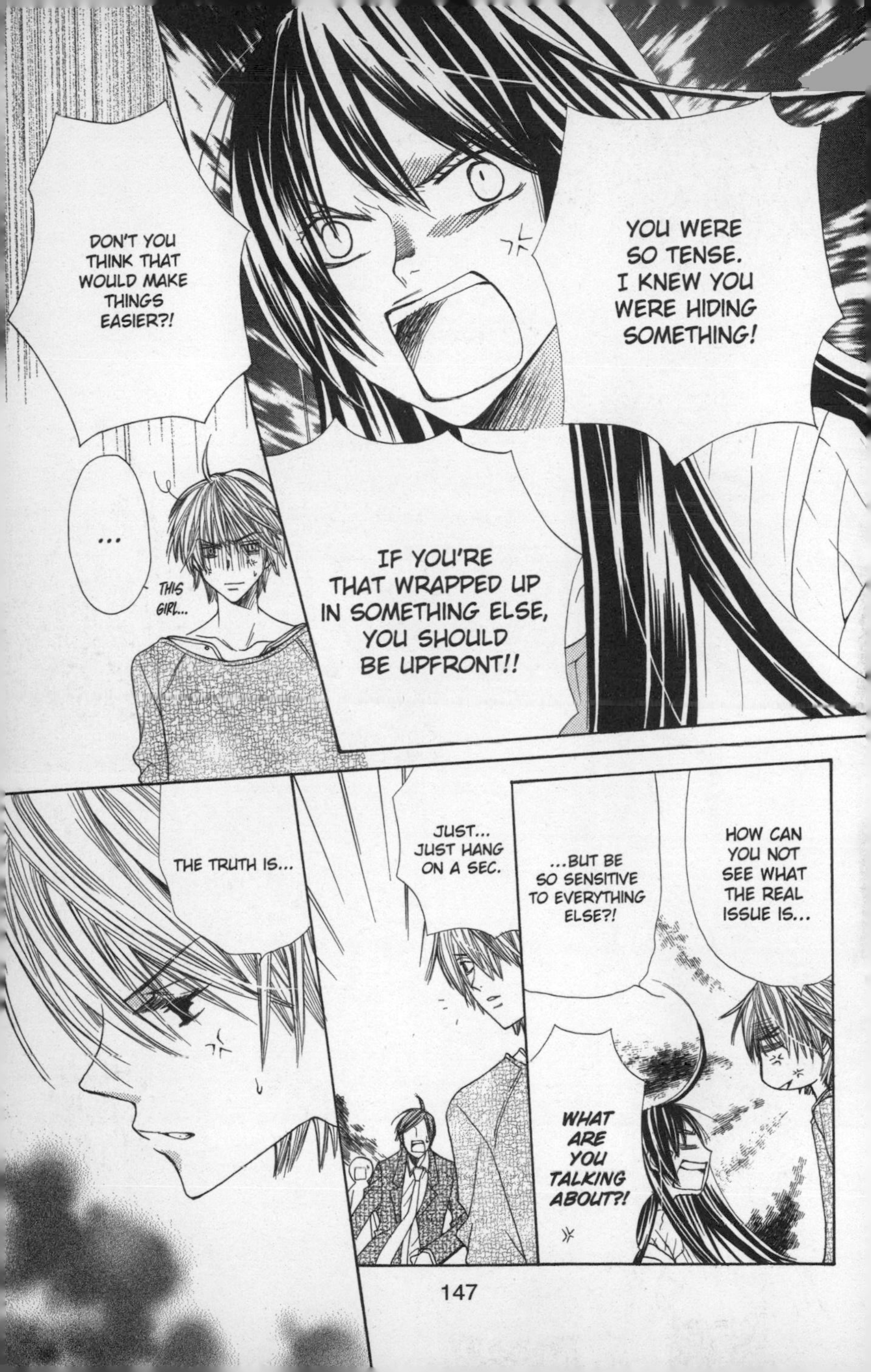
YOU WERE SO TENSE. I KNEW YOU WERE HIDING SOMETHING!
DON'T YOU THINK THAT WOULD MAKE THINGS EASIER?!
IF YOU'RE THAT WRAPPED UP IN SOMETHING ELSE, YOU SHOULD BE UPFRONT!!
...
THIS GIRL...
HOW CAN YOU NOT SEE WHAT THE REAL ISSUE IS...
...BUT BE SO SENSITIVE TO EVERYTHING ELSE?!
WHAT ARE YOU TALKING ABOUT?!
JUST... JUST HANG ON A SEC.
THE TRUTH IS...

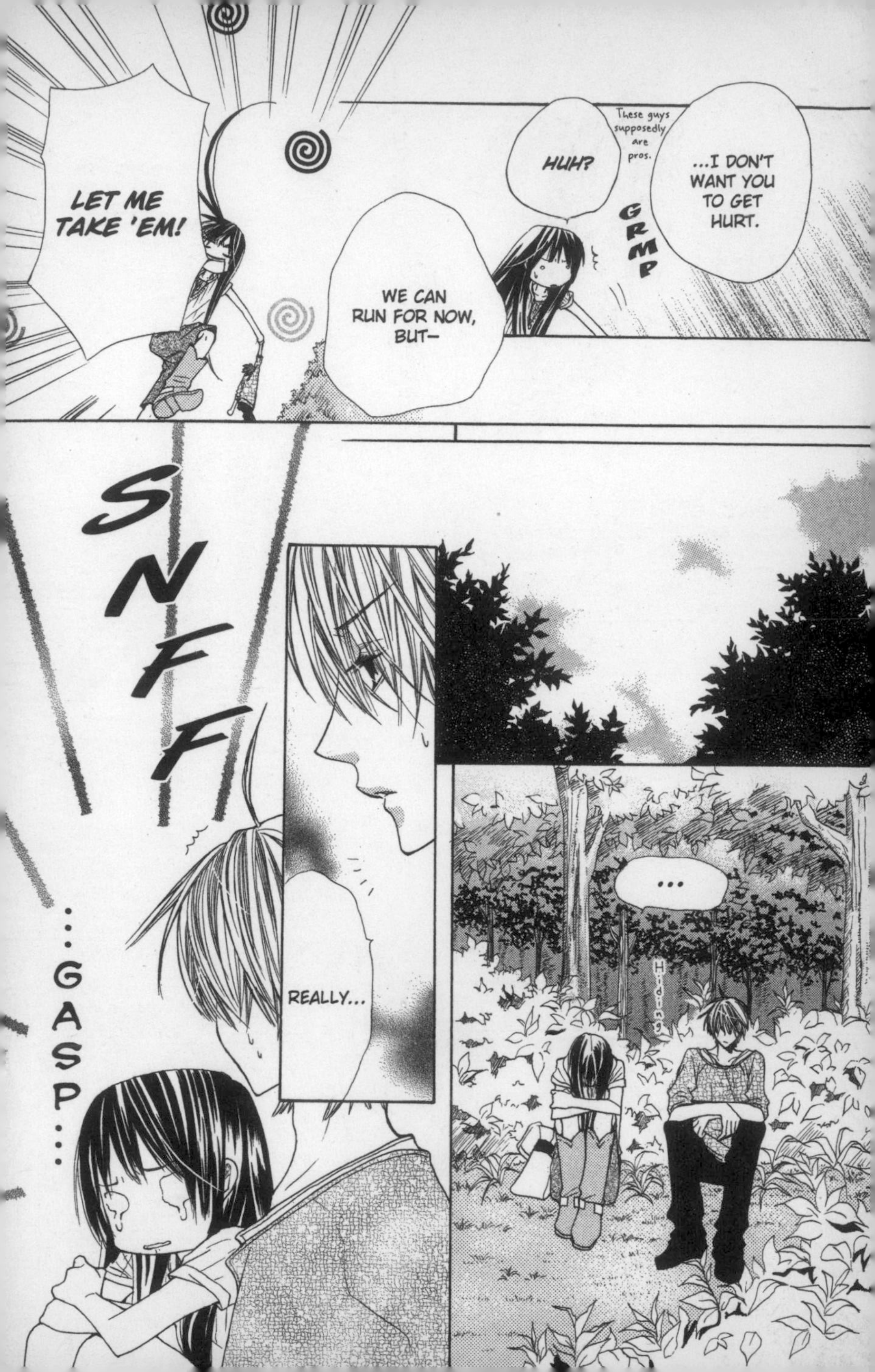
...I DON'T WANT YOU TO GET HURT.
HUH?
These guys supposedly are pros.
GRMP
WE CAN RUN FOR NOW, BUT–
LET ME TAKE 'EM!
...
Hiding
REALLY...
SNFF
...GASP...

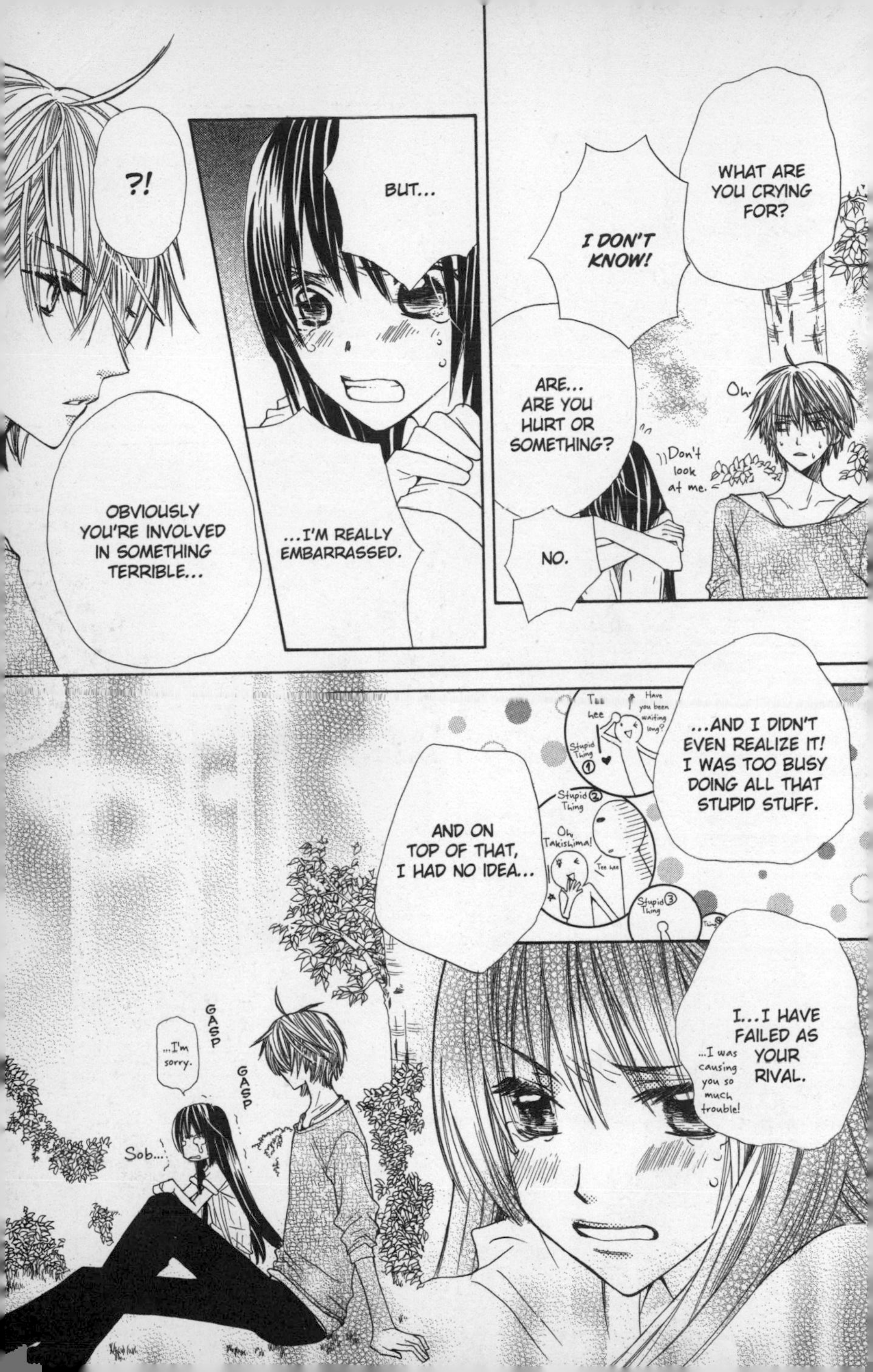
WHAT ARE YOU CRYING FOR?
I DON'T KNOW!
ARE... ARE YOU HURT OR SOMETHING?
Oh.
Don't look at me.
NO.
BUT...
...I'M REALLY EMBARRASSED.
?!
OBVIOUSLY YOU'RE INVOLVED IN SOMETHING TERRIBLE...
...AND I DIDN'T EVEN REALIZE IT! I WAS TOO BUSY DOING ALL THAT STUPID STUFF.
Have you been waiting long?
Tee hee
Stupid Thing ①
Stupid Thing ②
Tee hee
Oh, Takishima!
Stupid Thing ③
AND ON TOP OF THAT, I HAD NO IDEA...
I...I HAVE FAILED AS YOUR RIVAL.
...I was causing you so much trouble!
GASP
GASP
...I'm sorry.
Sob...

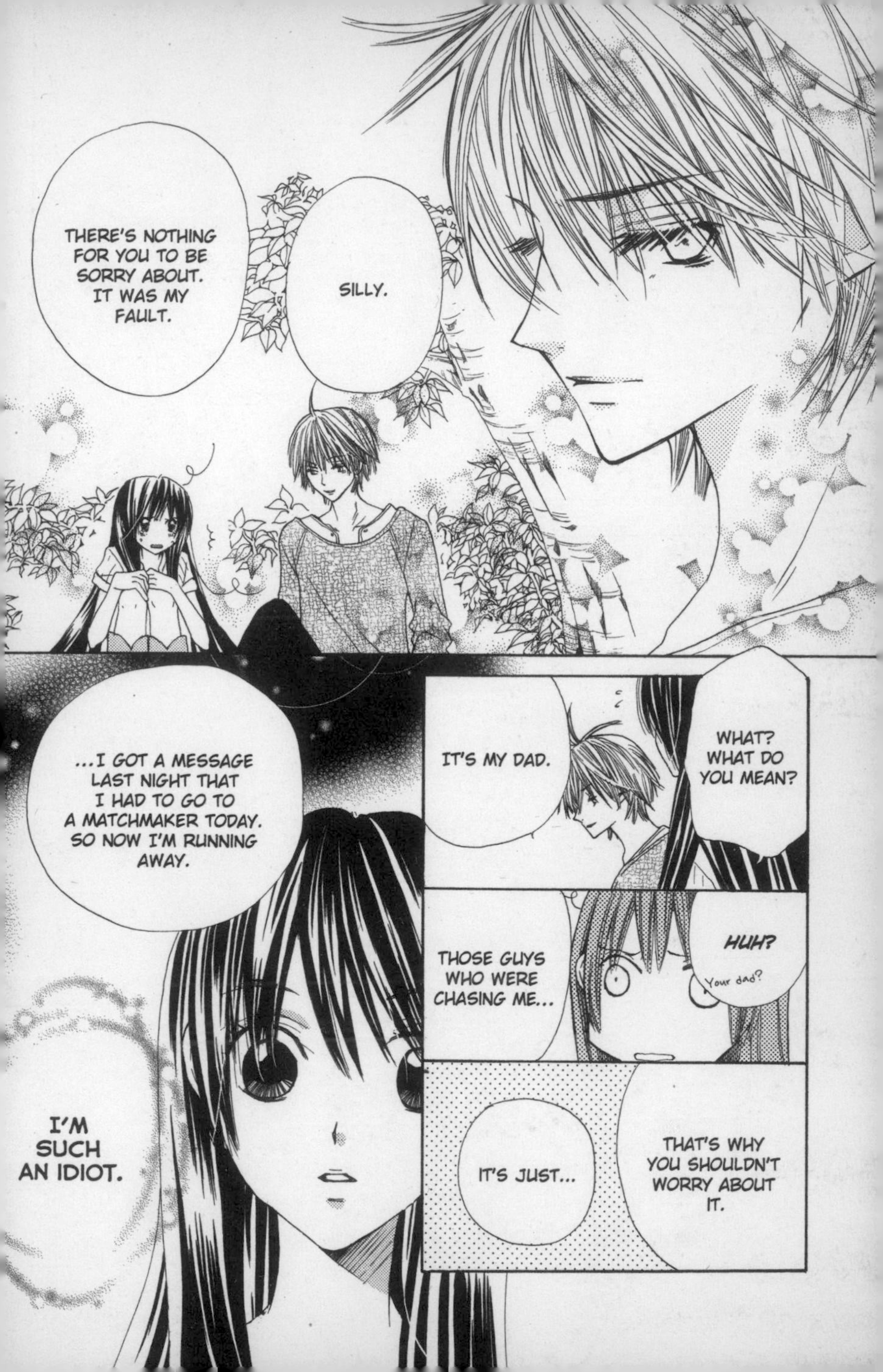
SILLY.
THERE'S NOTHING FOR YOU TO BE SORRY ABOUT. IT WAS MY FAULT.
WHAT? WHAT DO YOU MEAN?
IT'S MY DAD.
HUH?
Your dad?
THOSE GUYS WHO WERE CHASING ME...
THAT'S WHY YOU SHOULDN'T WORRY ABOUT IT.
IT'S JUST...
...I GOT A MESSAGE LAST NIGHT THAT I HAD TO GO TO A MATCHMAKER TODAY. SO NOW I'M RUNNING AWAY.
I'M SUCH AN IDIOT.

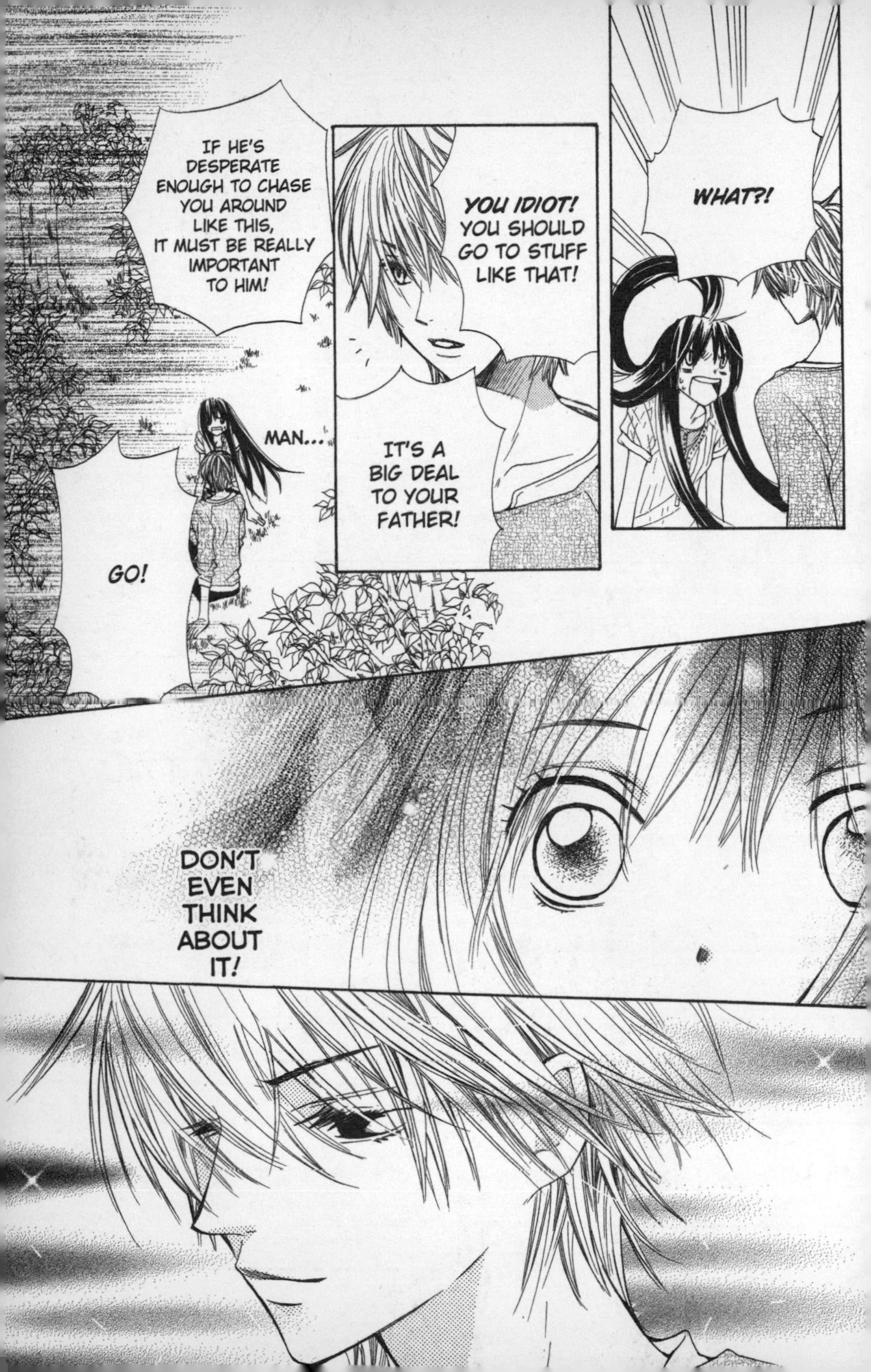
WHAT?!
YOU IDIOT! YOU SHOULD GO TO STUFF LIKE THAT!
IT'S A BIG DEAL TO YOUR FATHER!
IF HE'S DESPERATE ENOUGH TO CHASE YOU AROUND LIKE THIS, IT MUST BE REALLY IMPORTANT TO HIM!
MAN...
GO!
DON'T EVEN THINK ABOUT IT!

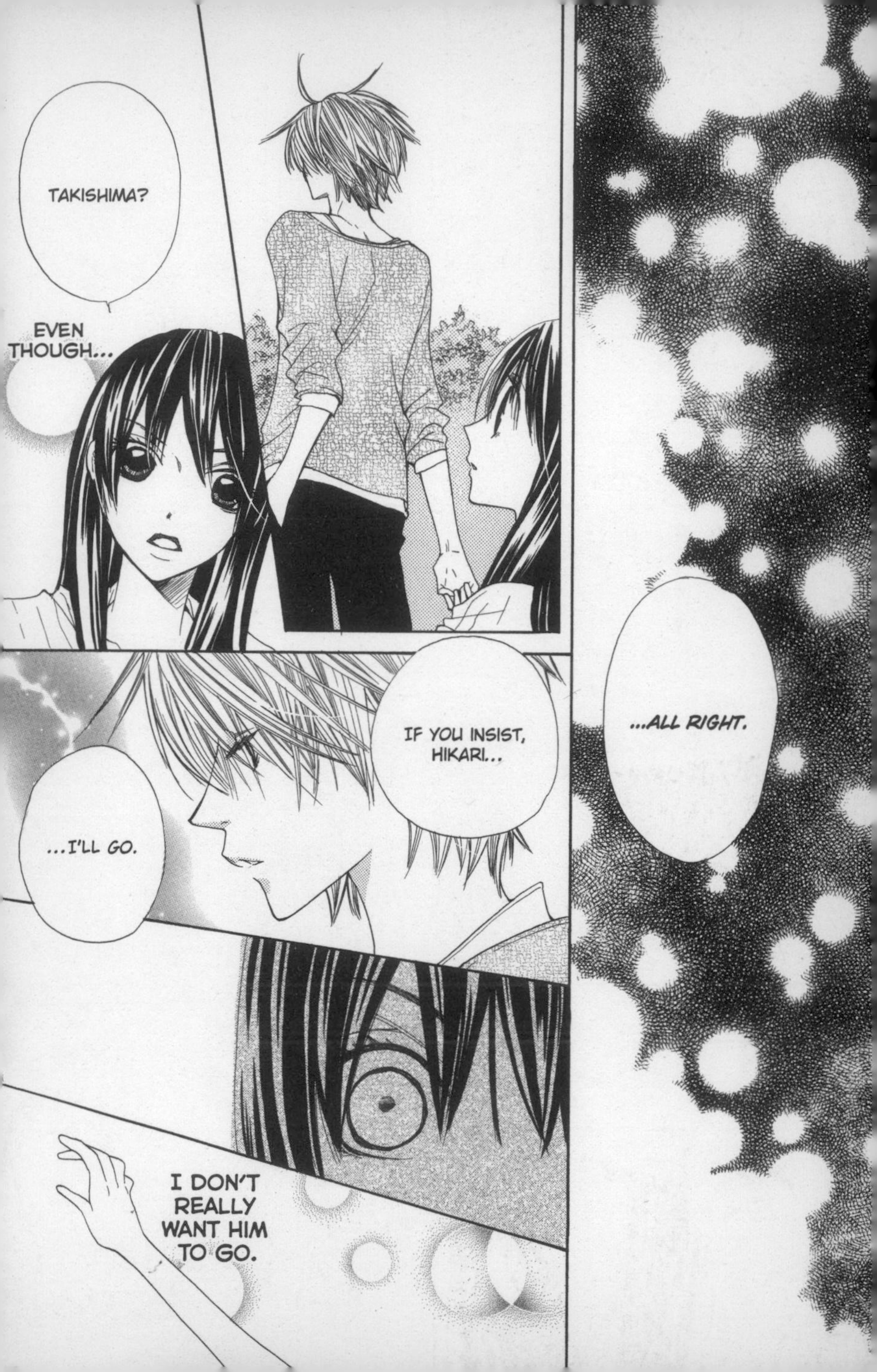
...ALL RIGHT.
TAKISHIMA?
EVEN THOUGH...
IF YOU INSIST, HIKARI...
...I'LL GO.
I DON'T REALLY WANT HIM TO GO.

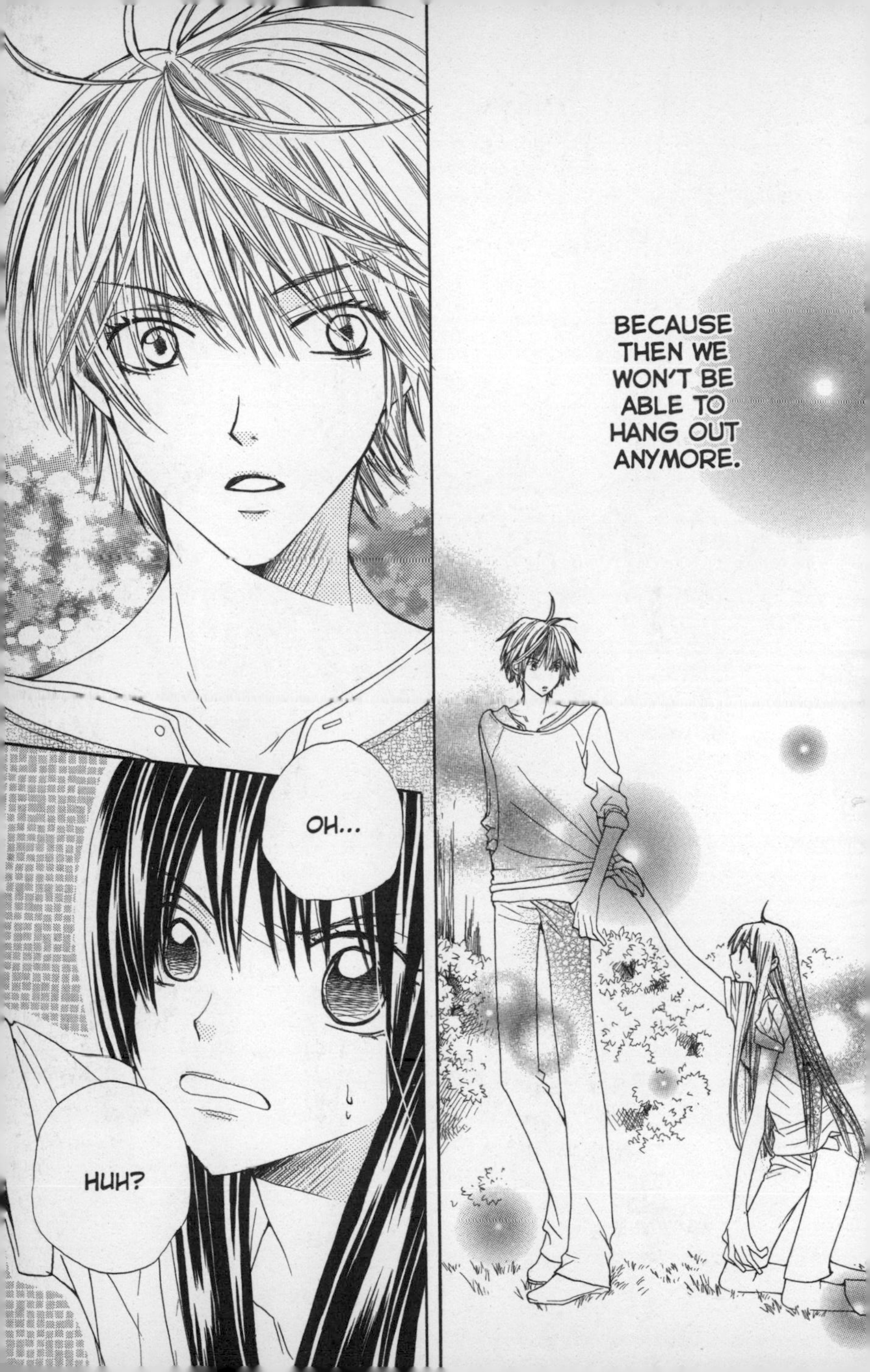
BECAUSE THEN WE WON'T BE ABLE TO HANG OUT ANYMORE.
OH...
HUH?

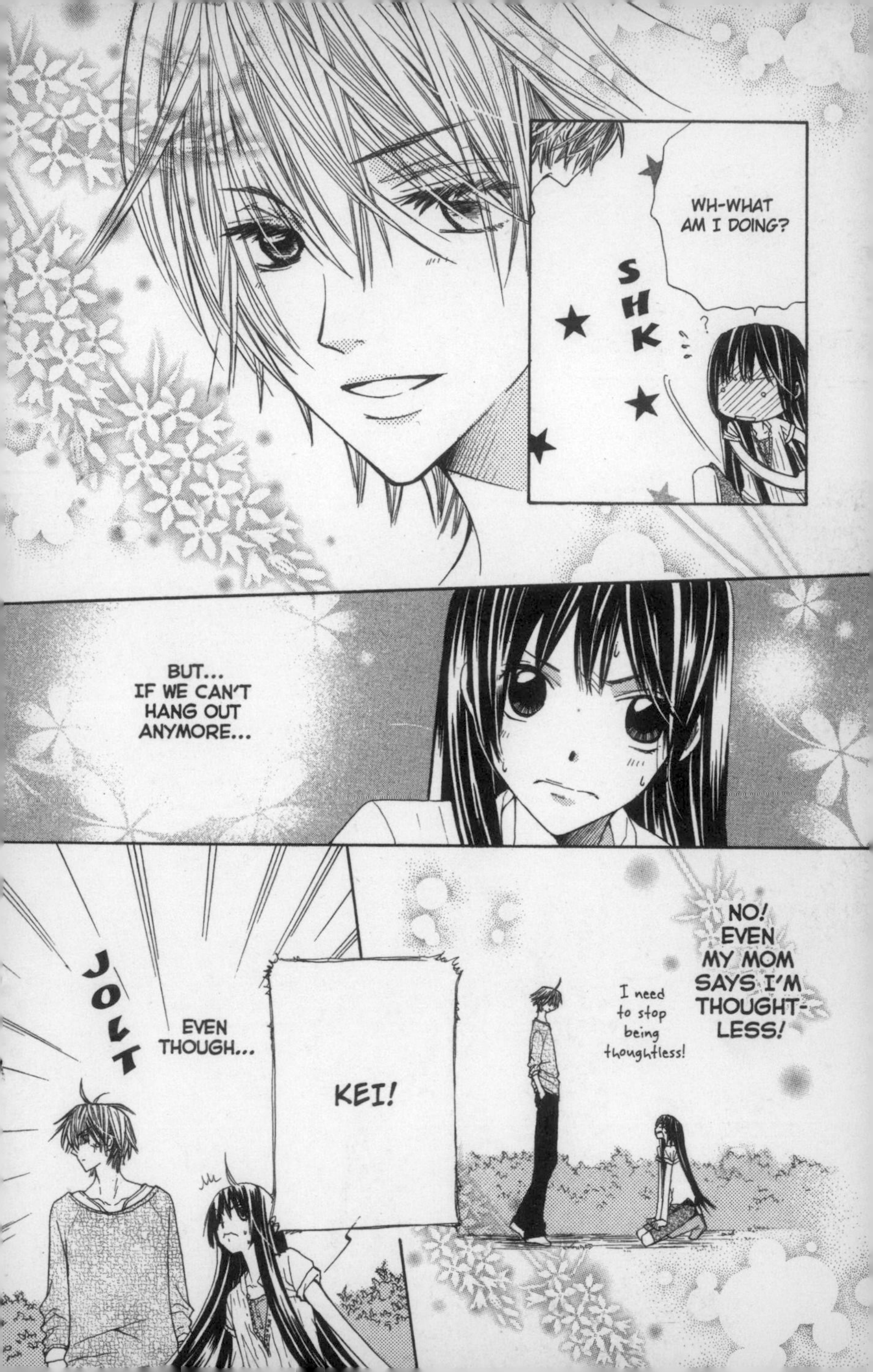
WH-WHAT AM I DOING?
SHK
BUT... IF WE CAN'T HANG OUT ANYMORE...
NO! EVEN MY MOM SAYS I'M THOUGHT-LESS!
I need to stop being thoughtless!
EVEN THOUGH...
JOLT
KEI!

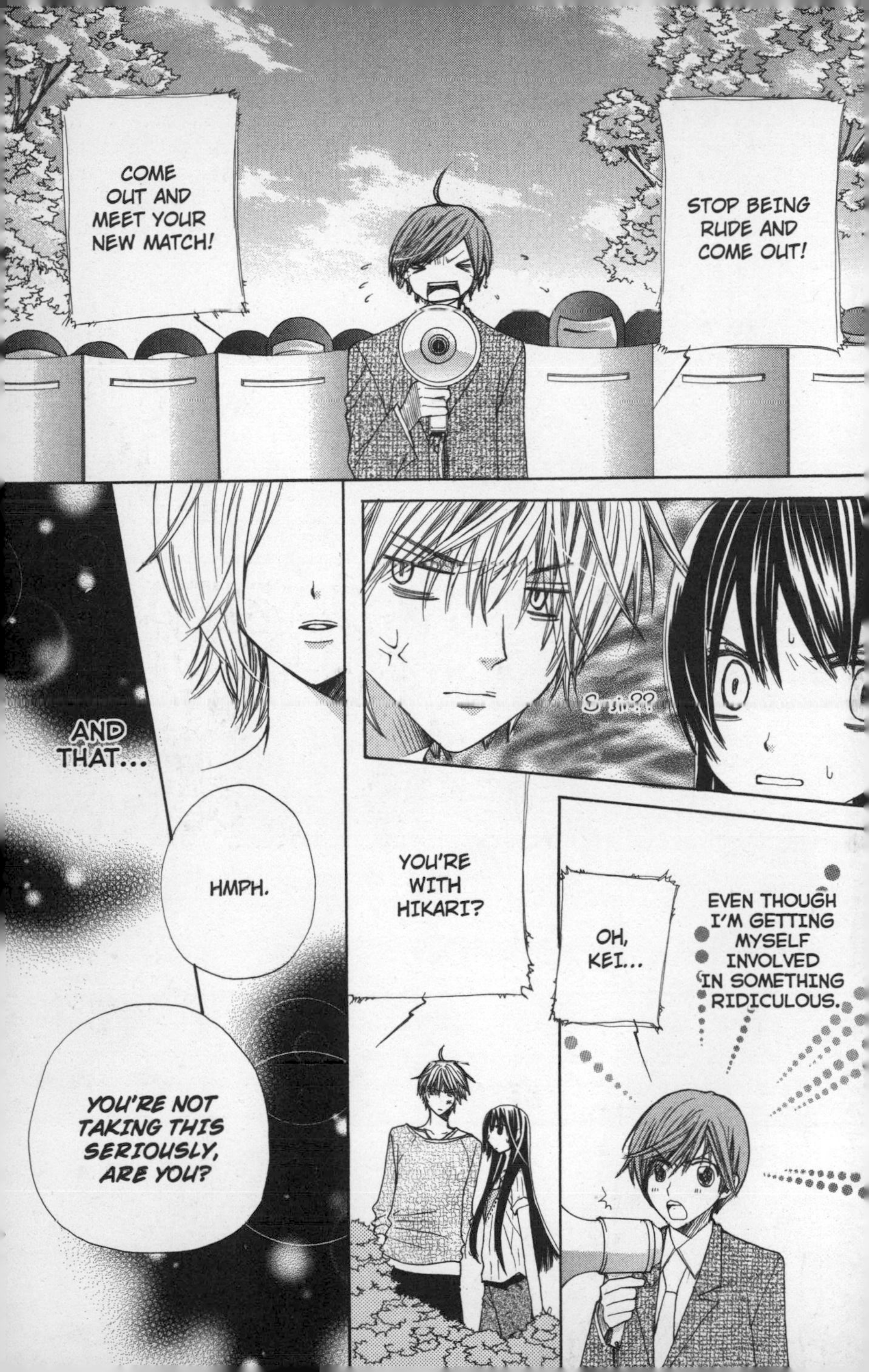
STOP BEING RUDE AND COME OUT!
COME OUT AND MEET YOUR NEW MATCH!
EVEN THOUGH I'M GETTING MYSELF INVOLVED IN SOMETHING RIDICULOUS.
OH, KEI...
YOU'RE WITH HIKARI?
AND THAT...
HMPH.
YOU'RE NOT TAKING THIS SERIOUSLY, ARE YOU?

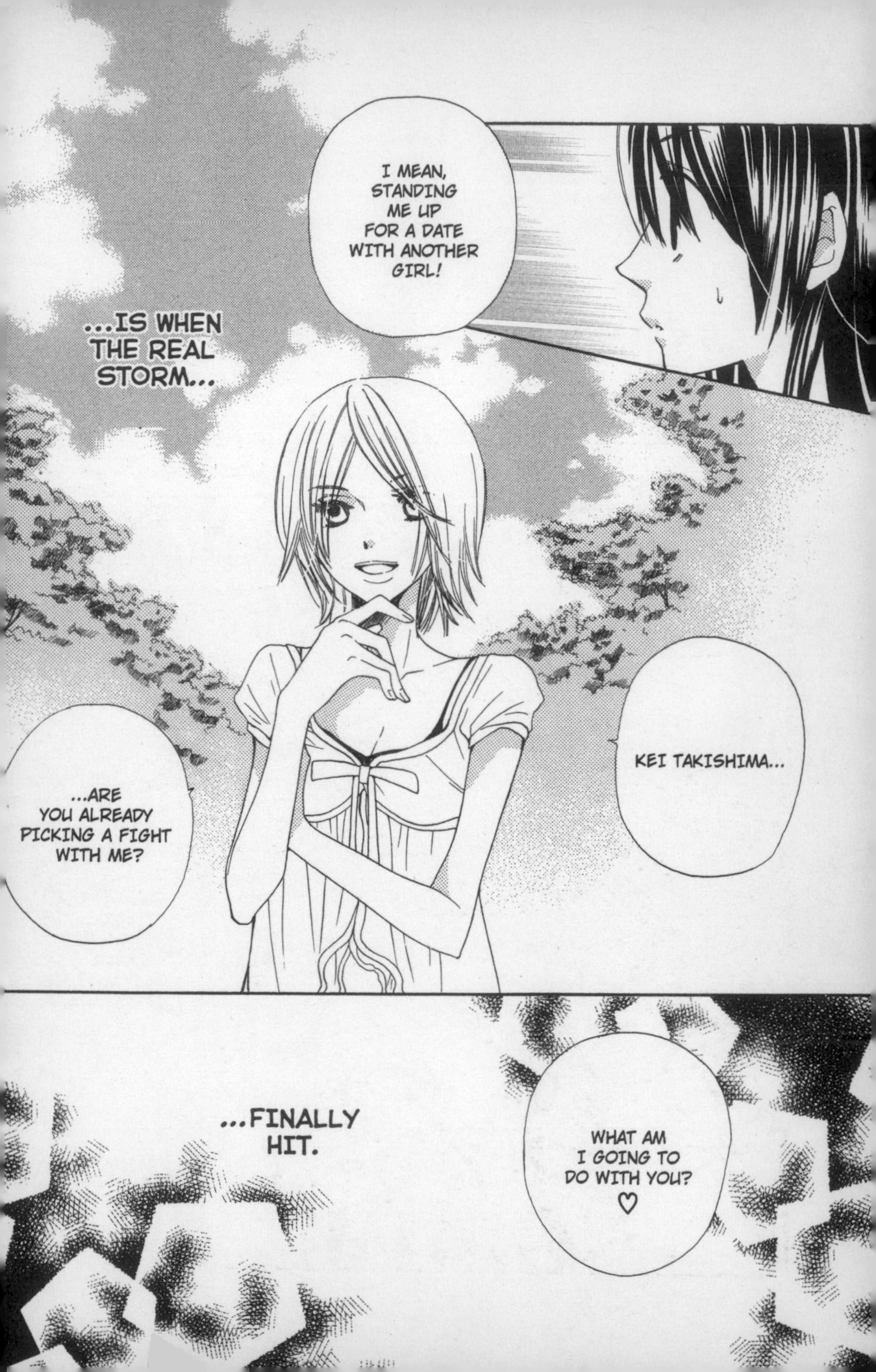
I MEAN, STANDING ME UP FOR A DATE WITH ANOTHER GIRL!
...IS WHEN THE REAL STORM...
KEI TAKISHIMA...
...ARE YOU ALREADY PICKING A FIGHT WITH ME?
WHAT AM I GOING TO DO WITH YOU? ♡
...FINALLY HIT.

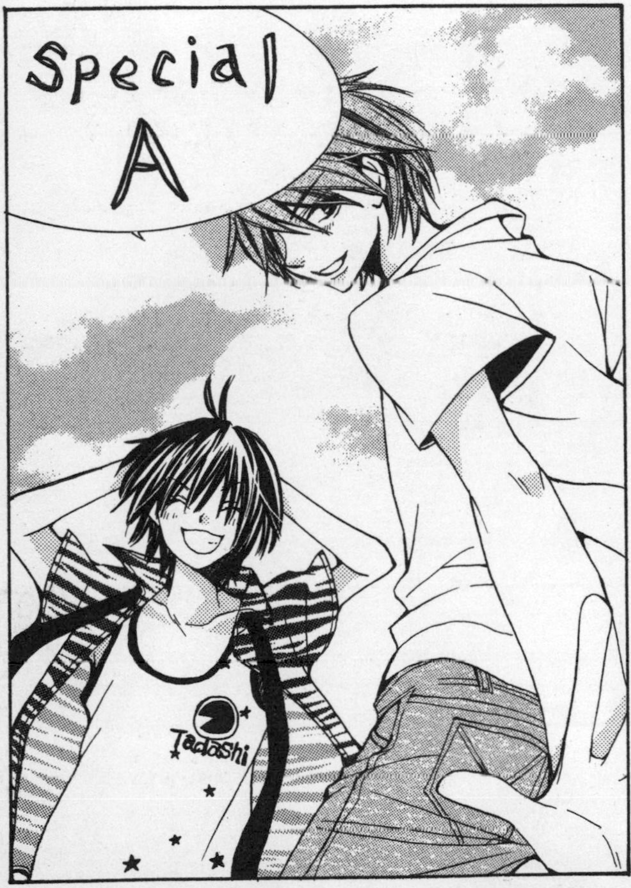
Special A
Tadashi

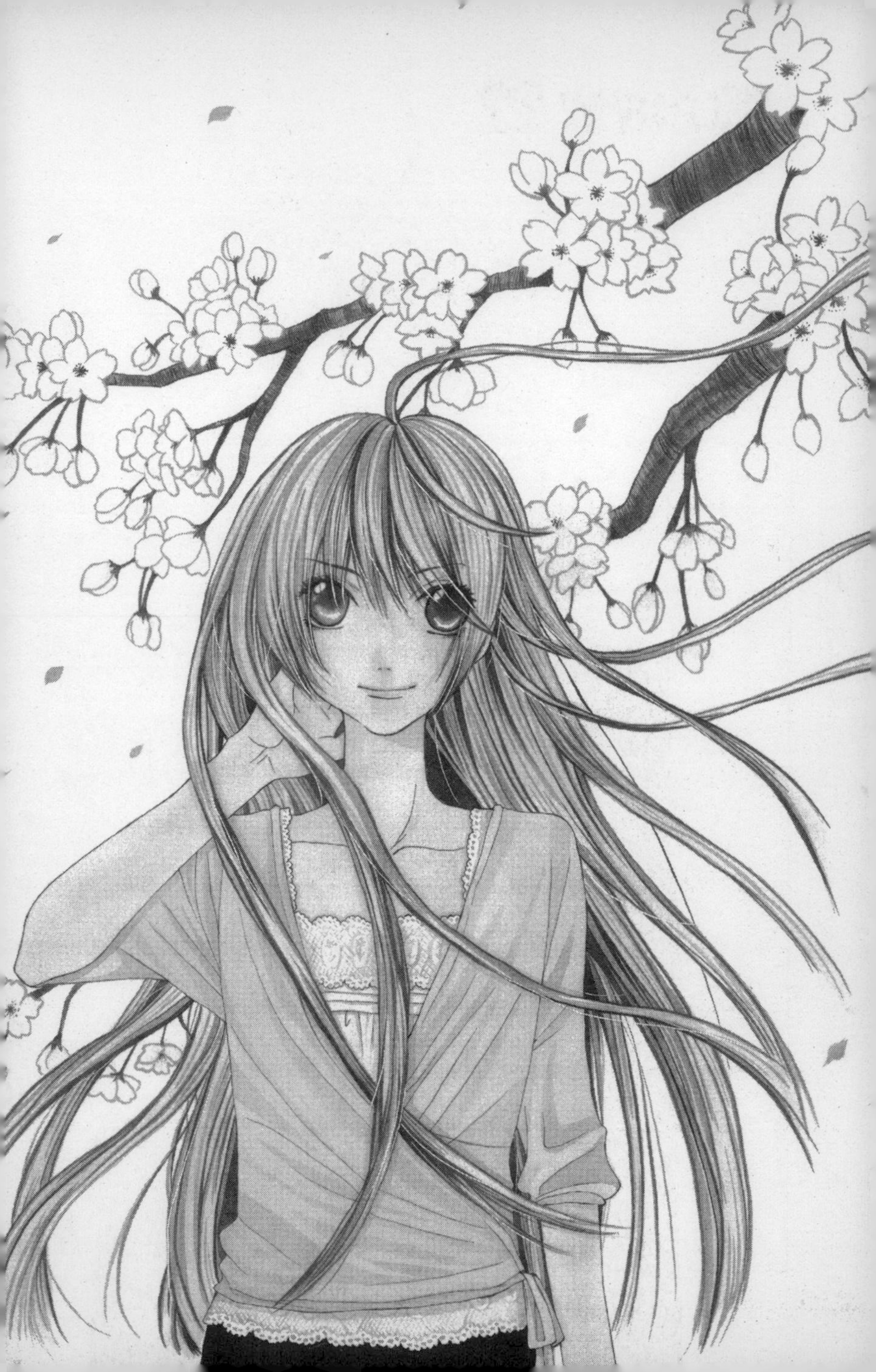

Chapter 22

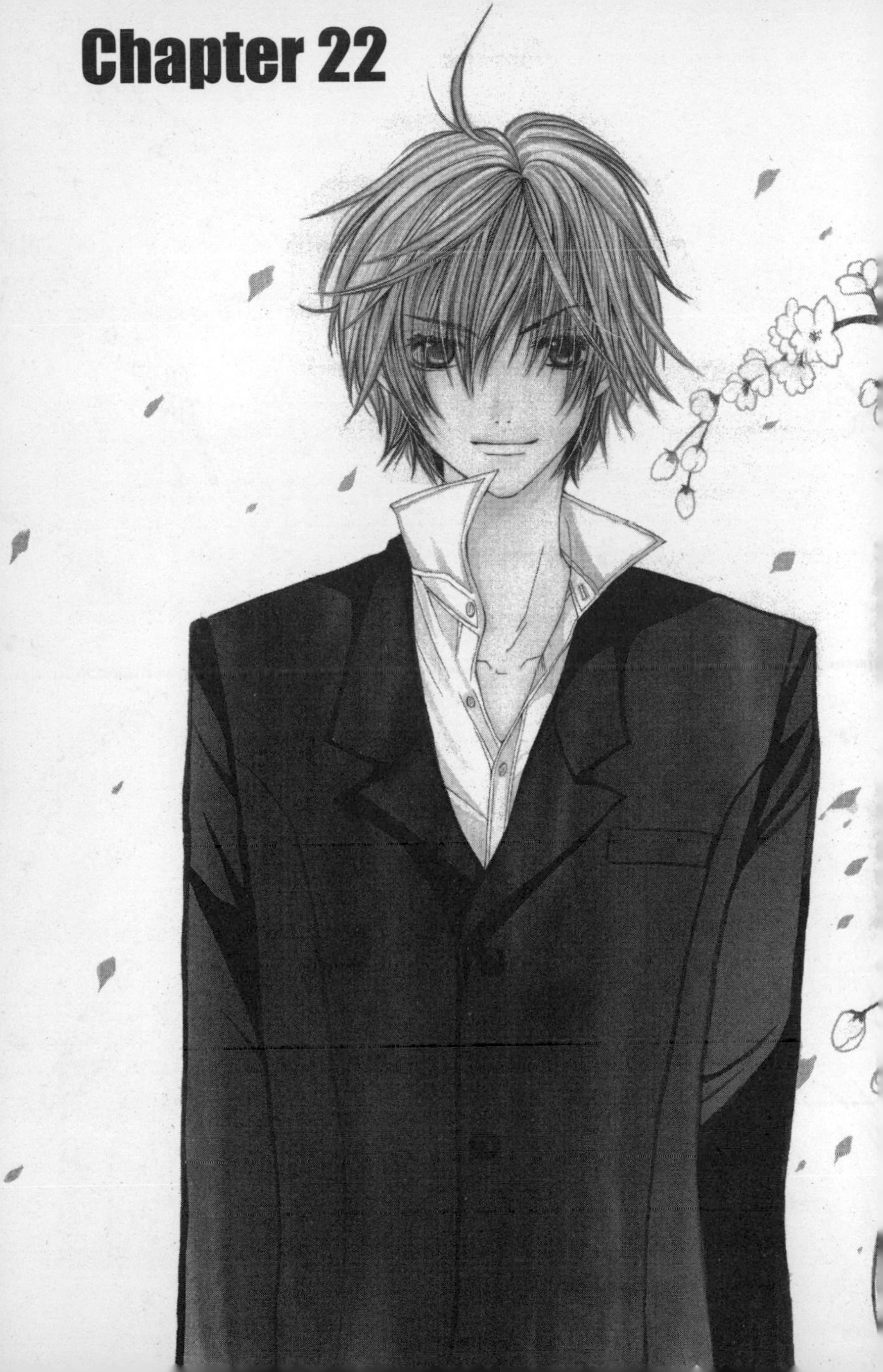

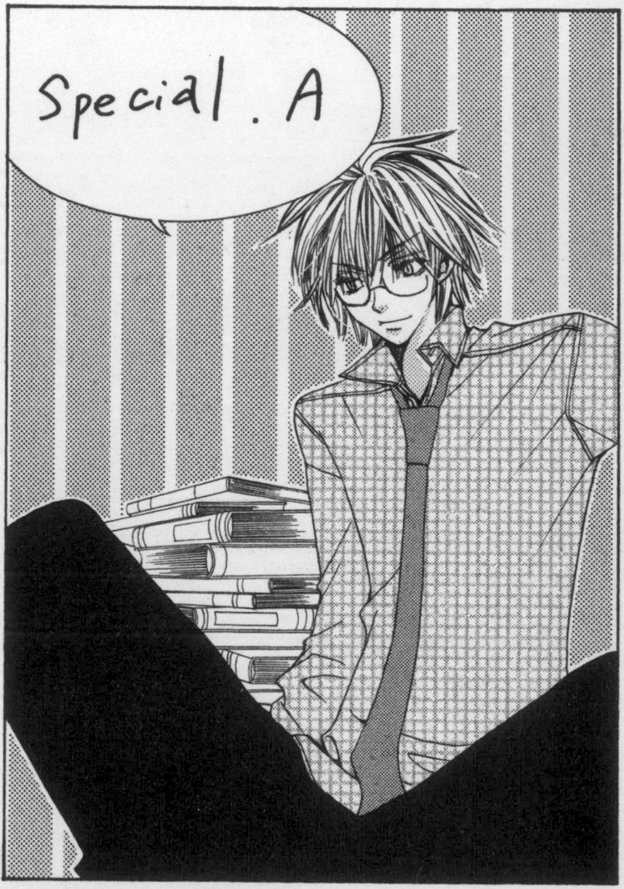
Special . A

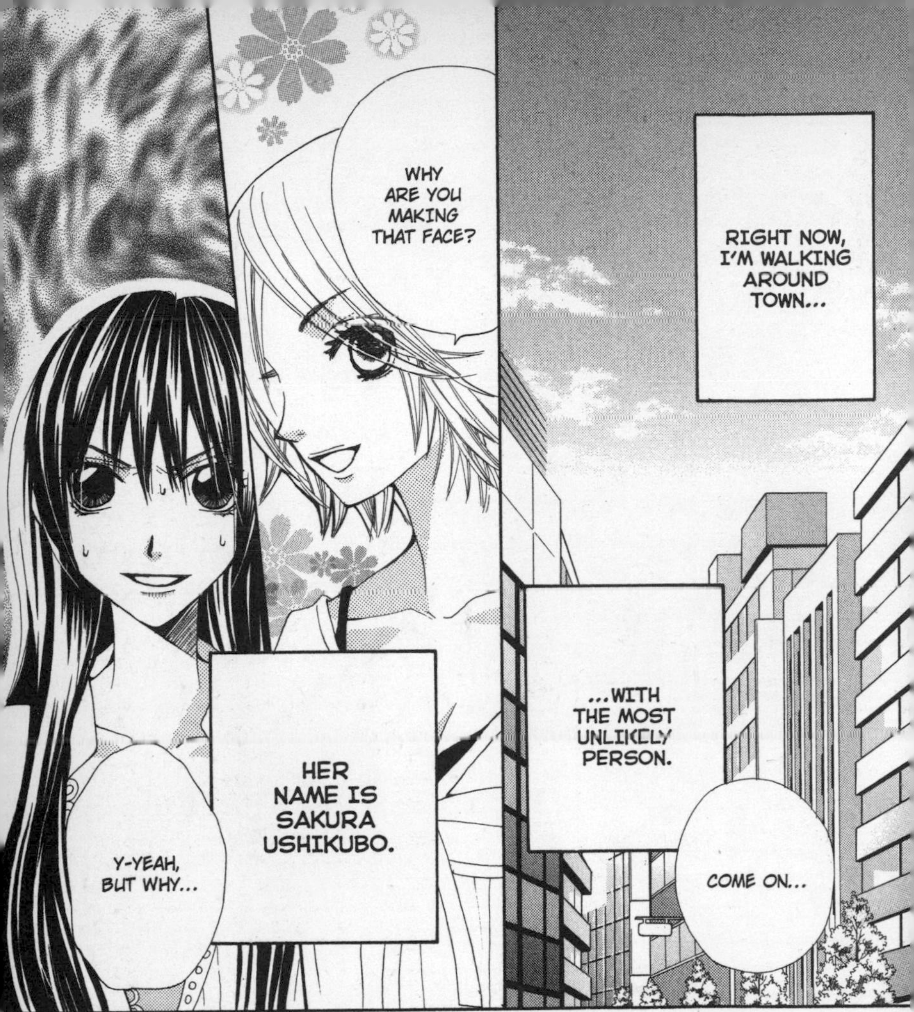
RIGHT NOW, I'M WALKING AROUND TOWN...
...WITH THE MOST UNLIKELY PERSON.
COME ON...
WHY ARE YOU MAKING THAT FACE?
HER NAME IS SAKURA USHIKUBO.
Y-YEAH, BUT WHY...

•THIS AND THAT•

THANK YOU SO MUCH FOR READING S.A!

IT MAKES ME SO HAPPY, EVEN THOUGH IT'S KIND OF JUST THE SAME OLD THING. TO EVERYONE WHO ALWAYS HELPS ME–AKIKOU AND NISSHI AND ATORI AND IGUCHI AND ALL MY FRIENDS—THANK YOU SO MUCH!!

AND SPECIAL THANKS TO ALL OF YOU WHO SEND ME LETTERS AND PURIKURA PHOTOS AND DRAWINGS! THEY'RE SO ENCOURAGING! I'M SORRY I TAKE SO LONG TO RESPOND.

HIKARI AND YAHIRO ARE ON THE COVER THIS TIME. WHO SHOULD I USE NEXT TIME? I HOPE THERE IS A NEXT TIME! ANYWAY...

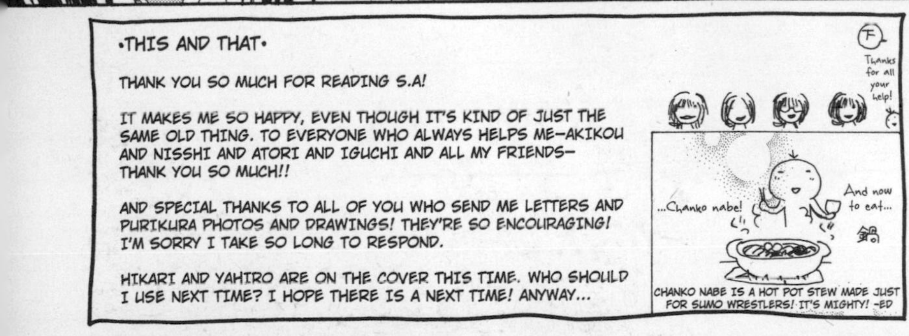
Thanks for all your help!
...Chanko nabe!
And now to eat...
鍋
CHANKO NABE IS A HOT POT STEW MADE JUST FOR SUMO WRESTLERS! IT'S MIGHTY! –ED

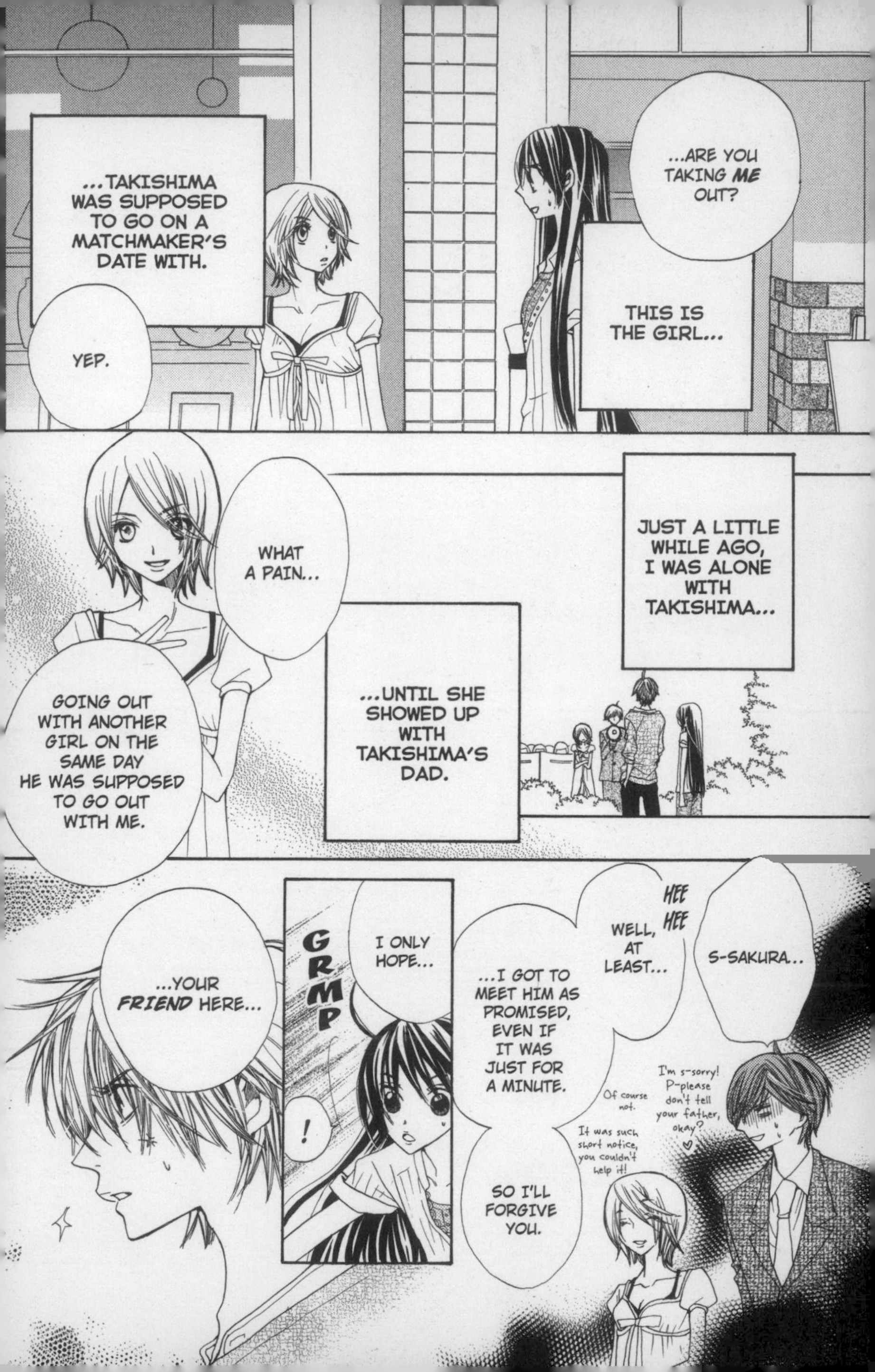
...ARE YOU TAKING *ME* OUT?
THIS IS THE GIRL...
...TAKISHIMA WAS SUPPOSED TO GO ON A MATCHMAKER'S DATE WITH.
YEP.
JUST A LITTLE WHILE AGO, I WAS ALONE WITH TAKISHIMA...
...UNTIL SHE SHOWED UP WITH TAKISHIMA'S DAD.
WHAT A PAIN...
GOING OUT WITH ANOTHER GIRL ON THE SAME DAY HE WAS SUPPOSED TO GO OUT WITH ME.
S-SAKURA...
HEE HEE
WELL, AT LEAST...
...I GOT TO MEET HIM AS PROMISED, EVEN IF IT WAS JUST FOR A MINUTE.
I'm s-sorry! P-please don't tell your father, okay?
Of course not.
It was such short notice, you couldn't help it!
SO I'LL FORGIVE YOU.
I ONLY HOPE...
GRMP
!
...YOUR *FRIEND* HERE...

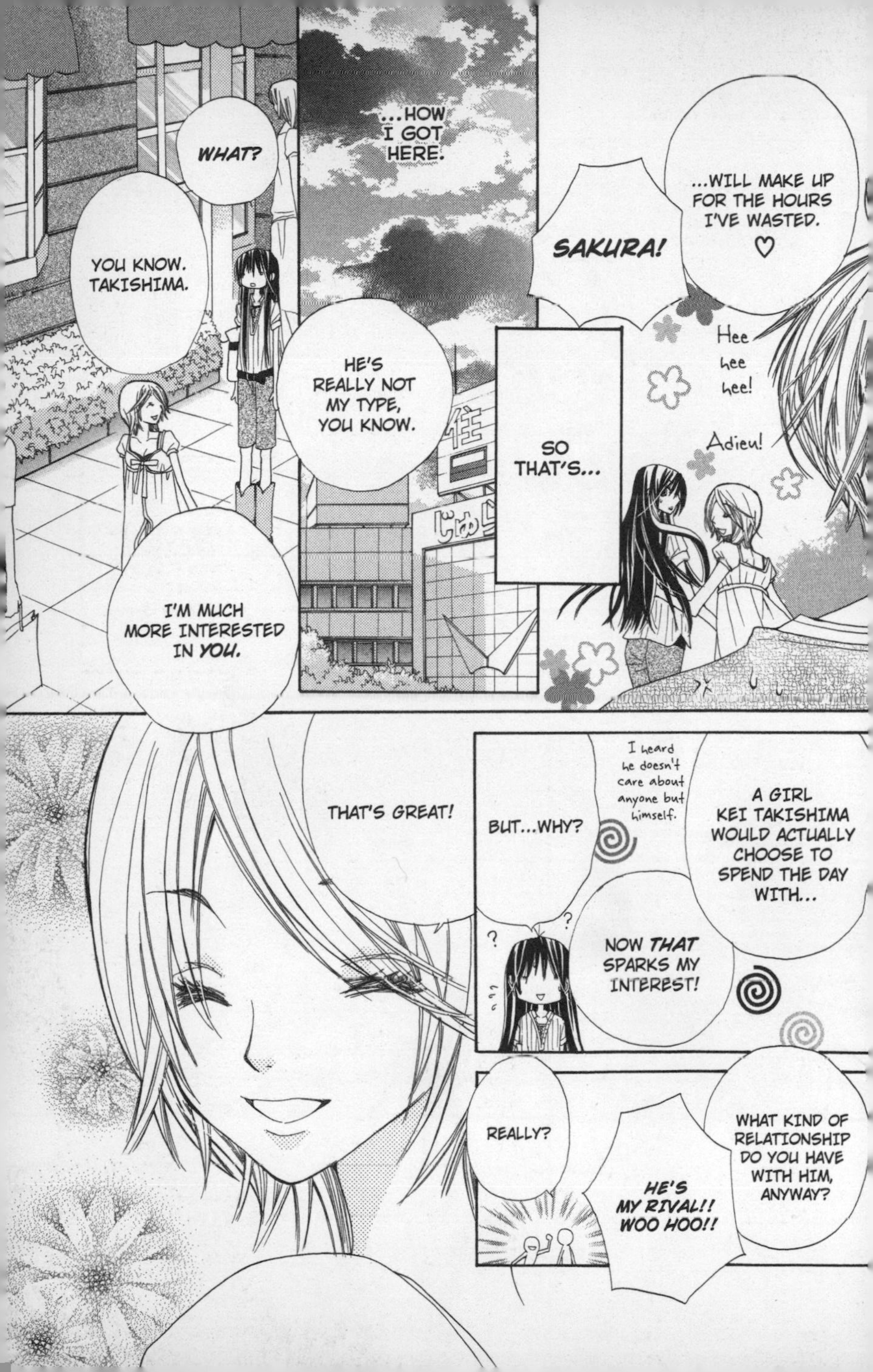
...WILL MAKE UP FOR THE HOURS I'VE WASTED. ♡
SAKURA!
Hee hee hee!
Adieu!
SO THAT'S...
...HOW I GOT HERE.
HE'S REALLY NOT MY TYPE, YOU KNOW.
WHAT?
YOU KNOW. TAKISHIMA.
I'M MUCH MORE INTERESTED IN YOU.
BUT...WHY?
A GIRL KEI TAKISHIMA WOULD ACTUALLY CHOOSE TO SPEND THE DAY WITH...
I heard he doesn't care about anyone but himself.
NOW THAT SPARKS MY INTEREST!
WHAT KIND OF RELATIONSHIP DO YOU HAVE WITH HIM, ANYWAY?
HE'S MY RIVAL!! WOO HOO!!
REALLY?
THAT'S GREAT!

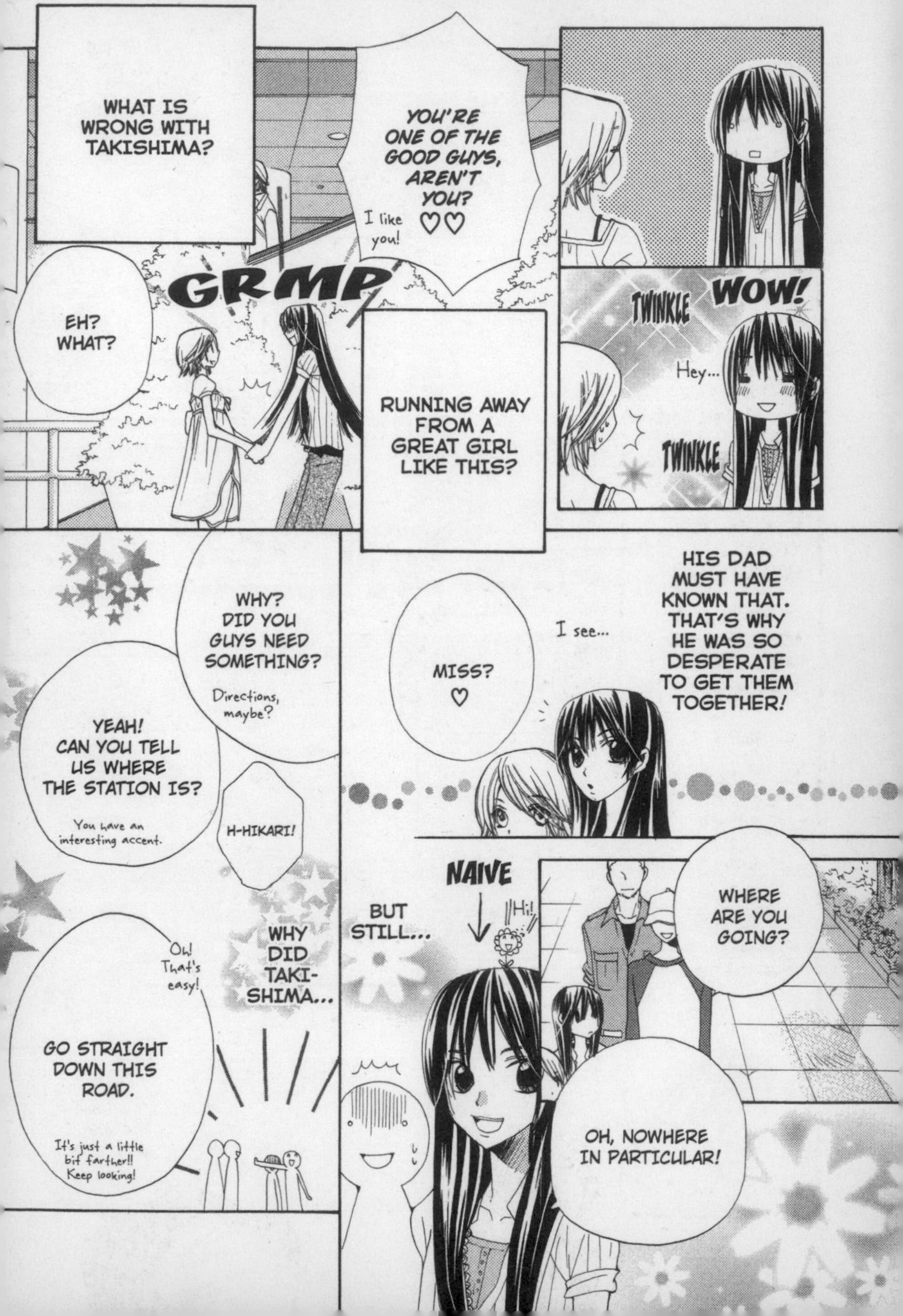
TWINKLE
WOW!
Hey...
TWINKLE
YOU'RE ONE OF THE GOOD GUYS, AREN'T YOU? ♡♡
I like you!
WHAT IS WRONG WITH TAKISHIMA?
RUNNING AWAY FROM A GREAT GIRL LIKE THIS?
GRMP
EH? WHAT?
HIS DAD MUST HAVE KNOWN THAT. THAT'S WHY HE WAS SO DESPERATE TO GET THEM TOGETHER!
I see...
MISS? ♡
WHY? DID YOU GUYS NEED SOMETHING?
Directions, maybe?
H-HIKARI!
YEAH! CAN YOU TELL US WHERE THE STATION IS?
You have an interesting accent.
WHERE ARE YOU GOING?
NAIVE
Hi!
BUT STILL...
OH, NOWHERE IN PARTICULAR!
WHY DID TAKI-SHIMA...
Oh! That's easy!
GO STRAIGHT DOWN THIS ROAD.
It's just a little bit farther!! Keep looking!

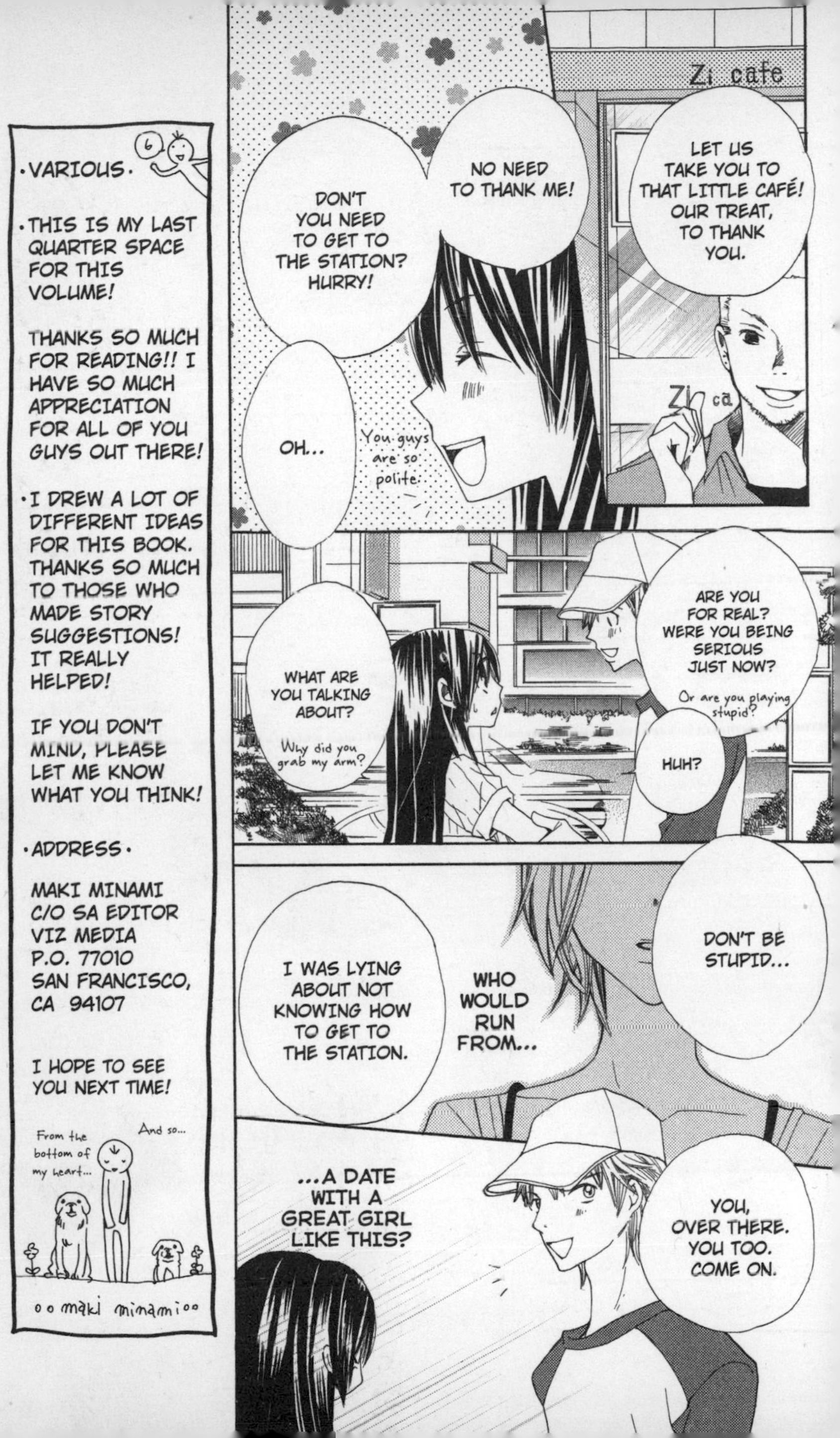
Zi cafe
LET US TAKE YOU TO THAT LITTLE CAFÉ! OUR TREAT, TO THANK YOU.
Zi ca
NO NEED TO THANK ME!
DON'T YOU NEED TO GET TO THE STATION? HURRY!
OH...
You guys are so polite.
ARE YOU FOR REAL? WERE YOU BEING SERIOUS JUST NOW?
Or are you playing stupid?
HUH?
WHAT ARE YOU TALKING ABOUT?
Why did you grab my arm?
DON'T BE STUPID...
WHO WOULD RUN FROM...
I WAS LYING ABOUT NOT KNOWING HOW TO GET TO THE STATION.
YOU, OVER THERE. YOU TOO. COME ON.
...A DATE WITH A GREAT GIRL LIKE THIS?

6

• VARIOUS •

• THIS IS MY LAST QUARTER SPACE FOR THIS VOLUME!

THANKS SO MUCH FOR READING!! I HAVE SO MUCH APPRECIATION FOR ALL OF YOU GUYS OUT THERE!

• I DREW A LOT OF DIFFERENT IDEAS FOR THIS BOOK. THANKS SO MUCH TO THOSE WHO MADE STORY SUGGESTIONS! IT REALLY HELPED!

IF YOU DON'T MIND, PLEASE LET ME KNOW WHAT YOU THINK!

• ADDRESS •

MAKI MINAMI
C/O SA EDITOR
VIZ MEDIA
P.O. 77010
SAN FRANCISCO,
CA 94107

I HOPE TO SEE YOU NEXT TIME!

From the bottom of my heart... And so...

oo maki minami oo

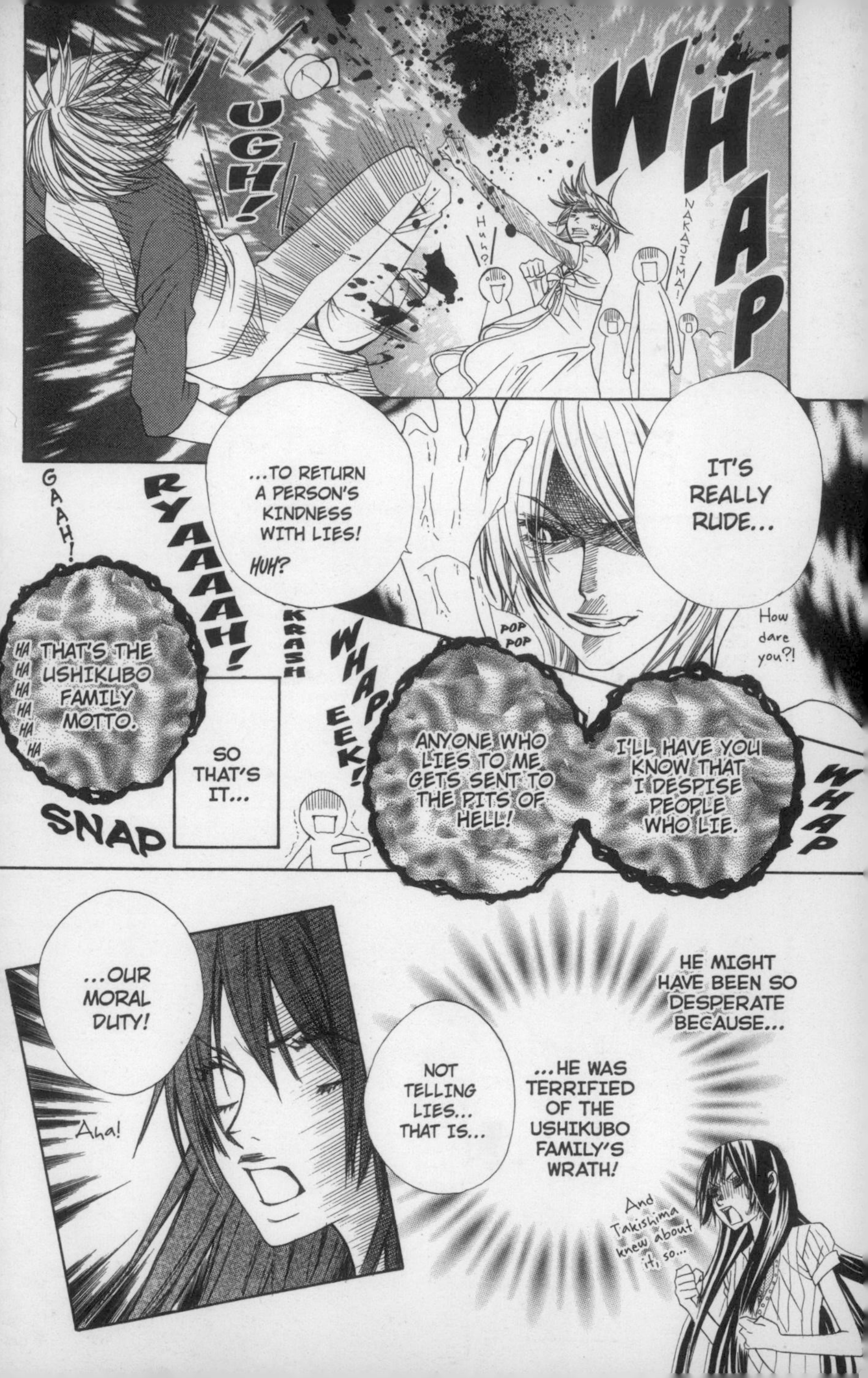
WHAP
NAKAJIMA!
Huh?
UGH!
IT'S REALLY RUDE...
...TO RETURN A PERSON'S KINDNESS WITH LIES!
HUH?
POP POP
How dare you?!
I'LL HAVE YOU KNOW THAT I DESPISE PEOPLE WHO LIE.
ANYONE WHO LIES TO ME GETS SENT TO THE PITS OF HELL!
WHAP
WHAP
EEK!
KRASH
RYAAAAAH!
GAAH!
SO THAT'S IT...
THAT'S THE USHIKUBO FAMILY MOTTO.
HA HA HA HA HA HA
SNAP
HE MIGHT HAVE BEEN SO DESPERATE BECAUSE...
...HE WAS TERRIFIED OF THE USHIKUBO FAMILY'S WRATH!
And Takishima knew about it, so...
NOT TELLING LIES... THAT IS...
...OUR MORAL DUTY!
Aha!

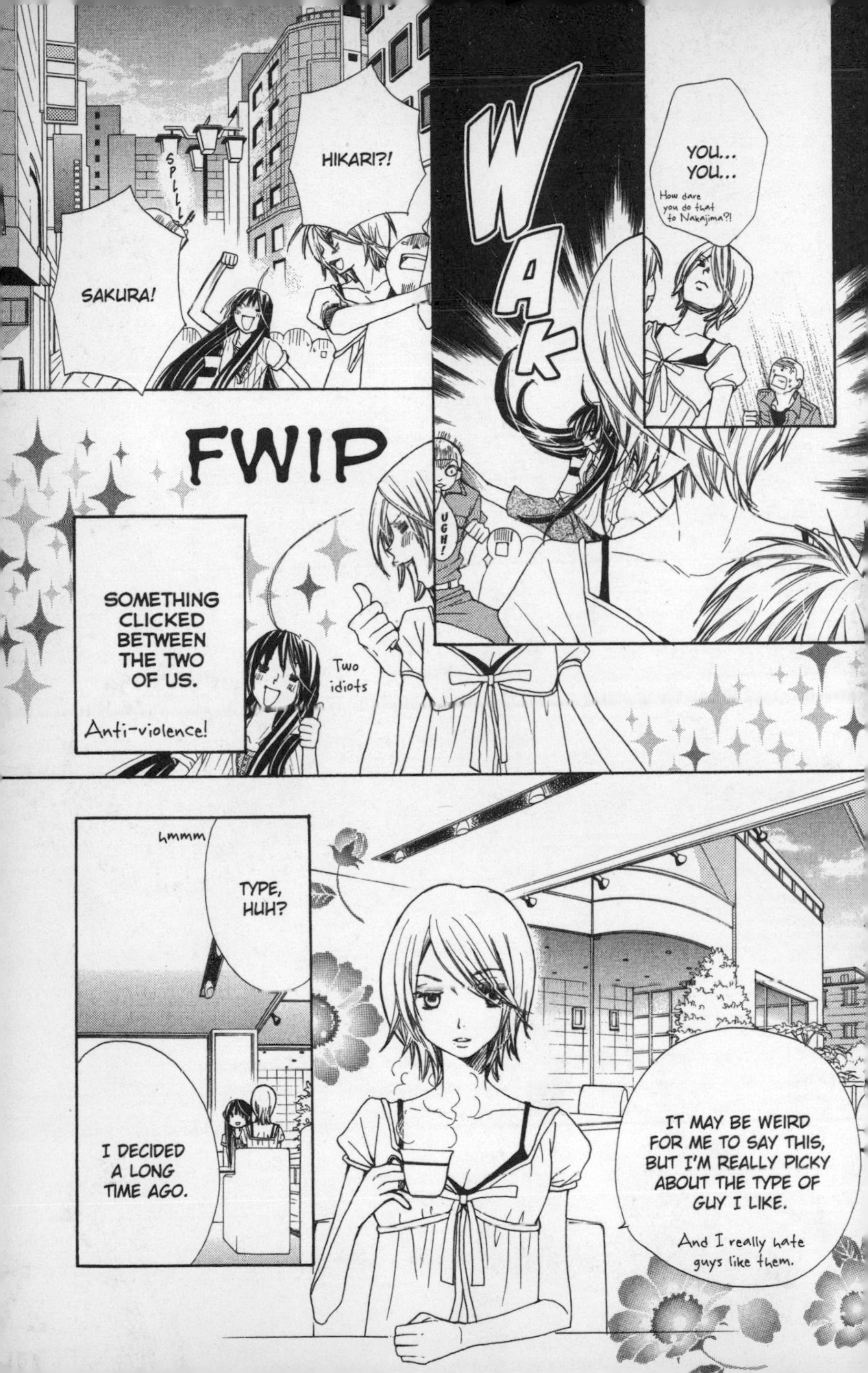
YOU... YOU...
How dare you do that to Nakajima?!
WAK
HIKARI?!
SPLLL
SAKURA!
FWIP
UGH!
SOMETHING CLICKED BETWEEN THE TWO OF US.
Anti-violence!
Two idiots
IT MAY BE WEIRD FOR ME TO SAY THIS, BUT I'M REALLY PICKY ABOUT THE TYPE OF GUY I LIKE.
And I really hate guys like them.
hmmm
TYPE, HUH?
I DECIDED A LONG TIME AGO.

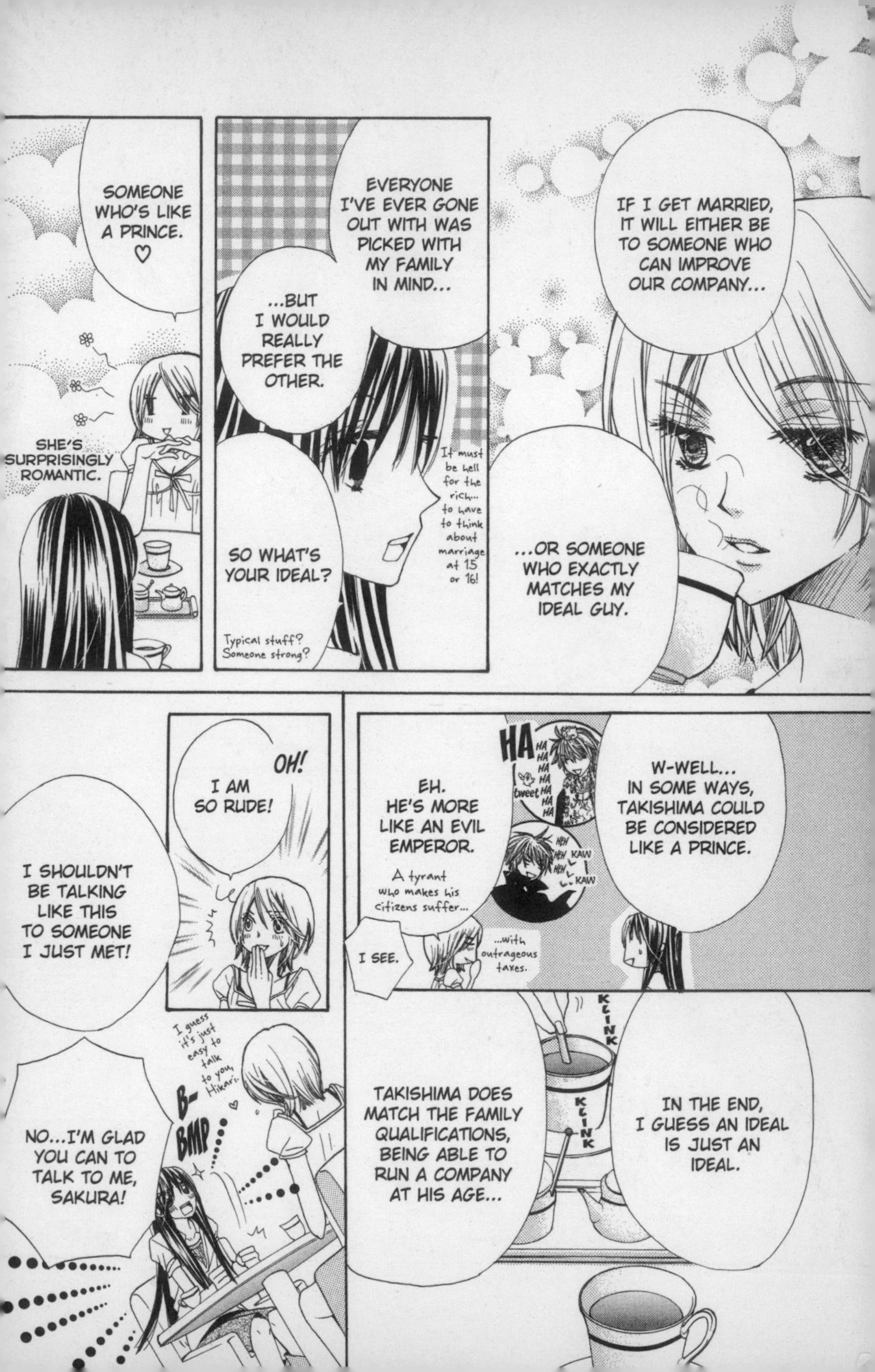
IF I GET MARRIED, IT WILL EITHER BE TO SOMEONE WHO CAN IMPROVE OUR COMPANY...
...OR SOMEONE WHO EXACTLY MATCHES MY IDEAL GUY.
EVERYONE I'VE EVER GONE OUT WITH WAS PICKED WITH MY FAMILY IN MIND...
...BUT I WOULD REALLY PREFER THE OTHER.
It must be hell for the rich... to have to think about marriage at 15 or 16!
SO WHAT'S YOUR IDEAL?
Typical stuff? Someone strong?
SOMEONE WHO'S LIKE A PRINCE. ♡
SHE'S SURPRISINGLY ROMANTIC.
W-WELL... IN SOME WAYS, TAKISHIMA COULD BE CONSIDERED LIKE A PRINCE.
HA HA HA HA HA HA HA HA
tweet
HEH HEH HEH KAW KAW
EH. HE'S MORE LIKE AN EVIL EMPEROR.
A tyrant who makes his citizens suffer...
...with outrageous taxes.
I SEE.
IN THE END, I GUESS AN IDEAL IS JUST AN IDEAL.
KLINK
KLINK
TAKISHIMA DOES MATCH THE FAMILY QUALIFICATIONS, BEING ABLE TO RUN A COMPANY AT HIS AGE...
OH!
I AM SO RUDE!
I SHOULDN'T BE TALKING LIKE THIS TO SOMEONE I JUST MET!
I guess it's just easy to talk to you, Hikari.
B-BMP
NO...I'M GLAD YOU CAN TO TALK TO ME, SAKURA!

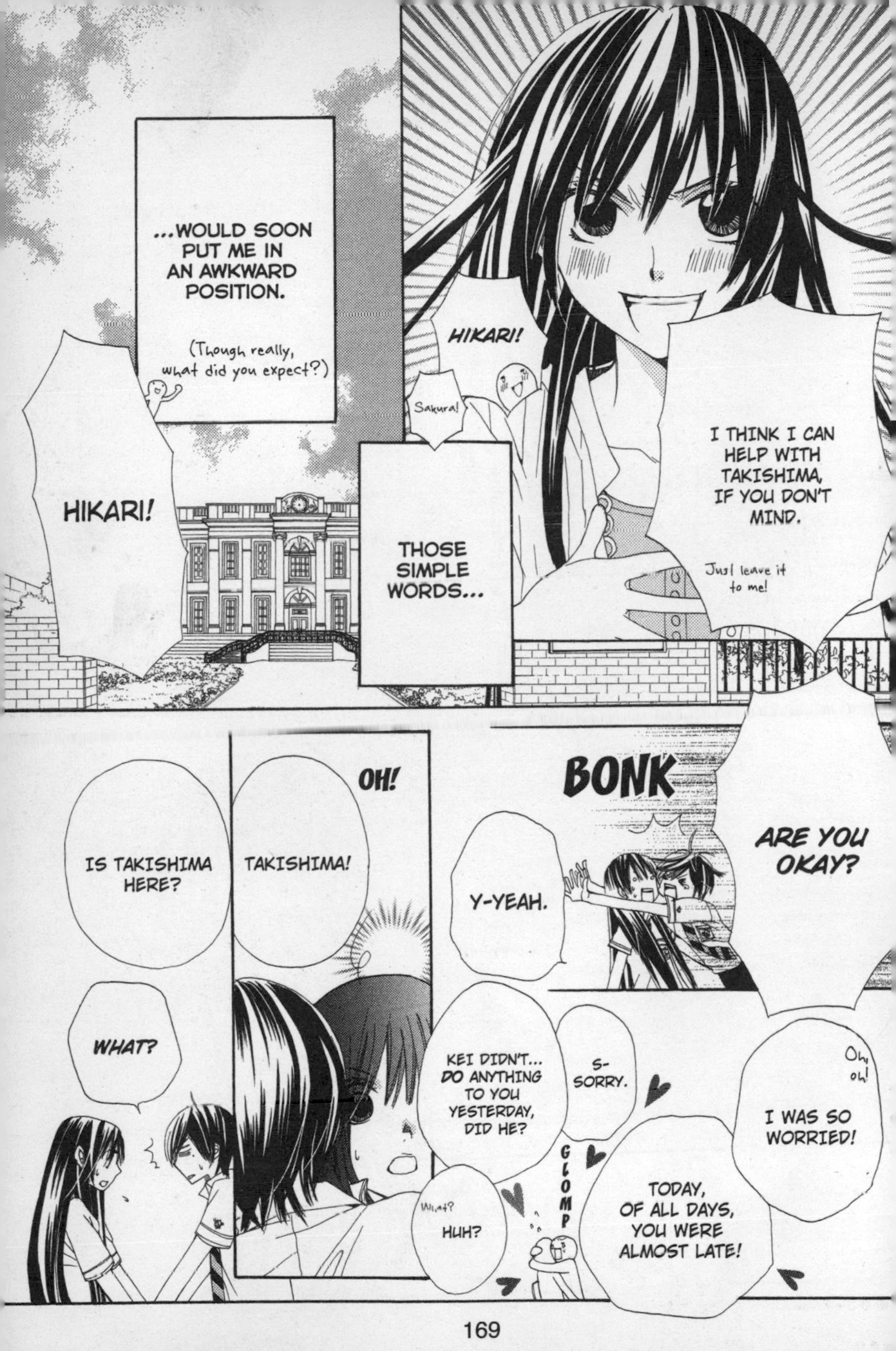
HIKARI!
Sakura!
I THINK I CAN HELP WITH TAKISHIMA, IF YOU DON'T MIND.
Just leave it to me!
THOSE SIMPLE WORDS...
HIKARI!
...WOULD SOON PUT ME IN AN AWKWARD POSITION.
(Though really, what did you expect?)
ARE YOU OKAY?
BONK
Y-YEAH.
Oh, oh!
I WAS SO WORRIED!
TODAY, OF ALL DAYS, YOU WERE ALMOST LATE!
GLOMP
S-SORRY.
KEI DIDN'T... DO ANYTHING TO YOU YESTERDAY, DID HE?
What?
HUH?
OH!
TAKISHIMA!
IS TAKISHIMA HERE?
WHAT?

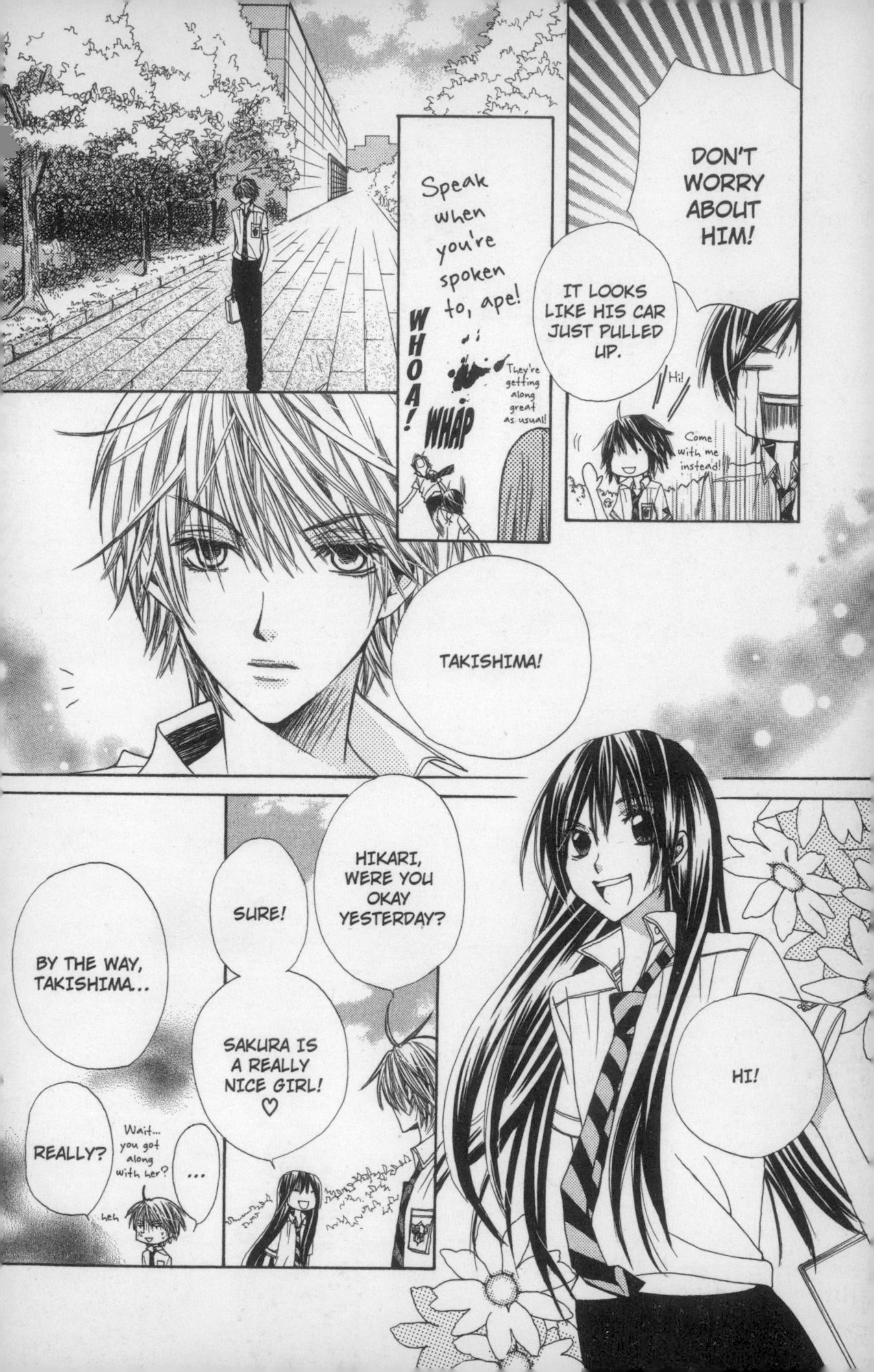
DON'T WORRY ABOUT HIM!
IT LOOKS LIKE HIS CAR JUST PULLED UP.
Hi!
Come with me instead!
Speak when you're spoken to, ape!
WHOA!
WHAP
They're getting along great as usual!
TAKISHIMA!
HI!
HIKARI, WERE YOU OKAY YESTERDAY?
SURE!
SAKURA IS A REALLY NICE GIRL! ♡
BY THE WAY, TAKISHIMA...
REALLY?
Wait... you got along with her?
...
heh

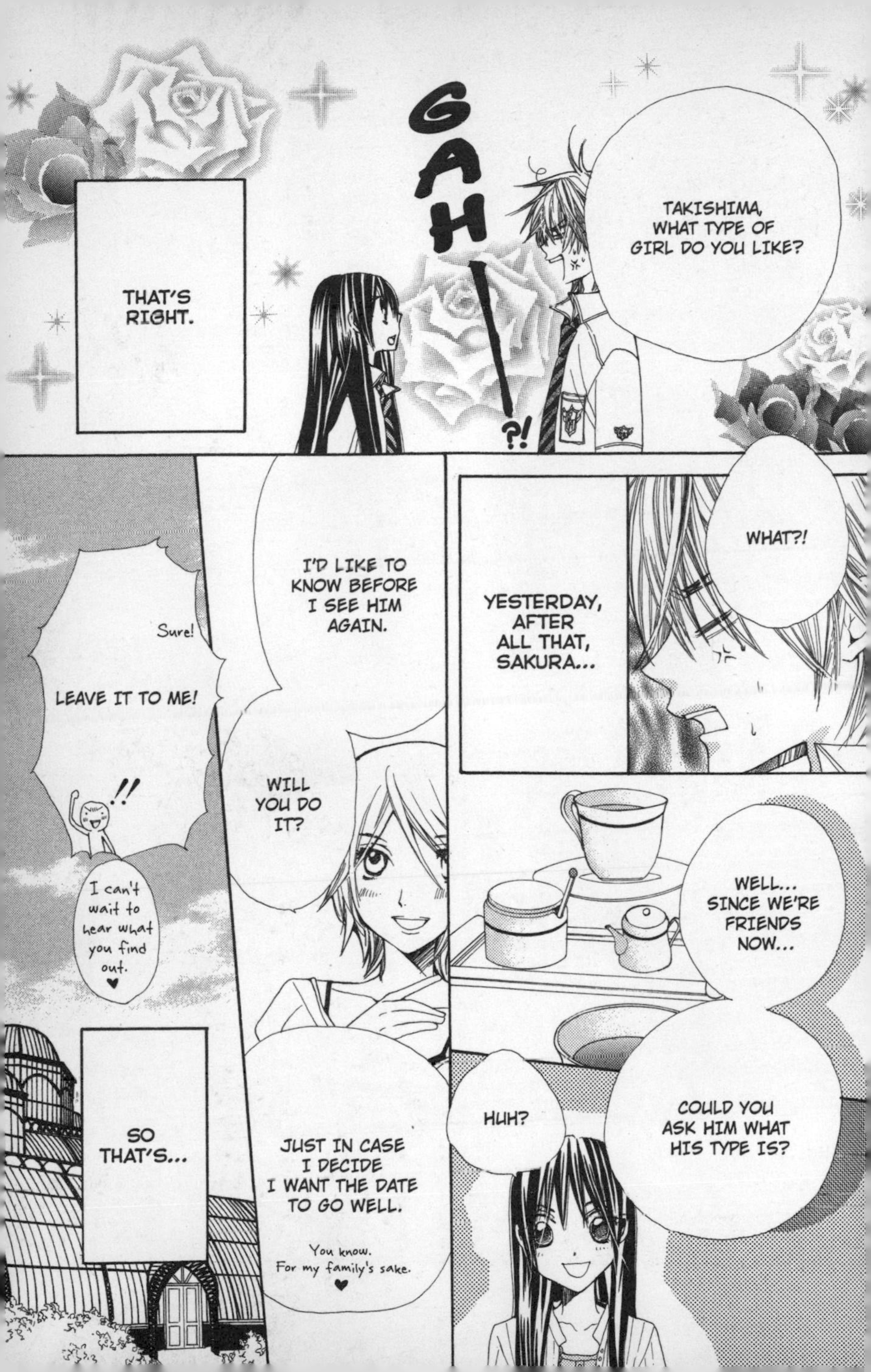
TAKISHIMA, WHAT TYPE OF GIRL DO YOU LIKE?
GAH!?!
THAT'S RIGHT.
WHAT?!
YESTERDAY, AFTER ALL THAT, SAKURA...
WELL... SINCE WE'RE FRIENDS NOW...
COULD YOU ASK HIM WHAT HIS TYPE IS?
HUH?
I'D LIKE TO KNOW BEFORE I SEE HIM AGAIN.
WILL YOU DO IT?
JUST IN CASE I DECIDE I WANT THE DATE TO GO WELL.
You know. For my family's sake.
Sure!
LEAVE IT TO ME!
!!
I can't wait to hear what you find out.
SO THAT'S...

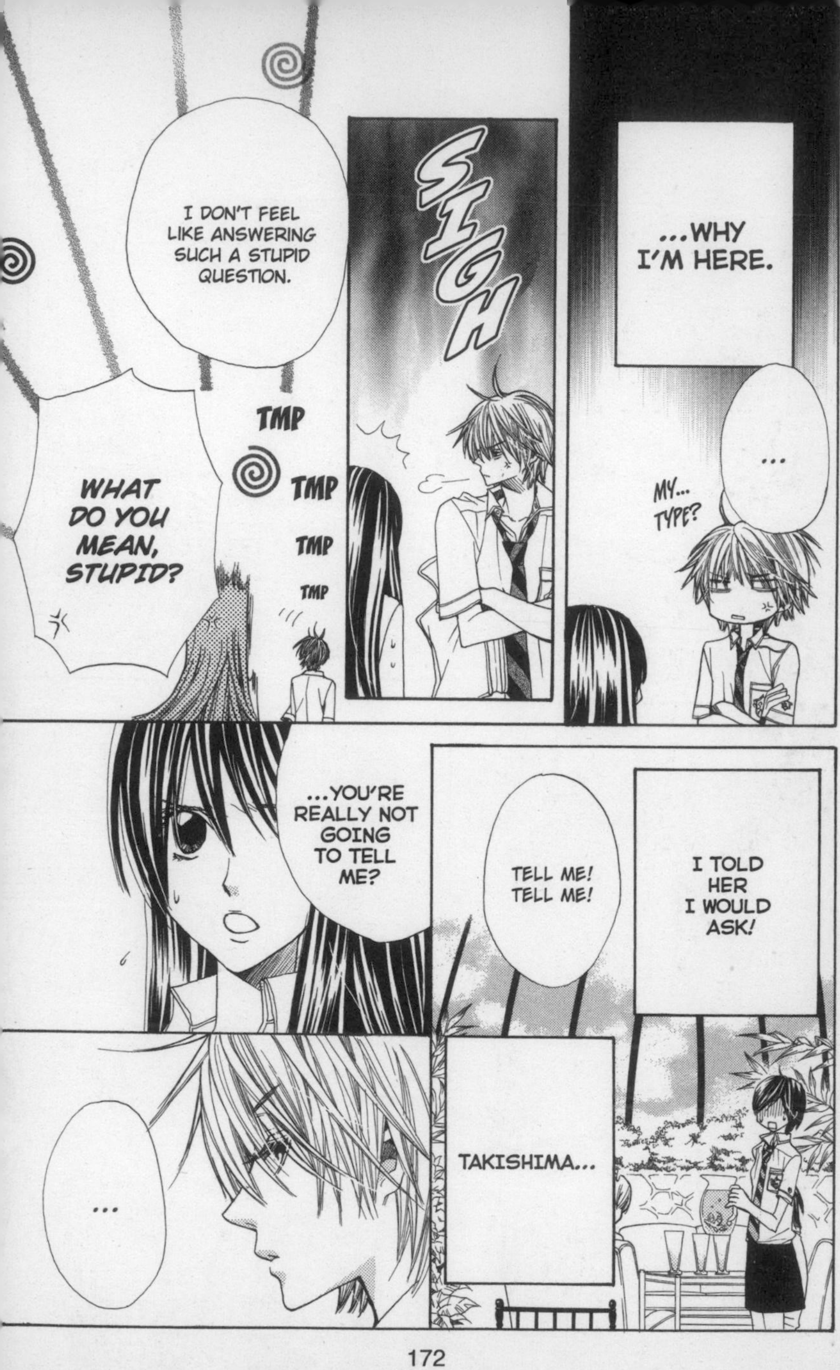
...WHY I'M HERE.
...
MY... TYPE?
SIGH
I DON'T FEEL LIKE ANSWERING SUCH A STUPID QUESTION.
TMP
TMP
TMP
TMP
WHAT DO YOU MEAN, STUPID?
I TOLD HER I WOULD ASK!
TELL ME! TELL ME!
TAKISHIMA...
...YOU'RE REALLY NOT GOING TO TELL ME?
...

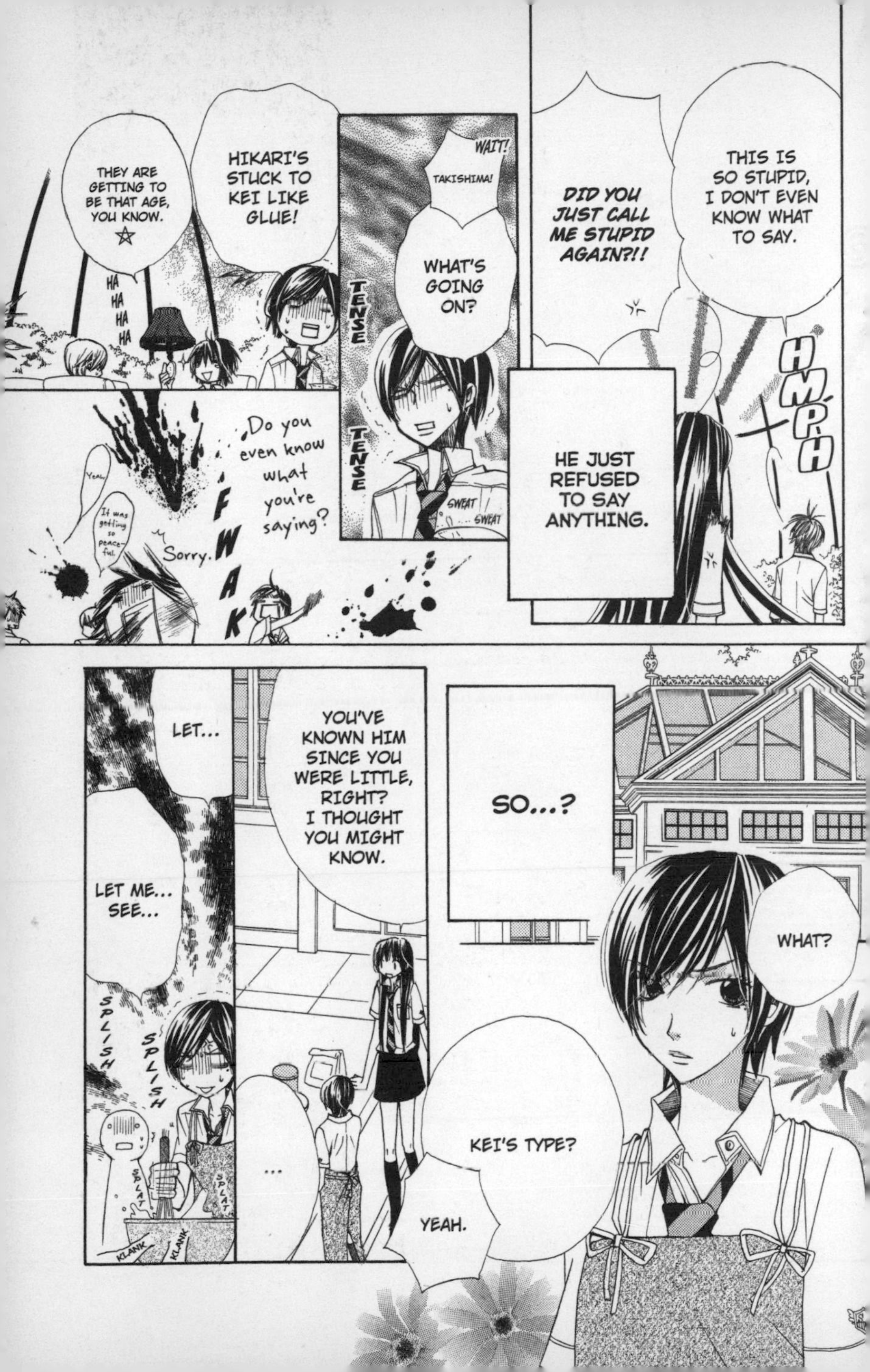
THIS IS SO STUPID, I DON'T EVEN KNOW WHAT TO SAY.
DID YOU JUST CALL ME STUPID AGAIN?!!
HMPH
HE JUST REFUSED TO SAY ANYTHING.
WAIT!
TAKISHIMA!
WHAT'S GOING ON?
TENSE
TENSE
SWEAT
SWEAT
HIKARI'S STUCK TO KEI LIKE GLUE!
THEY ARE GETTING TO BE THAT AGE, YOU KNOW. ☆
HA HA HA HA
Do you even know what you're saying?
FWAK
Yeah.
It was getting so peace-ful.
Sorry.
SO...?
WHAT?
KEI'S TYPE?
YEAH.
YOU'VE KNOWN HIM SINCE YOU WERE LITTLE, RIGHT? I THOUGHT YOU MIGHT KNOW.
...
LET...
LET ME... SEE...
SPLISH
SPLISH
SPLAT
SPLAT
KLANK
KLANK

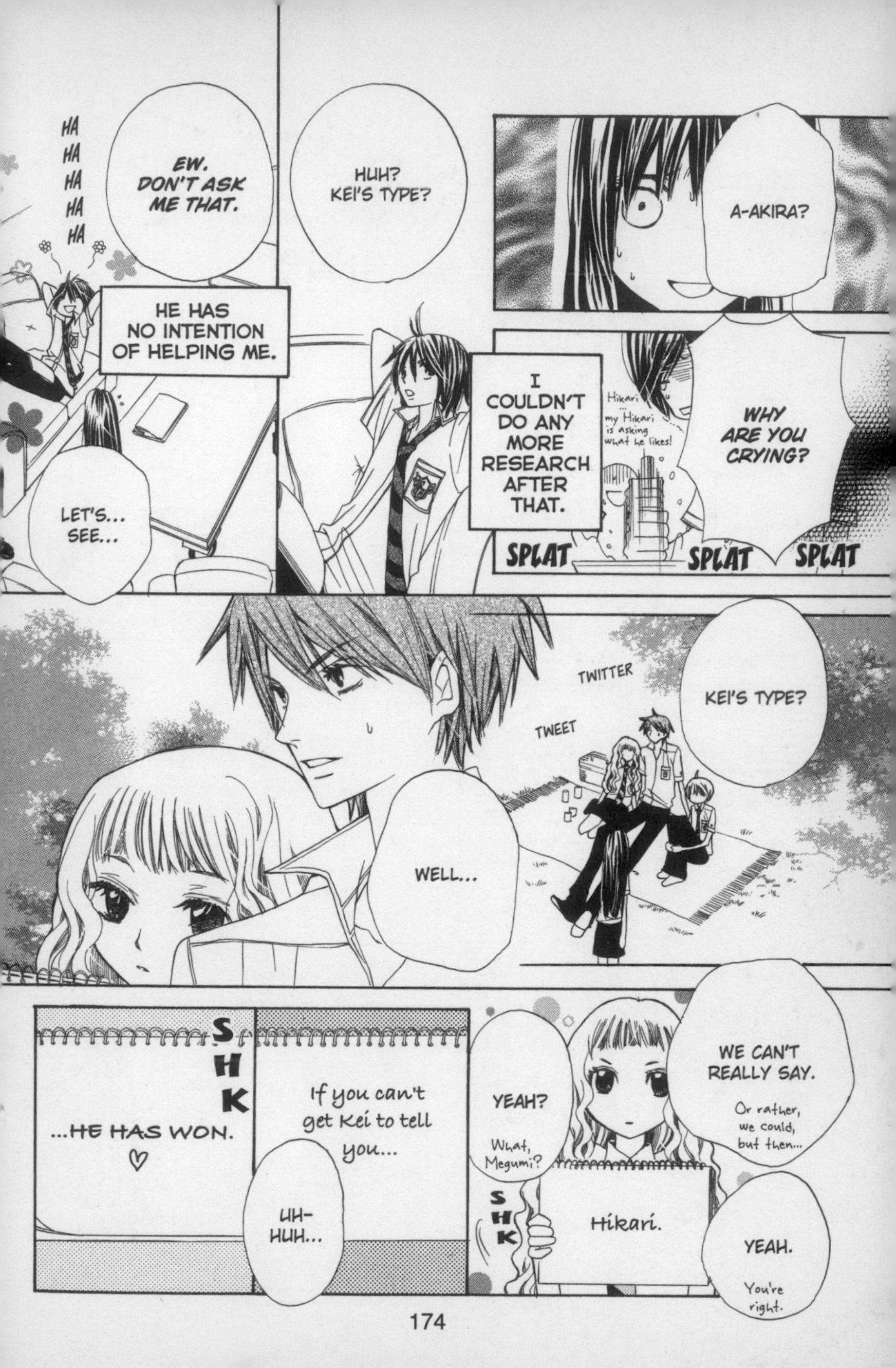
A-AKIRA?
WHY ARE YOU CRYING?
Hikari... my Hikari is asking what he likes!
I COULDN'T DO ANY MORE RESEARCH AFTER THAT.
SPLAT SPLAT SPLAT
HUH? KEI'S TYPE?
EW. DON'T ASK ME THAT.
HA HA HA HA HA
HE HAS NO INTENTION OF HELPING ME.
LET'S... SEE...
KEI'S TYPE?
TWITTER
TWEET
WELL...
WE CAN'T REALLY SAY.
Or rather, we could, but then...
YEAH?
What, Megumi?
Hikari.
SHK
YEAH.
You're right.
If you can't get Kei to tell you...
UH-HUH...
SHK
...HE HAS WON. ♡

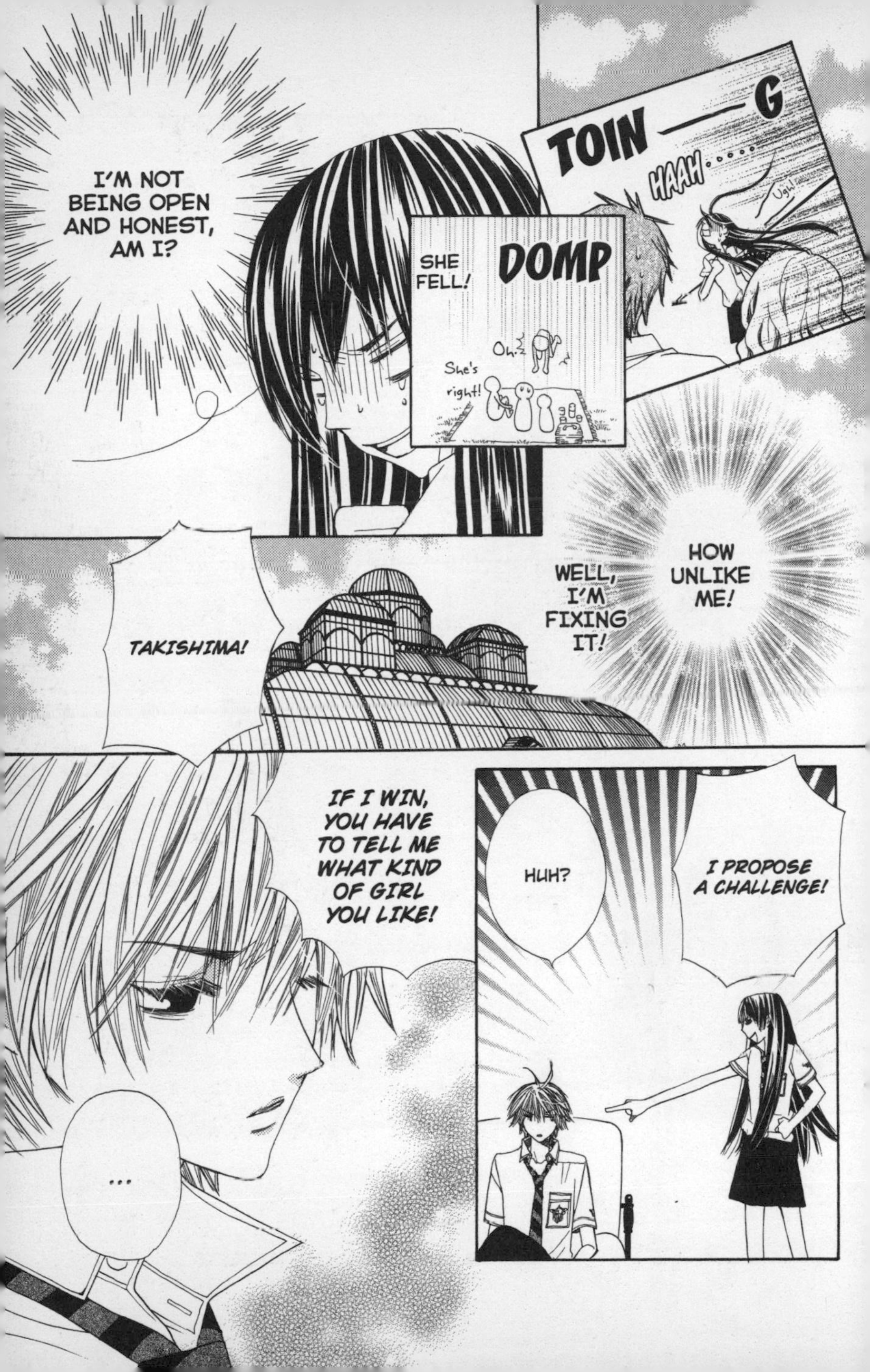
TOIN—G
HAAH.....
Ugh!
DOMP
SHE FELL!
Oh...
She's right!
I'M NOT BEING OPEN AND HONEST, AM I?
HOW UNLIKE ME!
WELL, I'M FIXING IT!
TAKISHIMA!
I PROPOSE A CHALLENGE!
HUH?
IF I WIN, YOU HAVE TO TELL ME WHAT KIND OF GIRL YOU LIKE!
...

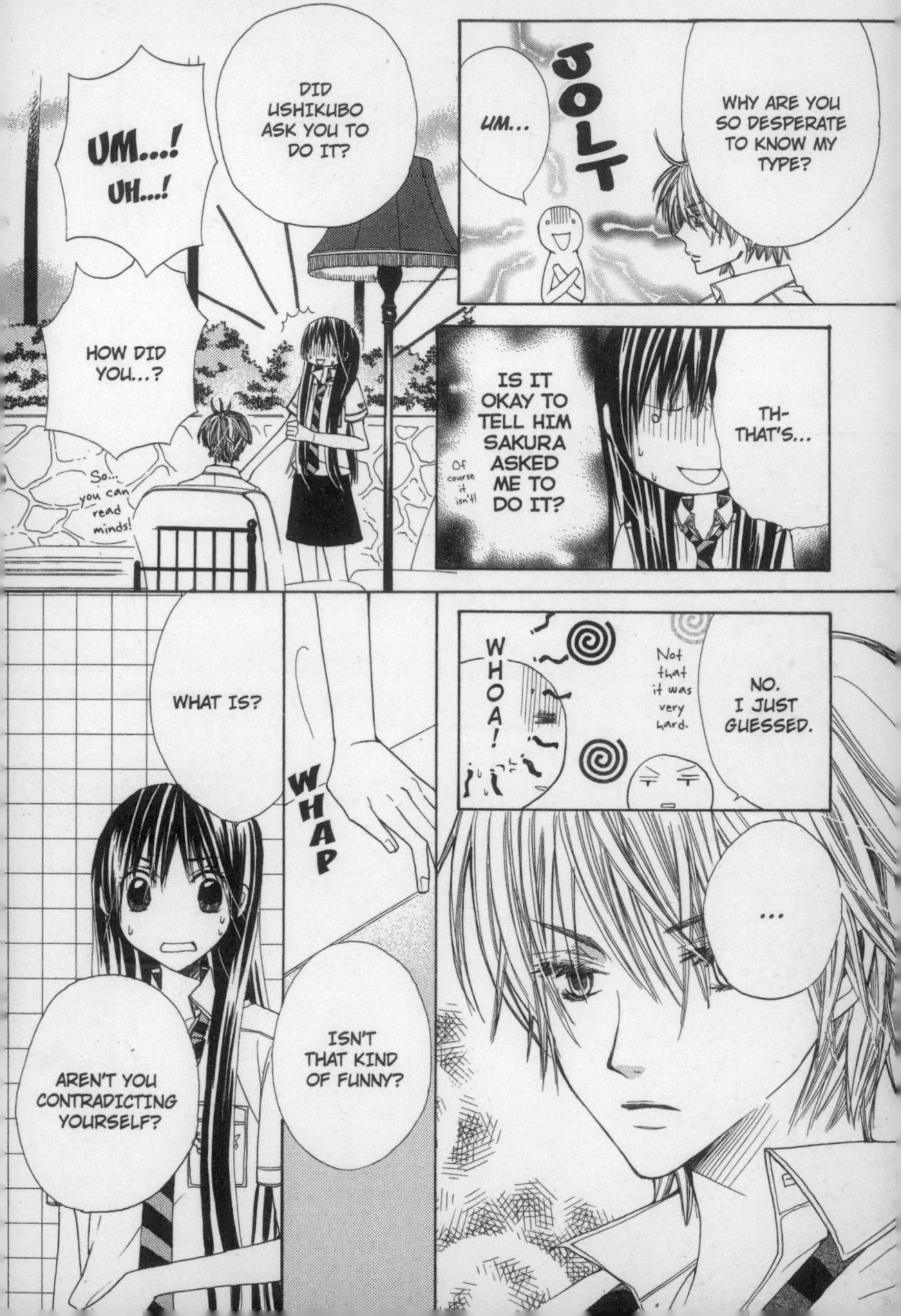
WHY ARE YOU SO DESPERATE TO KNOW MY TYPE?
JOLT
UM...
TH-THAT'S...
IS IT OKAY TO TELL HIM SAKURA ASKED ME TO DO IT?
Of course it isn't!
DID USHIKUBO ASK YOU TO DO IT?
UM...! UH...!
HOW DID YOU...?
So... you can read minds!
NO. I JUST GUESSED.
Not that it was very hard.
WHOA!
...
WHAP
ISN'T THAT KIND OF FUNNY?
WHAT IS?
AREN'T YOU CONTRADICTING YOURSELF?

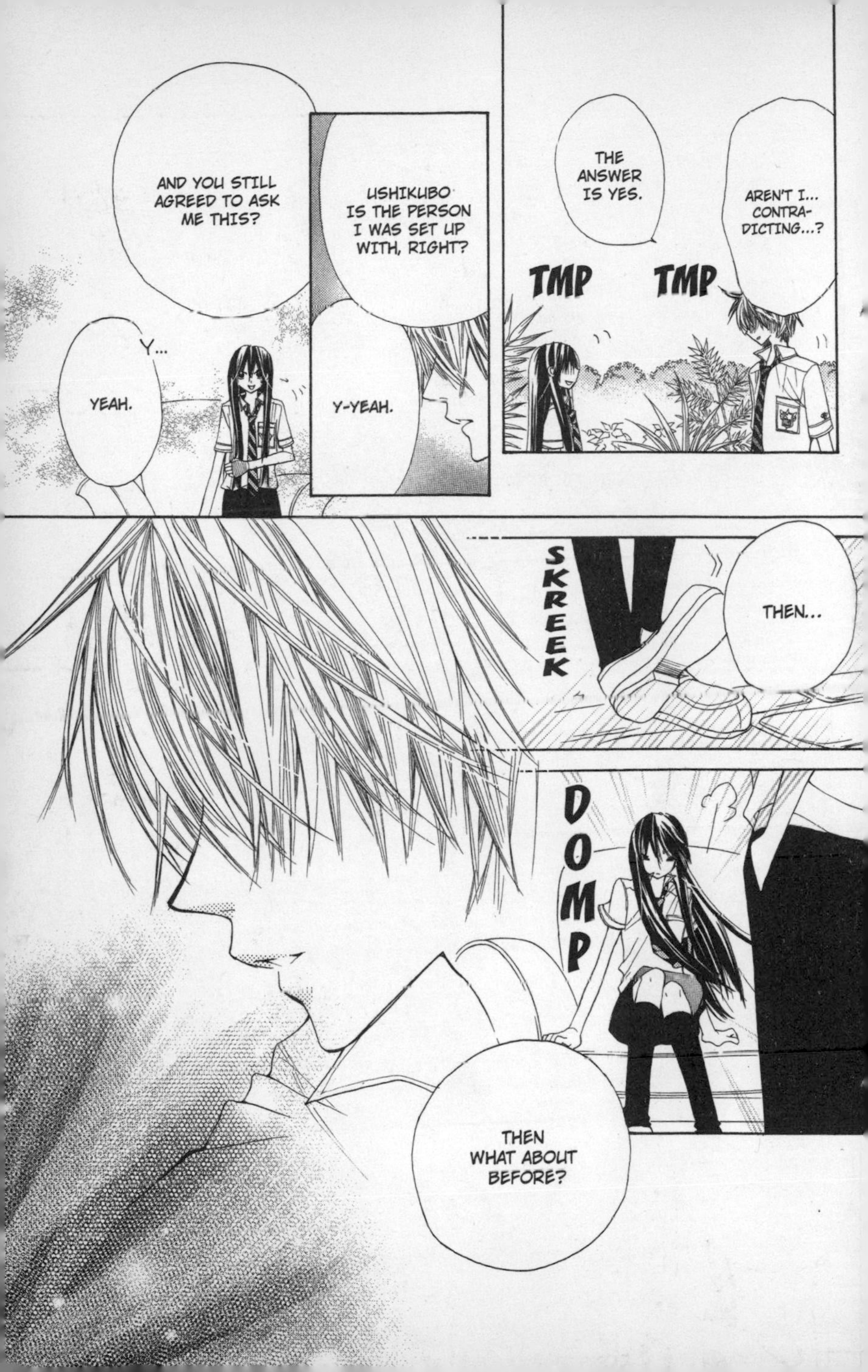
AREN'T I... CONTRA-DICTING...?
THE ANSWER IS YES.
TMP
TMP
USHIKUBO IS THE PERSON I WAS SET UP WITH, RIGHT?
Y-YEAH.
AND YOU STILL AGREED TO ASK ME THIS?
Y...
YEAH.
THEN...
SKREEK
DOMP
THEN WHAT ABOUT BEFORE?

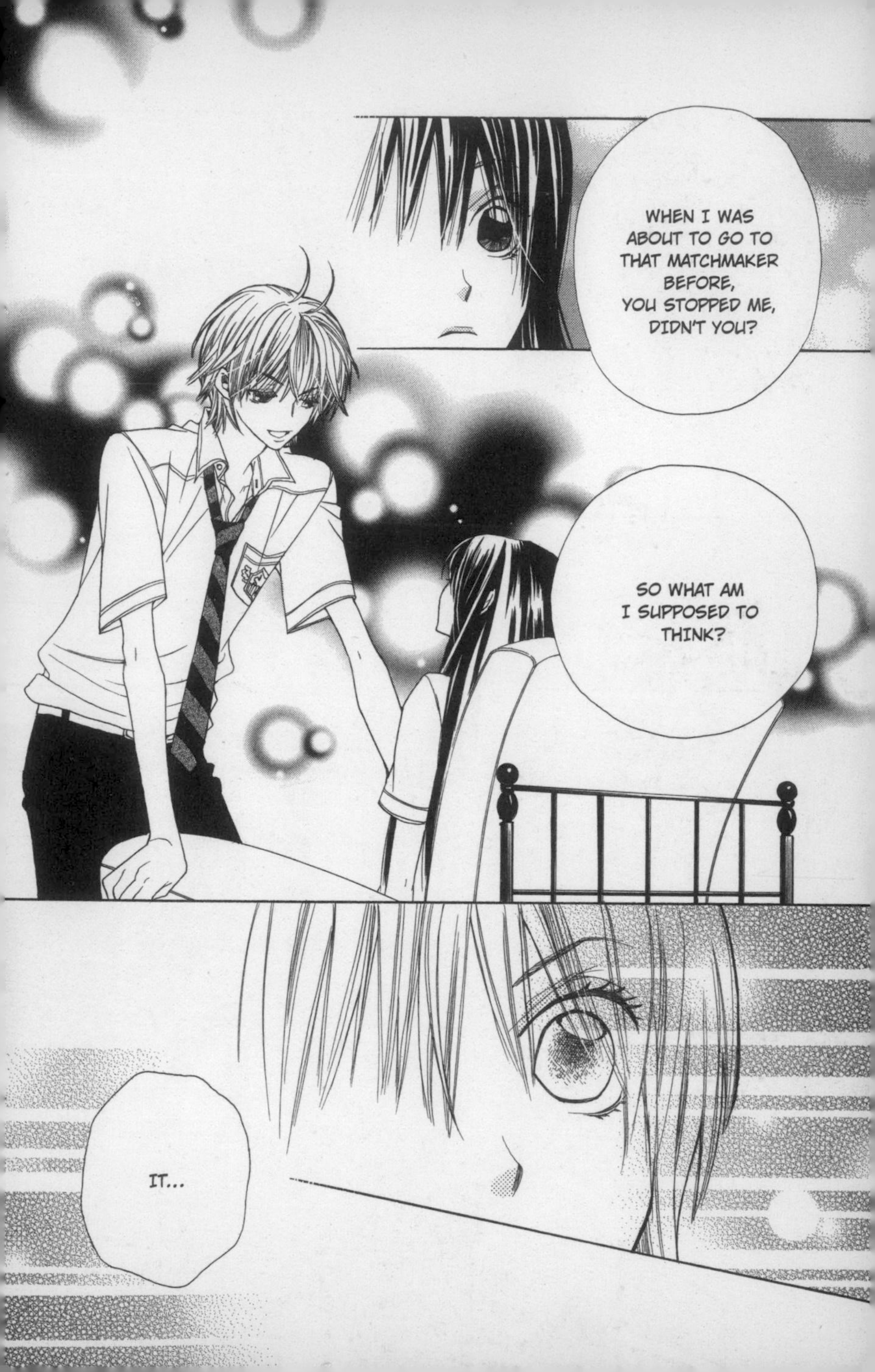
WHEN I WAS ABOUT TO GO TO THAT MATCHMAKER BEFORE, YOU STOPPED ME, DIDN'T YOU?
SO WHAT AM I SUPPOSED TO THINK?
IT...

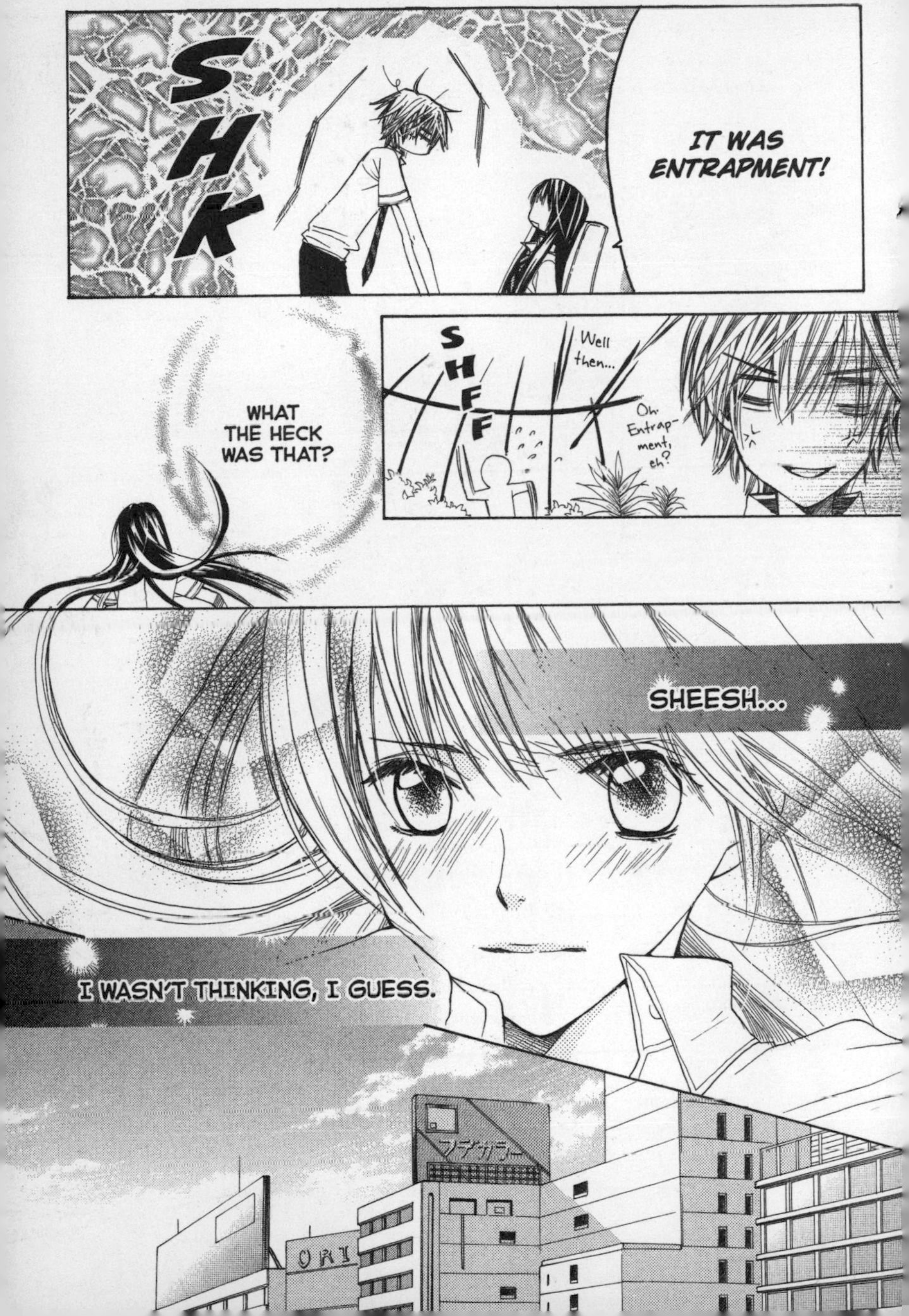
IT WAS ENTRAPMENT!
SHK
Well then...
Oh Entrapment, eh?
SHFF
WHAT THE HECK WAS THAT?
SHEESH...
I WASN'T THINKING, I GUESS.

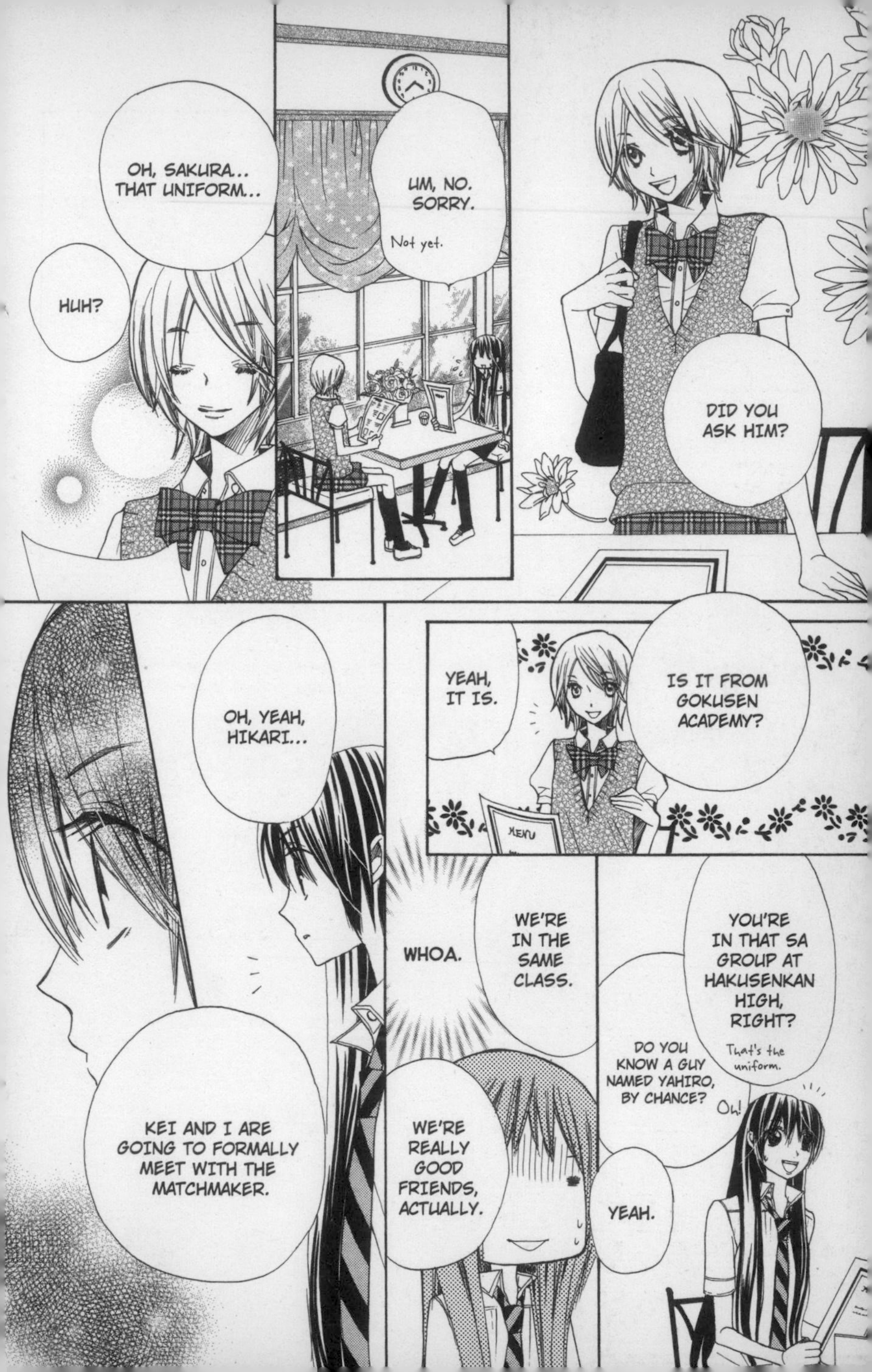
DID YOU ASK HIM?
UM, NO. SORRY.
Not yet.
OH, SAKURA... THAT UNIFORM...
HUH?
IS IT FROM GOKUSEN ACADEMY?
YEAH, IT IS.
YOU'RE IN THAT SA GROUP AT HAKUSENKAN HIGH, RIGHT?
That's the uniform.
Oh!
DO YOU KNOW A GUY NAMED YAHIRO, BY CHANCE?
YEAH.
WE'RE IN THE SAME CLASS.
WHOA.
WE'RE REALLY GOOD FRIENDS, ACTUALLY.
OH, YEAH, HIKARI...
KEI AND I ARE GOING TO FORMALLY MEET WITH THE MATCHMAKER.

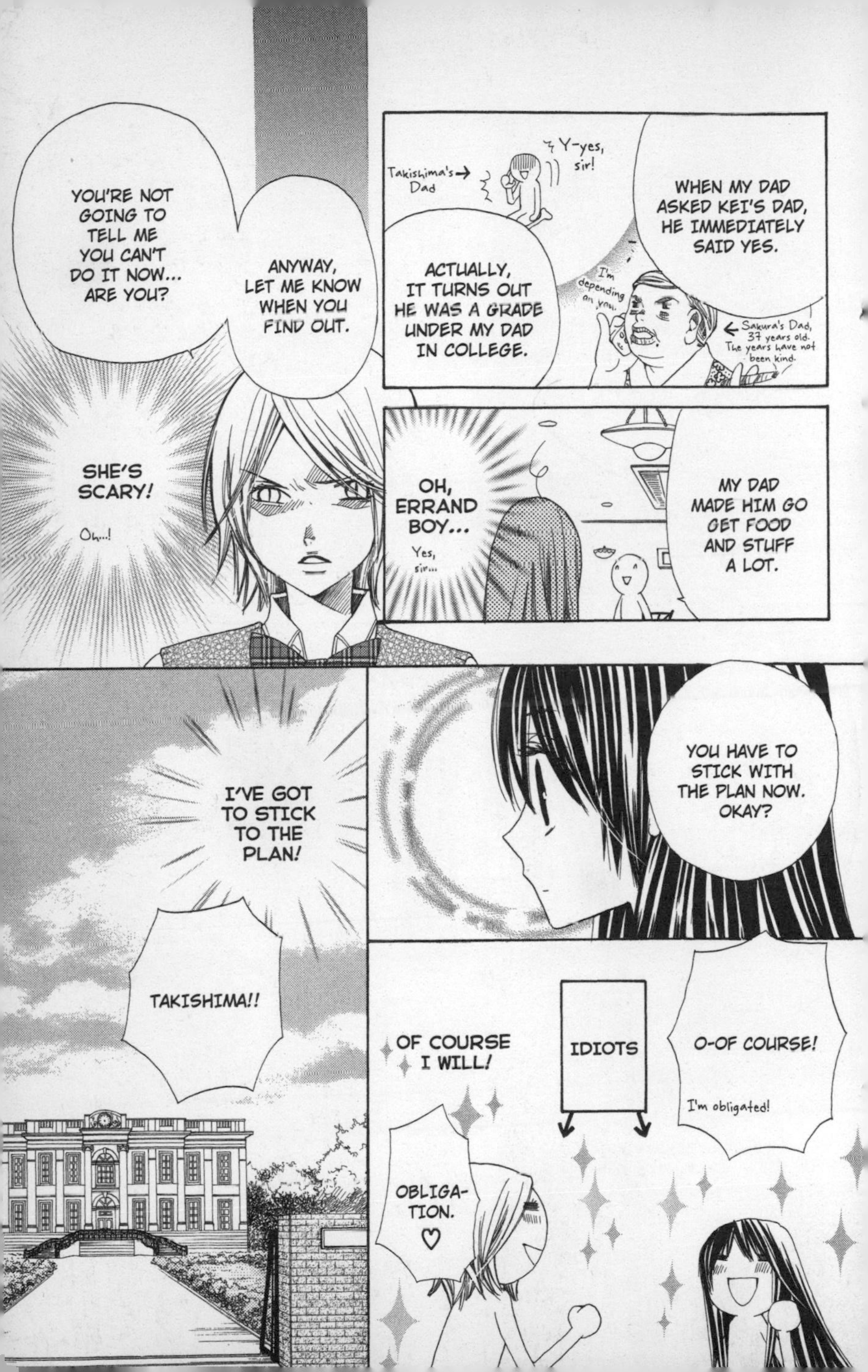
WHEN MY DAD ASKED KEI'S DAD, HE IMMEDIATELY SAID YES.
Y-yes, sir!
Takishima's Dad
I'm depending on you.
Sakura's Dad, 37 years old. The years have not been kind.
ACTUALLY, IT TURNS OUT HE WAS A GRADE UNDER MY DAD IN COLLEGE.
MY DAD MADE HIM GO GET FOOD AND STUFF A LOT.
OH, ERRAND BOY...
Yes, sir...
ANYWAY, LET ME KNOW WHEN YOU FIND OUT.
YOU'RE NOT GOING TO TELL ME YOU CAN'T DO IT NOW... ARE YOU?
SHE'S SCARY!
Oh...!
YOU HAVE TO STICK WITH THE PLAN NOW. OKAY?
O-OF COURSE!
I'm obligated!
IDIOTS
OF COURSE I WILL!
OBLIGA-TION. ♡
I'VE GOT TO STICK TO THE PLAN!
TAKISHIMA!!

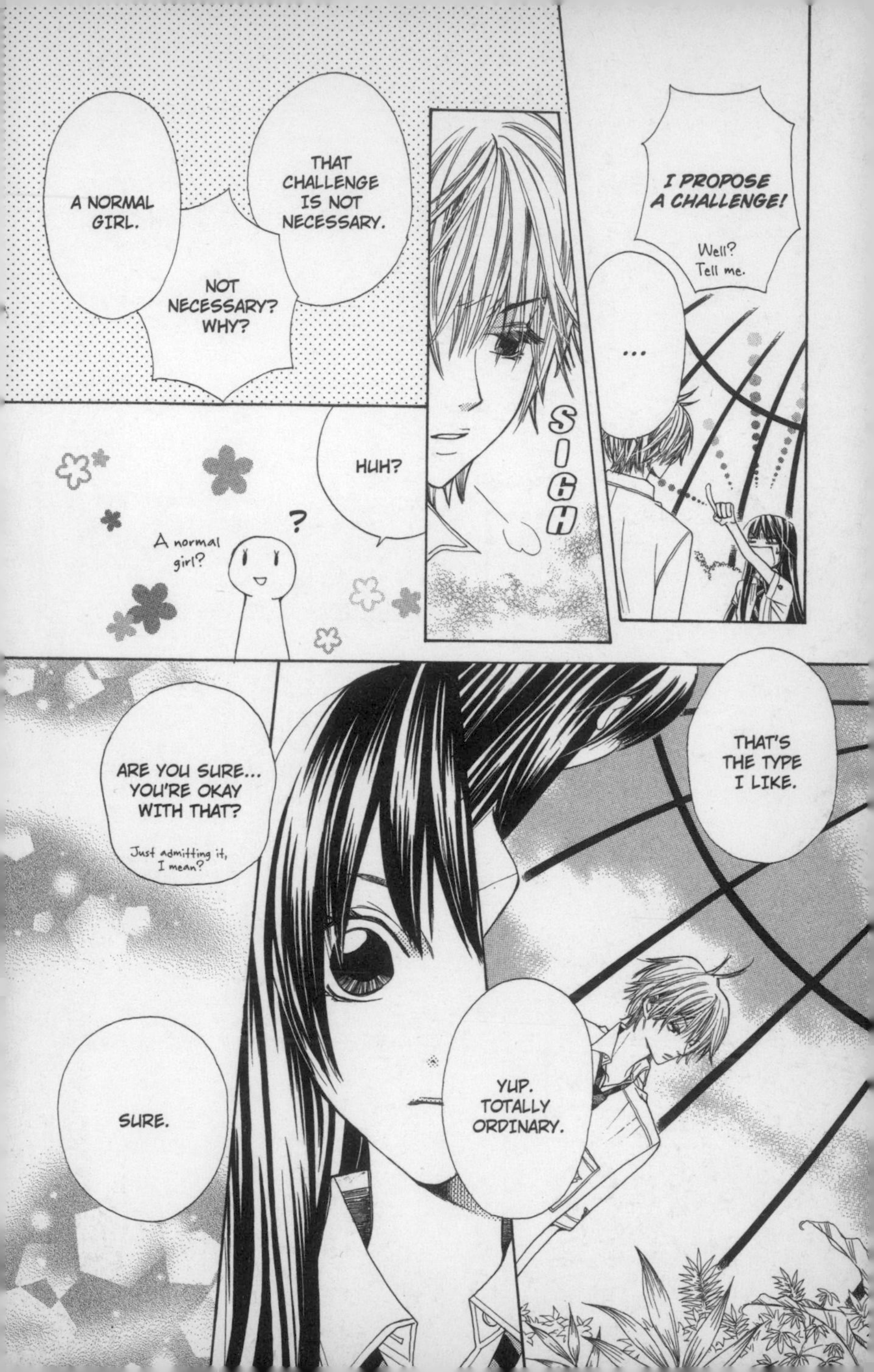
I PROPOSE A CHALLENGE!
Well? Tell me.
...
SIGH
THAT CHALLENGE IS NOT NECESSARY.
NOT NECESSARY? WHY?
A NORMAL GIRL.
HUH?
?
A normal girl?
THAT'S THE TYPE I LIKE.
ARE YOU SURE... YOU'RE OKAY WITH THAT?
Just admitting it, I mean?
YUP. TOTALLY ORDINARY.
SURE.

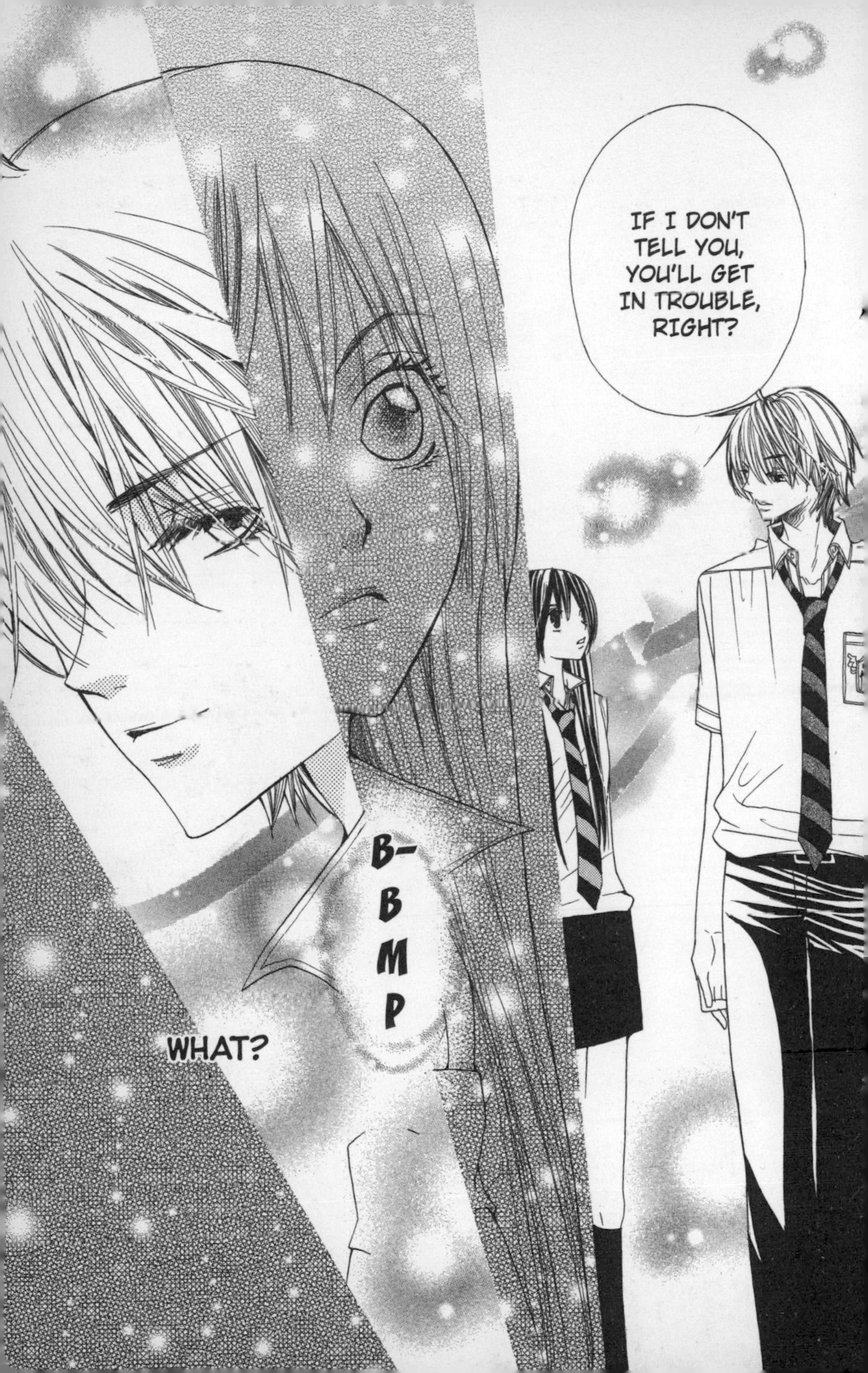
IF I DON'T TELL YOU, YOU'LL GET IN TROUBLE, RIGHT?
B-BMP
WHAT?

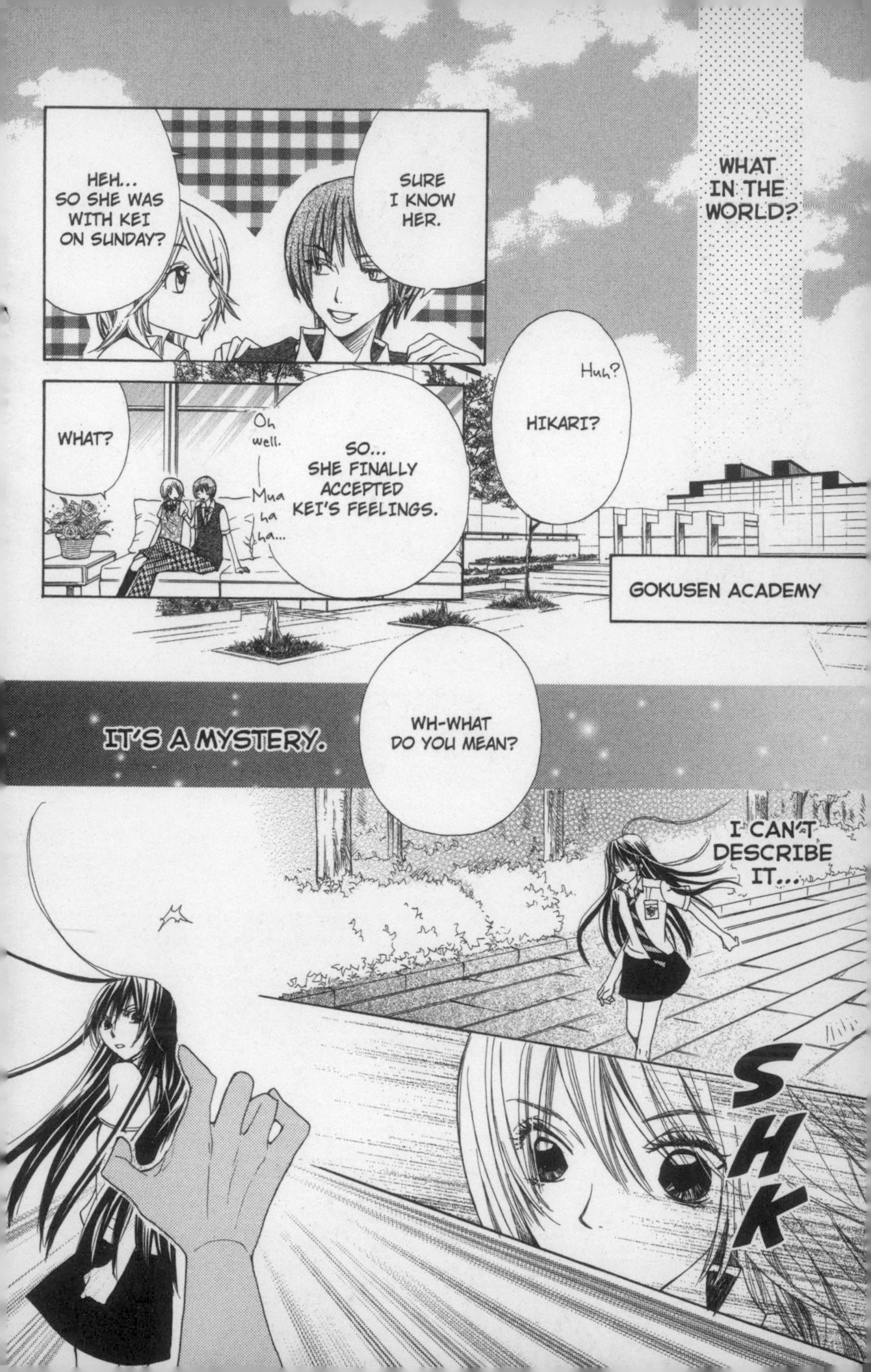
WHAT IN THE WORLD?
GOKUSEN ACADEMY
Huh?
HIKARI?
SURE I KNOW HER.
HEH... SO SHE WAS WITH KEI ON SUNDAY?
SO... SHE FINALLY ACCEPTED KEI'S FEELINGS.
Oh well.
Mua ha ha...
WHAT?
WH-WHAT DO YOU MEAN?
IT'S A MYSTERY.
I CAN'T DESCRIBE IT...
SHK

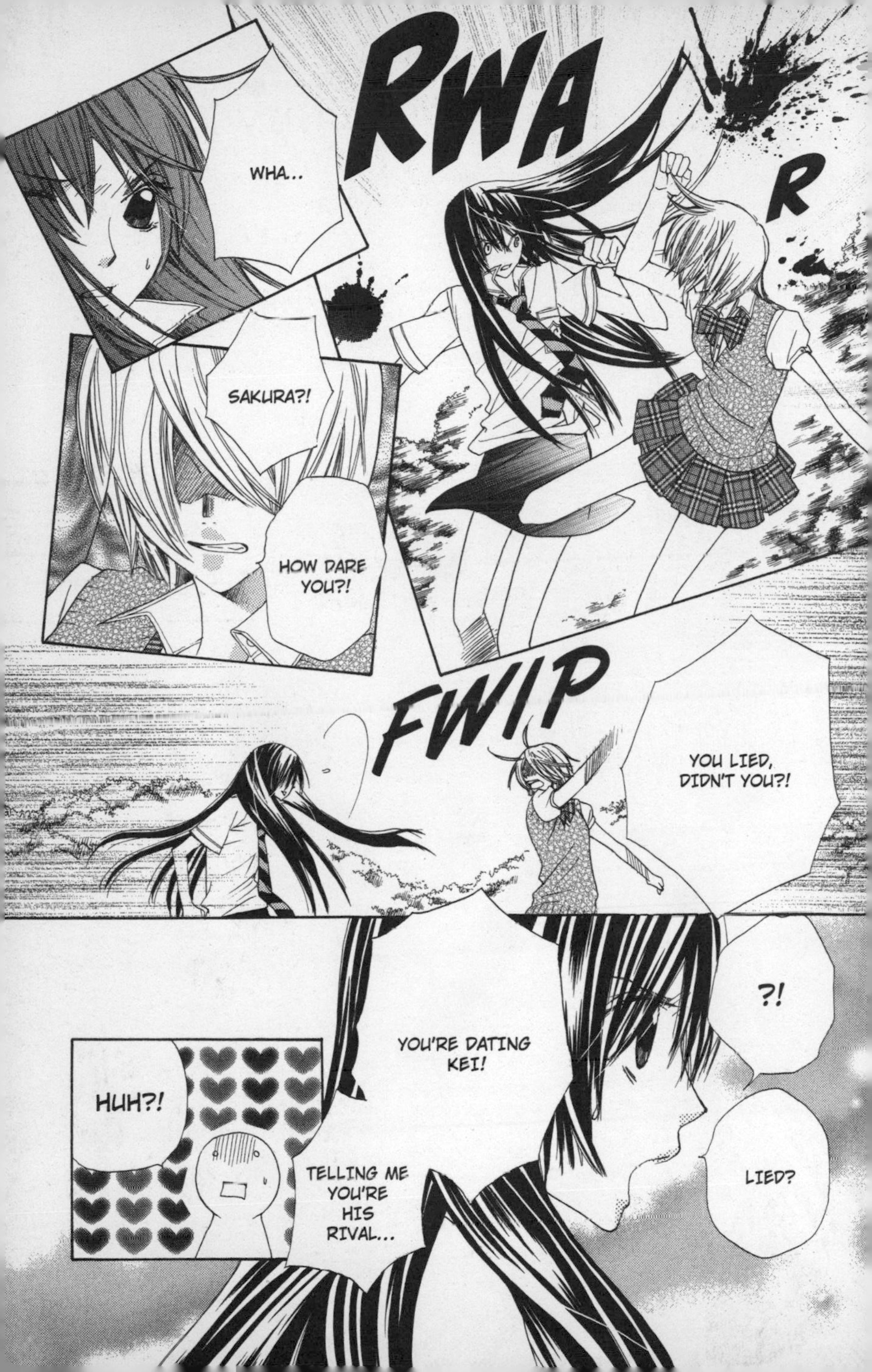
RWA
R
WHA...
SAKURA?!
HOW DARE YOU?!
FWIP
YOU LIED, DIDN'T YOU?!
?!
LIED?
YOU'RE DATING KEI!
TELLING ME YOU'RE HIS RIVAL...
HUH?!

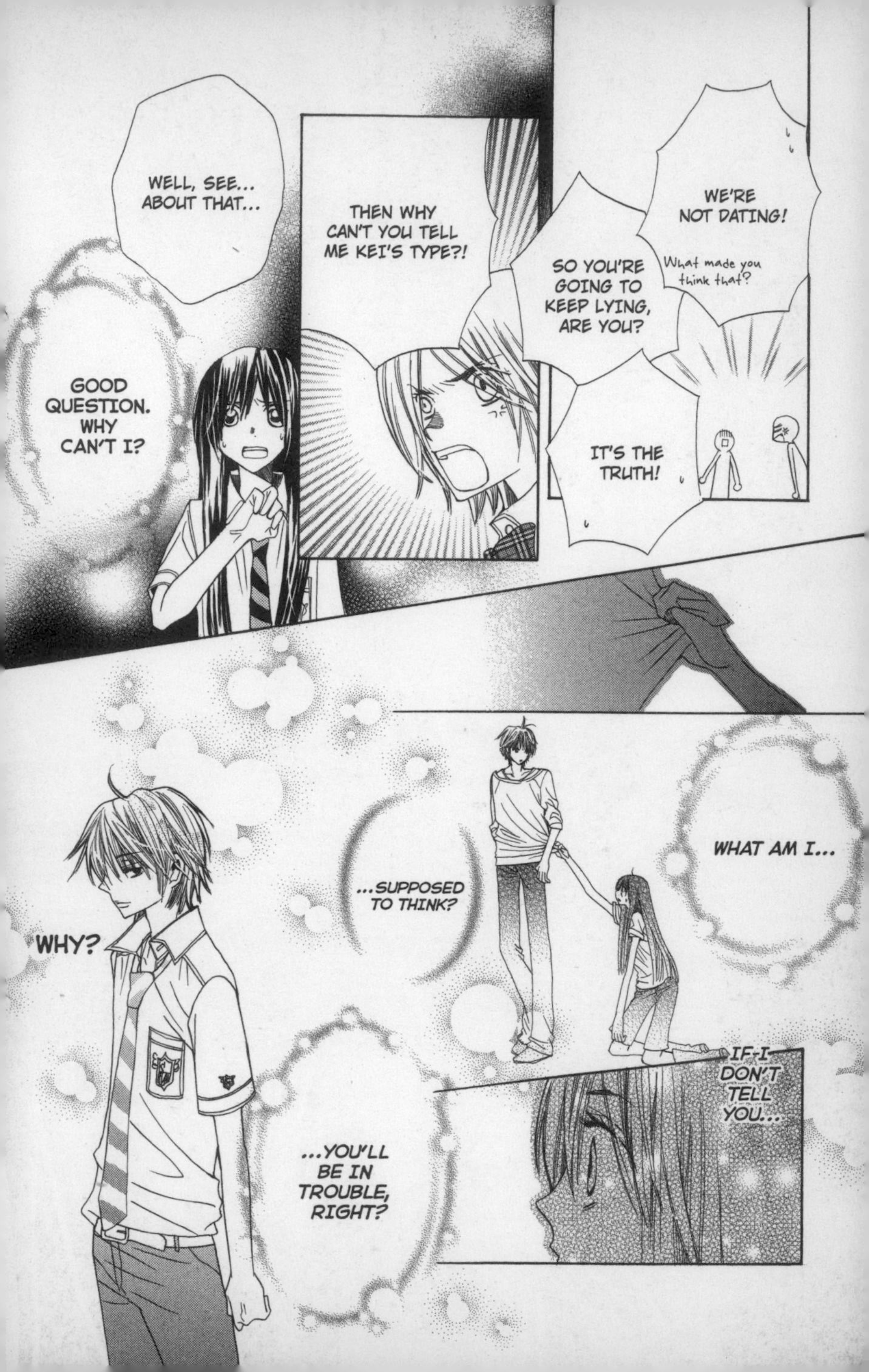
WE'RE NOT DATING!
What made you think that?
SO YOU'RE GOING TO KEEP LYING, ARE YOU?
IT'S THE TRUTH!
THEN WHY CAN'T YOU TELL ME KEI'S TYPE?!
WELL, SEE... ABOUT THAT...
GOOD QUESTION. WHY CAN'T I?
WHAT AM I...
...SUPPOSED TO THINK?
IF I DON'T TELL YOU...
...YOU'LL BE IN TROUBLE, RIGHT?
WHY?

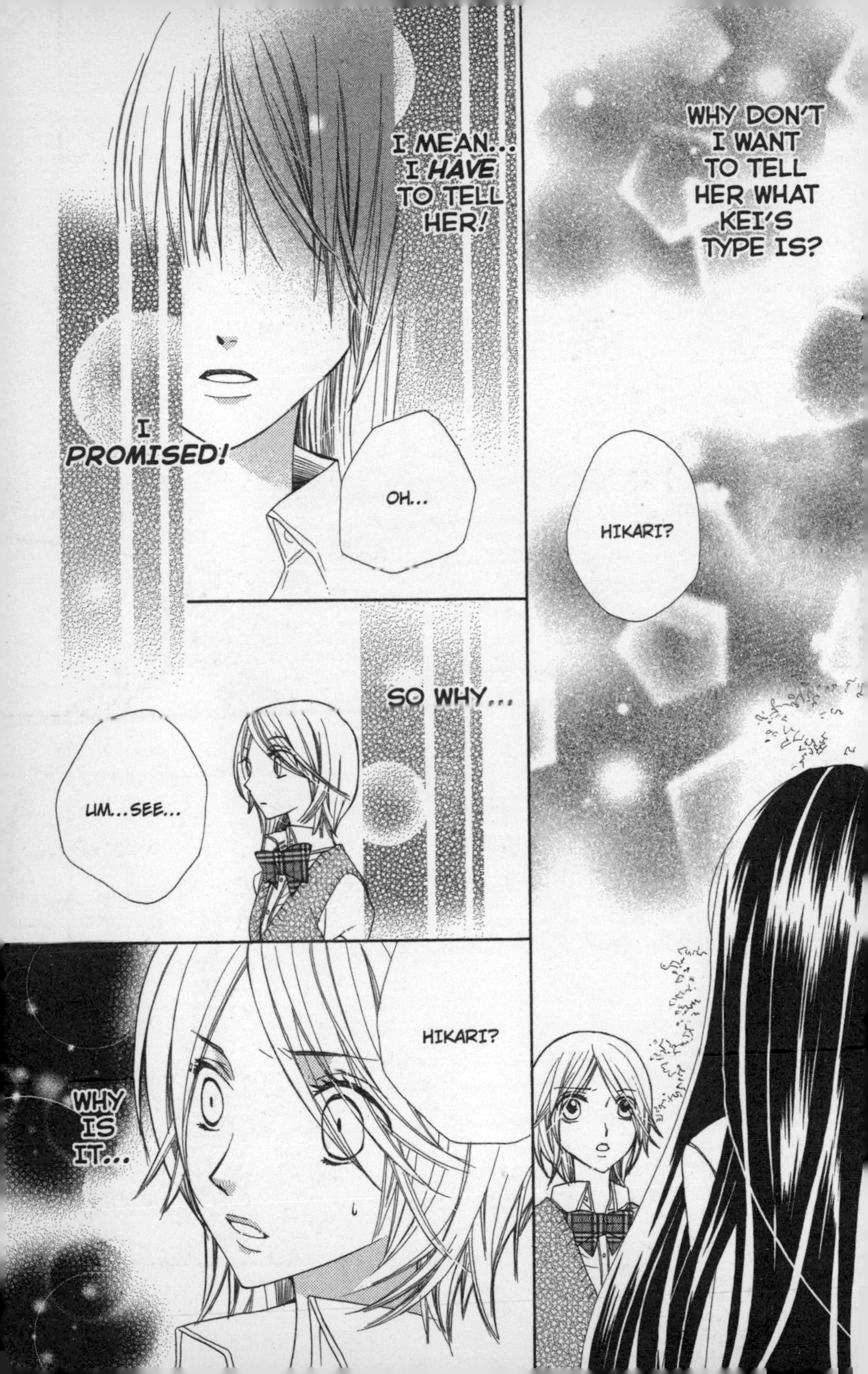
WHY DON'T I WANT TO TELL HER WHAT KEI'S TYPE IS?
HIKARI?
I MEAN... I *HAVE* TO TELL HER!
I PROMISED!
OH...
SO WHY...
UM...SEE...
HIKARI?
WHY IS IT...

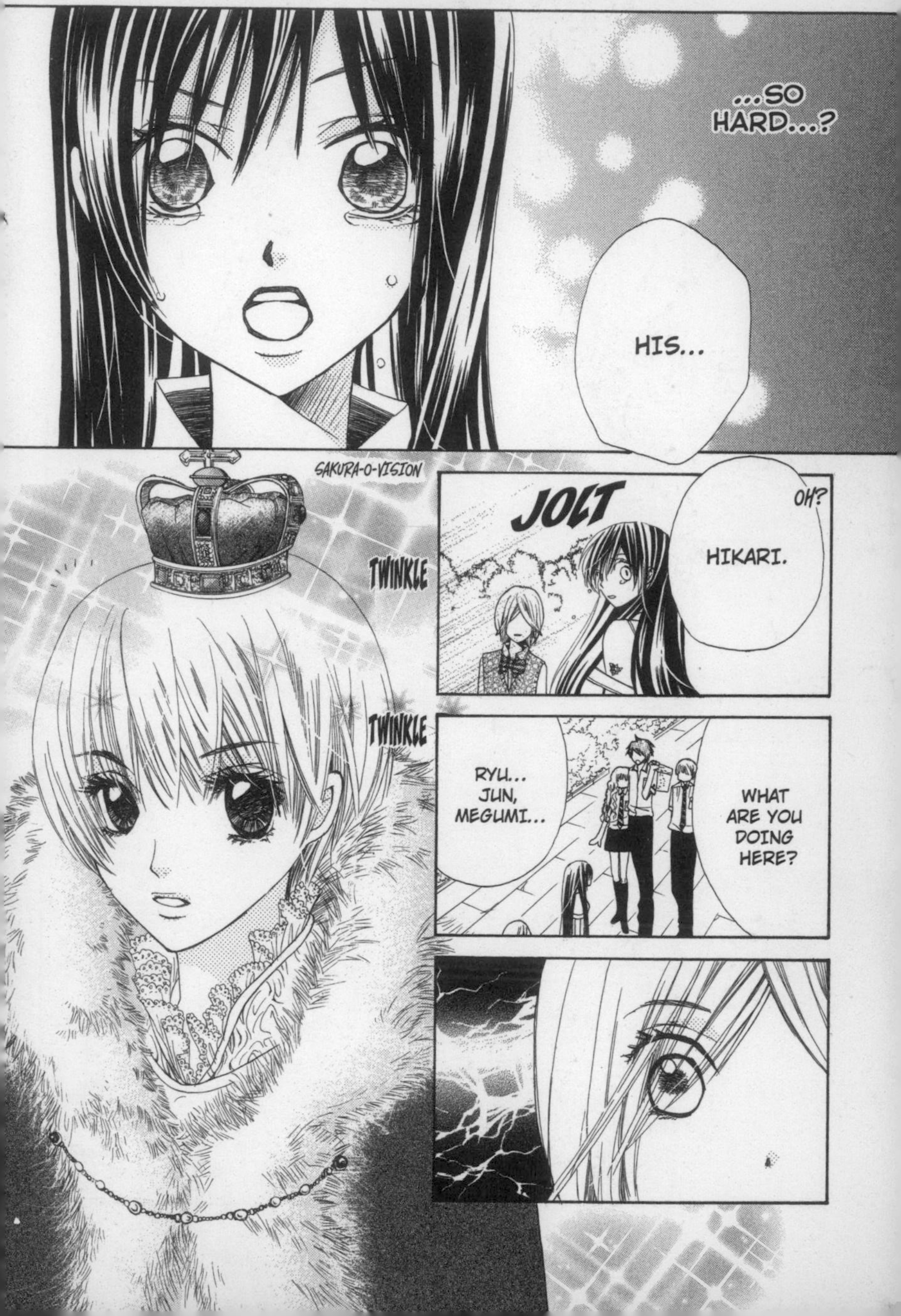
...SO HARD...?
HIS...
OH?
HIKARI.
JOLT
WHAT ARE YOU DOING HERE?
RYU... JUN, MEGUMI...
SAKURA-O-VISION
TWINKLE
TWINKLE

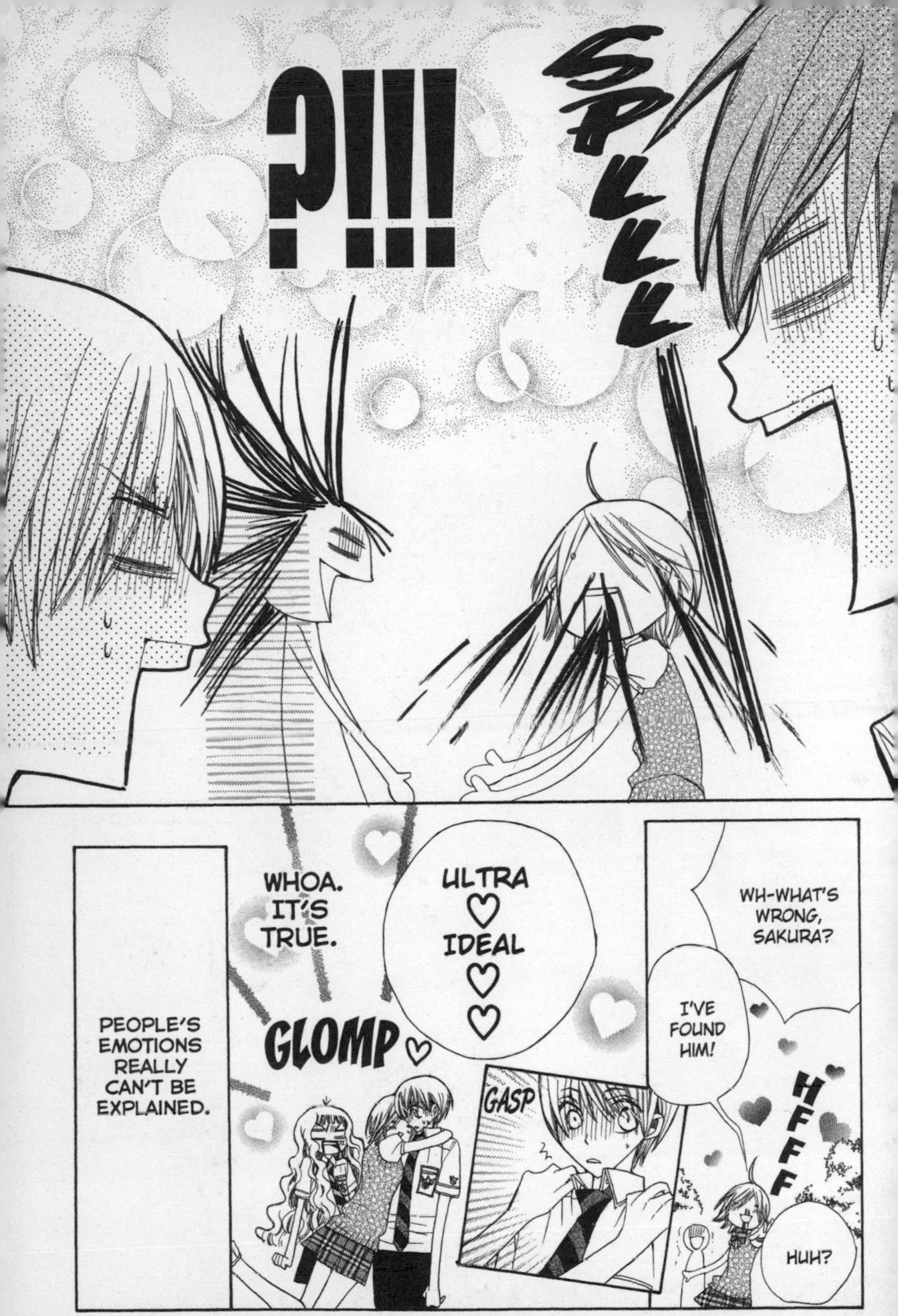
SPLLL
?!!!
WH-WHAT'S WRONG, SAKURA?
I'VE FOUND HIM!
HFFF
HUH?
GASP
ULTRA ♡ IDEAL ♡ ♡
WHOA. IT'S TRUE.
GLOMP ♡
PEOPLE'S EMOTIONS REALLY CAN'T BE EXPLAINED.

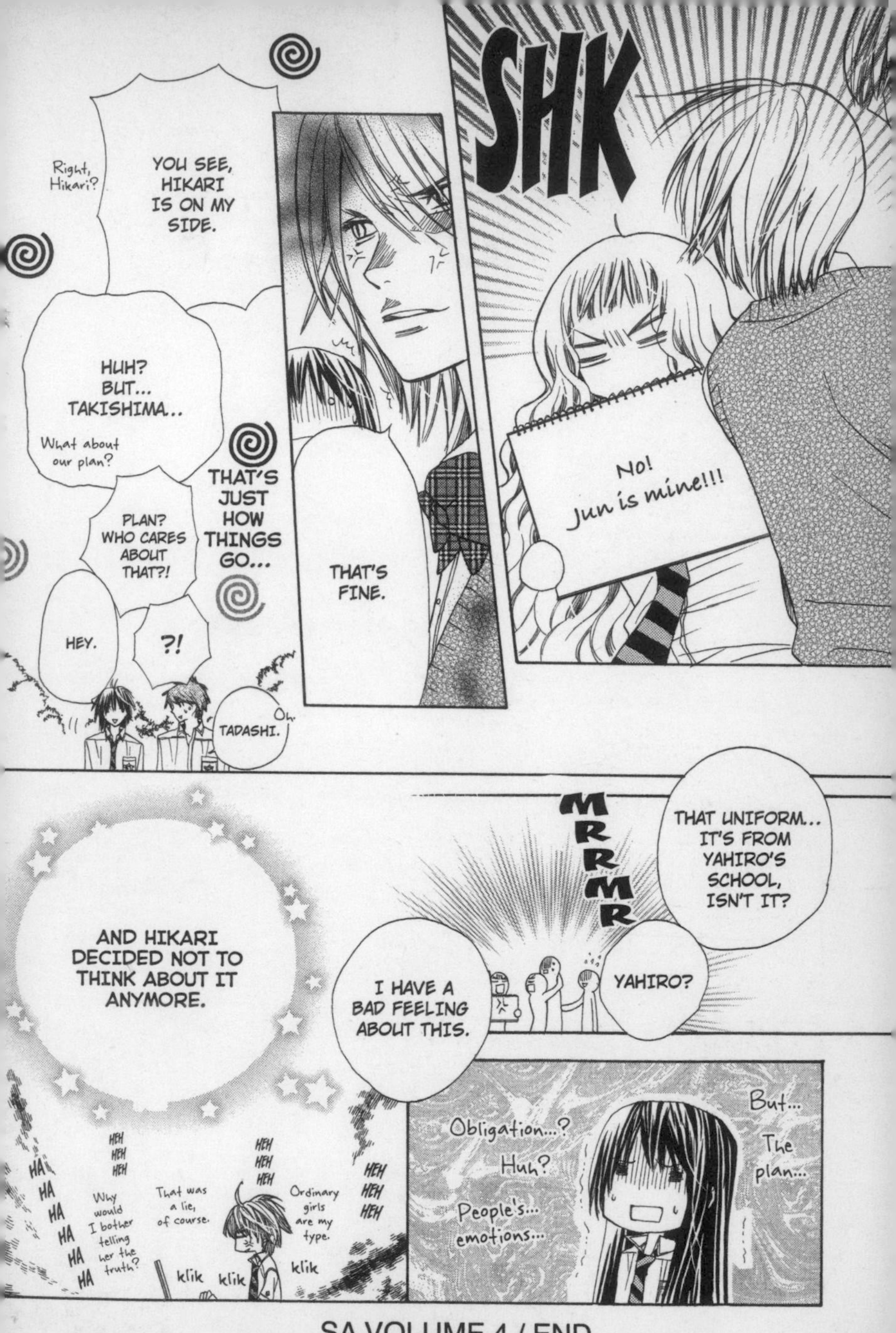
SHK
No! Jun is mine!!!
THAT'S FINE.
THAT'S JUST HOW THINGS GO...
YOU SEE, HIKARI IS ON MY SIDE.
Right, Hikari?
HUH? BUT... TAKISHIMA...
What about our plan?
PLAN? WHO CARES ABOUT THAT?!
?!
HEY.
Oh.
TADASHI.
THAT UNIFORM... IT'S FROM YAHIRO'S SCHOOL, ISN'T IT?
MRRMR
YAHIRO?
I HAVE A BAD FEELING ABOUT THIS.
AND HIKARI DECIDED NOT TO THINK ABOUT IT ANYMORE.
But...
The plan...
Obligation...?
Huh?
People's... emotions...
HEH HEH HEH
Ordinary girls are my type.
klik
HEH HEH HEH
That was a lie, of course.
klik klik
HEH HEH HEH
Why would I bother telling her the truth?
HA HA HA HA HA HA

SA VOLUME 4 / END

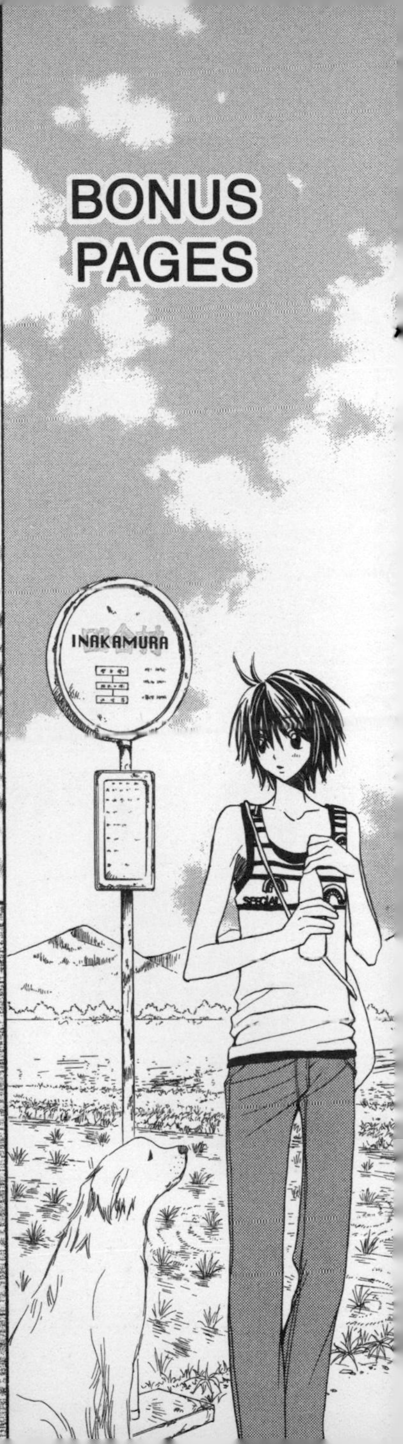
BONUS PAGES
INAKAMURA

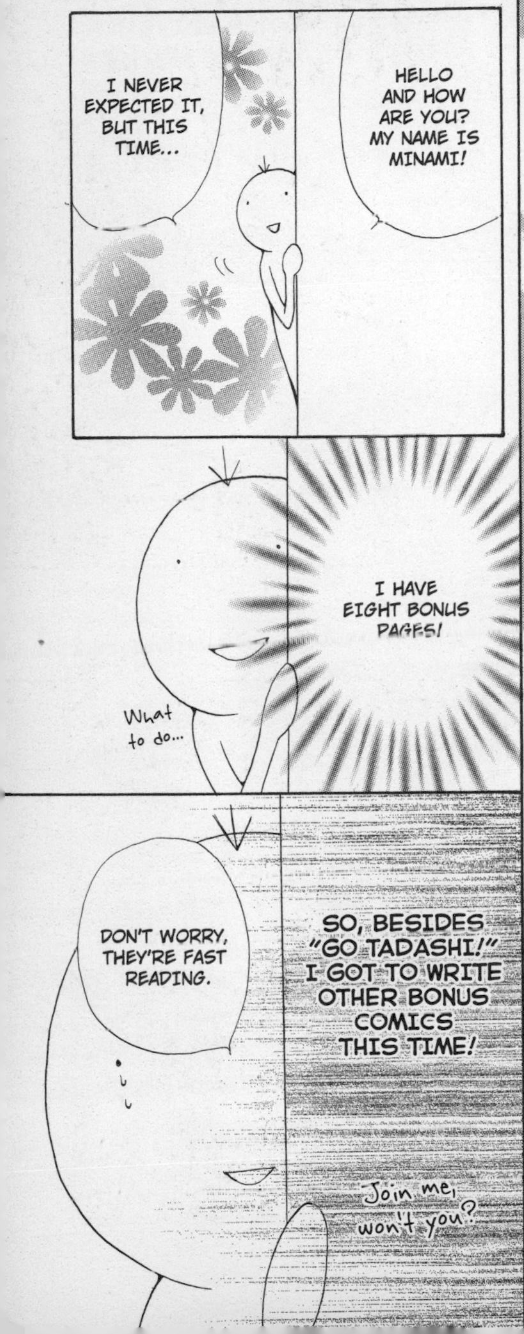
HELLO AND HOW ARE YOU? MY NAME IS MINAMI!
I NEVER EXPECTED IT, BUT THIS TIME...
I HAVE EIGHT BONUS PAGES!
What to do...
SO, BESIDES "GO TADASHI!" I GOT TO WRITE OTHER BONUS COMICS THIS TIME!
Join me, won't you?
DON'T WORRY, THEY'RE FAST READING.

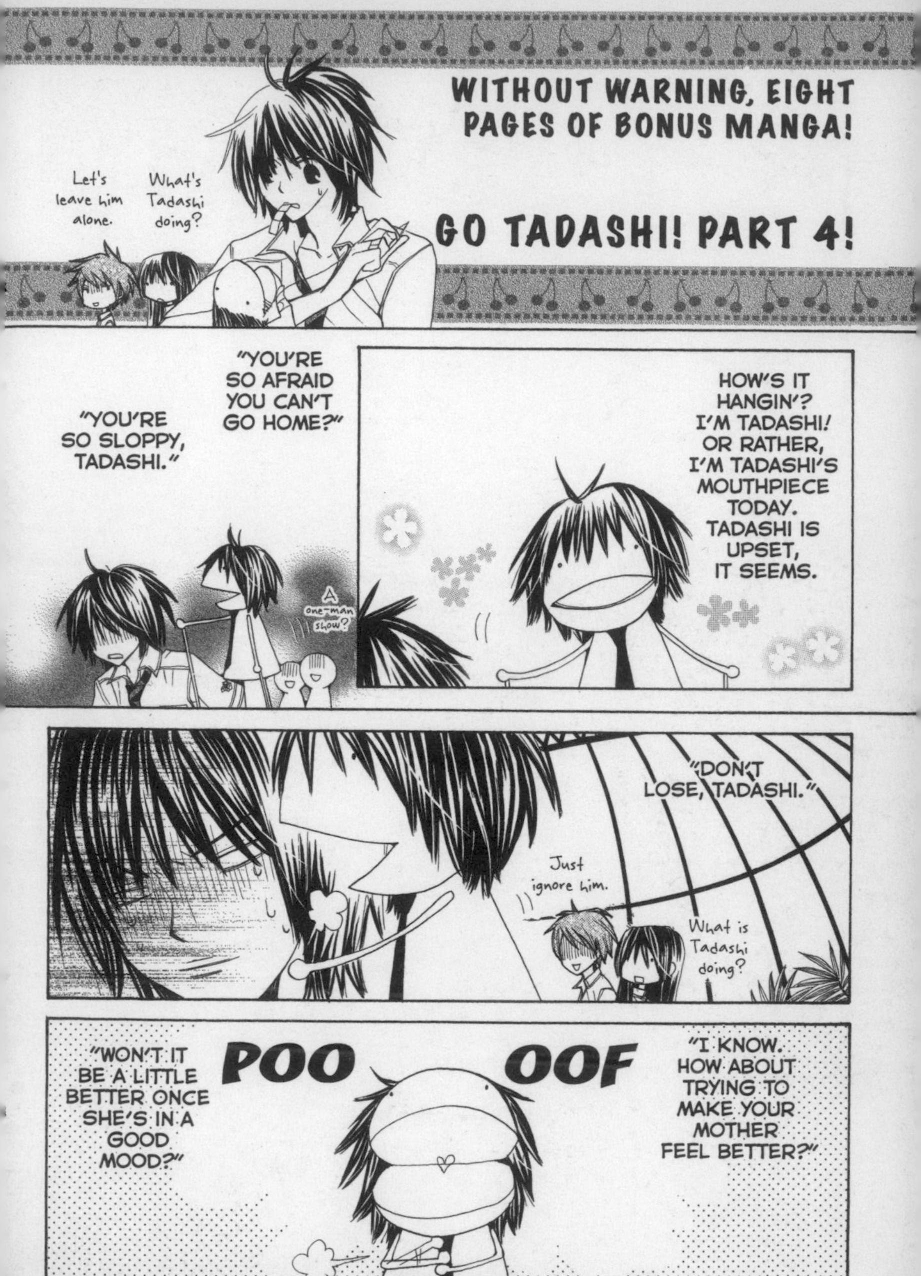
WITHOUT WARNING, EIGHT PAGES OF BONUS MANGA!
GO TADASHI! PART 4!
What's Tadashi doing?
Let's leave him alone.
HOW'S IT HANGIN'? I'M TADASHI! OR RATHER, I'M TADASHI'S MOUTHPIECE TODAY. TADASHI IS UPSET, IT SEEMS.
"YOU'RE SO AFRAID YOU CAN'T GO HOME?"
"YOU'RE SO SLOPPY, TADASHI."
A one-man show?
"DON'T LOSE, TADASHI."
Just ignore him.
What is Tadashi doing?
"I KNOW. HOW ABOUT TRYING TO MAKE YOUR MOTHER FEEL BETTER?"
OOF
POO
"WON'T IT BE A LITTLE BETTER ONCE SHE'S IN A GOOD MOOD?"

BONUS PAGE

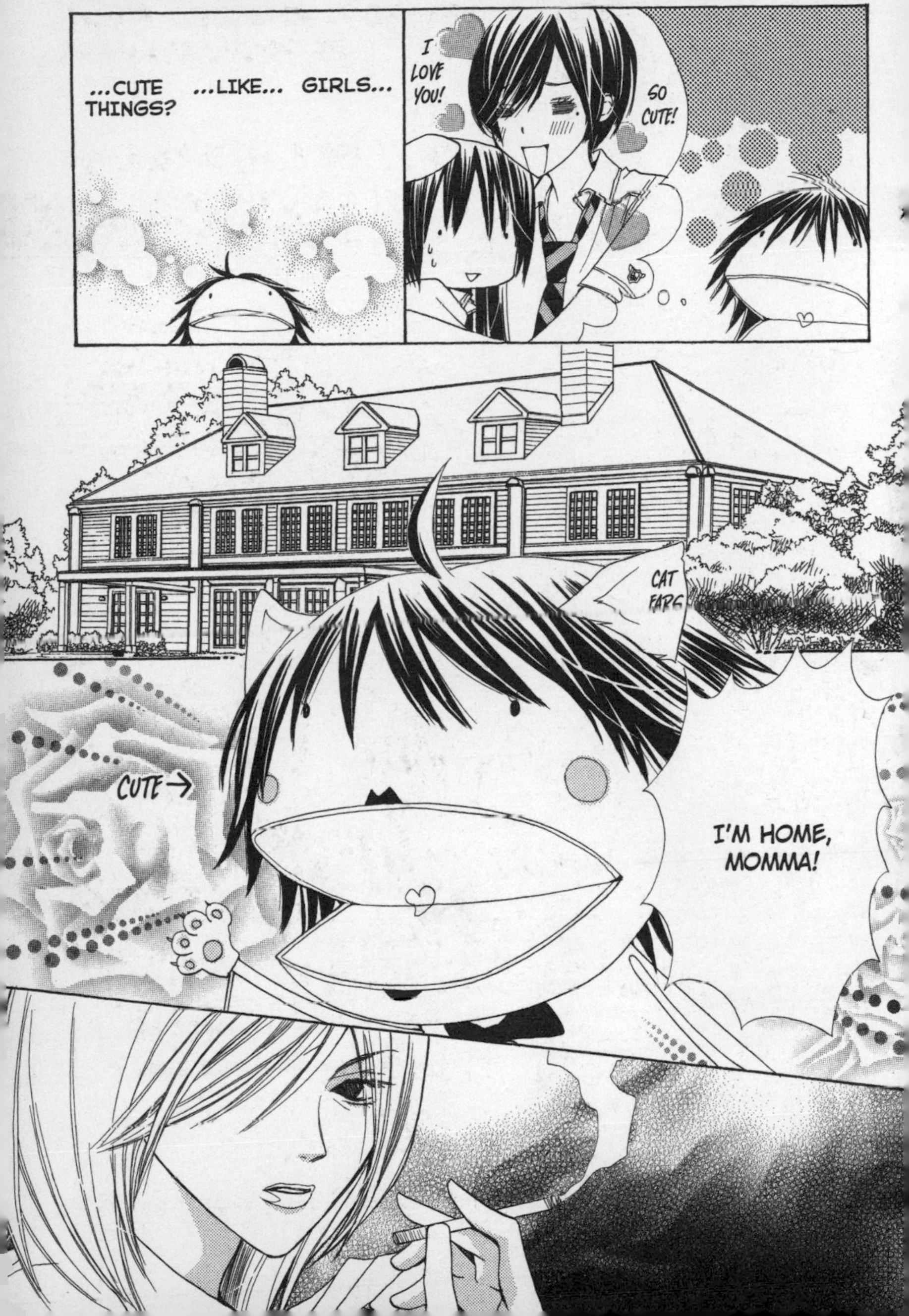
SO CUTE!
I LOVE YOU!
GIRLS...
...LIKE...
...CUTE THINGS?
CAT EARS
I'M HOME, MOMMA!
CUTE →

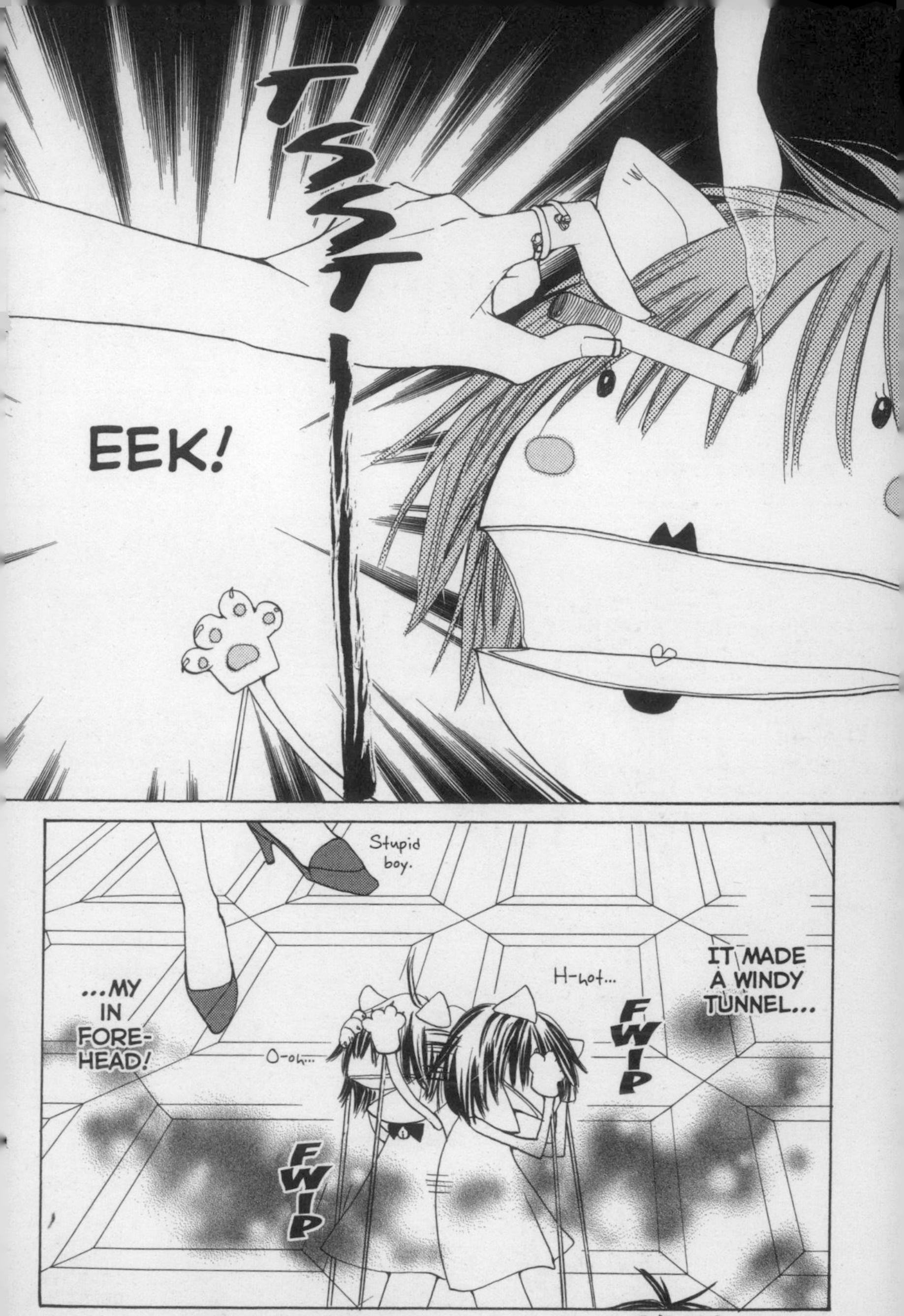
TSST
EEK!
Stupid boy.
IT MADE A WINDY TUNNEL...
H-hot...
FWIP
...MY IN FORE-HEAD!
O-oh...
FWIP

THE END

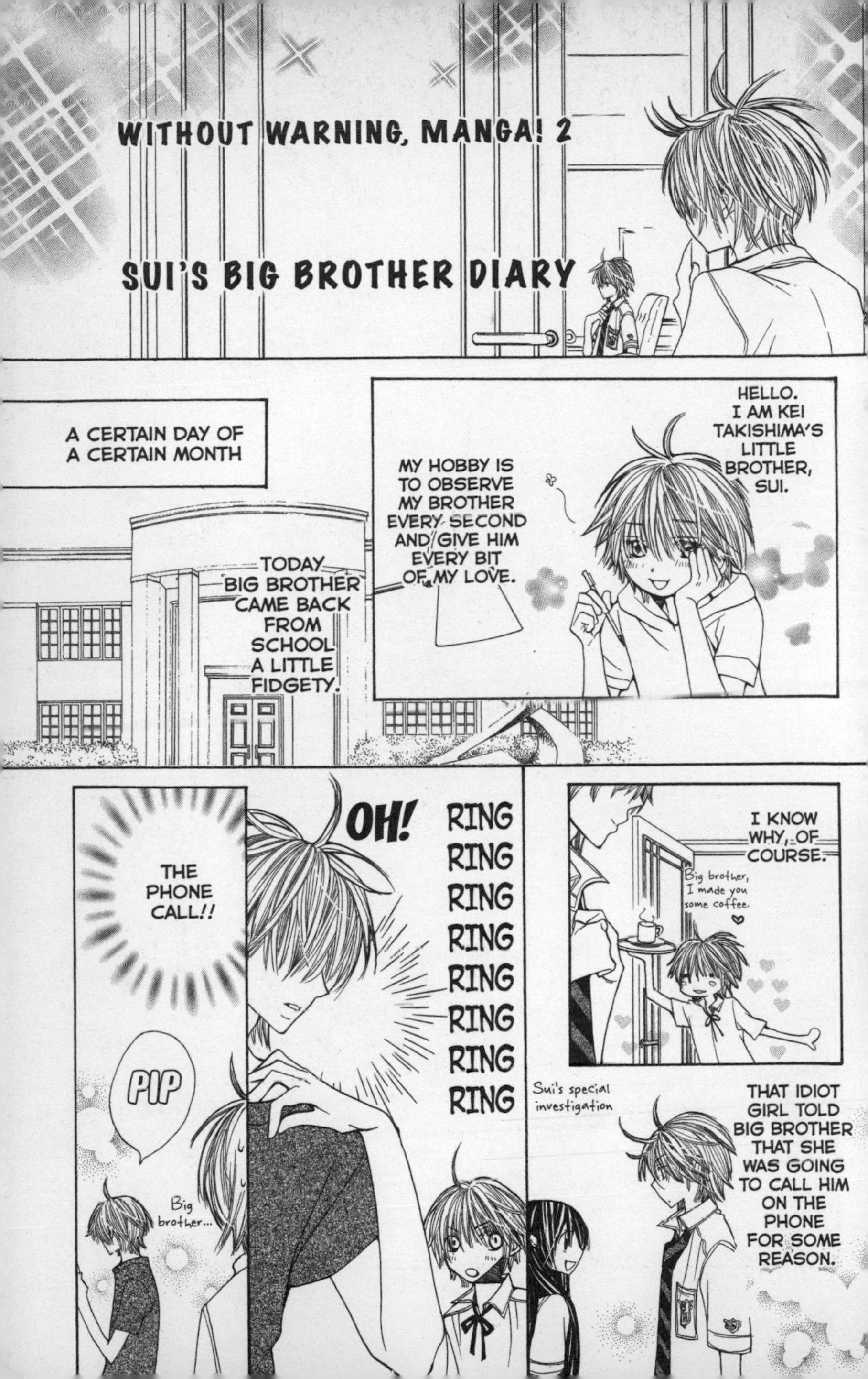
WITHOUT WARNING, MANGA! 2
SUI'S BIG BROTHER DIARY
HELLO. I AM KEI TAKISHIMA'S LITTLE BROTHER, SUI.
MY HOBBY IS TO OBSERVE MY BROTHER EVERY SECOND AND GIVE HIM EVERY BIT OF MY LOVE.
A CERTAIN DAY OF A CERTAIN MONTH
TODAY BIG BROTHER CAME BACK FROM SCHOOL A LITTLE FIDGETY.
I KNOW WHY, OF COURSE.
Big brother, I made you some coffee.
Sui's special investigation
THAT IDIOT GIRL TOLD BIG BROTHER THAT SHE WAS GOING TO CALL HIM ON THE PHONE FOR SOME REASON.
OH!
RING RING RING RING RING RING RING RING
THE PHONE CALL!!
PIP
Big brother...

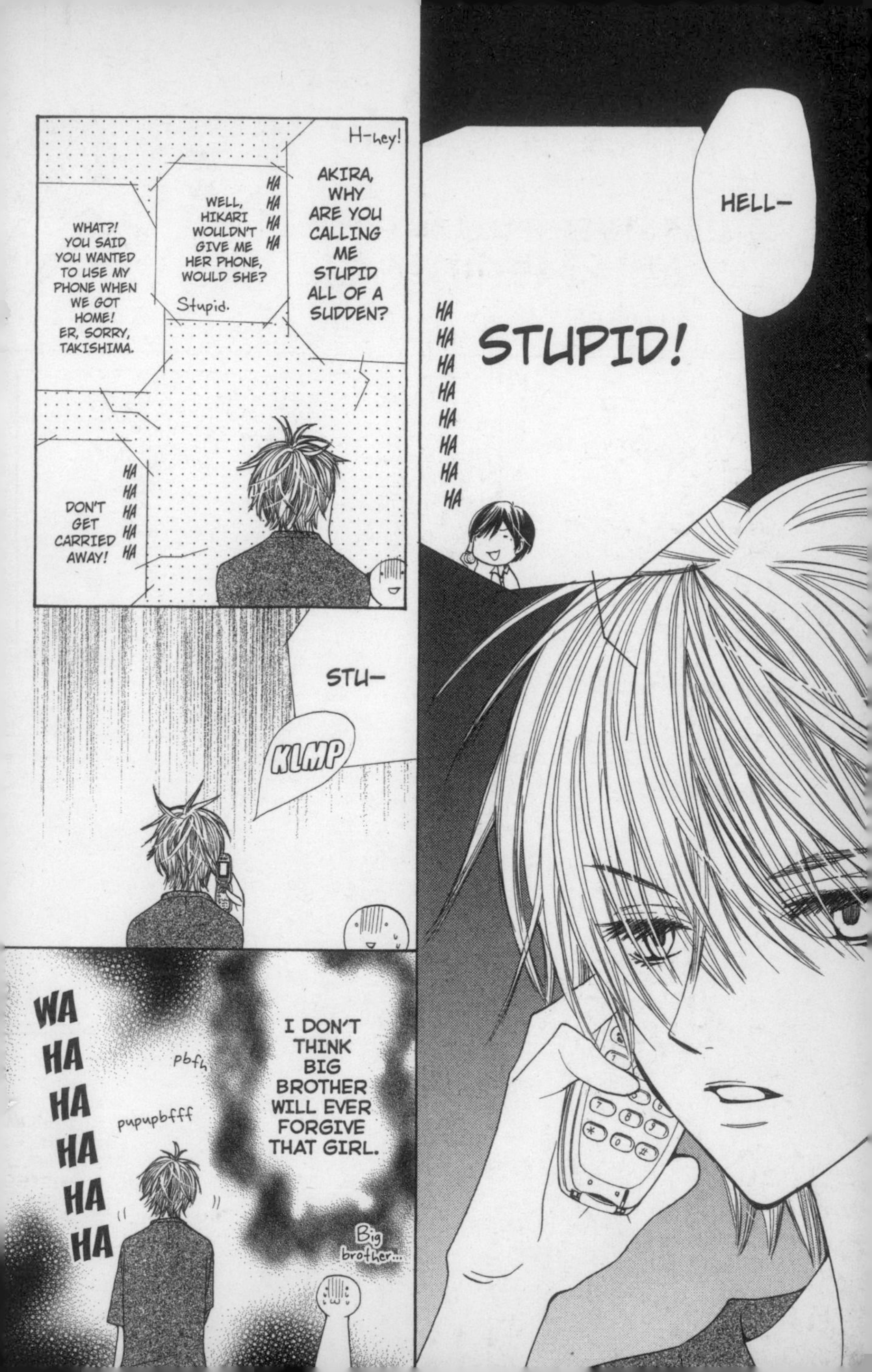
HELL-
STUPID!
HA HA HA HA HA HA HA HA
H-hey!
AKIRA, WHY ARE YOU CALLING ME STUPID ALL OF A SUDDEN?
HA HA HA HA
WELL, HIKARI WOULDN'T GIVE ME HER PHONE, WOULD SHE?
Stupid.
WHAT?! YOU SAID YOU WANTED TO USE MY PHONE WHEN WE GOT HOME! ER, SORRY, TAKISHIMA.
HA HA HA HA HA
DON'T GET CARRIED AWAY!
STU-
KLMP
I DON'T THINK BIG BROTHER WILL EVER FORGIVE THAT GIRL.
Big brother...
pbfh
pupupbfff
WA HA HA HA HA HA

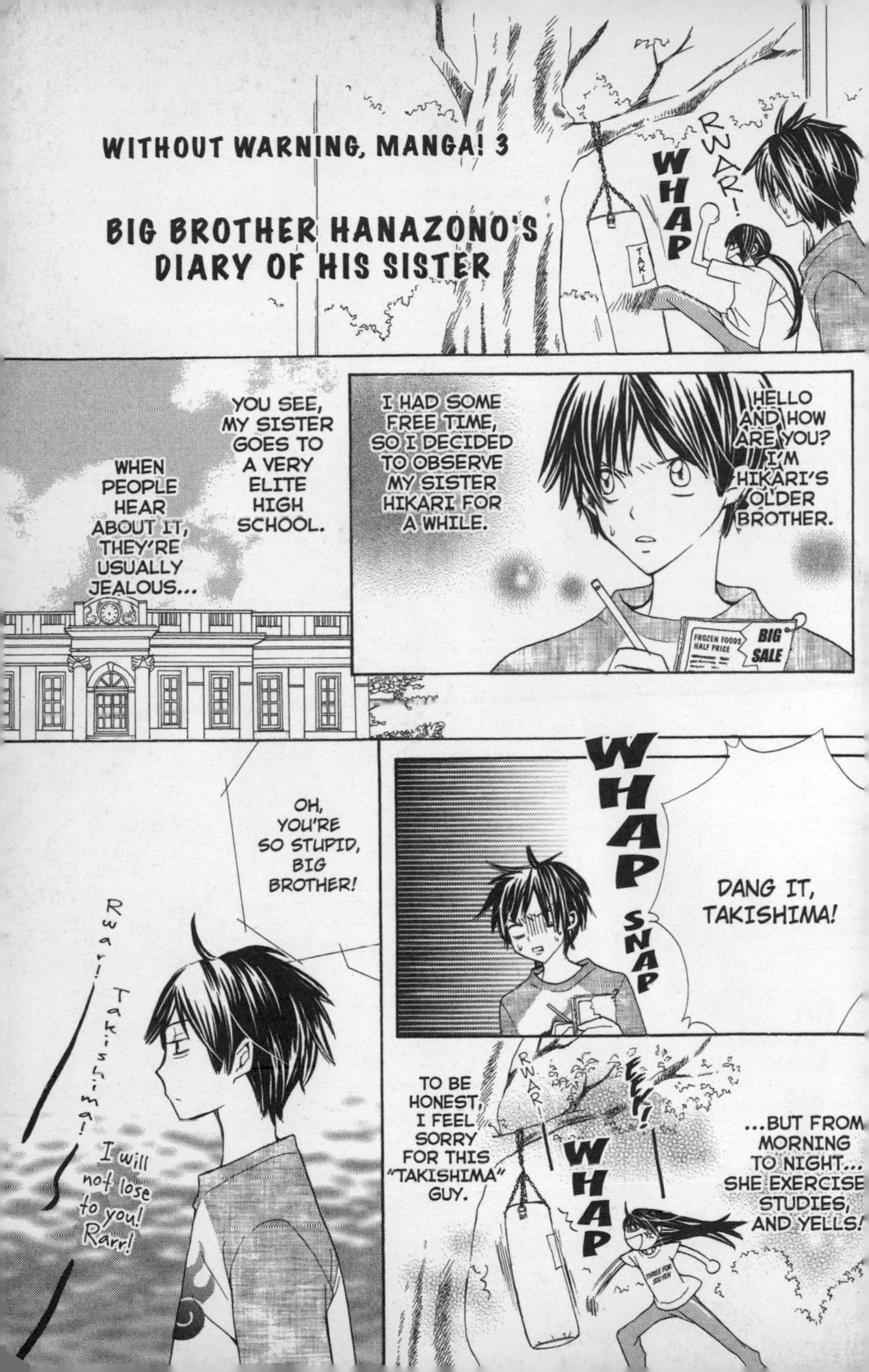
RWAR!
WHAP
TAKI
WITHOUT WARNING, MANGA! 3
BIG BROTHER HANAZONO'S DIARY OF HIS SISTER
HELLO AND HOW ARE YOU? I'M HIKARI'S OLDER BROTHER.
I HAD SOME FREE TIME, SO I DECIDED TO OBSERVE MY SISTER HIKARI FOR A WHILE.
FROZEN FOODS HALF PRICE
BIG SALE
YOU SEE, MY SISTER GOES TO A VERY ELITE HIGH SCHOOL.
WHEN PEOPLE HEAR ABOUT IT, THEY'RE USUALLY JEALOUS...
WHAP
WHAP
DANG IT, TAKISHIMA!
SNAP
...BUT FROM MORNING TO NIGHT... SHE EXERCISE STUDIES, AND YELLS!
RWAR!
EEK!
WHAP
WHAP
TO BE HONEST, I FEEL SORRY FOR THIS "TAKISHIMA" GUY.
THREE FOR 500 YEN
OH, YOU'RE SO STUPID, BIG BROTHER!
Rwar! Takishima!
I will not lose to you! Rarr!

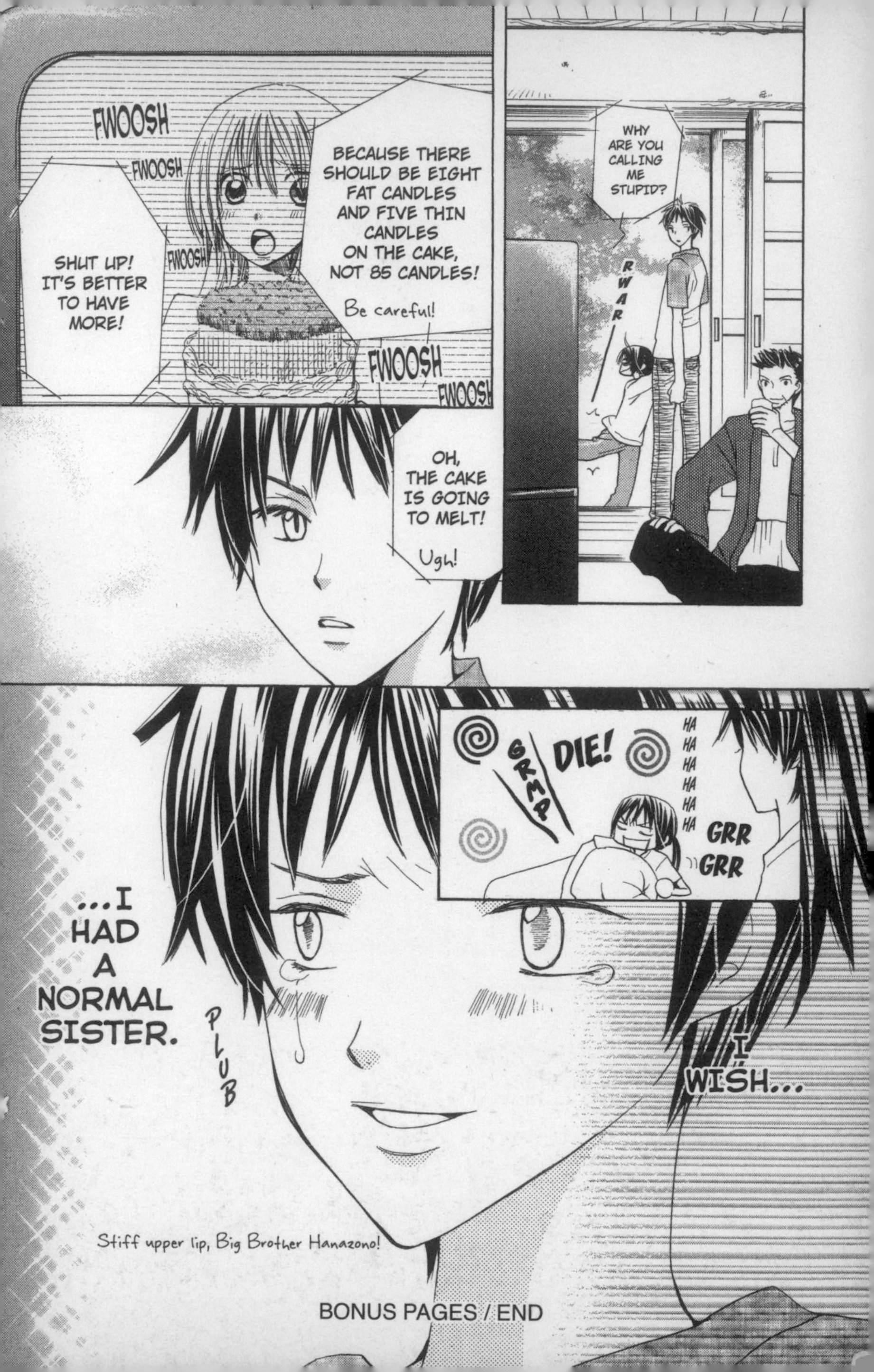
WHY ARE YOU CALLING ME STUPID?
RWAR
FWOOSH
FWOOSH
BECAUSE THERE SHOULD BE EIGHT FAT CANDLES AND FIVE THIN CANDLES ON THE CAKE, NOT 85 CANDLES!
FWOOSH
SHUT UP! IT'S BETTER TO HAVE MORE!
Be careful!
FWOOSH
FWOOSH
OH, THE CAKE IS GOING TO MELT!
Ugh!
HA HA HA HA HA HA
DIE!
GRMP
GRR GRR
I WISH...
...I HAD A NORMAL SISTER.
PLUB
Stiff upper lip, Big Brother Hanazono!
BONUS PAGES / END

Maki Minami is from Saitama
prefecture in Japan. She debuted
in 2001 with *Kanata no Ao*
(Faraway Blue). Her other works
include *Kimi wa Girlfriend*
(You're My Girlfriend), *Mainichi
ga Takaramono* (Every Day Is a
Treasure) and *Yuki Atataka*
(Warm Winter). *S•A* is her current
series in Japan's *Hana to Yume*
magazine.

S·A

Vol. 4
The Shojo Beat Manga Edition

STORY & ART BY
MAKI MINAMI

English Adaptation/Amanda Hubbard
Translation/JN Productions
Touch-up Art & Lettering/Rina Mapa
Design/Izumi Hirayama
Editor/Carol Fox

Editor in Chief, Books/Alvin Lu
Editor in Chief, Magazines/Marc Weidenbaum
VP of Publishing Licensing/Rika Inouye
VP of Sales/Gonzalo Ferreyra
Sr. VP of Marketing/Liza Coppola
Publisher/Hyoe Narita

Printed in Canada

Published by VIZ Media, LLC
P.O. Box 77010
San Francisco, CA 94107

Shojo Beat Manga Edition
10 9 8 7 6 5 4 3 2 1
First printing, May 2008

www.viz.com   store.viz.com

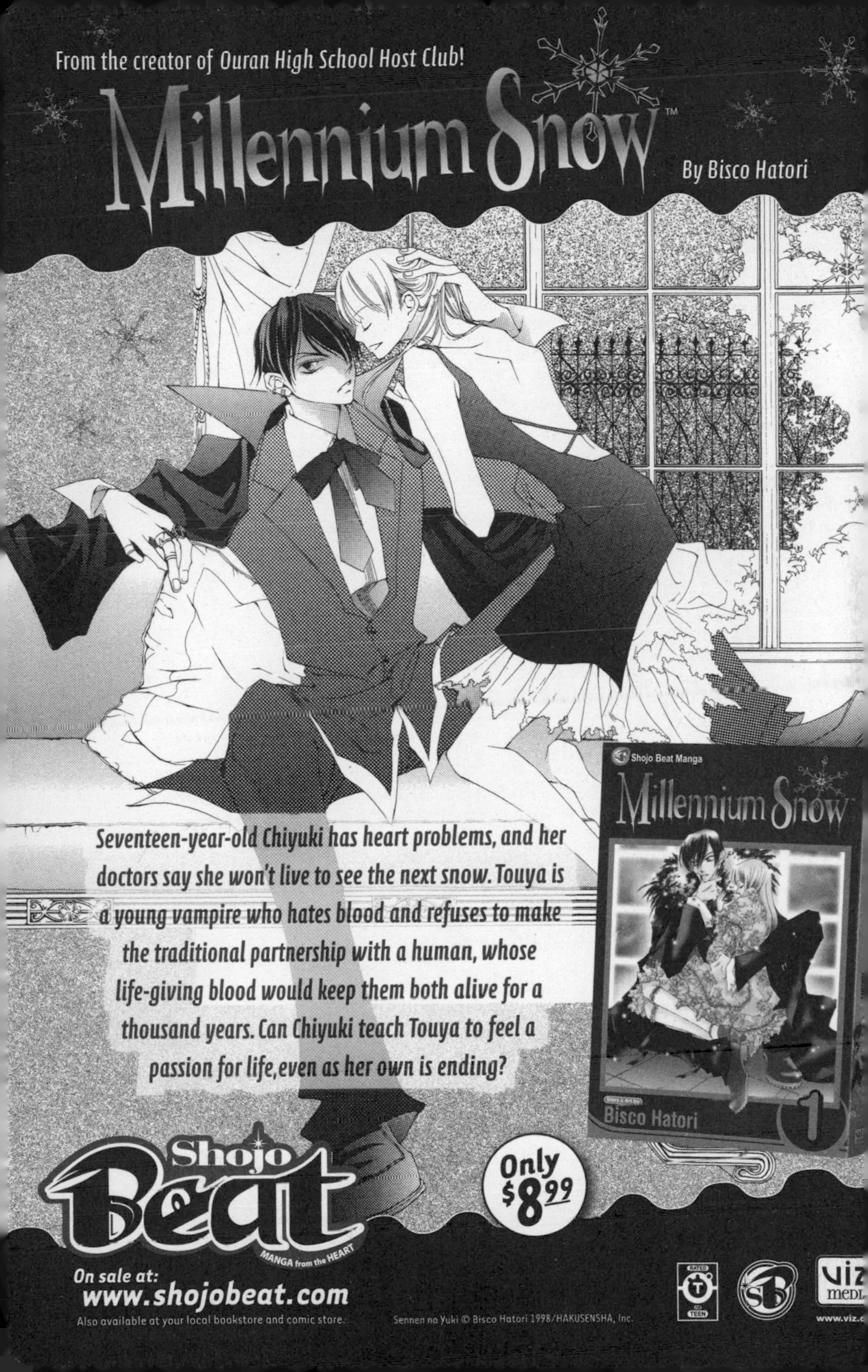
From the creator of Ouran High School Host Club!
Millennium Snow™
By Bisco Hatori
Seventeen-year-old Chiyuki has heart problems, and her doctors say she won't live to see the next snow. Touya is a young vampire who hates blood and refuses to make the traditional partnership with a human, whose life-giving blood would keep them both alive for a thousand years. Can Chiyuki teach Touya to feel a passion for life, even as her own is ending?
Shojo Beat Manga
Millennium Snow
Story & Art by
Bisco Hatori
1
Only $8.99
Shojo Beat
MANGA from the HEART
On sale at:
www.shojobeat.com
Also available at your local bookstore and comic store.
Sennen no Yuki © Bisco Hatori 1998/HAKUSENSHA, Inc.
RATED T TEEN
www.viz.c

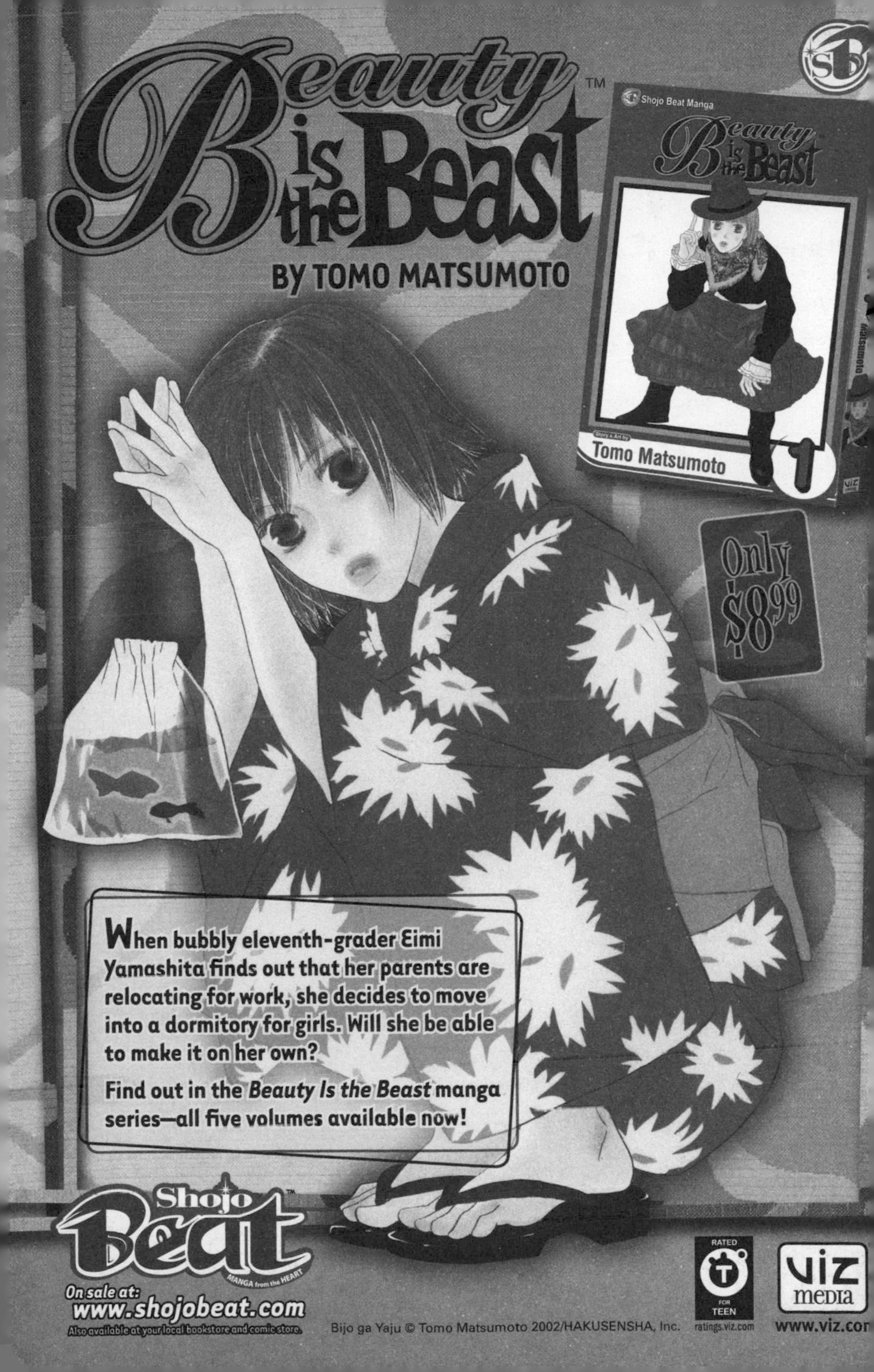
Beauty is the Beast™
BY TOMO MATSUMOTO
Shojo Beat Manga
Beauty is the Beast
Story & Art by
Tomo Matsumoto
1
Only $8.99
When bubbly eleventh-grader Eimi Yamashita finds out that her parents are relocating for work, she decides to move into a dormitory for girls. Will she be able to make it on her own?
Find out in the *Beauty Is the Beast* manga series—all five volumes available now!
Shojo Beat™
MANGA from the HEART
On sale at:
www.shojobeat.com
Also available at your local bookstore and comic store.
Bijo ga Yaju © Tomo Matsumoto 2002/HAKUSENSHA, Inc.
RATED T FOR TEEN
ratings.viz.com
VIZ media
www.viz.com

Tell us what you think about Shojo Beat Manga!

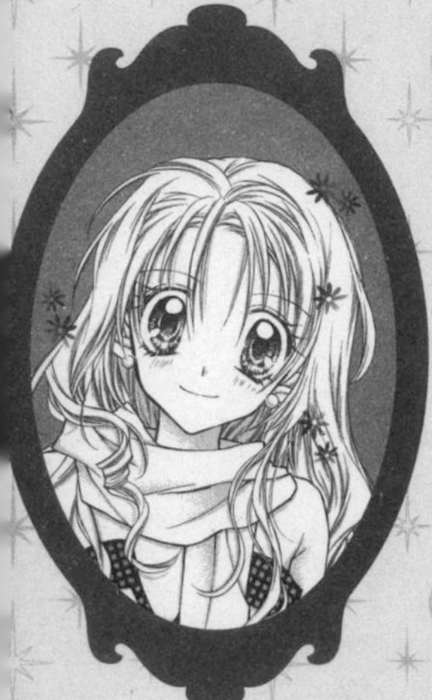

Our survey is now available online. Go to:

shojobeat.com/mangasurvey

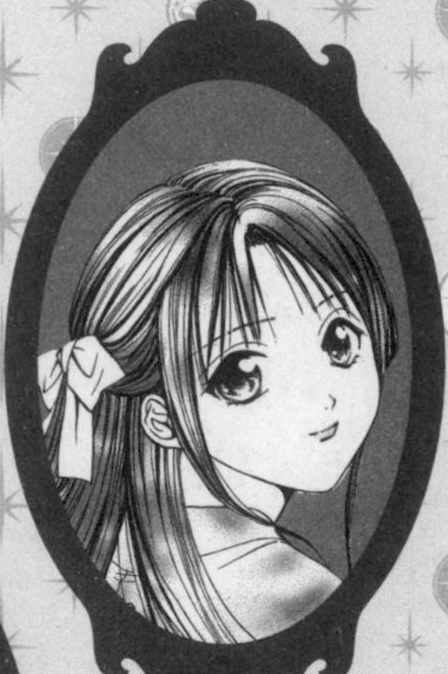

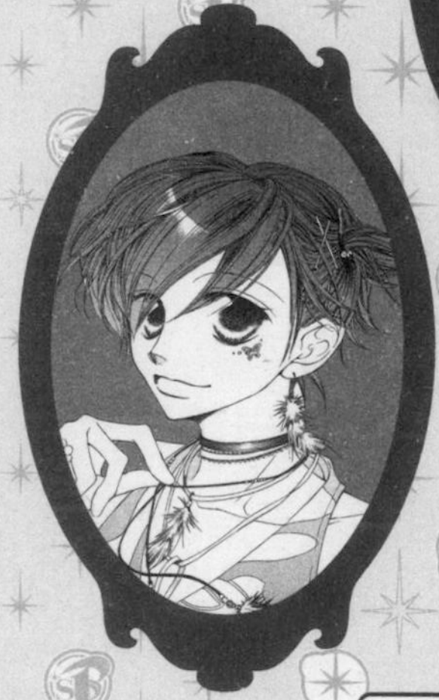

Help us make our product offerings better!

VIZ media

THE REAL DRAMA BEGINS IN... Shojo Beat

MANGA from the HEART

Shojo Beat™

MANGA from the HEART

The Shojo Manga Authority

12 GIANT issues for ONLY $34.99*

That's **51% OFF** the cover price!

The most **ADDICTIVE** shojo manga stories from Japan **PLUS** unique editorial coverage on the arts, music, culture, fashion, and much more!

Subscribe NOW and become a member of the ⑤ Sub Club!

- **SAVE** 51% OFF the cover price
- **ALWAYS** get every issue
- **ACCESS** exclusive areas of www.shojobeat.com
- **FREE** members-only gifts several times a year

Strictly VIP!

3 EASY WAYS TO SUBSCRIBE!

1) Send in the subscription order form from this book O
2) Log on to: www.shojobeat.com OR
3) Call 1-800-541-7876